CU00896826

Women Making News

THE HISTORY OF COMMUNICATION

Robert W. McChesney and
John C. Nerone, editors

*A list of books in the series appears
at the end of this book.*

Women Making News

Gender and Journalism in Modern Britain

MICHELLE ELIZABETH TUSAN

UNIVERSITY OF ILLINOIS PRESS

Urbana and Chicago

© 2005 by Michelle Elizabeth Tusan
All rights reserved
Manufactured in the United States of America
∞ This book is printed on acid-free paper.
C 5 4 3 2 1

Library of Congress Cataloging-in-Publication Data
Tusan, Michelle Elizabeth, 1971–
Women making news : gender and journalism in modern Britain /
Michelle Elizabeth Tusan.
p.   cm. — (The history of communication)
Includes bibliographical references and index.
ISBN 0-252-03015-x (cloth : alk. paper)
1. Women and journalism—Great Britain—History—20th century.
2. Press and politics—Great Britain—History—20th century.
3. Women's periodicals, English—History—20th century.
I. Title. II. Series.
PN5124.W58T87   2005
072'.082'09041—dc22   2005002728

Contents

Acknowledgments

My sister and I learned how to be advocates for causes big and small at an early age. Growing up in a relatively large ethnic community, we raised money for relief efforts and social events that we heard about from the bilingual Armenian newspapers and newsletters that found their way into our world in the San Joaquin Valley in California during the 1980s. The same community supported my entry into higher education through scholarships, though some must have privately wondered why a girl from what was once a small farming community would choose to study the past lives of middle-class British women. The Armenian-American Citizens League, the Mushetsies, Holy Trinity Armenian Apostolic Church, the UC Berkeley Armenian alumni, and a Magasarian Award all directly and indirectly contributed to the completion of this project.

The research for this book started as a senior research project at the University of California at Davis. The previous year I had won an award that supported a month of study in England, which inspired my interest in British history. I was fortunate to have at Davis the help of several wonderful historians who both took me seriously and treated me kindly, including Cathy Kudlick, Paula Findlen, Roland Marchand, and Michael Saler. Cathy and Paula, in particular, guided the early iterations of this work and supported me as mentors and friends during and after graduate school.

At Berkeley, Tom Laqueur and Carla Hesse helped give further form to my work on women journalists and British political culture. Tom let me chase down research whims on my own, intervening to offer intellectual guidance and thoughtful advice at crucial moments. Carla's seminar on French history really inspired me to think about doing women's history in a new way, and I remain grateful for her critical eye. Others, like Tom Metcalf, kept me on my toes by asking often hard but important questions of my work. Tom Leonard gave me a larger perspective on writing about journalism and journalists.

I also had the good fortune to be surrounded by a brilliant cohort of friends and scholars at Berkeley. To Chaela Pastore I am grateful for her honest criticism but most of all for her friendship. Hee Ko, too, helped me in countless ways. My "ladies knitting circle," as Tom Metcalf once called it, read, commented, and then tirelessly read again my oddly consistently fifty-two- to fifty-five-page chapters. Durba Ghosh and Deborah Cohler made our sessions significant intellectually and personally, over treats made with the bounties seemingly only present at markets within the Berkeley city limits.

Most of the research for this book was completed in Britain and funded largely by a grant from the Fulbright Program. The Mellon Foundation, the Berkeley Center of German and European Studies, and a Berkeley Humanities Research Grant funded other crucial stages of the project. While working in London I was privileged to have the ear of Peter Mandler, who served as my Fulbright sponsor. He subsequently generously agreed to read every word of the manuscript, offering the most careful of critiques while pushing me to think about the relationship between historical evidence and theoretical analysis. Angela John showed me kindheartedness and provided me with a venue to present my work in London. Colleagues Monica Rico, Andy Muldoon, and John Jenks helped make London seem more like home.

Working at archives in Britain was both a challenge and true pleasure, made easier by the generosity of the archivists who helped me complete my work. Kate Perry at the Girton College Archive in Cambridge went beyond the call of duty by giving me a lift here and there, arranging for a place to stay, and making sure I had a good lunch. She also introduced me to the most significant find of my research: tea chests full of uncatalogued correspondence relating to the founding of the *English Woman's Journal.* I am grateful to her for allowing me to be the first to examine these documents. I acknowledge The Mistress and Fellows, Girton College, Cambridge, for permission to cite from the collection.

I had the unusual opportunity of researching at two time-honored but now much changed institutions. The British Library, then on the premises of the British Museum, was an inspiring place to work, despite the cold December mornings and hot July afternoons spent in the reading room. The Fawcett Library, in the basement of Guildhall University, also inspired for different reasons. Absent the physical charm of the old BL, the archive, now the Women's Library, had the benefit of the expertise of the indefatigable David Doughan. I now know why he is thanked in almost every book on British women's history, and I add my gratitude to the long list. Both institutions now look very different. The modernization of these two research pilgrimages has made each more easily accessible, though I do miss the familiarity and the people of the old places.

The task of turning the manuscript into a book opened up new possibilities. A position as a Fellow in the Humanities at Stanford gave me the time to revise the manuscript while working with outstanding faculty, such as Mary Lou Roberts, who taught me as much about teaching as writing history. Cathy Kudlick and Susan Pedersen generously agreed to read the whole manuscript and offered their comments. Durba and Deb, too, kept reading long after we all had left Berkeley for good.

At the University of Nevada, Las Vegas, I have had the opportunity to work with a superb group of scholars who have welcomed me with open arms and provided much needed support. I feel fortunate to be part of such a strong, vibrant department of history. My former chair, Andy Fry, and current chair, Hal Rothman, both gave me departmental support to finish the manuscript. Participants in the History Department Faculty Seminar offered valuable advice on parts of the manuscript. They included: Paul Werth, Colin Loader, David Tanenhaus, Andrew Bell, and David Wrobel. Elizabeth White Nelson, Joanne Goodwin, Elspeth Whitney, Andy Kirk, Thomas Wright, Willard Rollings, Gene Moehring, Greg Brown, Raquel Casas, Barbara Wallace, and Elizabeth Fraterrigo at various times offered me encouragement and good advice. Kelly Mays remains an expert reader and dear friend. Despite my readers' attempts at prevention, any errors in the following text are my own.

My family has persevered with me through the many years of this project. My then elementary school–aged brother, David, asked several years ago when he would be able to find my book in the local county library. When I told my father that I had finished the book, he asked, "Is this the same project that you've been working on all this time about the women journalists?" Having once been a journalism graduate student and later a printer himself, I think he wondered why it took so long to write a book about something one did to make a living. My mother, too, I believe is proud that I have followed in her footsteps as a teacher. I have my sister, Christina Tusan, to thank for many hours of heated discussions both personal and political that energized me and inspired me to write about women and the culture of politics. My in-laws, Don and Marte Muelrath, deserve thanks both for their generosity and for encouraging me and their only son to take up our new life in Las Vegas.

I have dedicated this book to my husband, Scott Muelrath, and my son, Nicholas. I remember during a very frustrating time in graduate school standing in the living room of our first apartment. When I dramatically announced that I wanted to drop out of graduate school, he wisely said that once I found something that I could own in this process, I would think differently. Since then he has given me nothing but the most heartfelt support, not least of which included moving from green and mountainous Northern California to the desert where there is hardly a native trout to be found. Finally, to my little Nico: the first true "local" Las Vegan in the family. He has been an untold joy as he continues to amaze his parents and make this place feel real. To him I am most grateful for sleeping just long enough during his first months to allow his mommy to finish her manuscript. That must be him calling now.

A New Political Medium
for Women

In July 1911, American women's suffrage advocate Jessie Anthony went to London to sell *Votes for Women,* the official newspaper of the Women's Social and Political Union (WSPU). Placed on a busy London street corner, where she confined herself within a "sandwich board" advertising that day's news, Anthony paraded her political beliefs on hot summer days in front of mixed crowds of ardent antisuffragists, passionate supporters, and apathetic passersby. She had come to learn the methods of the WSPU and marveled at the varied voices, activities, and political ideals encompassed by the British women's movement. As a news seller, she participated in this political community in a way that she could not have experienced in a less public role. When her sales leader put her on the street in visible city places, she was forced to explain her stance to hostile antisuffragists "muttering something about homes and babies" while passing on news to supporters who were "glad to hear about the Monday afternoon meetings at Piccadilly Pavilion."[1] Defending her political convictions on the street enabled Anthony to sharpen her sense of commitment to the activist discourse preached in the meeting halls of America and London.

This book, in part, is about the making of a particular kind of female political subject who was shaped by her connection to women-run print journalism and its associated institutions. Between 1856 and 1930, female proprietors published over 150 political journals and newspapers targeted at a female audience. Suffrage papers, like the one sold on the street by Anthony, were by far the most successful of these publications. *Votes for Women* itself reached a circulation of over 50,000 papers weekly. By the early twentieth century, women reformers succeeded in transforming the periodical into both a real and imagined space for female intellectual and political community.

The women's press movement was started in the mid–nineteenth century when a small group of educated middle-class women took advantage of changes brought on by the liberalization of laws governing the press and small businesses. Together they formed one of the first modern advocacy institutions: the women's political press. Women began the business of press advocacy through the formation of corporate organizations and informal associational networks. By the late nineteenth century, new technologies and journalistic techniques embodied in the rise of what media critics have called the New Journalism made women's press advocacy into a small but increasingly influential industry.[2] As professional newspaperwomen, they opened up new markets for their ideas by engaging in contemporary political and economic debates regarding women's status in society. In the pages of "their" press, one explicitly identified as being both for and by women, social reform concerns advocated by women emerged as inextricably linked to the progress of the British nation.

Women found a way to enter British political life before they attained equal suffrage in 1928 through advocacy journalism that enabled them to learn a trade that advanced their political and professional interests. A print-based extraparliamentary approach to politics provided the basis for an alternative, gender-based political culture that maintained a strong hold on British society up through the 1930s.

This new genre of periodical defined itself by its purpose: to engage the public with the news as defined and shaped by women. In the case of Anthony, her experiences as a street seller gave her a sense of belonging to an international community of political activists. American women visiting London were thrilled to find one of their own passing on news of "votes for women" so far from home. A woman from Spain who approached Anthony remarked that "the Spanish women had no chance" of the suffrage and declared, "We need you there." Anthony was energized by these responses to her propaganda work and sold papers regardless of weather conditions and unpleasant run-ins. In the hot weather she found herself "almost tempted to take a vacation." She continued, however, despite slow sales and the difficult time she had approaching potential customers. She was reminded by one of her sales leaders that what was important was "not so much the number sold as . . . keeping the work before the public." That public had clearly expanded beyond any previously imagined political and national borders and was now united as a *gender*-identified community of female activists.

Anthony influenced the news' reception through anonymous interactions with curious passersby. Her "costume," advertising the main topics of the day's news, often invited explicit comment. "Does a Man Support his wife?" read one controversial placard. Anthony found it "amusing to watch the different expressions as (people) read it" and commented that she had had more women buyers "than on any other day." That a middle-class American woman held this controversial sign on a busy street corner certainly influenced the paper's sale that day, creating a silent dialogue between female passersby and Anthony. The placard sold papers while also making its holder a newsworthy spectacle herself. Tourists took pictures of Anthony holding her sign and were anxious to have the message clearly visible in the photograph. "'Pardon me,'" Anthony reported one onlooker commented, "'but we are trying to get a good snap of the wording on that placard.' Oh, I said, and immediately pulled the huge thing around in better view." Whether her presence amused, enlightened, or alarmed people on the street, it served as a reminder of a larger community of women already actively involved in public life.

Requiring the regular participation of members in highly visible aspects of propaganda work led to the development of a political identity that reconfigured the acceptable boundaries of public activism for women. During the nineteenth century, women's limited engagement in public forms of political debate meant that the periodical had the potential to serve as a primary mode for the exchange of ideas. Women gathered in the meeting rooms of women's clubs and institutions to discuss the news, much as men had done in decades past in coffeehouses, as well as read the news in the privacy of their own homes.[3] The successful rise of the women's political press in the late 1850s relied on the periodical's status as a semipublic medium that appealed to a largely female middle-class audience fearful of public notoriety through open association with radical causes such as women's suffrage. By the Edwardian era, as the example of Anthony and her WSPU colleagues demonstrates, a new kind of political culture based on public display emerged. The women's press created a very particular kind of community that utilized both the public and private characteristics of traditional modes of women's sociability. This "imagined community," to borrow Benedict Anderson's phrase, was made tangible for many participants through contact facilitated through the pages of their own papers. Correspondence sections of women's papers invited contributors to present their ideas in a relatively safe space understood as occupied by sympathetic readers. This created the opportunity for engagement with other politically minded women. Women's periodicals thus facilitated the growth of a gendered community of activists who met in a print-based Habermassian public sphere found in the pages of the women's press.[4]

By the early twentieth century, this loosely connected association of female activists had grown in strength, thanks to the focus imposed by the suffrage movement that demanded the unqualified dedication of members to projects such as street selling. Hawking newspapers provided a very particular type of political training that asked individuals to make personal sacrifices in the name of a larger movement. The experience of selling newspapers quickly made Anthony aware of the importance of physically asserting herself. At first, she "was not much of a success," selling only three papers, because she "stood there dumbly holding out the paper." By the second day, however, she "made (her) voice heard, and oh joy—sold all but two and lots of people stopped to talk and perhaps I made some converts." The street, in many ways, provided a training ground for Anthony where she practiced her arguments on those who were willing to listen.

Possible "converts" came from all social stations. One woman, "a very tall gaunt creature, bareheaded, wearing a ragged shawl and shabby black skirt," approached Anthony to talk about "the wrongs suffered by the poor":

> "I tell you," she said, "it is not the rich that help the poor, the poor support the rich; they get their living off the lives of us," and her eyes blazed and her voice faintly shrieked and had a note of challenge in it. It made me sick at heart there was so much truth in it and I put my hand on her thin old shoulder and said—"I know, but I am sure there will be better laws after a while when women help make them." Her face softened a little and she slowly walked away.

Couching women's suffrage in the language of liberal reform culture enabled Anthony to see "votes for women" as a call for solidarity. Poverty was appropriated as a woman's issue that would be solved with a simple act of Parliament. Anthony's education as a propagandist taught her to understand what she was doing on the street as a radical act of social reform that went beyond winning the vote. The idea of creating a political space where all women belonged, however patronizing or unrealistic, was essential in making participants believe that they could affect social change by creating a new, gender-based political culture.

As the example of Anthony's experiences in London reminds us, numerous elements of modern women's political culture culminated in the Edwardian suffrage movement. This book reveals that this new gendered politics had a long and distinctive history that did not just emerge fully formed with the breaking of the first shop window by militant suffragettes in 1912. Rather, through the slow development of what eventually emerged as "women's issues" as a subject for national concern during the second half of the nineteenth century, radical feminist politics found both its mode of expression and intellectual justification. By the middle of the nineteenth century, women reformers had begun to cast liberal reformist ideas as falling within the special purview of women. With the subsequent rise of the "Woman Question" as a subject of cultural debate, reform-minded women appropriated causes such as education, employment, and legal reform as issues of special interest to women. (I am using the term "women's issue" to signify the recognition by women reformers of the relationship between the rise of liberal critiques of society and female, single-issue campaigns as they related to the status of women during the late nineteenth to early twentieth centuries.)

The emergence of suffrage as a unifying issue for the early twentieth-century women's movement thus needs to be understood within the larger context of earlier single-issue reform campaigns run by female activists that helped create a multifaceted woman-centered political culture in Britain. Anthony's experiences reveal how the suffrage movement both drew upon and contributed to an institutional culture that asked women to make sacrifices for issues that placed women squarely in the center of debates about social reform, parliamentary politics, and even foreign policy. The women's political press, I argue, played a key role in creating and sustaining a modern female political culture starting as early as the late 1850s.

Although a good deal of overlap is evident, the women's press was not necessarily synonymous with what historians such as Philippa Levine have called the "feminist press." The voices of the women's press, despite declarations that each promoted women's interests broadly defined, included many groups that were disassociated from a feminist or protofeminist agenda. Religious organizations, advocates of temperance, sexual restraint, and moral reform all had their own women-run printed mediums. Some early pioneers of the women's press, such as Bessie Rayner Parkes, did not see the point in arguing for women's suffrage, claiming other issues such as employment needed to take priority over the political representation of women.[5] Figuring out exactly whom or what the women's press was meant to represent was part of the difficulty that continued to characterize the larger enterprise. Was the women's press to be a separatist press, or would it include male readers, correspondents, and financiers in its ranks? Supporters faced this question from the beginning in the late 1850s up through the mid-1930s, the twilight of the women's advocacy press movement.

The issue of class further influenced the development of a press "for and by women." Founded by educated women from the middling classes, the early periodicals of the late 1850s and early 1860s addressed women from the lower middle classes to the upper classes in their pages. Distribution patterns, along with a rhetoric that imagined the emergence of a cross-class "sisterhood" meant to appeal to women from a wide range of experiences, suggest that many developed a diverse readership starting in the late nineteenth century. Self-conscious attempts by publishers to steadily lower the prices of their periodical titles also points to a desire to attract less affluent readers. The turn-of-the-century publication *Shafts,* for example, addressed "women and the working classes." In 1914, Sylvia Pankhurst started the *Woman's Dreadnought,* a socialist paper directed at working-class women. The emergence of a paper explicitly for a working-class female audience revealed the inherent class bias of most women's papers, which had traditionally assumed a middle-class readership.

The question of who belonged to this political community continued to shift during the over seventy-five-year history of the women's press movement. A disparity between the actual versus intended audience further complicates the picture of a press that claimed to speak for all women, using language that addressed readers as part of a monolithic "womankind." In reality, the production and financing of these journals, including working-class papers, continued to rest in the hands of educated middle-class editors. This affected the process of selection and rejection that determined what women's papers printed in their pages. An article championing the cause of the seamstress, for example, appeared alongside an opinion piece on the difficulty of retaining good maidservants in the *English Woman's Journal.*[6] As Kate Flint has illustrated, although the experience of reading women's political journals created a "means of joining with other women," this sense of imagined commonality overlooked real differences between women in terms of class, regionalism, and sexual orientation.[7] The problem of representation on a practical level, I argue, intensified starting in the late nineteenth century with the proliferation of competing radical voices. The multiplicity of opinions among women in a host of movements, including suffrage, social reform, international and domestic feminism, and the peace movement, all found expression within the pages of women's periodicals.

What, then, bound this community together? In many ways, the plurality that characterized women's political culture proved a significant strength. As particular campaigns for social reform, political representation, and personal liberty waxed and waned, new agendas took their place. The rise of a modern women's political culture to sustain these ideas found strength not necessarily in terms of the continuities of the kinds of issues argued but in the methods and institutions that women set up to serve particular causes. This created associations that linked women's groups together, however loosely, in gender-identified political and business networks. Periodicals that proclaimed themselves to be both for and by women connected reformers to a large range of what these publications helped define as women's issues that eventually culminated in the campaign for equal suffrage. The appearance of long-term continuity resulted, in part, from the general spirit of reform embraced by women in multiple cultural and political arenas.

Attention to this diversity helps explain the crucial links between nineteenth- and twentieth-century women's activism that have largely been overlooked. Historians have traditionally divided modern women's history into three distinct categories: Victorian, Edwardian, and Interwar. Accounts that have narrated connections between these periods have focused on the importance of the legislative campaign for suffrage as providing an otherwise disparate movement with its continuity. The sustained expression of these myriad voices of reform within women's print culture adds a greater complexity to current historical interpretations that understand the vote as an inevitable outcome of nineteenth-century women's political activism. David Rubenstein's classic study of the suffrage issue has argued for the importance of suffrage as a liberal political issue for both politicians and the women's movement during the 1890s.[8] Renewed interest in women's political culture during the second half of the nineteenth century has led scholars to extend Rubenstein's project back to the 1850s. Recent attempts to understand women's political activism during this period have focused on explaining how the issue of the vote provided continuity to a movement plagued by innumerable stops and starts, disappointments and setbacks. Sandra Holton's work on the nineteenth-century suffrage movement, in both her book *Suffrage Days* and the collection of articles edited with June Purvis, *Votes for Women,* have more recently argued for the importance of suffrage as the key organizing principle for the nineteenth-century women's movement.[9] Sophia van Wingerden's survey of the history of the suffrage movement starting in the nineteenth century has pursued a similar agenda.[10]

Focusing mainly on how women's activism attempted to gain a foothold in formal politics through legislative appeals to the state has revealed only a partial view of the complex nature of nineteenth- and twentieth-century women's activism. This book attempts to understand the female activist within her larger cultural context. It thus participates in the project of "rethinking the political" as articulated by scholars such as Amanda Vickery, who have understood women's engagement with print, among other things, as crucial to understanding the extraparliamentary nature of women's political culture in Britain.[11] Key to what historian Ellen DuBois calls this "new political history" is to shift the focus away from studying formal politics to "recognizing the underlying values that characterized and distinguished the ways people thought about political life."[12] Rather than examining the history of women's political activism from the perspective of the successes or failures of individual campaigns for the franchise and improved legal status, *Women Making News* explores how women used cultural forms such as print journalism to advocate for social reform and construct their own identity as citizen subjects.

This approach does not rely on rejecting historical narratives that have explored how women engaged directly with the state through formal protests and the British political party system in order to advance their legal status. Studies by historians such as Sandra Holton, Martin Pugh, and many others have convincingly demonstrated the significance of this aspect of women's activism.[13] Rather, it asserts that we also need to examine the cultural side of women's politics in order to gain a more complete picture of the nature of nineteenth- and twentieth-century political activism in Britain. Here I draw on Lynn Hunt's interpretation of "politics as the creation of new strategies and tactics for wielding power."[14] This modern women's "political culture," as defined for the purposes of this study, relied on the emergence of a complex female-centered associational life that, when coupled with the beginnings of grass roots organizations during the second half of the nineteenth century, laid the foundation for new cultural institutions that served the interests of women as a political interest group. Women's journals and newspapers played a vital role in connecting communities of social reformers and political activists with a growing educated female public interested in numerous social reform issues. These associational networks provided the foundation for making women's political culture in Britain more than the culmination of the struggle for the vote. By the 1920s, a gender-identified community of intellectuals, reformers, and activists had established itself as a clearly recognizable presence in British political life.

Women's Political Culture and Advocacy Media

The central argument of this book, then, rests on the premise that historians can better understand the changing nature of political life during the late nineteenth and early twentieth centuries in Britain first, by examining particular alternative print-based political cultures that developed during this period and second, by understanding how British women subjects themselves forged a wide range of new political identities through the pages of their own press. Historians and literary critics have not yet fully explored the institution of the women's press in terms of this larger context. Recent work has examined women-run journals as an isolated phenomenon, comprised of a small number of fringe periodicals possessing very little importance outside of the community of women who supported them. Interesting studies of periodicals such as the *English Woman's Journal, Woman's Signal,* and *Time and Tide* and the women who wrote for them have added to our knowledge of women's political writing during this period.[15] These individual snapshots, however, tell us little about the larger world of print culture and gender politics.

This book places women's advocacy journals within the context of a well-developed network of institutions and individuals that supported women's entry into public life in order to better engage with current historical debates regarding the development of a modern women's political culture. The Society for Promoting the Employment of Women (known by its unfortunate acronym, SPEW), as discussed in chapter 1, emerged as one of the first such organizations. Previously undiscovered documents offer new perspectives on this important group of well-known Langham Place reformers. The Society's role in creating the infrastructure for a news medium built on the principles of "for and by women," I argue, reveals the importance of real institutional structures in the development of a larger sense of political community among women in modern Britain. Excellent histories of women's associational life have demonstrated that during the second half of the nineteenth century, new modes of female sociability fueled the formation of such gender-based networks. Educational and employment opportunities provided women with institutional structures that encouraged same-sex organizations and activities that allowed organizations like SPEW to thrive.[16] As Phillipa Levine and, most recently, Erika Rappaport have shown, the rise of women's clubs during the second half of the nineteenth century created further possibilities for women to come together while legitimating their presence in public and semipublic spaces.[17]

These modern social and cultural networks certainly played an important role in creating new gender-identified political communities, but taken on their own, they do not tell the whole story. Women's political culture also relied on gender-identified business practices to sustain a community-based activism. Economic institutions, of the kind pioneered by women in the press industry, provided a new kind of associational life built on liberal ideas of cooperation. New professional opportunities brought on by an expanding Victorian economy enabled women to learn the trade of journalism and to put into practice liberal economic practices championed at midcentury by John Stuart Mill.

Women reformers' interest in liberalism, in many ways, started with questions of political economy rather than political representation. A series of articles and debates in the early numbers of the *English Woman's Journal* encouraged women to "club together" and form business relationships to benefit members. As chapter 2 argues, Mill's ideas of cooperation deeply influenced the economic theories that informed early women's advocacy business networks. By the 1860s, these ideas guided an industry that tied economic and political theories to a model of community action. The changes brought about by improved printing technology, distribution techniques, and incorporation laws further enabled the successful formation of a female-based industry that helped make print media into a tool for women's own political mobilization. The Education Acts of the late nineteenth century further fueled these changes by facilitating the rise of a new class of potential women readers. This combination of community-centered initiatives and state-directed changes to women's status provided the necessary conditions for the development of a multifaceted female-centered political culture in Victorian Britain.

Located at the intersection of the study of women's political activism, liberalism, and the history of journalism, this book uses a social and cultural historical approach to trace the development of the institutions that made press advocacy into a key aspect of nineteenth- and twentieth-century extraparliamentary political culture. In many ways, advocacy journals and newspapers such as those started by women in the late 1850s represented a new liberal incarnation of the radical press tradition of the first half of the nineteenth century. The radical journals of 1819, the Unstamped press, and the Chartist press have each been the subject of thorough studies and provide interesting insights into pre-1850 political culture.[18] Scholars have done less work on the advocacy presses that supported particularized political agendas starting at midcentury. Socialist, ethnic, working-class, and race-identified presses emerged during this period as an alternative to mainstream print media.[19] Stephen Koss's two-volume study of what he defines as the "political press" in Britain does not discuss periodicals that fall outside of the rigid definition of mainstream party politics. Similarly, Lucy Brown's work on Victorian newspapers and Alan Lee's study of the rise and fall of the liberal press ignore the emergence of specialized political periodicals as part of a sustained effort by reformers to diversify mainstream media.

Alternative or advocacy news media, the main subject of this study, emerged as a small but important part of the larger British periodical industry. By the late nineteenth century, socialist, temperance, working-class, antivice, church reform, and ethnic presses such as the Yiddish press and the black press, to name a few, had developed significant audiences. Advocacy journalism was an integral part of the process of liberalization of print culture that started at midcentury with the abolition of the last newspaper taxes, a move credited with paving the way for a free, unfettered press in Britain. As press historians have argued, the mid-1850s witnessed the birth of a truly popular press supported by individual subscriptions and advertisers rather than subsidies from political parties or elite interests. By the turn of the century, press barons such as Alfred Harmsworth (later Lord Northcliffe) revolutionized the periodical market in Britain through the introduction of the elements that drove the New Journalism, such as mass marketing techniques and new technologies, in order to take advantage of an almost fully literate reading public. In less than half a century since the abolition of the "taxes on knowledge," as Richard Cobden had once called them, newspapers emerged as a self-proclaimed medium of the masses.

Nineteenth-century critics and journalists developed a particular vocabulary to talk about this increasingly diverse world of periodicals. For the purposes of this study, I have stayed as close as possible to the constantly evolving meanings of the terms used to describe British periodicals. The "mainstream press" typically denoted "Fleet Street" publications that held prestige and sometimes managed to achieve relatively high circulations. These papers very much remained part of the British "quality" press establishment during this period and included dailies, weeklies, and some monthly publications. The term "popular press" remains more problematic but is used here to refer to high-circulation daily and weekly periodicals, such as Northcliffe's *Daily Mail,* that emerged with the New Journalism at the end of the nineteenth century. Clearly, much overlap did exist between to the two aforementioned categories, but in this study the latter term is used to describe what we today might categorize as part of the mass media. Other specialized categories of journalism also emerged during this period. The "women's domestic press" remains an important counterpoint to the women's political press. Periodicals that focused on issues relating directly to women's relationship to home and hearth, such as the *Queen* and the *English Woman's Domestic Magazine,* were part of a growing specialized press that thrived during the late nineteenth century.

Historians such as Alan Lee and others have argued that the late nineteenth-century period of expansion was followed by decline and consolidation, where alternative voices were suppressed by large print media conglomerates brought on by the likes of Lord Northcliffe and other practitioners of the New Journalism.[20] This case study of women's advocacy journalism challenges the validity of Lucy Brown's claim that as "newspapers grew in social acceptance [during the second half of the nineteenth century], being no longer taxed or suspected, so they declined in critical vigor." More recently, Jean Chalaby has argued that the rise of journalism as a "discursive genre" in the mid-nineteenth century marked a shift away from earlier news reporting that "was political at heart and public in character."[21] Women's papers, in particular the suffrage press, offered some of the most pointed critiques of British governmental policy that continued well beyond the Edwardian era. Unlike many of their early nineteenth-century radical predecessors, these advocacy journals, as licit not-for-profit enterprises, remained free to dispel political ideas that fell outside of mainstream political culture.

Although starting in the 1850s Britain had two significant branches of legitimate print media, "advocacy" and "mainstream," much of the work done on the British press has concentrated on mainstream commercial publications. This focus is understandable, as these papers made up the most visible segment of the market. Advocacy papers, however, provided an important counterpoint to the thriving commercial press during this period. The advocacy press, despite being only tangentially connected to the larger market, played a complementary and sometimes contradictory role in relation to its mainstream counterpart. Advocacy journalists understood the function of periodicals differently from their commercial counterparts: newspapers served political communities by providing a medium of communication for women's organizations rather than profiting from them. Little concerned with the bottom line, these papers often existed on the margins. However, as their specialized audiences started to grow during the Edwardian era around the suffrage issue, women's papers developed a new prestige in the larger world of British news making.

In order to more fully understand the British press during this period, then, we must look more closely at alternative political print media. The periodicals that made up the women's press during its early years were weekly and monthly publications—and, in one case, a quarterly publication—that included discussions of nontraditional employment for women, university education, suffrage, feminism, and social reform. Despite the absence of a women's political daily, women's papers recorded and commented upon current events both at home and abroad that included discussions of parliamentary debates. Their format, however, varied considerably. Early titles tended to look more like journals, each page measuring approximately eight by five inches and containing fifty to seventy pages on average. They often included serialized stories and lengthy essays, lending such periodicals a more literary style. After 1870, women's publications adopted a larger, newspaper-like format, complete with columns and mastheads. Advertisements also became more prevalent as the century progressed with women editors employing some of the same New Journalism techniques used by their mainstream counterparts. Women's periodicals continued to grow in size and sophistication, like other papers of this period, with popular suffrage newspapers such as the *Common Cause* and the *Vote* appearing as large tabloid-size productions measuring as large as over ten by fourteen inches.

It is important to note that the women's press started largely as a privately funded and noncommercial enterprise, leaving editors free from advertiser's censure to promote their own agendas. An independent editorial voice mediated the content and tone of the journal and guided the majority of these journals. Often such editors provided the financial backing to keep the periodical afloat. In addition, these periodicals typically served as the voices of particular organizations. Influence over content was thus split between an independently motivated editor and a politically focused institution. Through serving in this capacity as a noncommercial medium for the exchange of ideas, the women's press first took its place as a specialized advocacy press at midcentury.

Consumers and Producers: A Modern Medium for the Modern Woman

Readers themselves played an important role in creating a female-based political culture. According to Kate Flint, reading for women provided "a means of becoming part of a broader community." As she argues: "Such a community may stretch far beyond the reader's immediate social world to incorporate other readers whom she may never meet in person, but with whom she shares horizons of expectations which have to a significant extent been built up through their common reading material."[22] Women's reading of political papers, I argue, helped forge both real and imagined bonds between women who often found themselves compelled to advocate for particular campaigns. Readers in London, the provinces, and around the world were constantly reminded in articles and editorials of the shared nature of their commitment to particular reform agendas.

During the 1890s, the growth in print culture ultimately helped fuel women's appetite for news. Chapter 3 demonstrates the ways in which women's advocacy journals challenged mainstream discourses about gender and the private sphere by creating a semipublic space for the woman reader to engage with ideas not covered in popular periodicals. At the same time, publishers and advertisers courted the female reader, starting at the turn of the century, because of her status as primary household consumer. Northcliffe himself tried on three separate occasions to target the middle-class woman reader with a blend of household tips and more serious "women's news." Although each of these papers was a commercial failure, he had recognized something newspapers today take for granted: advertisers would pay the way of periodicals that promised a particularized readership. Advocacy journals used this knowledge to their advantage. Whether they supported the politics of a particular organization or not, by the early twentieth century, advertisers such as Selfridges and Debenhams department stores found women's periodicals an ideal place to hawk their wares to largely middle-class readers.

Through careful manipulation of the commercial marketplace, editors found a way to reach a growing constituency of readers interested in women's politics. Women's political papers imitated the changes brought about by the mainstream press, while creating some of their own innovations. For example, advocacy papers used the commercialism that historians have long considered to be the hallmark of the New Journalism—and to have ushered in the decline of serious political journalism—to fund and promote political campaigns in their pages. Lisa Ticker's classic study of the use of mass propaganda techniques by suffrage campaigners revealed how women volunteers organized to create grand political spectacles in Edwardian Britain.[23] Women's newspapers, I argue, proved central in the orchestration not only of suffrage spectacle but also of more mundane daily operations that ensured the continuance of women's political culture throughout the 1920s. Media spectacles, generally the regular, staged street sales of papers advertising bold, shocking headlines, provided for a new type of political stage in which the women's movement of the twentieth century operated. In addition, advocacy papers provided a constant link for activists during the times between mass meetings and marches, lectures, and regular propaganda work. A particular kind of political subject emerges in chapter 4, one whose activism was characterized by both her volunteerism and the politics of her reading and spending habits.

Women Making News is thus also the story of the people who made the women's press into a viable, working institution. Women readers, writers, publishers, and printers all contributed to the expansion of a press that opened up journalism as an arena for women's own professional advancement. Largely confined to publishing their work in domestic and literary magazines, women had few opportunities to build a professional identity as serious political journalists. Those who did faced serious prejudice in making a career out of journalism during the nineteenth century, as Barbara Onslow has illustrated.[24] This book takes the story of the women journalists through to the twentieth century in order to better understand the changes brought on by the New Journalism, improved printing technologies, and changes in the management of periodicals in Britain to women's status in the professions. The narrative also reveals the importance of a specialized press in promoting women in journalism. Women's papers provided reporters and writers with a new opportunity to build careers in the publishing industry. Although many contributors received little or no payment for their work, women-run newspapers provided a venue for women writers to practice their trade and build their reputations as serious journalists.

As the organizations, periodicals, and business networks discussed in the following pages demonstrate, the growth of a complex network of supporting institutions played an important role in promoting the economic, cultural, and social interests of professional women within the broader context of print culture. Certainly, women writers had succeeded in the marketplace as writers well before the 1850s.[25] During the second half of the nineteenth century, women such as Harriet Martineau and Francis Power Cobbe rose to prominence by writing lead articles for such popular publications as the *Daily News* during the course of their careers.[26] Other lesser known journalists, as any brief examination of *The Wellesley Index to Victorian Periodicals* (the key research guide to Victorian periodicals) demonstrates, published both anonymous and signed work regularly in a variety of periodical publications. The vast majority of these women, however, maintained a marginal existence in the profession. In the pages of women-run periodicals, women journalists held a new prominent position as valued contributors. The reach of the women's press extended beyond assisting the educated middle-class woman find a space for her writings. Working- and lower-middle-class women also benefited from the networks created by the women's press industry. Printing houses that primarily employed women emerged as part of an expanding set of business relationships both for and by women. These industry-based organizations found success through a combination of subsidies and consumer patronage from women-run organizations. The women's press movement, through its myriad organizations and institutions, thus provided new professional and industrial opportunities for both unemployed and underemployed women.

In addition to providing new employment opportunities for women, these networks enabled the articulation of a particularized female political voice starting in the late 1850s. Despite the small but significant number of women writing both as novelists and journalists well before the emergence of a press for and by women, women did not have an independent forum to promote agendas that fell outside of the realm of mainstream politics. The women's press during the second half of the nineteenth century attempted to create a political medium that spoke for women unmediated by commercial market forces. Activists like Teresa Billington-Greig, for example, came to believe that such a "noncommercial" articulation of political protest was crucial to the success of the suffrage campaign.[27] Largely ignored in modern scholarship, women journalists, printers, and publishers played a crucial role in producing and sustaining such a voice.[28] Finding a "female voice" was not only about the actual expression of particular ideas regarding women's status (pamphlet literature and essays had done that since Wollstonecraft's *Vindication of the Rights of Woman*) but also a case of literally securing a permanent gendered space in which readers and writers could develop and disseminate ideas to an informed constituency in a periodic format.

By the beginning of the twentieth century, new modes of communication brought a small advocacy institution into the larger world of political discourse. In many ways, consumerism, image making, and mass-market propaganda of the Edwardian era, discussed in chapter 4, had the potential to make women's periodicals into a viable international medium. World War I, however, as Nicoletta Gullace has shown, posed challenges for the female activist by asking her to reassess her political identity as a citizen patriot.[29] The seeming unity lent by the campaign for the vote was tested when women activists began to reassess liberal democratic notions of citizenship as a result of the war. Chapter 5 turns attention to the role of the wartime women's press in attempting to hold a dynamic and rapidly changing women's movement together.

The economic and cultural disruptions caused by the war resulted in a shift in news-making practices that had a significant effect on British political culture. As Stephen Koss has argued, this period witnessed the beginning of the decline of the prestige of political weeklies, a style of reporting that most women-run periodicals took up in the 1920s.[30] With the emergence of radio and the general decline of political newspapers, women's periodicals faced new difficulties. Intense competition for readers during a period of world economic depression prompted papers to create more modern and "eye-catching" papers in order to survive. This new economy of print challenged the noncommercial foundations upon which the women's press was built. Chapter 6 discusses how women's papers adjusted to these changes and the kinds of challenges that the 1930s posed for the continuation of advocacy journalism as a political medium. The book concludes by reflecting on the journals of the women's movement during the 1970s and provides a final assessment of the relationship between gender, community, print culture, and political subjectivity. It ends by contemplating the limitations of the media as a forum for politics within the context of contemporary concerns. By briefly recounting the story of *Spare Rib,* a radical feminist periodical started in Britain in 1972, I explore the return by women to print as a viable alternative political forum.

The history of the women's press was by no means one of a progressive and ultimately triumphant success, although some individual papers did enjoy widespread popularity. Rather, it remains a story of a series of stops and starts, disappointments and successes, under which supporters persisted, due to a combination of the sometimes single-minded dedication of editors willing to sink personal fortunes into failing publications and middle-class women volunteers deciding to transgress class and gender boundaries to sell papers on the streets. Despite continuing difficulties, by the opening years of the twentieth century, a well-established infrastructure for the women's press industry was firmly in place. A relatively small but dedicated reading audience supported the gender-based business practices of their favorite weekly, monthly, and/or quarterly advocacy periodicals. As a space of alternative political discourse, these publications provided an invaluable medium for the organizations that used them as a forum for issues that included concerns over women's education, employment, suffrage, and a host of social causes such as antivivisection, temperance, and antivice campaigns. Advocacy journalism emerged as a primary means through which women's organizations both discussed and disseminated these agendas.

The importance of this kind of community in the formation of political identities remains crucial to understanding the development of a woman-centered political culture in Britain. Scholars have long mined women's political periodicals as sources rather than studied them as a discrete historical subject. This book historicizes these publications for the first time as a crucial part of women's political culture. Tracing the history of a women-run institution that spanned over seventy-five years reveals important links between Victorian political forms and those of the later twentieth century.[31] The debate over suffrage, as June Purvis and Sandra Holton have demonstrated, extended back to the second half of the nineteenth century. The successful suffrage papers of the Edwardian era, as this book reveals, emerged out of a fifty-year tradition of women's advocacy journalism, whose development was shaped by the successes and failures of earlier women's news journals. The rise of institutions such as the women's advocacy press played a crucial role in both articulating and promoting these early suffrage debates. Uncovering these connections between ideas and the institutions that supported them emphasizes the very real continuities that existed between nineteenth- and twentieth-century forms of women's political culture.

1

Making Women Their Business: The Origins of the Women's Political Press in Britain

"A periodical is enormous power," remarked Bessie Parkes in a letter to Barbara Bodichon in 1857. These two pioneers of the women's press joined together in the mid-1850s in the hopes of starting a forum for women to voice concerns about employment, education, and their political status. Friends since the late 1840s, they began their careers as political activists by forming the Married Women's Property Committee in 1855 to petition Parliament for the passage of legislation that would give married women limited rights to their own property. Although the petition failed, the publicity generated by the campaign influenced them to coordinate a series of piecemeal propaganda efforts and create a medium that would give disenfranchised middle-class women a forum to express political opinions. Parkes and Bodichon thought that through publishing a women's paper they could further focus public attention directly on the issue of women's changing economic status in the emerging Victorian liberal democratic state. With this ambitious objective in mind, these two women laid the foundation for the women's press movement by creating a journal and a set of supporting institutions that encouraged the educated, independent, and politically minded woman reader to believe in the power of print to affect social change.

Parkes and Bodichon had significant journalism experience, publishing articles in both local newspapers and the radical press in the 1840s on the education and employment of women.[1] By the late 1850s, they became convinced that a women-run paper would serve as a sympathetic space where they could publish their own ideas and better advocate for these issues. At the same time, such a journal would connect them to a larger community of readers and journalists interested in women's economic advancement. By March 1858, Parkes and Bodichon had formed a limited liability company, "the necessary money having been collected from various good friends of the cause," and the first number of the *English Woman's Journal,* with Bessie Parkes and fellow reformer Matilda Hayes as coeditors, came off the presses (fig. 1).[2]

The ability of a small group of middle-class women with limited financial resources to start a publication both "for and by women" developed out of the particular historical circumstance of mid-nineteenth-century Britain. The rise of the liberal state supported the development of civic institutions that facilitated the growth of a nascent women's movement, led by educated middle-class women. At the same time, the government loosened its grip on political expression by doing away with the longtime practice of press regulation through the abolition of the newspaper taxes. Britain during the mid–nineteenth century witnessed the birth of a new genre of female-run "advocacy" political journals largely because of the convergence of these two events.

This chapter traces the institutional infrastructure of the women's press movement in order to explore how a gender-based political culture first emerged in Britain during the second half of the nineteenth century. It also discusses the ideological and historical factors behind the founding of early women's advocacy journals, while analyzing the broader project of creating a women's press industry. More than simply a series of loosely related women-run periodical publications, the women's press relied on a sustaining set of business networks that consisted primarily of well-funded women's organizations to support their programs. Promoting what these publications defined as "women's causes," middle-class women editors, publishers, and printers harnessed print media as a powerful and, more important, accessible tool for use in furthering their own nascent political agendas. These journals and their associated institutions played a crucial role in establishing a new politically minded community of intellectuals and activists based not on more familiar divisions of class but on gender.

Creating a Press "For and By Women" at Midcentury

During the 1860s, a growing debate over the economic and educational needs of women helped establish the women's advocacy press as a viable and lasting institution. Victorians who started women's periodicals found themselves, like Parkes and Bodichon, inspired by these issues. Radical religious groups

THE

ENGLISH WOMAN'S JOURNAL.

PUBLISHED MONTHLY.

| Vol. XII. | February 1, 1864. | No. 72. |

LXVI.—A REVIEW OF THE LAST SIX YEARS.

SIX YEARS have now elapsed since the "English Woman's Journal" was started, and this number for February, 1864, being the last of the twelfth volume, I have thought that it might be useful to say a few words to our readers regarding the motives which led to its commencement, and the reasons which have induced those who started it to carry out their undertaking in one particular way. Numerous questions are constantly (and very naturally) asked by friends who come to the office, of those who conduct its practical business; observations are made as to the relative size and the special nature of the contents of the Journal, and many suggestions made in a kindly spirit for its supposed possible improvement. It is to the answering of these questions, observations, or suggestions that I would now address myself; and I do so individually, because until lately I possessed immediate control over the matter in hand; and because considerable sums of money have been, from first to last, practically confided to me for the purposes of our cause.

Ten years ago, although there was an earnest and active group of people, deeply interested in all that relates to female education and industry, and to the reform of the laws affecting the property of married women, and though efforts were being made in many directions for the bettering of the condition of the mass of single women in this country, there was no centre of meeting, nor any one work which could be said to draw together the names of the ladies so actively employed. But the separate exertions carried on were surely and solidly laying the foundations of what has now taken its place as one of the chief social "movements" of the day. In Education, a great start was made by the erection of the "Ladies' Colleges." Both at the one located in Harley Street, and at the one carried on in Bedford Square, under the auspices of a most generous and indefatigable foundress, the girl pupils were brought in

Figure 1. Lead article from the *English Woman's Journal.*

such as the Unitarians and Quakers brought public attention to questions regarding women's cultural status prior to 1850 by promoting the improved status of women and the egalitarian schooling of the sexes. Although small in number when compared to other dissenting Protestant groups, Unitarians, in particular, played a central role in developing an early feminist consciousness in Britain through encouraging the link between women's education and female responsibility.[3] Like other early feminist reformers, Parkes, the daughter of a radical lawyer, and Bodichon, the daughter of a reformist member of Parliament (MP), came from Unitarian backgrounds, where they received new educational opportunities.[4] Other groups, such as the early Owenite socialists, so well described by Barbara Taylor, promoted a program of sexual equality during the early nineteenth century that attempted to radically reconfigure women's role in British society.[5]

Educated women from the middling classes, many with their own independent incomes, started and led the first women's political periodicals. Like the radical "Unstamped" journalists of the early nineteenth century who came before them,[6] they believed in the transformative power of press advocacy. Much early inspiration came from new theories on the relationship between women and paid labor. A series of two lectures given by Unitarian Anna Jameson in the early 1850s and later published as "Sisters of Charity and The Communion of Labour" articulated justifications for women's right to work. She described a model of cooperation between the sexes in the labor market that in turn would lead to a greater social role for women through their service to the community. Jameson was personally connected with women advocacy journalists of the 1850s and 1860s; her theories acted as a guiding force for women journalists who sought to reimagine economic and social relationships in Victorian Britain.[7]

Harriet Martineau's work on women's status in British society provided further inspiration for the early women's press. Her writing on women's employment helped to fuel the debate over the "redundant woman" that took place in the mainstream press during midcentury. In a widely read article published in the *Edinburgh Review,* Martineau used figures from the 1851 census to identify a new class of woman: unmarried, unsupported, and unemployed. Many of the half a million women Martineau categorized in this group came from a lower-middle-class background and could expect to receive support neither from a husband nor their own families. These "odd women," as George Gissing later famously labeled them, existed on the social margins, often as underpaid governesses or seamstresses.[8] Martineau's well-publicized findings greatly influenced early advocacy journalists to focus on women's employment and financial independence.

This well-rehearsed story of what many historians have understood as the beginnings of the feminist movement has been used recently to help understand the "gendered nature of politics" in Britain.[9] Jane Rendall, Catherine Hall, and Amanda Vickery have explored how women participated in nation building during the second half of the nineteenth century. A new liberalism, according to Rendall, emerged during the 1860s, linked to a radical Unitarianism that facilitated women's entry into public life.[10] Through her analysis of suffrage agitation surrounding the 1867 Reform Bill, Rendall maintains that women's presence on the boundaries of the political nation was not insignificant.[11] Citizenship during this period came to be framed in terms of not only rights but also a collective British identity of which women had to prove they were a part. As Vickery observed, "there was more to politics than Parliament."[12]

Print, for each of these historians, played an important role in fostering women's inclusion in the nation, although none develops an argument as to why or how this occurs within the context of the emergent liberal state. The growth of an extraparliamentary political culture by and for women, I argue, found its expression not only in the moment of suffrage controversy in 1867 described by Rendall but in the long-term networks created by women's newspapers and their associated institutions throughout Great Britain. Placing the familiar story of women's political activism within the larger narrative of the growth of a popular liberal reform culture thus can further our understanding of the historical relationship between gender, politics, and nation.

This new gendered culture of politics was facilitated, in part, by the liberalization of press and business laws. During the second half of the nineteenth century, the periodical press underwent a number of fundamental legislative and technological changes that made periodicals easier to establish and cheaper to produce and distribute.[13] Paper taxes, advertising taxes, and the Stamp Duty had all contributed to restrictions on the free flow of information in the early nineteenth century. The government first abolished the advertising tax in 1853; the abolition of the Stamp Duty, the most hated of the press taxes, followed. This tax had required all official newspapers to pay for and receive a stamp from the government in order to legitimately sell their publications. Although a thriving "Unstamped" alternative press did emerge during this period, laws and practices that limited an editor's ability to distribute information greatly restricted its broader influence.[14] By 1861, Britain abolished the last of the "taxes on knowledge," the paper tax. The circulation potential of this new free press dramatically increased with the growth of a complete railway network that came to replace the slower, more expensive stagecoach transportation system during the 1850s.[15]

The Limited Liability Acts of 1856 and 1857 played a further role in both expanding and diversifying the press. Before limited liability legislation, shareholders of a company could be held liable for the whole amount of a company's losses, making it difficult to find shareholders to start a business. Investors could now raise money to start periodicals more easily and with less financial risk. "There must be a joint-stock," declared Bessie Parkes before starting the *English Woman's Journal*.[16] In addition to legal protections, women's advocacy journalists came to realize, such a corporation would ensure the financial backing necessary to create a relatively independent journalistic enterprise.

Women's political journalism developed as part of this newly unfettered British liberal press. Newspapers and journals, once restricted by the state, now found themselves regulated by the economy of the marketplace. Publishers, printers, and private investors embarked on a broad range of journalistic enterprises during this period, as new commercial political dailies grew alongside less profit-conscious political advocacy publications.[17] Hundreds of political periodicals started and failed in London and the provinces in the decades following the repeals. As Alan Lee has argued, this new and highly diverse press served the growing needs of an emergent liberal political culture that took root in Britain during this period.[18] Postrepeal newspapers played an important role in shaping the character of Victorian liberal society by providing a wide range of both information and analysis for a growing middle-class readership. The "Fourth Estate," as journalists and proprietors came to call the press during this period, claimed its place at midcentury as a cultural institution that presumed to preserve the rights of citizens as an arbiter of the people. Some contemporaries went as far as to boldly declare that this new press represented "a power, a branch of government, with inalienable weight in law-making."[19] Regardless of whether there was evidence to support such hyperbolic statements, this attitude found increasing currency among nineteenth-century printers, publishers, and readers.

Why did female reformers believe that women readers needed a specialized space to engage in political discourse as part of this new Fourth Estate? Women's advocacy journals made up a distinct and highly specialized part of the large constellation of print media and addressed the serious-minded woman reader, a woman concerned with the political, economic, and social advancement of herself and her fellow "sisters." These journals clearly distinguished themselves from other types of periodicals targeted at women that also thrived during this period. Publications written for but not necessarily by women had long helped constitute women into a community of consumers who shared common interests linked to the issues of household management, dress, and entertaining. Scholarly studies of commercially driven domestic women's magazines run mainly by men for women have demonstrated the ways in which domestic women's magazines constituted an apolitical female reader.[20] Commercial magazines such as the *Lady's Magazine* (1770–1832), the *Lady's Monthly Museum* (1798–1832), and *La Belle Assemblee* (1806–32) held an established place in British culture and maintained a strong cultural influence because of their large readerships.[21] The type of gendered communities that grew up around these journals remained distinct from those of the women's press. As Kathryn Shevelow has argued, periodicals for women during this early period provided little opportunity for women readers or writers to represent themselves as subjects outside of a privatized domestic realm and instead "offered normative constructions of domestic femininity."[22] Separating women out from male readers, the earliest periodicals targeted women as a consumer group linked together through a common concern over manners and morals.[23] Rather than constructing women as public citizens, as the women's press attempted to do, the women's domestic press represented a woman reader whose interests fell outside of the realm of politics.

As the popularity of domestic magazines increased, this community of women readers increasingly found itself bound by contemporary beliefs governing traditional feminine behavior. The market for women's domestic magazines greatly expanded during this period, as the nineteenth century witnessed the publication of over a thousand women's domestic magazine titles.[24] In these domestic magazines, women found highly prescriptive domestic advice, dress patterns, "cookery," and fashion plates. Critics of women's magazines, such as Alice Adburgham and Cynthia White, have read these publications primarily as instruments of female oppression through their imposition of a model of middle-class domesticity on their readers.[25] Margaret Beetham has rejected this formulation of the domestic magazine and attempted to understand the potential of women's magazines as a "feminized space" to become "a medium of exchange among a community of women."[26] In both cases, the domestic women's magazine provided a means of constituting the woman reader and writer as a domestic subject who found ways to sometimes subvert the hegemonic aspects of domestic femininity through her own responses and interpretations of the text. Women's domestic magazines thus located reader agency firmly in the private sphere.

Mainstream newspapers and journals offered similar fare to female readers. Although the press extensively covered topics relating to women starting as early as the 1830s, in the majority of newspapers, according to E. M. Palmegiano, "women were not news but features."[27] The mainstream, provincial, and radical press only occasionally published articles on women's education and employment in the late 1840s and 1850s.[28] By the late nineteenth century, mainstream newspapers had started to mimic the success of women's domestic magazines with the advent of the "women's page," a feature that highlighted fashion, cooking, and domestic advice columns. Women, of course, could read beyond the women's page, if they chose. However, as Stephen Koss has argued about this period, political newspapers remained "distinctly a gentleman's press as much in sex as in class."[29] Even the handful of "advanced" mainstream newspapers directed at a female audience steered women away from public concerns. Arnold Bennett, the editor of the penny illustrated weekly *Woman* (1896–1900), claimed that "politics were excluded from its pages." As he explained his editorial policy: "A woman's politics were those of her husband, if she had one; and those of her male relatives if she was unmarried."[30] The interests of this community of women readers, as constructed by the mainstream and domestic presses, fell entirely outside of the public realm.

Women like Parkes and Bodichon created a woman-run paper largely in response to the unavailability of serious features in the press directed at the woman reader. In this new genre of periodical, politics, opinion pieces, and advice articles on issues of employment and education of use to women replaced the more standard home-centered fare of domestic magazines. Unlike the domestic women's press, advocacy journals engaged their readers in contemporary political questions and debates. Thus, the women's press provided women with an alternative vision of community based on women's direct involvement in public concerns. In contrast to the project of women's magazines and mainstream periodicals directed at women as described by Palmegiano, Adburgham, White, and Beetham, the women's advocacy press self-consciously constituted women as political rather than domestic subjects.

The women's press thus helped facilitate women's entry into public life by developing a sophisticated institutional infrastructure that drew upon an emergent liberal journalistic tradition. Women's advocacy journals, like other periodicals of this period, performed the role of political watchdog by reporting on political issues of the day. This small, ambitious press, however, tested many of the limits of the liberal press model. Although founded on the principles of individual freedom and political justice, the disenfranchised status of the woman reader meant that women's advocacy journals did not pay allegiance to any particular political party. At the same time, advocacy journals placed themselves outside of the commercial marketplace because they relied on donated capital and a volunteer work force. Leaders of women's organizations actively promoted the production and maintenance of a female literary space by asking members not only to purchase but also to participate directly in the daily workings of those women-run journals that supported their own political, economic, and cultural ideals.

BUILDING POLITICAL NETWORKS

As the foregoing brief history of the British press at midcentury suggests, little opportunity existed for women to engage in open political debate before the founding of the *English Woman's Journal.* The National Association for the Promotion of Social Science (NAPSS) was a notable exception. Formed in 1856 out of a group of liberal-minded politicians and thinkers, led by Lord Brougham, the Society remained one of the few public societies that accepted women as members. The NAPSS debated at their annual conferences such varied topics as juvenile delinquency, sewage systems, housing, and women's rights, all with an eye to improving the conditions of Britain through the application of the "science of society."[31] According to Lawrence Goldman, the organization helped diffuse a "popular liberalism" by serving as an effective extraparliamentary institution that brought a social reform agenda into the realm of formal Liberal politics.[32]

The NAPSS played an important role in establishing a women's press industry by providing both an inspiration for leaders and a model for its institutional infrastructure. The Society's reformist agenda immediately attracted several women who had been active in the agitation over the passage of the first Married Women's Property Act. Prominent members included early founders of the women's advocacy press, including: suffrage advocates Lydia Becker and Helen Blackburn; Girton College founder Emily Davies; Emily Faithfull, proprietor of the Victoria Press; and journalists, editors, and proprietors Barbara Bodichon, Jessie Boucherett, and Bessie Rayner Parkes.[33] Isa Craig, a women's press contributor, served as secretary of the organization in 1857. Many of these women, such as Lydia Becker and Barbara Bodichon, possessed independent incomes, enabling them later to own the papers that supported their agendas.

In this venue, women reformers publicly engaged in social reform debates for the first time. One of the central issues regularly taken up by the NAPSS related to the plight of unemployable, "redundant" women. Jessie Boucherett's paper "The Industrial Employment of Women" and Bessie Parkes's paper "The Market for Educated Female Labour" represented two of the first and most influential pieces by women presented at early NAPSS meetings.[34] The organization, however, did not allow women to read their own work during the first two annual conferences. At the urging of its female members, this policy changed in 1859. Parkes wrote to Bodichon of the excitement of speaking in public, a rare opportunity granted to women during this period: "I had a most successful week at Leeds and Bradford. I read our paper to a crowded section; two hundred people listening at the very least, Mrs. Jameson and Miss Twinning on the platform besides me. . . . We . . . stayed on the platform all day. . . . Did you ever hear of such a thing!"[35] This new authoritative position on the podium opened up women such as Parkes to numerous criticisms. The mainstream press parodied "Lord Brougham's little corps of lady orators," and called the "unladylike" NAPSS women inappropriate speakers. *Blackwood's* magazine complained of women's "inaudible" voices and urged the public to discourage women's future presence on the podium.[36] Significantly, the reviewers praised the actual *content* of the papers. They only criticized their public *delivery* by women members. The NAPSS later reprinted many of the papers written by women. Clearly, even within the progressive space of the NAPSS, the British public during the late 1850s and 1860s had more difficulty with women expressing ideas on the speaker's podium than on paper.

Outside of the confines of the NAPSS, women generally did not express political opinions, verbally or in print. Early supporters of the women's press believed that in their own newspapers they could deal with issues of women's employment and social reform while paying little regard to the cultural limitations imposed on them by traditional gender roles. In this anonymous print medium, female journalists believed that they might remain free from the embarrassment of public ridicule and accusations of unfeminine behavior. A woman-run venue could potentially provide to women a voice in shaping contemporary debates over issues such as employment and education.

Their experience with the NAPSS taught women reformers, however, that they needed a strong institutional base to accompany such an enterprise if they were to fulfill the ambition of offering a gendered critique of liberal society. The start of the *English Woman's Journal* in 1858 thus soon was followed by the founding of the Society for Promoting the Employment of Women (SPEW) in January of 1860.[37] Separate but intimately connected in both purpose and administration, each provided mutual assistance for the creation and promotion of a woman's collective voice within a gender-specific literary space. Bodichon and Parkes used the *Journal* to provide an opportunity for women to discuss topics first addressed at NAPSS meetings. However, they strategically suppressed the question of women's political status. As Parkes claimed, "the only subject which I steadily refused to discuss was the political one, believing it too impractical, in the present constitution of the world to make it worth while to risk very vital and practical interests by the introduction of so unpopular an element."[38]

SPEW complemented the *Journal* by offering real-world solutions to women's social and economic concerns. Both modeled on and affiliated with the NAPSS, SPEW understood its female-centered liberal agenda in the following practical "social scientific" terms: "to promote the Employment of Women in occupations suitable for their sex, by collecting and diffusing useful information on the subject by establishing an office which shall be a centre for inquiry, by practically ascertaining the capacity of women for some of the occupations hitherto closed to them and by encouraging their better and more complete education."[39] Holding its first official meeting in January 1860, the Society incorporated in 1879[40] and enjoyed a distinguished list of members, due to its loose affiliation with the NAPSS.[41]

Together with the *Journal,* SPEW provided the framework for a press that advocated for a newly created gender-identified constituency, not of the "ladies," "servants," or "girls" addressed by domestic magazines but of "women." The following series of stories about the early institutions of the women's press reveals how a group of educated middle-class women came to join Parkes and Bodichon in promoting the women's press movement. During the late 1850s and 1860s, the formation of volunteer networks came together with the willingness to experiment with new modes of doing business to create a lasting model for the women's press. Women began to participate in and shape larger cultural discussions regarding the social, political, and economic status of women in Britain in a bold new way. By drawing public attention to issues of particular intcrest to women, the women's press supported a community of readers and writers who understood print media as a potentially powerful tool in creating political communities in the name of social reform.

The Early Institutions of the Women's Press

A key characteristic of women's political culture after 1850 was the importance of middle-class female leadership. According to Phillipa Levine, a

strong sense of woman-centered community motivated this new generation of organizer.[42] In contrast to the women of the 1840s studied by Kathryn
Gleadle, who attached themselves to radical humanitarian causes, usually led
by Unitarian men, midcentury female reformers looked to promote more
clearly gendered causes.[43] Employment, rather than the question of women's
political representation, soon took center stage as the first reform program
taken up under the banner of a campaign launched "for and by women." As
Parkes later recalled in her book *Essays on Women's Work,* the actual impetus
for starting the *English Woman's Journal* came from her desire to start "a
magazine" devoted "to the special objects of woman's work."[44]

Parkes's vision of helping unemployed and underemployed women find
work found inspiration not in England but in Scotland. After sighting a
copy of a Scottish journal "Edited and Published by Ladies" called the *Waverley Journal* on a visit to Edinburgh in October 1856, Parkes—along with
Bodichon, who used her own income to help fund the project—entered
into negotiations with the editor to turn the *Waverley* into a journal that
advocated for British "working women." Remaking the *Waverley* into a
broad-based national journal of women's work proved untenable. The editor, while sympathetic to Parkes's project, believed that the journal should
maintain a Scottish and literary focus, and thus prevented the possibility
of collaboration. "The *Waverley Journal* certainly shall not have my name
unless it is entirely given up into my hands," Parkes ultimately proclaimed.[45]
At the advice of an influential member of the NAPSS, Parkes and Bodichon
decided "not to spend money and effort over a property which did not appear to be worth either but to start afresh with a new journal of our own
in London."[46]

This episode illustrates one of the early lessons learned by the proponents
of women's press advocacy: the necessity of securing full editorial control.
Like other periodicals published in Britain during this period, the power of
the editor-proprietor journalist loomed large in the business of advocacy
journalism. As Alan Lee has argued in the case of the mainstream press,
securing financing and keeping a strong hold on the editorial direction of a
paper enabled the editor-proprietor to determine its focus.[47] Throughout the
second half of the nineteenth century, editors of women's advocacy journals
kept tight control over content.

The account of the failed attempt to take over the *Waverly* illustrates another eventual pattern in women-run journalism. London, as the British
metropole, immediately developed as the center of the women's press movement. Not only did most women's advocacy papers get their start there but

also the handful of papers that started outside of the city moved to the capital city as soon as they had secured a regular audience. The establishment of London as a hub for women's journalism proved crucial in terms of creating a cosmopolitan medium for exchange while helping to better facilitate distribution and secure publicity. More important, the capital provided women journalists with the opportunity to create social and business networks that expanded both the scope and influence of their social reform projects. The networks established alongside particular journals thus often proved as important to the project of press advocacy as the periodicals themselves.

The establishment of the *English Woman's Journal* in 1858 in London, for example, also inspired the founding at its Langham Place headquarters of a Ladies Institute, reading room, lunch room, and employment register. The *Journal,* in a very particular way, also influenced the founding of SPEW later that year by Jessie Boucherett. Well educated and possessing her own independent income, she had developed an interest in the plight of the redundant woman after reading Martineau's article on women's employment. The *English Woman's Journal* quite literally prompted Boucherett to take action. Helen Blackburn recalled Boucherett's decision to spend her annual income on founding an organization to assist unemployed women:

> She was consuming her soul in solitary desire to help women to better economic conditions when one day she caught sight on a railway bookstall of a number of the *English Woman's Journal.* She bought it, attracted by the title but expecting nothing better than the inanities commonly considered fit for women. To her surprise and joy she found her own unspoken aspirations reflected in its pages. She lost no time repairing to the office of the journal. . . . She began forthwith to plan the desire of her life, a society for promoting the employment of women.[48]

Boucherett made her way to Langham Place to meet the staff of the *Journal,* who offered her office space and encouraged her to put the periodical's message of expanding employment opportunities for women into practice. Soon, she convinced both the editors and other women she met in the reading room to make the *Journal* SPEW's official organ.

The connection between the *Journal* and SPEW enabled the development of a complete program of women-run political advocacy. In both organizations, women acted as the primary shareholders and participants. Leaders charted an extraparliamentary political course along the lines of the NAPSS. Rather than starting petitions supporting changes in women's legal status, a program Parkes considered as "too impractical" during this period,[49] both institutions worked to mobilize public opinion in favor of practical campaigns to support women's economic advancement:

> Here stands our case. . . . We ask but to throw down the barrier so that women may be free to choose their own way of life—to earn their living independently and to marry or not to marry as they may see it well or prudent. We ask for a wider field of employment so that poor milliners, whose condition benevolent gentlemen have striven in vain to improve under the present state of the market for their labour may not be compelled with wasted cheeked [sic] and glassy eyes to work all hours of Sunday and of week-day or to starve. We ask but to let things find a more natural and healthy level, hoping and trusting that all women, down at least to those who now struggle honestly upon the brink of a shameful and degraded life, may gather hope and walk with firmer footing.[50]

These words, printed in the *Journal* in 1858, laid the foundation of a liberal reform agenda that sought to establish a moral political economy in the midst of the capitalist marketplace. Before the founding of SPEW, however, such rhetoric did not have the force of action behind it. Ultimately, SPEW provided the organizational infrastructure that enabled the practical implementation of a "social scientific" agenda, while the *Journal* mobilized public opinion in favor of the cause of the female worker.

SPEW thus emerged as the institutional medium that put into practice the *English Woman's Journal*'s philosophy of creating networks both "for woman and by women." In many ways, this organization played a crucial role in expanding the community that had developed at Langham Place in the reading rooms and in the pages of the *English Woman's Journal* itself. The actual work of SPEW during this period constituted a radical program of reimagining traditional definitions of women's work by opening up what they defined as "occupations suitable for their sex." This included financing women's entry into seventy nontraditional fields, including printing, bookkeeping, wood engraving, wig making, and book binding. SPEW encouraged women throughout Britain in need of employment assistance to apply directly to the office by post and helped facilitate the entry of a small, but symbolically significant, number of women into industrial employments through its financial assistance programs.

In creating a network of reform-centered projects linked to the larger project of the *Journal,* SPEW served as an important link between disparate Victorian women's organizations by lending support to other groups that assisted women. Members of the General Committee often sent delegations to conferences and meetings at the request of other women's organizations and endorsed various woman-run enterprises. Money for these projects usually came out of SPEW's general fund, although donations or loans from members also helped SPEW to carry out its obligations. As the activities of SPEW expanded, the Committee came to rely on these at times substantial donations from members. This direct involvement by committee members helped create a sense of common purpose among midcentury reformers, who for the first time found it possible to imagine themselves as part of a larger community of female activists.

The collaboration of SPEW and the *English Woman's Journal* reveals an important characteristic of this new brand of gender-identified community: the mutual assistance of women. Members often became involved in advocacy on multiple levels. Having offices centrally located in London enabled both organizations to draw on the resources of an informal community structure, supported by the reading room, employment registry, and a growing staff of volunteer and paid workers. Through this collaboration, the *Journal* itself emerged as a space for this community to expand beyond the confines of Langham Place by providing a sympathetic forum for the discussion of economic issues relating to women. As the *Journal* grew in influence in the coming years, this narrow agenda broadened to invite discussion on a wide range of topics traditionally considered off limits for the female sex, such as parliamentary politics, international news, and political theory. This shift had important consequences in expanding the market for and influence of political publications directed at the middle-class woman reader. Understanding how and why the *Journal* took the form that it did provides significant insight into the development of the women's press as a viable advocacy institution that emerged as part of the modern British liberal democratic reform tradition.

READING THE *ENGLISH WOMAN'S JOURNAL*

"When the *Times* is offered to a lady, the sheet containing the advertisements, and the births, deaths and marriages, is considerately selected," wryly observed one-time *Journal* editor Emily Davies in 1864.[51] One of the early challenges of the women's advocacy press was to teach middle-class women how to read differently. The mainstream press, as Davies comment indicates, failed to consider the woman reader as a serious reader, offering her only social features and commercial fare. In other mediums for women, current events, political commentary, and an open forum for debate over contemporary issues simply did not have a place. Female editors responded by introducing a number of journalistic innovations intended to pique reader interest in political topics in the hopes of drawing them into the larger women's advocacy community. The women's press thus attempted to transform both cultural understandings as well as personal perceptions of the woman reader who had yet to see herself as a political subject.

This reality reveals an important underlying assumption about women's reading during this period: women had their own particular relationship to print when compared to men. Periodicals like the *English Woman's Journal* attempted to redefine its audience's relationship to the news by claiming political topics as "women's concerns." Middle-class women had not participated in the long-established British tradition of visiting coffeehouses and other public places to hear and discuss the news with one's peers. The reading room at Langham Place, coupled with the information provided in the *Journal,* provided a female space where women for the first time could go to read and discuss current events. Through these semipublic and print media venues, the educated woman reader found herself surrounded with new ways of imagining her relationship to British society and politics. As Benedict Anderson has claimed in his famous study of the link between nationalism and print culture, newspapers serve as important vehicles for connecting readers to a larger political community.[52] For women, according to Kate Flint, reading can be seen as "a means of becoming part of a broader community."[53] Through the "ritual" act of regularly reading advocacy journals, women participated in a new kind of woman-centered political community that helped create a collective gender-based identity.

Who was this group of readers envisioned by the *Journal*'s editors, contributors, and correspondents? Those at Langham Place intended the *Journal* to serve as a space for an imagined community of middle-class female readers, broadly defined. Letters addressed editors as "Madam" or as "Ladies," creating the sense that the *Journal* remained a place for women, in particular, to exchange ideas. The actual reader, however, probably varied from the imagined reader. Parkes claimed that she wanted to remake the *Waverley* into a periodical for "working women." This most likely included those lower-middle-class women not in possession of an independent income. That working-*class* women read the *Journal* is doubtful. As a reader, in the words of Flint, "the working-class woman was doubly other, distanced by class as well as sex" from the burgeoning culture of print.[54] Priced at one shilling, the *English Woman's Journal* remained out of the reach of the working classes. The average reader most likely came from the upper middle class, judging from the content of the *Journal,* although no actual subscriber lists have survived.

For example, articles on the problems of finding good maidservants and letters to the editor commented on how one could appropriately educate those working-class women in their charge.

Men also read the *Journal*. Editors encouraged the participation of prominent male supporters, as they believed they helped bring in needed funds while keeping the *Journal* in the public eye. As one reader wrote:

> I heard it asserted that your *Journal* was not true to its name because some of your articles were written by gentlemen. Am I not right in having delivered my firm belief that from the first your desire has been strongly expressed that all men who heartily wish for the good and happiness of women in our social and domestic arrangements should lend us their aid in every possible way, whether that may be by their co-operation in the numerous philanthropic modes of action your *Journal* is constantly keeping before the public?[55]

The editor heartily agreed: "We have from the first invited the cooperation of men and women." She went on to praise the "very valuable assistance and encouragement" of their male and female supporters.[56] However, although the *Journal* encouraged "aid" from gentlemen, that assistance also remained largely invisible. The *Saturday Review* observed that the *Journal* "carefully excluded (men) from its compositions." Although men signed a small percentage of articles (most articles were unsigned), women were the primary shareholders and held all paid and unpaid positions.

The *Journal* quickly established a wide and respected following. "We recommend our lady readers to give this Magazine a trial," the *Leicester Chronicle* advised, while the *Welshman* declared it "certain" that the *Journal* would "be appreciated by a large class of women." The *Daily News* called it "simple, earnest, vigorous, and yet feminine," claiming that "the topics it treats are of the deepest social interest and these are discussed broadly and thoroughly, with great intelligence, with considerable ability, and with perfect good taste."[57] In cultivating women's interest in political topics, the *Journal* nevertheless maintained a reputation as both "vigorous" and "feminine" and thus thoroughly appropriate for the middle-class woman reader. The *Illustrated News of the World* also offered its approval: "We are much mistaken if the *English Woman's Journal* does not become a universal household favorite."[58] Circulation increased from four hundred in 1858 to reach its peak at one thousand copies monthly in 1860, and the *Journal* was reportedly read as far away as New Zealand.[59]

Although the *Journal* did not fulfill the ambitious predictions of the *Illustrated News,* it did sustain for its readers a unique forum for the exchange of ideas among women on "topics . . . of the deepest social interest." The monthly presence of this publication on newsstands helped ensure continued visibility of the *Journal*'s main concern: women's employment. Articles on this topic previously had appeared only occasionally in mainstream and radical journals or in the form of pamphlet literature such as Bodichon's *Women and Work* (1857). The characteristic regularity of the periodical format encouraged a continuous dialogue to emerge between readers, journalists, and the public regarding the plight of the underemployed woman.

Commitment to this diet of social reform and political news required the potential willingness to forego commercial success. When compared to its counterparts in the domestic women's press, the circulation of the *Journal* itself appears quite small. (One of the most popular periodicals of this genre, the *Englishwoman's Domestic Magazine,* claimed a readership of fifty thousand.)[60] The different projects of these journals, one to sell goods and services to women through the promotion of domestic ideals and the other to encourage women's political activism through debate and discussion, largely determined the terms by which each periodical understood its wider influence. Domestic women's periodicals, as Margaret Beetham has shown, needed to first attract advertisements in order to turn a profit and often maintained a close relationship with their advertisers.[61] Political journals such as the *English Woman's Journal* could rely less on profits from sales because of the financial support of shareholders and donors. The *English Woman's Journal* thus could afford to focus its attention on subjects of interest to a smaller community of readers.

The case of the *Queen,* a domestic women's newspaper that survives today, dramatically illustrates the potential impact of market pressure on midcentury periodicals. Started in 1861 by Samuel Beeton as a ladies' paper, complete with fashion tips and domestic advice, the magazine also covered issues such as women's employment and education in the hopes of competing for the same educated woman reader courted by the *Journal.* Davies called their new rival at first a "vulgar" imitation and later labeled it "a low kind of thing" that "no educated person would think of looking at."[62] When the *Queen* fell into difficulties within the first year, Parkes expressed relief to Bodichon: "The *English Woman's Journal* is doing its work . . . and the *Queen* newspaper which started with such a flourish is being—sold by auction!—You feared it would be a rival and so did I; so it might have been! but it wasn't!"[63] Later that year Beeton revived the *Queen* as a "ladies" paper, devoid of any "advanced" articles. The new series of the *Queen* defined news, according to Beetham, as novelty, not politics. Indeed, fashion news came to dominate the periodical in its search for advertisers and profits.[64]

In contrast, the *Journal* continued to engage readers in discussions of domestic and international news. Thus by focusing on content rather than advertisers, the *Journal* held itself to a different standard, measuring its influence as an advocacy rather than commercial enterprise. This enabled editors to introduce journalistic innovations that periodicals such as the *Queen,* with their eye on the bottom line, could not. The periodical pioneered the development of several regular features to encourage reader interest in contemporary issues beyond women's employment and education. The "Notice of Books" feature heavily weighted content in favor of books by and about women, as well as reviewing a diverse range of subjects that included Coventry Patmore's book *The Angel in the House,* a series of pamphlets on workhouse legislation, and W. E. Gladstone's book *Homer and the Homeric Age.* "Open Council," a feature borrowed from the *Waverley Journal,* published reader opinions, hoping to promote "general discussion." Correspondents did not always agree with one another. As one reader began a letter on divorce, "I hope you will admit the following letter, although its object is to express dissent from the view taken by one of the writers in the last number of your *Journal.*"[65] The publication of such correspondence placed readers in conversation with both the editors and each other in the relatively anonymous space of the periodical.

The editors understood keeping women up to date with the current events as a particular problem. Parkes explained that the column "Passing Events" should give readers an appetite for serious "news":

> It is obviously impossible for a publication, making its appearance only once a month, to compete in mere novelty of intelligence with daily contemporaries; though it has some compensatory advantage in being able to exercise some discrimination as to what is deserving of being recorded instead of being obliged in the haste of daily publication to shoot loads of matter into its columns and leave the reader to pick out from the heap what he may consider worth preserving. The purpose of these slight sketches of public occurrences has had reference rather to the future than to the moment in which they are read.[66]

The *Journal* provided readers with an original summary of selected news for readers to digest and later contemplate that included the prince consort's death, the American Civil War, and the Indian Mutiny. Readers responded by archiving individual issues both to refer to in the future and lend to friends. Women's periodicals, as Parkes's statement implied, should cultivate women's sustained interest in contemporary events rather than "novelty" news. "Women's news" included information for the sophisticated reader who imagined herself as part of a community of like-minded women. Reports on the activities of Garibaldi in Sicily, for example, included discussion of the Ladies' Garibaldi Benevolent Association, which collected money for the "relief of the wounded" in order to demonstrate women's involvement in world events.[67] Other features turned reform issues into women's causes. The "Social and Industrial" section reported on institutions such as the London Female and Preventative and Reformatory Institution, which aided "friendless and fallen females." Through careful selection and storytelling, the *Journal* offered readers a gendered perspective of contemporary events located in the realm of women's concerns for the first time.

Educating women to read in this new way was essential to sustaining advocacy journalism as a noncommercial medium that relied on female-run networks rather than the marketplace for success:

> It now needs to be considered in what relation this journal could be expected to stand to the rest of the periodical press. Had it from the first any hope, any expectation, any wish to come forward in the same field with the able monthlies which contained the best writing of the day? To this question an emphatic "No" must at once be given. . . . If it had been wished to start a brilliant and successful magazine, some eminent publisher should have been secured and persuaded to undertake active pecuniary interest and risk; all the best known female writers should have been engaged, "regardless of expense" and then—good-bye to the advocacy of any subject which would have entailed a breath of ridicule; good-bye to any thorough expression of opinion; good-bye to the humble but ceaseless struggle of all these years, the small office where so many workers collected together because the purpose and the plan were honestly conceived and carried out.[68]

Advocacy journalism thus came to define itself through its reliance on a community of dedicated workers. Engaging in competition with domestic magazines such as the refashioned *Queen*, Parkes believed, would actually inhibit the *Journal* from following its own course. Even quality monthlies such as the *Fortnightly Review* had to concern themselves with profits. Rather, success would be come through putting "women's issues" before the public. "People read the *Journal* with so much more attention than other magazines and . . . an article read by 1000 people in the *English Woman's Journal* tells more than one read by 60,000 in *Good Words*," Parkes claimed.[69] The *Journal* thus demanded much more of its audience than for-profit magazines: the ideal reader of the advocacy journal remained an engaged reader.

Through such support, the women's press avoided total dependence on the marketplace for survival throughout its seventy-five year history. In "A Few Words to Our Friends and Subscribers," Parkes echoed the sentiments of most other future editors in urging readers

> to bear in mind that the unrelaxing exertions of those who are interested in our work are absolutely necessary to ensure its continued prosperity. This *Journal* cannot rival amusing periodicals in its circulation, neither, being serious in its character, can it rely upon that principle of cheapness, which might otherwise ensure a large trade sale. It will, generally speaking, only be bought and read by those who really care for its objects.[70]

Why would middle-class women, many with limited resources, contribute to a profitless enterprise? From the beginning, Parkes and her colleagues understood the success of the *Journal* not in terms of copies sold but rather in light of a periodical's larger influence as an agent for improving women's status. "The result of this six months' labor," Parkes claimed, "has … most abundantly and satisfactorily proved that, judiciously urged, the claims of women to be allowed wider fields of work and to take their place naturally among the industrial and money getting classes of society are sure of continuance and support from the best and most enlightened members, male and female, of the community."[71] Quasi-philanthropic in its scope, the *Journal* offered assistance and advice to readers who believed in the project of creating a political, social, and economic community founded on the principles of "for and by women." Throughout her tenure as editor during the first several years and as financier during its last two, Parkes found a means of keeping her "experiment" afloat by rethinking journalism's relationship to the commercial marketplace.

By the early 1860s, the *Journal* had established a key tenet of advocacy journalism: unlike their counterparts in the mainstream press who depended on advertisers for support, advocacy journals relied on a community of dedicated readers for survival. The series of networks that emerged as an outgrowth of the activities of the *Journal* cultivated a new participatory reader. The rooms at 19 Langham Place served as an extension of the forum found in the pages of the *Journal* by providing a place where women could read and discuss the news, as well as buy pamphlets published by SPEW. The employment registry ensured that women's work remained a central issue.

Applications poured into 19 Langham Place, which continued to grow as a center of activity. Parkes remarked on the virtual impossibility of providing for the large number of applicants from "literally hundreds of women neither well trained nor picked; out numbering ... demand by ninety nine percent."[72] Those at the *Journal* soon discovered that they had drawn attention to a problem that they could not solve within the spaces of the periodical or reading room.

Concerns over finding solutions to women's employment led to further innovation and experiment in the business of press advocacy. Just as the marketplace had failed to support the publication of the *Journal,* it had also proved unable to provide the woman worker with adequate employment. Through the support of readers and patrons, Langham Place promoted new women-run industrial institutions linked to the project of press advocacy. SPEW's founding of a woman-run printing house in the late 1850s helped strengthen both the philosophical foundations and practical work of the *Journal* as an advocate for women's employment. Subsidizing a women-run printing house also insulated the *Journal* from the world of free market competition. By the early 1860s, an activist community of readers began to engage in projects that expanded the boundaries of existing women's advocacy networks.

Women Printers and the Case for Vertical Integration

The overwhelming response to the employment register resulted in Parkes's decision to collaborate with SPEW in seeking nontraditional solutions for finding remunerative work for women. "The first trade we thought of was printing," Jessie Boucherett recalled.[73] This decision represented a radical departure for women's employment advocates, as it went against conventional thinking about the relationship of women to work. Male printers had long considered themselves part of a "labor aristocracy," receiving high wages for producing culturally valued commodities.[74] Unions responded to the scheme by labeling women "unsuited" for the rigors of this "unladylike" employment,[75] claiming that the *Journal* operated "entirely from mistaken notions of philanthropy" in attempting to gain women entry into the more prestigious aspects of the trade.[76] As Sonya Rose has argued, gender played a crucial role in the construction of this nineteenth-century industrial order.[77] The rise of a sexual division of labor during the Industrial Revolution, according to Sally Alexander, resulted in limiting women's opportunities to traditional "feminized" trades such as textile manufacture.[78] This new gendered hierarchy of the industrial period resulted in a mixed bag for the female worker. Mechanization, while providing new opportunities for women in the industrial trades, also contributed to leaving women with deskilled, low-paying jobs.[79] Although the efforts of the Langham Place women did not dramatically increase women's overall presence in the printer's "labor aristocracy," this emblematic challenge to Victorian gendered hierarchies strengthened the development of a middle-class community of reformers dedicated to advocating better employment opportunities for women.

Establishing women-run printing enterprises strengthened women's advocacy networks by involving more women in the practical aspects of social reform. At the same time, getting women involved in printing solved a real problem for the *Journal:* controlling printing expenses. Volunteers had distributed the periodical and solicited subscriptions from the beginning, but printing had always been contracted out.[80] Getting involved in the printing of their own periodical, many believed, would help the Society lower costs. They did, after all, produce an increasing number of documents that needed printing, including the *Journal* itself, pamphlets, and reports. Vertically integrating publishing and distribution with printing could thus serve a double purpose: money already being spent on printing would also go toward promoting employment opportunities for women.

The women's press community tested the boundaries of the industrial gender hierarchy by reimagining Victorian business practices. SPEW developed a woman-run printing training program after Parkes bought a small press and recruited Emily Faithfull, a clergyman's daughter associated with the *Journal* since 1858, to learn the art of printing. SPEW provided the first five apprentices from the employment register for the new press now under Faithfull's management. Opened on March 25, 1860, at Great Coram Street in Russell Square, the Victoria Press, named in honor of the queen, published books, pamphlets and, of course, periodicals. The industry watched the Victoria Press closely, maintaining that women printers could only exist as a philanthropic project: "This pet printing establishment still continues to receive kindly and considerate treatment under which, of course, it is developing and increasing its business capacities."[81] These criticisms revealed the difficulties faced in creating an enterprise that relied on women's advocacy networks rather than profits—it was a semicommercial institution supported by subsidies from a volunteer organization.

Supporters of the Victoria Press thus played an important role in determining its success. The NAPSS discussed the progress of the press at their annual meetings, while offering their patronage. The *Queen* even lent its endorsement, asserting that "[Faithfull] has sought to open to her countrywomen a handicraft which has hitherto been closed to them, and to give those women, whose education and ability qualify them to undertake skilled labour, the opportunity of freeing themselves from the slopseller's sordid tyranny and the dull drudgery of the mill."[82] One women's advocacy paper "urg[ed] upon all ladies who require printing to be done to inquire whether the printer they select employs women in his office and to give the preference where it is possible to anyone who is doing his best to help on a very laborious class of women in a comparatively new and arduous undertaking."[83] By challenging the rules of the capitalist labor market through their own women-run enterprises, organizations such as SPEW created new opportunities for women. At the same time, they called upon their members and related institutions, such as the *English Woman's Journal,* to play a direct role in the success of these "for and by women" projects.

The increasing support offered by a growing community of middle-class female activists reflected a prevailing class bias. While attempting to rethink gender hierarchies, the press upheld rigid class divisions. Lower- and upper-middle-class women from throughout Britain who had read about the registry in the *Journal* applied to the offices at Langham Place for assistance. Parkes proposed a class-based division of labor in order to maintain a hierarchy that kept women of her class firmly in charge of the project. In reality, women only performed two tasks in the printing trade: the job of compositor (performed by lower-middle-class women) and that of reading and correcting manuscripts (performed by "the most cultivated class of women"). Men performed the lifting and positioning of printing equipment and type, as well as other strenuous physical tasks, which fell into line with SPEW's ideal of finding only "respectable employment" for women.

Consistent with the program of the *Journal,* concern for the well-being of workers remained important regardless of class. Faithfull created a relatively healthy environment free from the hazards of the typical print shop, where compositors sat in poorly ventilated rooms, forced to take in lead-contaminated air produced by the dust from type. She chose the original premises because of the location of "light and airy" rooms in a "quiet respectable neighborhood." The press instituted a "no talking" policy to facilitate an efficient work environment and provided high stools for women to sit on while performing their tasks. Female compositors came for training from all over Great Britain with varying abilities and physical limitations. One compositor, trained in printing by her father, came from Limerick, while another came from the "Asylum for the Deaf and Dumb."[84] Faithfull emphasized that the Victoria Press, in contrast to other printing houses, cultivated women's mental capacities and regarded it as "a mistake to regard women as mere machines—hands without heads."[85] The press thus reconceived printing industry standards in order to focus on the well-being of workers.

The Victoria Press also challenged the for-profit business model of commercial printing houses. It was a relatively expensive business to run, and the NAPSS initially subsidized the enterprise. SPEW also contributed by paying apprentice fees. Even Queen Victoria offered her support in the form of granting Faithful the title of "printer and publisher in ordinary to Her Majesty" in 1862.[86] Patronage aside, SPEW considered the press a private business enterprise from the outset. Members agreed "that it would not be advisable for the Society to undertake the business of Printer," as they believed that the "Society was formed more for helping women into remunerative occupation than for employing them itself."[87] Thus SPEW only offered support to individual workers and did not accept any liability for the business side of the press. The Victoria Press thus developed as a cross between a for-profit business and a philanthropic organization, thanks to the constant supply of printing orders, mainly from women interested in helping women break down gendered hierarchies of work.[88] This hybrid business model attempted to reform free market capitalist practices in the name of promoting women's visibility in the printing industry.

This press model soon spread to Dublin and Edinburgh through the branch organizations of SPEW in Ireland and Scotland. Though little is known of the Dublin enterprise, it was started around the same time as its Scottish counterpart. The Edinburgh-based Caledonian Press began to train women as printers, thanks to the patronage of the duchess of Kent and the financial backing of Mary Anne Thomson, the daughter of a wealthy Scottish family, in 1862.[89] Like the Victoria Press, the Caledonian Press had both the support of the queen and private capital.[90] The press listed NAPSS leader Lord Brougham as president, though evidence indicates he remained in charge in name only. The Scottish National Institution for Promoting the Employment of Women in the Art of Printing and Mary Anne Thomson herself actually started and ran the organization. "The Promoters of this Institution," claimed one advertisement bearing the foregoing names, "will be prepared with an organized and efficient Staff of *Female Compositors*, to execute *any description of Printing*."[91]

Like the Victoria Press, the Caledonian Press published a woman-run periodical, the *Rose, Shamrock, and Thistle* (fig. 2).

Figure 2. *The Rose, the Shamrock, and the Thistle,* title page.

The periodical appeared monthly starting in May 1862, "for the Fair Daughters of Great Britain and Ireland." Priced at one shilling, the periodical mirrored the *Journal*, with articles on women's employment appearing alongside serialized stories and reports of current events. Accusations of "philanthropy" also abounded. "Take away benevolence, sympathy, and patronage and all institutions for promoting the employment of women in the art of printing will very soon go quietly to Hades," asserted members of the Scottish Typographical Union.[92] The *Thistle*, however, rejected this assessment, embracing the hybrid business model of the Victoria Press: "we have in view a two-fold object. To amuse, to interest and . . . to instruct our patrons and . . . to give assistance to women walking the rugged road of life alone. But we do not ask alms for our protégés: nor are they paupers: we solicit subscriptions." By issuing a periodical "printed by women," they hoped to add printing "to the number of trades by the exercise of which women can earn honourable bread." "We hope by its production," the editors claimed, "to give greater publicity to the Institution, to provide a certain amount of regular employment for our 'hands,' and—is it too presumptuous?—to assist our treasury."[93]

These small but closely watched "experiments" in women's employment questioned gender hierarchies of work during the late 1850s and early 1860s, while at the same time vertically integrating the fledgling institutions of the women's press. The new business model developed by these organizations, however, was not strong enough to overcome what still remained a competitive marketplace. The Caledonian's "treasury" never filled to an adequate level, and in 1864 it folded, along with the *Rose, Shamrock, and Thistle.* During this same period, the Victoria Press had staffing problems and fell behind in its print orders. "My chief worry," wrote Parkes to Bodichon in 1862, "has been the Victoria Press which never by any chance keeps an engagement as to time; while Emily Faithfull is herself worried by twenty half trained female printers and I often wonder she gets through *at all.*" The *English Woman's Journal* itself had experienced a continual drop in circulation, starting in 1863. Emily Davies believed that the periodical needed to look to the larger periodicals market for readers. To attract a more general reader, she maintained, the *Journal* had to pay more money to contributors for better articles. This proposal, however, remained untenable, as the *Journal* began losing fifty pounds per year.[94] By August 25, 1864, the responsibility for the *Journal* was placed solely in the hands of Parkes, and the limited liability company soon was "wound up voluntarily."[95]

By the mid-1860s, leaders began to look for new solutions to sustain the early momentum of the press advocacy movement. Despite its growing network of readers and writers and the consolidation of print work, the periodical business remained a highly competitive industry, even for a relatively well-supported advocacy journal. Parkes attributed the difficulties of the *Journal* to the shifting marketplace of the 1860s. "The condition of the periodical markets have [*sic*] quite changed in the last four years," wrote Parkes. "It has become the great field for *speculation,* each serial pitted against the other which shall try the cleverest article. At the same time, the trade is very uncertain; the circulation of these different serials rise and fall and it has become a race which seems to me unwholesome and foolish and with which I cannot possibly cope."[96]

Parkes had observed one of the problematic aspects of what some critics have called the "golden age" of postrepeal periodical production. Increased competition from the numerical expansion of regional and special interest for-profit periodicals in both London and the provinces occurred as a result of the repeal of the press laws, improved paper-making and printing technology, and more liberal incorporation laws.[97] Parkes and her supporters, rather than giving up, came to believe that they could rely on this improved and expanding periodical marketplace to help sustain their enterprise. The mixture of private capital and institutional support from organizations such as SPEW and the NAPSS had not yet covered the costs of publishing a monthly journal, which amounted to 550 pounds per annum, exclusive of administrative support costs. As the early founders discovered, the semicommercial model of press advocacy remained difficult to sustain in the face of challenges from not only the marketplace but also within the nascent institutions of the women's press itself.

REINVENTING THE WOMEN'S PRESS

The problem of keeping this community of reform institutions and supporters together led to the decision by those at Langham Place to broaden the scope of their projects while widening the appeal of women's press advocacy. Continued attention to the question of women's employment by the women's press during the late 1850s and early 1860s contributed to the shaping of what came to be known as the "Woman Question" during the 1860s and 1870s. Concerns over women's employment, education, and rights within marriage made up the constellation of issues debated by liberal reformers. This period witnessed the passage of Married Women's Property rights legislation, the early origins of the women's suffrage movement with the petition offered by John Stuart Mill to Parliament in 1867, and the rise of new institutions to support women's education. Journals, newspapers, and pamphlets all discussed and debated the effect of these changes on British society and women. Critics such as Eliza Lynn Linton—with her negative depiction of the educated and independently minded "Girl of the Period," a series of articles that appeared the *Saturday Review* starting in 1868—fueled heated debates. Whether one supported the slowly emerging legislative and cultural changes to women's status or not, one thing remained clear: the mainstream media and domestic magazines had begun to pay closer attention to the same issues that women first debated in reading rooms, committee meetings, and, most notably, in the pages of the *English Woman's Journal.*

Rather than seeing their work as done, the women at Langham Place capitalized on the publicity generated by the Woman Question debates. As Parkes argued:

> It has been frequently urged, why not trust to the diffusion of ideas through the general press, now that editors and readers are so much more willing to accept them than they once were; and while each article thus written is certain to circulate far more widely than anything printed in a special magazine? But I am convinced there is something in a re-iterated effort which far outweighs the effect of the separate thoughts. It is not this or that number of a magazine, this or that article from a given pen, which does the work; it is partly the effect of repetition—line upon line—and partly the knowledge that there is in the world a distinct embodiment of certain principles. Even if this embodiment be in itself far from mighty, it serves to sustain a great amount of scattered energy, and may be a rallying point of much value to the whole of the field.[98]

Despite this new attention given to the Woman Question, Parkes's assessment of the coverage of such topics in the mainstream media spoke directly to the issue of control. Advocacy journalism provided a "rallying point" for the support of particular "principles," as it represented a permanent and lasting institution that would ensure the "repetition" of the ideals promoted by periodicals and the institutions that supported them. In no other medium could these women articulate concerns and ideas in a regular forum. The problem for Parkes and her supporters remained how to preserve this space as a voice of popular female-led reform in the increasingly competitive periodicals market of the mid-1860s.

As early as April 1864, Parkes had plans in place to replace the *English*

Woman's Journal with a new publication. She wrote to Bodichon regarding her idea to dissolve the limited liability company to raise more funds from supporters for a new journal that would "be nearly the same size and half the price."[99] Through increasing subscribers by lowering the per-copy cost, Parkes believed that the new periodical would avoid the financial difficulties by embracing a more broad-based commercial model. More subscribers would lessen the operating costs and the periodical's dependence on cash from supporters while increasing its influence. Parkes incorporated the *Alexandra Magazine and Woman's Social and Industrial Advocate* in May 1864. That September, subscribers to the *English Woman's Journal* received their first issue of the *Alexandra Magazine and Englishwoman's Journal* (*sic;* see fig. 3).

Employing a woman from Cork, Ireland, Susanna Meredith, as editor sent the message that the new *Magazine* would be more than a periodical for and by English women.[100] Pricing the periodical at sixpence rather than one shilling monthly also made it more accessible to a larger class of reader. "The time has come when it appears desirable to secure the diffusion of practical principles over a larger class of society, and in a cheaper form," claimed Parkes. The joint periodical, it was hoped, would, "by reason of its greater cheapness, reach many homes into which the *Englishwoman's Journal* [*sic*] could not penetrate."[101] Setting up its offices at 19 Langham Place, the magazine maintained a close connection with SPEW and advocated "all suitable employment for women" in its pages. Serial stories and poetry by women "of well known literary merit" appeared alongside regular columns that included "Monthly Memoranda," "Open Correspondence," "Quarterly Notices of Books," and "Notices of Benevolent Institutions."

The excitement at Langham Place over the new periodical was tempered by problems with the Victoria Press that threatened to undercut the "respectable" middle-class character of this new endeavor. Management difficulties and public scandal distanced Faithfull from the women at Langham Place. In 1864, Faithfull found herself involved in the notorious Codrington divorce case. Faithfull had apparently witnessed Mr. Codrington's cruelty against his wife and supported Mrs. Codrington's claim that he had at one time attempted to rape Faithfull herself. A long, complicated trial resulted in dragging Faithfull's name and reputation all over the press. The *Times*'s coverage of the trial implied that Mr. Codrington had blackmailed Faithfull into ultimately not supporting the charges of his wife. "I find social opinion running high against Emily Faithfull," wrote Parkes in 1864. "But tho' nothing whatever was proved against her as with regards complicity, there seems a strong feeling

THE

Alexandra

MAGAZINE,

&

Englishwoman's Journal.

SEPTEMBER, 1864.

LONDON:

JACKSON, WALFORD, AND HODDER,

27, PATERNOSTER ROW.

PRICE SIXPENCE.

Figure 3. *Alexandra* magazine, cover page.

against her as having been mixed up with such a set of people."[102] According to Parkes, the *English Woman's Journal* could not recommend itself to its genteel readers if it maintained a connection to Faithfull's Victoria Press. After the trial, the Victoria Press no longer served as the official printer of the women of Langham Place.[103] Readers and contributors, they believed, would not support a journal affiliated with Faithfull's now very public life.

As the problems with Faithfull illustrate, achieving a loosely configured vertical integration of the women's press proved difficult. This semicommercial printing venture had not provided the intended result of greater private control and increased public influence for an industry unable to compete in the larger periodical marketplace. The next five years proved difficult for the floundering institutions of the women's press. In addition to problems with Faithfull, the *Alexandra Magazine and Englishwoman's Journal* failed to emerge as a cheaper, more successful version of the *English Woman's Journal* and folded in August 1865. Boucherett had to pick up the pieces, and in October 1866, she formed a new periodical based on the principles of the failed *Journal*.[104] According to Boucherett, the *Englishwoman's Review: A Journal of Women's Work* would "follow the plan traced out by those who established the *Englishwoman's Journal* . . . for we believe the favorable change of opinion, and the more respectful tone with regard to women, which may be observed in the literature of the present day, to be in no small degree to the influence of the *Englishwoman's Journal*."[105] Innovation, not replication, ultimately defined the project of the *Review*. For although Boucherett, as editor and patron, set out to have the *Review* follow the "plan" of the *Journal,* she did not intend it to be a carbon copy of its predecessors—the *Alexandra Magazine* had done that and had folded in less than a year.

From the beginning, Boucherett supported broadening the *Review*'s reform agenda in the hopes of further shaping the direction of the Woman Question. The *Review* soon emerged as one of the first public voices on women's franchise and attempted to spawn serious debate over this heated political issue. The first number of the *Review* contained two items concerned with the status of women: "Some Probable Consequences of Extending the Franchise to Female Householders," and "Public Opinion on Questions Concerning Women." The latter piece reported on articles that had appeared in the mainstream press and soon became a regular feature. Excerpts from the *Times,* the *Daily News,* and the *Spectator* appeared frequently. Less literary overall than the *Journal,* the *Review* instead featured information on parliamentary politics in columns such as "Incidents and Remarks." A supplement to the *Review* published with the April 1867 issue consisted of a "List of Petitions presented to Parliament for the Enfranchisement of Qualified Women."[106] The "Review of Books" and "Letters to the Editor" columns continued. Women's employment also continued to be an important theme. Soon, however, the periodical shifted to a more overtly political agenda.

Boucherett's decision to focus on suffrage reflected and shaped contemporary debates over the political status of women. When Parkes and Bodichon started the *English Woman's Journal* in 1858, they considered the franchise issue a "distraction" that might possibly exile their endeavor to the radical fringe. By the mid-1860s, the political climate had changed. John Stuart Mill included the women's franchise in his 1865 election address, and women, including Parkes and Bodichon, played an important role in his successful campaign. During the debate over the Second Reform Bill the following year, Bodichon asked Mill to present a petition to Parliament to grant votes to women. The ultimate failure of the petition of fifteen hundred signatures and the slow pace of suffrage organizing after this period revealed the relatively marginalized status of this issue in British politics. Information on this issue did appear in publications such as the *Westminster Review,* but publicity remained inconsistent at best. The *Review* provided a regular forum for the articulation of ideas about women's citizenship that had just begun to capture the attention of the British public.

Despite the relative lack of parliamentary interest in women's suffrage during the mid–nineteenth century, voices of protest among women continued to be part of a larger public discourse surrounding the passage of the Reform Bills of 1867 and 1884. Historians have connected the small-scale prosuffrage agitation of the mid-1860s to the mass movement for women's suffrage of the early twentieth century by focusing attention on parliamentary debates over women's status and early suffrage organizations. Petitions, dynamic individuals, and women's organizations certainly played an important role in creating a foundation for the movement for women's political representation during the nineteenth century.[107] The extraparliamentary activities of the *Review* helped sustain the debate over suffrage in a regular, periodic format. Much of the unifying work of the early movement occurred in the space of women-run journals and their associated networks. As the first women's periodical to address women's suffrage on a regular basis, the *Review* created a vital, consistent link between politically minded women. In Parkes's words, quoted earlier, "there is something in a re-iterated effort which far outweighs the effect of the separate thoughts." Through its steady attention to the Woman Question, the women's press functioned as a cultural institution that provided a consistent forum where reformers could engage in political issues outside of formal parliamentary discourse.

This broader, more overtly political perspective, in part, helped make the *Review* a success. Boucherett relied on the hybrid, semicommercial model established by the *English Woman's Journal,* based on an already existing institutional infrastructure. To make the *Review* pay its way, Boucherett cut overhead to free up money for paying contributors and staff salaries. Priced at one shilling, the *Review* started as a quarterly rather than monthly. Boucherett looked for further opportunities to cut costs. Sharing offices with SPEW, Boucherett requested "the use of the office after hours for addressing and sending out the numbers, keeping accounts, etc." She paid a ten-pound fee for rent, in addition to five pounds toward the SPEW secretary's salary, "to make up for the loss of time" occasioned by the interruptions that would occur during the day owing to the *Review.*[108] Essentially, each institution acted to subsidize the other. Boucherett's ability to rely on an infrastructure that advocated for the mutual assistance of women enabled her to dedicate more energy on women's advocacy than press management.

Although Boucherett only edited the *Review* herself for a few years, she continued to subsidize the periodical throughout her lifetime. After she died in 1905, she left a sizable legacy for the continuation of the periodical, which lasted until 1910.[109] With the help of a dedicated staff and the institutional support of SPEW, Boucherett maintained the *Review* as a viable enterprise by helping to fund its production during and after her tenure as editor. Parkes and Bodichon had attempted to make the *English Woman's Journal* work as a for-profit company yet ended up embracing the opportunity to not have to answer to shareholders or bow to commercial pressures. Only through creating an independent periodical free from the interests of advertisers, publishers, and distributors, as these early editors did, could a women's paper expect to succeed at and maintain the single-minded goal of creating a medium both for and by women in the increasingly competitive periodicals market of the 1860s.

In many ways, the story of Boucherett's *Review* mirrored that of her predecessors. At the same time, her decision to include commentary on suffrage influenced the course of later women's journalistic endeavors by expanding women's engagement in a larger range of topics affecting their political status. Whether circulation rose or fell, the patronage of women like Boucherett guaranteed that the next issue of a given women's political periodical would appear and continue to serve as a forum of reasoned debate for educated women. As the story of subsequent advocacy journals would prove, having a dedicated patron determined the continuation of a press industry both for and by women during midcentury and beyond. This model ensured that the women's press could maintain its position as a voice for women while insulating itself from competition from the commercial periodical marketplace. Marginalized opinions, such as those promoting women's suffrage, thus had a regular forum for expression, even after publicity surrounding events like the 1867 Reform Bill debates had ended. Through this model, the women's press guaranteed the perpetuation of its role, in the words of Parkes, as a "rallying point of much value" for female reform advocates and their public.

New Directions

As the institutional foundations of the women's press took shape, the early 1860s witnessed the publication of several new periodicals that sought to broaden the appeal of women's press advocacy. One such periodical, the *Victoria* magazine, started as a monthly publication in the spring of 1863 by the one-time *Journal* editor Emily Davies and Emily Faithfull. Davies took the idea from Bodichon, who had suggested that "a magazine jointly managed by men and women" be tried as an "experiment." Unlike the more narrowly focused *English Woman's Journal,* the *Victoria* magazine intended to serve as a literary magazine that would appeal to both men and women: "The *Victoria Magazine* will afford an outlet for the expression of moderate and well considered opinion on those questions which while more directly bearing on the condition of women are in their wider aspects, of the highest importance to society generally."[110]

The *Victoria* magazine marked a new departure in women's journalism with its self-conscious attempt to compete with mainstream literary periodicals by addressing broad social issues and drawing in male readers. As a completely separate enterprise, *Victoria* did not intend to rival the *English Woman's Journal* or its predecessors. Rather, it worked within the ideological framework of the women's press, including coverage of the NAPSS and the plight of the unemployed female worker. For example, the June 1865 issue of *Victoria* included "Miss Parkes' Essay on Women's Work," an article on the Social Science Association that included commentary on the suffrage question. At the same time, *Victoria* moved gradually into the mainstream as a commercial publication. Modeled on the great reviews of the day and priced at one shilling, it strove not only to be self-sustaining but to make a profit as well. The "Literature of the Month" column, for example, imitated a similar column that appeared in the *Westminster Review*. It also included the publication of poems by Christina Rossetti and serialized stories by T. A. Trollope, which lent it a strong literary tone. The *Illustrated London News* described *Victoria* as having "sterling qualities and a character of its own; it is a sort of milder *Macmillan*."

The *Victoria* magazine also provided a forum for discussion for the debate over the Woman Question, although in a more self-consciously mixed-sex environment than its counterparts in the women's press. Male and female authors contributed in almost equal number. The Victoria Discussion Society, an organization affiliated with *Victoria,* included prominent male and female members of London society. *Victoria* reported regularly on issues discussed at the Society, which included the reform of laws and practices governing such things as women's employment, education, and training. Readers were expected to participate by reading debates by their educated betters.[111]

In its attempts to create a professionally run and popular "advanced" publication, this literary women's periodical for the upper middle classes had its share of difficulties. Davies complained that Faithfull had gone too far in her attempts to make the *Victoria* a popular periodical: "It has not paid and Miss Faithfull is going to try if she can make it do so by new methods. It is to be of lighter quality and the expenses to be reduced. I cannot edit a light Magazine, nor can I edit one at all unless I may go to the best writers and pay them properly."[112] In addition, Faithfull's involvement in the Codrington divorce case damaged her credibility as a "respectable" reformer.[113] Davies's frustration led to her departure, upon which Faithfull took over full control of *Victoria.* Though she continued to seek commercial success for her "light" political paper, the periodical ended up largely following the model of other women's periodicals because of its steady reliance on the patronage of Faithfull. Despite its failure as a profitable political magazine, *Victoria* continued for seventeen years as a women's advocacy publication that brought further attention to the Woman Question in its broadest social, cultural, and political context.

The story of the *Victoria* magazine demonstrates the ways in which the women's press movement began to grow beyond the walls of 19 Langham Place. In experimenting with a commercial periodical for women's concerns, *Victoria* attempted to expand the audience for progressive ideas about women's status. It ended up, however, confirming the importance of patronage in determining the success of advocacy publications. Revenue from subscribers and individual issues could only go so far. As it was an enterprise bent on social reform, women publishers and editors realized the importance of maintaining networks of supporters and institutions. The 1860s continued to witness the slow expansion of both the number of periodicals and diversity of issues covered in such women-run forums. By the late 1860s, improved and cheaper technology, as well as a growing general awareness of the Woman Question, led to the development of single-issue journals that sought to wield a larger influence on public opinion than their predecessors. Nowhere was this more apparent than in the attempt to start a new internationalist women's paper.

Josephine Butler provided the inspiration for this new journal. Before starting her well-known campaign against the Contagious Disease Acts, she had begun to think about starting a periodical for the discussion of women's issues, including suffrage, employment, and education, not only in Britain but throughout Europe and America as well, during the late 1860s.[114] Butler had written articles for *Women's World,* a periodical with slight feminist leanings, in 1868.[115] After less than a year, for reasons that are not entirely clear, its editors decided to take the periodical in a more serious direction. "*Kettledrum* with which is united *Women's World*" was inaugurated in January 1869 and contained serial stories and articles, including some on suffrage, "by distinguished authors." The fashion supplement of *Woman's World* quickly disappeared. Critics summed up its purpose as "appeal[ing] to the softer sex through their literary taste rather than through their love of dress."[116]

Kettledrum, though it lasted only six months, was the first women-run periodical to assert the right of British women to exercise authority over domestic and colonial affairs. Using the metaphor of the tea-table as women's only "true" sphere of influence, *Kettledrum* argued for women's "natural" role in international affairs:

> The natural dominion which woman possesses over the tea-pot, gives us the right of discussing all particulars concerning tea. Its growth, manufacture, the taxes it pays on importation, our connection with the Celestial Empire, our amiable English custom of supplying the tea growers with opium in exchange for their invigorating herb, our noble behavior in going to war with the Chinese, when that government was unreasonable enough to object to this arrangement—all come within our province.[117]

Women's duties could thus expand within the bounds of respectable behavior into a world of political action that gave them new authority in the arena of imperial politics. As the article concluded, "it may be objected that *Kettledrum* has another meaning, signifying a noisy musical instrument, and that is this sense the word is inappropriate to a magazine. We beg to differ. The word seems to us vastly appropriate, for we intend to make a noise in the world. 'Kettledrum' is woman's signal for action."[118]

In June 1869, *Kettledrum* changed its name to the more current affairs–focused title *Now-a-Days,* in the hope of better directing its readers in this new leadership role. The editors immediately sought Boucherett's support, convincing her that amalgamating their two periodicals would better link the domestic concerns of the *Englishwoman's Review* with the internationalist ideals of *Kettledrum.* In 1869, Boucherett announced that *Now-a-Days* would replace the *Englishwoman's Review.* In business terms, this change, like the previous amalgamation of the *English Woman's Journal* with the *Alexandra Magazine,* appeared to be an attempt to strengthen the position of the *Englishwoman's Review* in the larger periodical market.

Publishing an international version of the *Review,* Butler believed, would enable her to claim a place for British women at the head of an international women's coalition. This included the formation of an "International Association for the advancement of the education of women," whose object consisted of "mutual helpfulness and sympathy and the common advantage through the composition of various plans for Education or for the amelioration of the position of women." Support came from "Her Royal Highness the Princess of Russia," who approved "of the idea of a little 'International Review of women's work and education.'" The new journal asked readers to offer their "encouragement and help" to women in both Britain and Europe "who are labouring under greater disadvantage than we ourselves are."[119] Published monthly, *Now-a-Days* would "contain some account of the wants and the work of women in various countries and would publish appeals for help or advice and answers to these appeals."[120]

Now-a-Days was "ephemeral, of a day," in the words of one supporter.[121] This statement had more than an element of truth in it, as only one issue of the periodical appears to have been printed.[122] Disappointed with the results of this new departure, Boucherett started a new series of the *Englishwoman's Review* in January 1870. As she explained to readers, "much regret having been expressed at the discontinuance of the *Englishwoman's Review,* especially of the Record of Events, and 'Now-A-Days,' which it was hoped would supply its place, having been suspended, I have determined to start the *Review* again."[123] The women's press movement had not yet established a strong enough infrastructure to move too far beyond its modest Langham Place beginnings. Despite new innovations and ambitions, women editors remained unable to export their new industry and British women's assumed moral authority abroad.

This short-lived experiment with an international women's journal ultimately introduced the possibility of representing the woman reader as a "respectable" reformer whose activism would not require her to transgress traditional gender boundaries. The new series of the *Review* continued the project of *Now-a-Days* by supplying readers with international and domestic news while meticulously recording women's political activities. "It shall be my humble task," wrote Boucherett, "to chronicle the doings of others." Boucherett also added a "Foreign Letter" column that contained "information of the women's movement abroad." The extent of these changes, she noted, remained contingent on subscriber interest, although this time Boucherett made the guarantee that "under any circumstances the records will be continued."[124] Though her guidance and financial assistance, the *Review* provided a continuous record of women's activism, while acting as a forum for women's political expression. The *Review* thus created a role for itself as both a historian of a budding movement and a guiding force for the promotion of its principles. In the competitive world of periodical publishing of the second half of the nineteenth century, Boucherett's patronage protected the *Review* from the whims of the commercial marketplace for the benefit of readers seeking to take a place in public life.

Although *Now-a-Days* and *Kettledrum* never really got off the ground, their short lives foreshadowed key changes in store for women's advocacy journalism during the 1870s and 1880s. A host of single-issue periodicals emerged that advocated everything from suffrage to women's unionization to the repeal of the Contagious Disease Acts and the international cooperation of women under British imperial leadership. The *Review* continued its role as the steady recorder of women's activities, while new periodicals dedicated to single-issue advocacy programs began to proliferate. However, old problems remained as others emerged including circulation, funding, and disagreements among individual editors. The infrastructure built during the early 1860s thus remained crucial in helping to maintain a cohesive program for women's political journalism. In particular, SPEW continued as a link between the numerous organizations connected with the production of women-run periodicals. Through these institutions, the printing and publishing of women's journals found new means of maintaining themselves as female-run enterprises for reform-minded women.

In assessing the early years of the women's press, several patterns emerge. As advocacy periodicals, women's papers catered to a highly particularized clientele that initially had little wider appeal. They were also expensive for all but the most dedicated middle-class reader to afford. Their relatively small circulation potential made finding distributors difficult. Even when editors found newspaper agents willing to sell their periodicals outside London, it soon became evident that these early papers generally appealed to a cosmopolitan readership. "The *Victoria* has done pretty well in London, but in the country it has been a dead failure," Davies claimed in 1864. "The provincial booksellers report that their customers won't look at it."[125] As this chapter has demonstrated, other types of motivations sustained this press. Advocacy journalism could not follow a model of journalism based on a commercial model of success. Nonpartisan women's political journalism emerged in the late 1850s *because* editors controlled their own enterprise completely.

Readers ultimately played a crucial role in determining how these journals were used through their participation in discussions and financial support. Features such as the "Letters to the Editor" column attempted to provoke readers into action. Articles and advertisements promoting women-run enterprises also shaped the character of female-centered reform networks. Making readers aware of women's role in the actual printing, editing, and financing of the text that they read each month or quarter added to a further sense of community. Women's periodicals allowed disenfranchised women to imagine themselves as citizens, in part due to their representation as political actors in the women's press. This new kind of extraparliamentary political culture had an important impact on the direction that women's activism would take in the second half of the nineteenth century. Lobbying for citizenship did not revolve solely around political inclusion but rather consisted of a host of other social, economic, and cultural demands. Within the pages of their press, women debated the particular direction of positions on employment, education, civil rights, and political enfranchisement.

The institutional infrastructure of the women's advocacy press was firmly in place by the end of 1860. A loose affiliation of periodicals, printers, and women's organizations found itself linked by the dual purpose of providing information and advocating for social reform. The support of these institutions demonstrated the faith that a growing constituency of women reformers placed in a gender-identified news institution. In the coming decades, this medium for and by women grew into an effective alternative political voice for encouraging reader interest in "women's issues." The rise of a liberal reform press, coupled with the development of a semicommercial business model, enabled advocacy journalists to represent the ideals of the growing number of women's organizations that emerged in Britain during the 1870s and 1880s. The women's press movement emerged as a broad-based project that perpetuated itself by drawing dedicated readers and workers continually into its fold. This included the practices of publishing and printing that engaged readers in seeking practical solutions for problems facing women.

Women readers, editors, and printers themselves thus refashioned and fine-tuned mainstream discussions over the Woman Question in the very public space of the women's advocacy journal. During the 1870s and 1880s, the women's press grew in both circulation and size. A new, more overtly political advocacy "newssheet," driven by special interests, emerged out of the early efforts of the women at Langham Place. Within the pages of the women's press a thriving, polyvocal, female-centered political culture grew. The next chapter traces the newssheet's revision of the postrepeal model of journalism that the mainstream press continued to follow. The development of new specialized periodicals for and by women, along with their accompanying networks, enabled the proliferation of a host of diverse political agendas aimed at reimagining women's status in Victorian society. At the same time, the institutional infrastructure of the women's press continued to provide new opportunities for women in nontraditional employments in the journalism, printing, and publishing worlds.

2

Building Networks:
The Rise of a Woman-Identified
Publishing Community

"Our periodical literature is essentially a classified literature," *Black-wood's* magazine observed regarding the British press in 1859. "The sphere of every new publication is more and more limited. Every class has its organ; every topic finds a journal; every interest has a friend in the press."[1] This belief that the press represented a print-based public sphere that served an increasingly large range of specialized interests continued to grow throughout the Victorian period. As chapter 1 demonstrated, the repeal of the newspaper taxes, the passage of limited liability corporation acts, and improved printing technologies in the late 1850s fueled the rapid expansion of this "classified" periodical literature. Nowhere was the rise of the new special interest genre of periodical described by *Blackwood's* more apparent than in the women's advocacy press.

During the 1870s and 1880s, a burgeoning association-based women's culture provided a solid infrastructure for the growth of a women's press industry that supported highly specialized publications. Proclaiming allegiance to "women's causes," a category that advocacy journals continued to help define in relation to the Woman Question, these specialized newssheets, or "organs," linked themselves together in a loose network of mutual support and promotion. Women's organizations published periodicals on a wide range of subjects, including women's suffrage, education, employment, and the status of women in the Empire. This chapter examines the evolving world of the women's press movement and the organizational culture it shaped. Together these institutions supported gender-based business practices that fueled the growth of an extraparliamentary political culture through the medium of women's advocacy journalism. As a space to read "women's news," the newssheet provided a vehicle for the dissemination of the progressively liberal agendas embodied in nascent women's organizations of the mid-Victorian era. Regardless of the veracity of the claim by editors and readers that women's newssheets represented a popular liberal forum, this perception helped create a sustained vision of an activist political identity for the female reformer.

The market for periodicals grew dramatically during this period. This "golden age" witnessed the expansion of the press in terms of both quantity and quality, as prices fell as a result of faster and cheaper printing technologies and lower costs for raw materials such as paper.[2] The increased flow of advertising money into periodicals, due to an expanding consumer-based economy, provided new support for fledgling publications and consequently affected both the number and types of printed material available to the public. Most mainstream periodicals and newspapers, according to Alan Lee, developed a ratio of "half news and editorial matter, half advertising," to increase their profitability.[3] Commercial periodicals increased in influence, due to business and technological innovations that put potential readers within the reach of advertisers. A growing railway network continued to improve timely distribution while expanding the market for periodicals beyond urban centers and into the provinces. As a result of these developments, hundreds of newspaper companies sprung up, while the number and variety of titles that appeared on newsstands proliferated.[4]

Rising literacy rates had a considerable impact on the periodical industry and its readership. The Education Act of 1870, along with the series of educational reforms that followed, as G. A. Cranfield has argued, played an important role in the development of an emerging reading public among both men and women.[5] Women's literacy had risen considerably by the end of the nineteenth century. The percentage of women able to sign their names, often used as an indicator for literacy, increased from 50.5 percent in 1839 to 74.6 percent in 1873 and to 94.3 percent in 1893. For men, these figures were 66.3 percent in 1839, 81.2 percent in 1873, and 95 percent in 1893, thus indicating that the gap between male and female literacy had greatly diminished by the end of the century.[6] Commercial publications included mass circulating "ladies newspapers" such as the *Queen*. Women's domestic magazines targeted these new upper- and middle-class women readers in their role as consumers in order to increase advertising profits.[7] Nearly universal literacy coupled with market-oriented business practices of the press industry made periodical reading into an everyday part of British life during the Victorian era.

For upper- and middle-class women, improved educational opportunities and the expansion of print culture resulted in a new voluntary associational life for women. Residential colleges founded in Cambridge, Oxford, and London provided women with new opportunities to engage in gender-segregated intellectual and personal communities.[8] Outside of universities, women formed clubs in increasing numbers. As Philippa Levine has demonstrated, the growth of women's social clubs, starting in the 1870s in London and the provinces, "provided middle class women . . . with an alternative social environment to that of their homes." By 1899 at least twenty-four such organizations existed in London alone. In addition to providing a social outlet, these women-only networks formed the basis of late nineteenth-century political organizations that participated in debates over the Woman Question by arguing for social reforms such as improvements in education, better employment opportunities, and new labor laws.[9]

The expansion of these associational networks encouraged the growth of a women's press industry, in part by providing a space where gender-based social and economic agendas could develop in an independent political forum. Like the coffeehouse sociability that men had enjoyed since the eighteenth century, women's clubs offered women a place to discuss news and contemporary events.[10] Reading rooms, a common feature at the headquarters of women's organizations during this period, were filled with periodicals, pamphlets, and other publications for female patrons. Organizations such as Lydia Becker's suffrage society and Emma Paterson's Women's Education Union ran bookstores that sold directly to the public. Through the sale of their own subsidized publications, such organizations linked like-minded women together, while they publicized problems regarding women's status and welfare to a wider audience.

Newssheet publications of women's reform organizations proved vital to the development of women's political culture in the nineteenth century.[11] Distinguishing themselves from commercially focused domestic magazines such as the *Queen,* these periodicals catalogued the happenings and promoted the agendas of a growing number of women-run associations, many of which had started publishing companies to support their own publications. Newssheets offered readers a heavy diet of political news, drawing subscribers from a growing pool of educated women readers, many of whom were solicited from the membership lists of other women's organizations.

Like their predecessors in the 1860s, women's advocacy newssheets developed as semicommercial and nonpartisan enterprises. This followed the pattern of mainstream periodicals that began to break the prerepeal tradition of serving as the mouthpiece of either the Whig or Tory party. As the British press came more and more to address itself "to every educated man of whatever party," women's periodicals found their audience in the general educated woman reader.[12] Women's newssheets, in this way, followed general trends in Victorian journalism by diversifying in terms of content, readership, and ownership.

The woman's newssheet, as a specialized news genre, redefined itself by the late 1870s as a vehicle to promote a broad-based social critique of the status of women. Unlike mainstream newspapers that might occasionally discuss the Woman Question or ladies' magazines focused on domestic life, women's periodicals, according to the *Englishwoman's Review,* covered all aspects of subjects of interest to women:

> a "Woman's newspaper" ... is obliged to record all events that bear upon the subject from the highest to the most insignificant, it is bound by its raison d'être to keep on "pegging away" at the risk of being a bore, it is carried on for principle, not for profit, to further a cause, not to pay a dividend. It has to compile statistics which are confessedly dull reading, to chronicle opinions which, scattered, have but little weight, but gathered together from an irresistible mass of evidence and experience. It must be the concave lens that concentrates the scattered rays into one focus for the increase of light and vital warmth.[13]

In addition to providing "women's news," such periodicals repeatedly addressed the question of women's political freedom "in innumerable parallel grooves."[14] This meant providing readers with a regular venue for the discussion of suffrage and topics relating to "the amelioration of the position of women."[15]

Establishing themselves as sites of information for the educated woman reader, many papers were tied to reform organizations. Feature articles included reports of institutional news and organizational business reports. Based on a business model of "principles not profits," women's advocacy periodicals had thus developed an identity as "newssheets": periodicals that provided information for subscribers interested in a diverse set of women's causes while connecting readers to women's organizations that ran particular papers.

Through publishing newssheets, women's organizations helped further shape debates over the Woman Question, as it continued to develop during the 1870s and 1880s. The institutions that grew up alongside the women's press promoted the early Langham Place issues of employment and education. At the same time, new concerns over women's social and political status began to take center stage. Many of the issues taken on by such woman-identified institutions and periodicals mirrored the liberal spirit of reform of the larger political climate of the period. As Parliament addressed questions regarding expanding the electorate, the organization and regulation of labor, calls for a universal system of primary education, and limited constitutional reform during the 1870s and 1880s, women's advocacy journals championed such causes as distinctly within the sphere of women. Female reformers thus claimed to represent the larger interests of the nation by developing a woman-centered culture of politics on the margins of formal political structures. Although unable to participate directly in politics as voters, female reformers played an important role in the social purity, the unionization of women workers, and temperance movements. Women's newssheets provided an important space for the development of such agendas, while at the same time encouraged the growth of a broad-based social reform culture that bolstered women's citizenship claims as servants of the nation. Middle-class reformers used the women's press during the mid-Victorian era to enter the world of social and political reform and to have a voice in shaping what they defined as the interests of their sex.

This reading of "the gendering of public life" during the Victorian period offers a new perspective on the importance of women's participation in an informal liberal political culture that, according to Hall, McClelland, and Rendall, has been "rarely placed at the center of historical concerns."[16] In the wake of debates over women's citizenship claims during the 1867 Reform Bill agitation, growing numbers of women's organizations encouraged members to take a more active part in reform activities.[17] The development of the newssheet as a potential mobilizing force for women reflected this increasingly activist-oriented women's organizational culture. By waging highly visible campaigns against the Contagious Diseases Acts, increasing suffrage agitation, and promoting women's intellectual and social advancement, women began to make news themselves. Women's newssheets developed as a specialized genre to provide a regular space for the coverage of these issues. While continuing the work of their predecessors of the 1860s, women's newssheets of the 1870s and 1880s expanded the program of creating a medium "for and by women" by publishing a "classified literature," in the words of *Blackwood's* magazine, that understood social reform crusades as especially related to the interests of women.

Concerns over the lack of attention and possible misrepresentation of women's activities by the mainstream press led organizations to look to women's newssheets to represent the views of female reformers. Although the mainstream press covered suffrage (male and female), labor union formation, and social purity during the Victorian period, women campaigners complained of the quality and extent of coverage.[18] Contemporary journalist Evelyn March Phillips credited advocacy journalism with increasing the coverage of women's reform activities. Such periodicals had historically provided both women and the larger public with information unavailable in the mainstream press or in domestic magazines:

> No doubt the intellectual woman will habitually turn for her news to the ordinary paper, but the diverse subjects with which she is now specially connected in this country demand a fuller treatment than the ordinary paper will give them. For instance, when the Woman Workers' Conference takes place in the autumn, an event of deep interest to hundreds, if not thousands, of women, the general papers scarcely touch upon it. . . . The views and interests of women are crowded out or receive but scant notice in the ordinary newspaper; in ladies' journals they are usually treated in a weak, dull way which can arrest the attention of no one.[19]

By contrast, women's newssheets provided information for the reform-minded reader in a periodic format. Although Phillips argued that women's newssheets often dealt with topics such as the aforementioned conference "*ad nauseam,*" she claimed that they nevertheless created a space for women to produce, record, and receive news, while imagining themselves as part of a larger community of "hundreds, if not thousands" fellow workers. This space produced what Benedict Anderson has called a "community in anonymity," making it possible for such women to "think about themselves and to relate to others in profoundly new ways."[20] Special interest periodicals, detached from commercial concerns, provided an alternative medium for women to read "their news" in a sympathetic, gender-identified arena.

The Single-Issue Newssheet and the Woman-Identified Reformer

The need for an arena to identify and communicate with fellow activists developed, in part, due to women's increased engagement in political life in mid-Victorian Britain. Agitation surrounding the failed attempt to gain women the vote under the 1867 Reform Bill resulted in a sustained Victorian suffrage movement that, according to Martin Pugh, historians have "under-rated" because of their lopsided focus on the Edwardian period.[21] According to Jane Rendall, women's involvement in the suffrage movement emerged from a combination of a woman-centered culture with a midcentury liberal mandate to create the impetus for reforms that brought "some women to the gates of the political nation," though by no means the majority.[22] Serious divisions regarding whether or not class or marital status should play a role in determining women's eligibility for the franchise gave the movement an uneven quality that historians such as Rendall and Pugh have begun to examine more closely. Lending continuity to the fits and starts of the Victorian suffrage movement requires a fuller understanding of the institutions and ideas that held together a nascent woman-centered reform culture. This reassessment thus calls for a more careful consideration of the organizational culture that grew up around franchise reform as well as other single-issue campaigns.

The world that women reformers created out of these new opportunities opened up the possibility for both formal and informal participation in British political culture. Previously limited to more informal activities such as philanthropy, some reform legislation allowed a small number of ambitious women to take a more active role in public politics. The municipal franchise was granted to English and Welsh women in 1869, while the 1870 Education Act extended to such women the right to vote and sit on school boards. Although Irish women remained disenfranchised, Scottish women received the municipal franchise in 1882. Such legislation helped legitimize women's newly distinguished role in England, Scotland, and Wales as guardians of child welfare and education, a belief that had started to gain wider cultural acceptance because of the gendered nature of such reform work. This period also witnessed the beginning of women's formal involvement with the political party structure. The Conservative and Liberal parties formed the Primrose League (1885) and the Women's Liberal Federation (1887), respectively, in order to recruit volunteer women canvassers after the passage of the Corrupt Practices Act in 1883 limited the expenditures of parliamentary candidates. Despite the popularity of these organizations, male politicians never intended women to play anything more than an auxiliary role. Nevertheless, women's participation in Victorian political life had clearly started to increase and take on a more formal character.

Whether women joined auxiliary party organizations or formed their own campaigns, advocacy journalism helped forge links among reformers. Almost every women's reform organization that was started during this period had its own newssheet. Both Conservative and Liberal women's auxiliary organizations also had their own women-run publications supported by member subscription. In associations where women played a supporting role, an organization-based publication enabled members to have something that was theirs, apart from the official organizational structure.

The arena where women found the most autonomy was that of the single-issue reform campaign. Crusades against the Contagious Diseases Acts, pro-Temperance organizations, and prosuffrage organizations were all started and run by women during this period. Identifying themselves as women's organizations allowed a fair amount of independence from partisan politics. Like earlier journals, women's newssheets of the 1870s and 1880s used institutional affiliations to advance causes including women's suffrage, union formation, temperance, and women's employment, as well as the status of women in the colonies. A number of factors made the advocacy of such potentially controversial issues possible. Staying insulated from the larger periodical market freed newssheets from the censor of advertisers. Rather than rely on the commercial success, women such as Lydia Becker started periodicals with personal funds and used limited advertising. Some women's periodicals, such as the *Women's Education Union* (1873–82), were started with membership fees, while still others, such as *Women and Work* (1874–76), were funded by a wealthy patron, revenue raised from sales and some advertising.

Newssheet editors sought ways of increasing a paper's influence by taking advantage of changes that made the "popular cheap press" of the 1870s possible. Lower production costs meant that most women's newssheets sold for a penny after 1870. Organizations such as SPEW and the Manchester Women's Suffrage Society could now afford to include newssheets with membership dues. Reading rooms, cheap pamphlet reprints, circulating libraries, and organization-based distribution networks that offered free "specimen copies" further encouraged circulation among potential readers. Lydia Becker's *Women's Suffrage Journal,* for example, encouraged readers to come by the office to examine the paper and purchase reprints of prosuffrage-related material.[23] Other newssheets, such as the *Women's Union Journal,* set up circulating libraries for union members and opened up their offices as meeting spaces and lecture halls.[24] Josephine Butler's *Dawn* offered free or reduced priced copies to reading rooms and subscribers who purchased multiple copies for distribution. Readers themselves also archived newssheets for later reference and to pass on to friends.

Despite increasing specialization, newssheets addressed "women," broadly defined. In the past, periodicals had taken on titles such as the *English*

Woman's Journal or the *Englishwoman's Review*. Some, such as the *Victoria* magazine and the *Alexandra* magazine, took the name of a female royal. The *Rose, Shamrock, and Thistle* had identified itself as a national paper for women belonging to the three kingdoms. These periodicals implicitly limited their audience to a particular kind of woman, differentiated by class and/or national identity. Later journals elided these distinctions. After 1870, with few exceptions, woman's advocacy papers used "woman" in their title unmodified, addressing a universal female subject defined first by gender rather than class or national origin.

There is evidence that by thee late 1880s, having the word "woman" or "women" in a periodical title indicated a relatively progressive political stance. When Oscar Wilde took over *Lady's World* in 1887, he wanted to create a periodical "for the expression of women's opinions on all subjects of literature, art, and modern life." He changed the name to *Woman's World*, to separate it from other "ladies magazines." The kind of women writers and readers he hoped to attract Wilde believed would find the word lady "vulgar" and would not look at the magazine as relevant to their concerns. Wilde ran the periodical until 1889. *Woman's World* remained relatively high priced, at one shilling per monthly issue, and placed an emphasis on questions of "fashion and dress." At the same time, Wilde declared: "contributions will be received from all women who are engaged in any practical work tending towards the intellectual and social advancement of the community." Writers who wrote articles on topics such as women's suffrage and women in the printing trade and in journalism included Millicent Garrett Fawcett, Olive Schreiner, and Emily Faithfull.

At any rate, this project of defining "woman" as an audience continued to be problematic after the emergence of the first periodicals targeted at female readers, according to Margaret Beetham. Domestic magazines traditionally understood "gender as axiomatic," while at the same time represented femininity as "fractured, not least because it is simultaneously assumed as given and as still to be achieved."[25] In the case of women's advocacy journals, defining the woman reader was part of a process that attempted to erase differences among women while emphasizing similarities based primarily on sex, creating the notion of an always existing female-identified reading subject. "Woman," as defined in the pages of organizational newssheets, came to represent a complex identity based in large part on the individual's identification with a particular set of social issues that affected "their sex." By grouping causes under the rubric of "women's concerns," women's organizations produced a gendered political identity that found expression in the pages of their own women's newssheets.

Editors promoted this vision of a gender-identified community by cooperating with other journalists. Competing periodicals often supported one another through professional and personal ties. The potential for rivalry aside, such connections created a congenial relationship among those in the women's periodical business. "Publications Received" columns, for example, "highly recommended" other newssheets to readers and included tables of contents and information on how to subscribe, as well as favorable reviews of particular news items and stories. These efforts amounted to free advertising space to potential competitors.[26] Through such cooperation, newssheets helped cultivate reader interest in women's news.

Newssheets' characteristic periodicity contributed to a new consciousness among readers of a community that existed for the mutual assistance of women. Advocacy journalism emerged as a trusted and durable institution that provided news unavailable in any other medium. As the number of women's newssheets grew during the 1870s and 1880s, they became standard fare in reading rooms of women's organizations, meeting halls, and in the private homes of those, such as Elizabeth Wolstenholme Elmy, who read, passed around, and regularly saved them.[27] Editors assumed that they addressed an informed constituency who would work with them for a common cause. Readers thus had a new responsibility: they figured as active participants, rather than passive recipients of information, in promoting causes advocated by women's newssheets. The modest employment journals of the 1860s had given way to a reform-centered news medium that invented a new activist reader.

By the 1870s, this woman-centered brand of cooperation came to define the larger project of advocacy journalism. Held together by a loose collaboration of institutions, the women's press depended on the support of its readers in producing a female literary space. Although men's names did appear on subscription lists and in the letters to the editor columns, editors self-consciously addressed a female audience, electing to use "she" rather than the customary "he" in editorials. Advertising copy also assumed an all-female audience and included pitches for women's clothing, beauty items, and household products. Calls for subscribers, advertisements, and editorials reminded readers, as part of the women's press advocacy community, of their responsibility to the larger world of women's industry. Patronizing one of their journal's advertisers, for example, enabled such readers to participate in the support of a larger network built on the maintenance of women's political, economic, and cultural interests.

Although most newssheets failed to turn a profit, the women's press continued as an independent medium, in part due to business models based on the "for and by woman" principle, the dedication of individual editors, and institutional support. Many newssheets also incorporated new commercial business practices pioneered by mainstream newspaper publications and women's domestic magazines such as advertising. Although newssheets never came close to the standard "50/50" ratio of a mainstream paper (half advertising and half copy)[28] they did start to use small-scale advertising, usually around 10 percent of total space, to subsidize costs. To make newssheets look more like newspapers, editors took advantage of improved technology that lowered the production cost of larger, more sophisticated editions. The steady fall in production prices provided women's newssheets, as Lucy Brown has argued about the mainstream press, with "a variety of opportunities," including the ability to "increase size without an increase of price" and "to improve or expand the coverage of news."[29] This allowed newssheet editors to imitate the eye-catching "newsy" format of many mainstream periodicals of this period.

Women's newssheets thus remained both separate from and embedded in the larger industry. Although by no means part of the mainstream news media in terms of circulation or influence, newssheets began to establish themselves as viable sources for news in appearance and content. The business of press advocacy had entered a new stage: insulating itself from the commercial marketplace while taking advantage of many of the innovations in the periodicals industry, newssheets served the needs of a growing community of women engaged in single-issue reform campaigns.

What kind of community did these papers help constitute? As chapter 1 demonstrated, a political program based on the philosophy of "for and by women" relied on creating business and social networks. The next section offers a case study of how expanding women's printing networks supported press advocacy by making "for and by women" a rallying cry for women reformers who wanted to participate in the debate over women's employment in a meaningful way. By patronizing women-run printing shops, organizations carved out a place for their newssheets in the marketplace, while offering an emblematic challenge to contemporary understandings of women's capacity for remunerative employment. In the process, newssheets found themselves part of a woman-run industry that created a space for women in the masculine world of business and Victorian liberal reform culture.

Publishing Networks

By the 1870s, supporting a women's advocacy newssheet often meant participating in a political program. From production to distribution, women's periodicals cultivated a network of relationships that connected patrons to a host of social and economic reform projects. Faithfull's Victoria Press, in association with SPEW, had introduced the idea that a press run both for and by women could provide employment for women while publicizing their ability to master a male-run trade. Newssheets continued to advocate this vertically integrated, gender-based business model throughout the 1870s and 1880s. Women-run printing "experiments," as Bessie Parkes called them, granted middle-class women entry into larger debates with trade unions and political economists over working conditions, business standards, and fair labor practices. More than simply a precursor to later suffrage struggles, women's attempt to participate in the economy as business owners and well-paid workers helped shape the ideals of a woman-identified reform culture regarding the relationship between political and economic reform.

Improved employment opportunities for middle- and working-class women made the imagining of a gendered business community possible. According to Lee Holcombe, Victorian women had two employment options: traditional feminine occupations such as teaching and nursing and new fields that included distributive trades, clerical work, and the civil service.[30] Though by no means a mass force, the number of women in the fifteen-to-twenty-four age range employed from 1851 to 1900 rose by about 10 percent.[31] The *types* of women employed, which included those from the middling classes for the first time, and the diversity of their choice of employment reveals an important trend in women's increasing participation in the labor market.

Employment reformers understood changes in the Victorian economy and technology as an opportunity to make a case for women's ability to perform nontraditional work. New prospects in the printing trades grew as the middle-class appetite for print steadily increased. The dramatic fall in production costs was due to the invention of new machines that made printing faster, cheaper, and less labor intensive, requiring fewer workers to run more efficient machines.[32] Although women printers generally still continued to be segregated from heavy work, the widespread introduction of easy-to-use linotype mechanical typesetting during this period opened possibilities in the composing room. These innovations bolstered reformers' arguments that women belonged in this relatively high-status industry where sex difference coupled with age-old tradition had threatened to block their entry during the late 1850s.

The question of whether women could or should seek remunerative work continued as a contentious debate throughout the second half of the nineteenth century. SPEW played an important role in opening up new opportunities for women in traditionally male-dominated sectors of the economy. Dramatic changes in the types of employment open to women occurred from 1850 to 1900, largely due to what Ellen Jordan has called the "pull factor" of SPEW's innovative attempts to train women in the trades and professions.[33] Throughout the 1870s and 1880s, the Society provided support for women seeking training and financial assistance while challenging cultural prejudices regarding women's capacity for work. By creating connections with other women's organizations, SPEW cultivated a series of informal relationships that, in turn, helped support a vision of "for and by women" as a political and business philosophy.

Through its association with the NAPSS, SPEW remained connected with the larger Victorian liberal reform project. Influential men such as Lord Brougham and George Hastings supported projects of the NAPSS's sister organization by pushing such things as the passage of the Married Women's Property Acts and supporting research on labor issues. SPEW continued to draw upon a web of networks that included influential liberal thinkers and female reformers after the NAPSS disbanded in 1886. Unlike the NAPSS, which could tap into the machinery of the Liberal Party to influence parliamentary legislation, SPEW exerted less formal political pressure up through the twentieth century by pushing its gendered political agenda in forums such as *Englishwoman's Review*. Its rational economic approach to issues including women's employment made SPEW a voice for female reformers whose sex barred them from participating in formal politics. In attempting to mirror the NAPSS as a "Parliament of Social Causes,"[34] SPEW understood its mission as an extraparliamentary voice for the female citizen, a program that it promoted through its support of women-run institutions.

By maintaining its commitment to single-issue campaigns such as women's employment, SPEW continued during the 1870s and 1880s to be an important coordinating force behind the women's press. The Society used the *Review* to keep readers informed of "the position of the women's cause throughout the world."[35] Each quarterly issue recorded the activities of other women's organization by condensing information previously published in women's newssheets, including reports on the legal campaigns for women's property rights, anti–Contagious Disease Act reform, suffrage, and education from periodicals such as the *Shield,* the *Women's Suffrage Journal,* and the *Women's Education Union Journal,* as well as many others. SPEW's commitment to maintaining a forum to record women's political activities in the *Review* was an important factor in holding the women's advocacy publishing community together.

Both the *Review* and SPEW relied on the generous support of wealthy patrons interested in promoting women's work in nontraditional trades. SPEW maintained a nonpartisan stance and refused to become involved directly with any of the political institutions that it supported through its subsidies. When the National Union of Women Workers asked SPEW to send delegates to its conferences, for example, members participated in discussions while maintaining their distance as independent observers. In another instance, the Women's Employment Defense League requested closer affiliation with SPEW. The organization made it very clear that such a relationship would not "implicate the Society with Trades Unions in any way," enabling it to avoid partisan affiliations that might potentially alienate its upper-class patrons.[36] SPEW's nonpartisan stance, according to members of the committee, enabled the *Review* to keep its neutral status as a "chronicle of events" while promoting mutual assistance among women.

To fulfill its project, SPEW provided generous subsidies to organizations interested in employing women. The London printer Bale and Sons benefited greatly from SPEW's patronage during the 1870s.[37] SPEW had previously apprenticed women to Bale as compositors and pledged not only to loan money to women for apprentice fees but also to rent expensive printing equipment for women's use in the shop.[38] Through such encouragement and subsidies, SPEW attempted to induce other printers "to open their doors to women."[39] This commitment to providing employment for women in the printing trades carried important implications for the future business dealings of the women's printing and publishing industry. SPEW subsidized other print shops, although not to the same extent as it had Bale, hoping to firmly establish women's foothold in the trade. According to the 1904 study, *Women in the Printing Trades,* women gained a small but significant presence in the industry.[40] Considerable resistance to this trend, similar to that of the 1860s, came from the influential London Union of Compositors.[41] Women printers, they claimed, lowered wages for men, as women willingly worked for less money. Ironically, since the Union refused membership to females, they had no recourse but to keep rates high.

This ongoing debate regarding women status in male-dominated trades had both ideological and structural roots. As Jordan has argued, ideas about femininity and appropriate gender roles during the nineteenth century deeply informed assumptions about the ability of the woman worker.[42] The rise of a sexual division of labor during the Industrial Revolution, according to Sally Alexander, resulted in limiting women's opportunities to traditional "feminized" trades such as textile work.[43] This meant that potential employers had difficulty imagining women succeeding in traditionally male pursuits. Such prejudices concerning traditional definitions of women's work limited women's mobility in the printing trade. Employers at the bidding of the Union, for example, readily hired women to do the "lower tasks" of bookbinding and paper folding, since the former required sewing skills and both demanded little physical strength.[44] Men in the union were not the only ones who believed in a more traditional division of labor. Women too rejected "men's work." One woman asked to varnish books remarked, "I know my place, and I'm not going to take men's work from them." When asked why she would not allow the women working under her to use easier processes employed by men in the shop, a forewoman replied: "Why, that is men's work, and we shouldn't think of doing it."[45]

This gendering of work further manifested itself in traditional male-centered culture of work-related rituals. In addition to ideological, economic, and physical arguments against female labor, the persistence of sixteenth-century initiation rituals up through to the beginning of the twentieth century ensured that printing maintained its status as a male trade. Secret ceremonies initiated teenage men into a fraternity that required, among other things, a pledge to celibacy and total obedience "towards his said Master."[46] Though a woman, in theory, could take these vows, they clearly did not apply in spirit to the "gentler sex" raised to pursue marriage. Reformers thus had to reimagine both traditional beliefs about women's abilities and overcome deeply embedded ritual practices in order to improve women's status in the industrial trades.

Despite these challenges, SPEW encouraged organizations to support women-friendly print shops. Creating a world where women came to rely on services provided by other women resulted in new ways of thinking about doing business. In her 1865 *Essays on Women's Work*, Bessie Parkes discussed the importance of women making inroads in business as employees *and* as owners. According to Parkes, two factors prevented women from owning their own businesses. First, women lacked the necessary startup money to begin such enterprises on their own. Second, unlike boys, who were trained early for either a trade or the management of the family estate, girls had only limited financial experience. Managing their pocket money was as close to money management as most girls could expect to get. "Girls never have any capital, they hardly know what it means," Parkes claimed, "yet without it the very first move is impossible; they may *enter* a shop, but they cannot *own* one."[47] By the 1870s, the idea of female ownership of businesses gained strong currency in employment projects supported by SPEW. Continuing to support women-run print shops, SPEW provided institutional support for an emerging woman-run publishing community.

Parkes's theories about women in business amounted to a rational economic response to the women's employment debate. She believed that a key obstacle for girls starting out on their own was the parental concern over "due and proper protection" for their daughters entering the trades. Owning a business clearly did not qualify as feminine work. Parkes recommended a system based on John Stuart Mill's theories of political economy to ameliorate this problem. His premise that "the peculiar characteristic, in short of civilized beings, is the capacity of cooperation" gave Parkes the idea for a system of shared ownership and profits. She defined her theory of business as follows.

> Cooperation, in the commercial sense, implies an application of the joint-stock principle; that the money with which a concern—say a grocer's shop, or a tailor's business, or even a factory—is carried on, has been clubbed together by different people, who appoint a manager and share the profits. . . . There must be a joint-stock, a common fund, clubbed together, yet nominally divided and actually divisible . . . [and] self-governed.[48]

Under Parkes's system, women-owned and -operated business could thus control profits and labor conditions. The passage of the 1855 and 1856 Limited Liability Acts made the formation of joint-stock "cooperative" companies possible and provided a solution for women reformers who believed that improvements to women's status would come primarily through their economic advancement.

These ideas influenced the action of reformers. The founding of the Women's Cooperative Printing Society by Emma Paterson in 1876 best illustrates the practical application of Parkes's "for and by women" business principle.[49] A close friend of Emily Faithfull, Paterson started this women-run and -funded organization to provide workers with high wages and a secure working environment. Born Emma Smith in 1843, she first sought employment as a bookbinder after her father's sudden death from typhoid fever when she was sixteen years old. Later, she took a job as a clerk at the Working Men's Club in 1860, where she met her future husband, Thomas Paterson. Deeply concerned with issues of gender inequality, she joined the Women's Suffrage Association, serving as secretary in 1872. Paterson soon became disillusioned with suffrage agitation and turned her attention to advancing women's interests in the "respectable" trades. "I don't think the vote the only panacea for all the sufferings of the weaker sex," Paterson commented, after leaving the Suffrage Association in 1873. "I am a working woman myself and my work for this society has brought me into contact with large bodies of women in other trades. . . . I hope to induce Englishwomen to try whether they cannot help themselves, as men have done, by combination."[50] Paterson dedicated her life to helping women succeed in the labor market. She organized over thirty women's labor societies after founding, in 1874, the Women's Protective and Provident League (WPPL), which included bookbinding, dressmaking and millinery.[51]

Paterson drew upon SPEW's business networks to start the women's Printing Society in 1876. The Society's first employees came from the Victoria Press. Like SPEW, the core of the directors were not workers themselves but patrons drawn from the middle and upper classes, including artisan bookbinders Sarah Prideaux and Mabel Winkworth, socialist Stewart Duckworth Headlam, and several lesser known "ladies of position," many with titles and exclusive West End addresses. Paterson also worked closely with fellow reformers Lady Dilke and Gertrude Tuckwell.[52] She immediately announced the founding of the WPS to SPEW which quickly apprenticed girls to the business. "They have a very good prospect of work and need more hands," remarked SPEW's secretary.[53] Affiliating with upper-class patrons and well-established organizations cultivated support among reformers while it legitimated the company as a "respectable" woman-run enterprise. The *Englishwoman's Review* reassured readers that parents should feel comfortable with their daughters working at the WPS, "especially as several ladies of position are on the Board of Directors." With the help of her female patrons, Paterson cast printing as an appropriate female employment and a truly "cooperative" business. Employees received bonuses every year based on company profitability. This amounted, on average, from 5 to 7 percent of their regular wages, a figure slightly above those set by the Union. Shareholders received yearly dividends of no more than 5 percent and only received further returns after employee bonuses were paid.[54]

The WPS expanded its operations, claiming by January 1881 that girls were "taught all branches of printing." "Girls and women are employed not merely as compositors but in other branches of the printer's work, commonly supposed to be beyond the intellect of 'females,' together with proof-reading and the general management of the business," one source claimed.[55] Men and boys did not work as compositors but performed the more physically demanding tasks of "pressmen and feeders."[56] Like boys in the trade, girls entering the WPS were legally bound as apprentices. Female apprentices did have some extra privileges, which included earning wages during the term of the apprenticeship. After this time, they could expect to earn fifteen to twenty-five shillings per week as compositors, with forewomen earning more. In addition, female apprenticeships ranged from three to four years. Boys entering the trade had to serve seven years as apprentices and work longer hours.[57] This difference resulted from the exclusion of training women on the heavy machine work required by men in such offices as well as the longer time boys had to spend "sweeping, cleaning, running errands, etc." Girl apprentices, in contrast, gave "practically their entire time to printing."[58]

SPEW continued its informal support of this female-run business throughout the 1870s and 1880s by providing employees and advertising and offering legal advice. The continued contact between these two institutions illustrated the importance of SPEW's advisory function during the late nineteenth century. As a well-funded advocacy organization, SPEW provided a place where institutions connected with the women's press could garner assistance for their projects as well as discuss their difficulties. In addition, smaller women's organizations could rely on the *Englishwoman's Review* to announce their meetings and chart their progress to members while promoting highly specialized causes to a wider audience. In this way, reform organizations found support through a series of loosely affiliated female-centered community networks.

The practical realities of cooperation formed a solid foundation for new gender-based business practices and promoted women's involvement in the debate over the women's employment issue. The WPS solicited women as shareholders and clients of this women-run, for-profit company. Like the Victoria Press before it, however, critics rejected this cooperative business model as unfair, accusing the WPS of "pos[ing] as philanthropists."[59] This charge had little weight behind it, as the WPS by the 1880s had become a thriving business. Although dependent on the patronage of wealthy board members in the beginning, the WPS's annual reports showed continued growth and an increasing profit margin for shareholders and employees. By the final decades of the nineteenth century, the Society printed and published material for a small but loyal reform-minded clientele. The WPS had

contracts for books, pamphlets, and periodicals from a variety of organizations, including socialist, labor, radical religious philosophy, and, of course,
women's advocacy titles.

As more of the British public heard about the cause of women's employment, the project of creating a space where women could help themselves
through remunerative employment gained a small but significant audience.
The WPS received extensive coverage in printer's trade journals, reviews,
and domestic magazines—even the *London Times*[60]—though its clientele
came mainly from liberal, socialist, and radical supporters.[61] Radical socialist minister Stewart Headlam choose the WPS out of principle: "The
printer's estimate was not the lowest estimate, but [I] was influenced by the
desire to encourage movements which enabled women to earn enough to
support themselves and by the knowledge that the WPS were considerate
to their employees and kept them on during the slack summer months."[62]
Other clients pledged their continued loyalty and praised the organization's
promptness and professionalism.[63] After the fading of the Victoria Press,[64]
the WPS emerged as a viable alternative for organizations with print work
that also supported the women's employment issue.

The overarching project of the WPS, to help women find steady, well-paid
work, advanced the program of editors of single-issue newssheets. Other
printers could have printed their publications, but the appeal of a journalism
completely dominated by women continued to drew in readers and, later,
advertisers in Britain and beyond. Perhaps inspired by the much-publicized
Victoria Press, American Susan B. Anthony wanted her women's paper, the
Revolution, to be printed entirely by women. "One of Miss Anthony's most
cherished plans," Elizabeth Cady Stanton claimed, "is to have a magnificent
printing establishment, and a daily paper, owned and controlled and all the
work done by women, thus giving employment to hundreds and making the
world ring with the new evangel for women."[65] Although the project failed, it
points to the cross-national appeal of the notion that women should control
the entire business of their own periodicals from production to distribution.
In Britain, the *Women's Penny Paper* marketed itself as "The only Paper Conducted, Written and Published by Women." This claim ultimately embodied
the project of patrons, workers, and readers of women-run periodicals during
the late nineteenth century.

The WPS inspired the work of reformers by offering them a practical means
of entering the employment debate. Its success reveals the stakes involved
in creating an economic and literary space for women through publishing.
Many of the most dedicated customers of the Society were women's orga-

nizations. Of the hundreds of titles published and printed by the WPS that I have located, the majority were either written by women or about topics related to women or, in some cases, both. Some late nineteenth-century titles included: *Speech of J. S. Mill, MP, on the Admission of Women to the Electoral Franchise* (1867); Eva Shaw MacLaren, *The Civil Rights of Women* (1897); Florence Dismore, *The Position of Women* (1896); and Mrs. Martindale, *Women in India* (1896). As Headlam's statements and the claims of the *Women's Penny Paper* illustrate, patronizing a women's printer made a strong statement about women's abilities while legitimating their role as workers, readers, and authors. The small act of selecting a printer, therefore, entailed more than convenience or financial consideration. Evidence—the nature of the titles published and printed by the Society—suggests that many women reformers chose a printer on the basis of their politics rather than their pocketbooks.

Suffrage Politics and the Woman's Newssheet

By the 1880s, specialized women's advocacy periodicals, covering everything from women's employment to social reform issues, emerged as a well-established part of Britain's journalistic landscape. Lydia Becker's *Women's Suffrage Journal* (1870–90) developed into the most successful newssheet of this period in terms of influence, longevity, and circulation (fig. 4). Becker was the eldest daughter of a well-established Manchester family; her interest in women's politics developed as a result of the influence of the early pioneers of the women's press. In 1866 she attended the annual meeting of the Social Science Association in Manchester, where she heard Barbara Bodichon read her paper "On Reasons for the Enfranchisement of Women." Bodichon argued that suffrage would awaken "a healthy sense of responsibility" in women regarding "social questions," issues previously considered "men's business."[66] This belief in the importance of voting as a means of civic participation greatly influenced Becker in the coming years. She herself made history by winning election to the Manchester school board in 1870. As a result of her own political activity, correspondence with the Langham Place circle, and writings for the *Englishwoman's Review,* Becker developed a political philosophy that linked women's economic and personal liberty with their direct participation in politics.[67]

Becker emerged as a key voice in what historians have begun to recognize as the vibrant and well-sustained Victorian women's suffrage movement. The movement took on a decidedly formal political character starting with

MANCHESTER
NATIONAL SOCIETY FOR WOMEN'S SUFFRAGE
Journal.

NO. 1.—PUBLISHED MONTHLY.   MARCH 1, 1870.   PRICE ONE PENNY.

IN issuing the first number of their Journal, the Manchester Executive Committee are actuated by a desire to furnish a medium of communication among the members, and a record of the work done by the different branches of the NATIONAL SOCIETY FOR WOMEN'S SUFFRAGE. They believe that many persons would gladly help the cause if they knew exactly what to do, and when to do it, and if they understood the great importance of individual effort at this crisis. If persons interested in the movement could receive every month an account of what has been done in other places, they might be tempted to try what could be done in their own locality. If they saw that one person, by taking the trouble—and it is not much trouble—of writing out the petition, obtaining a few names to it, and sending it to their own member to be presented, did something which was really useful, many might be incited to the same effort. For there is a pleasure in helping a good cause—a pleasure which too many deny themselves, because they fancy that the little they can do is not worth doing. Individuals are too apt to undervalue the importance of individual effort; forgetting that it is by the combination of individual efforts—each one seemingly insignificant—that collective force is accumulated and great results obtained. The movement would receive an enormous impetus if every person who has it in his or her power to do something for the cause would resolutely determine that however little CAN be done that little SHALL be done.

Isolation is another cause of weakness. No one can work well without sympathy and encouragement from others who are likeminded. It is the object of the promoters of this Journal to extend to every isolated well-wisher the firm grasp of an outstretched hand, offering and seeking help. Let every one who reads these pages, and who is thereby moved with a wish to give some help, however little, to the cause, write at once to the Editor, who will find for such a place among the band of workers.

Particular attention is requested to the announcement of the progress of the Women's Disabilities Bill, the second reading of which is fixed for the 4th of May. Petitions, to be of use, must be sent in before that date, and the sooner the better. Many people fancy that petitions are of little or no use; but this is a very great mistake. Mr. Disraeli, when Chancellor of the Exchequer, stated on one occasion, in the House of Commons, that "there was no right really more valuable than the

"right of petition; nor could any opinion be more erroneous "than that which supposed it to be a mere form. Because the "petitions presented did not now lead to discussion, it was "supposed that the House did not attend to them, but the fact "was not so. The Committee on Public Petitions strictly ex-"amined every petition, and the more important were printed "with the votes. Opinions expressed in petitions had great "influence on the judgment of the House."

The Reports of the Committee on Public Petitions are issued every three or four days, and placed in the hands of each member of the House of Commons. The total number of petitions and of signatures is carried forward from one report to another, so that the numbers of signatures to petitions for any special object, which are given in the first report, reappear to swell the total in every subsequent report throughout the session. This shows the advantage of petitioning early, for the sooner a petition is sent in, the greater the number of times that the amount of signatures appended is brought before the House. Up to the present date, March 1st, the total number of signatures to petitions in favour of Women's Suffrage is 20,166. These numbers will be brought forward in every future report. But if they had been delayed till nearly the end of April, the numbers would only have been brought once or twice under the notice of members before the second reading of the Bill, and they would have been of comparatively little use. So much of the Parliamentary report as refers to the Women's Disabilities Bill is given in another column, and attention is particularly directed to the continually increasing number of petitions, and the way in which the accumulated force is brought forward. It is most important to keep sending in a constant succession of petitions up to the time of the second reading of the Bill.

Besides recording the progress of the Women's Disabilities Bill and the number of petitions presented in its favour, it is intended that this Journal shall contain an account of public meetings and lectures held during the past month—of arrangements for forthcoming meetings—expressions of opinion from members of Parliament and other influential persons—extracts from newspapers bearing on the question—correspondence on the subject of women's suffrage, and original articles advocating the principle. It is hoped that friends throughout the country will assist the promoters by communicating such intelli-

Figure 4. *Woman's Suffrage Journal,* lead article.

the 1867 Reform Bill debates, as a result of women reformers' collaboration with male liberal and radical politicians, including John Stuart Mill, Henry Fawcett, and Jacob Bright.[68] Between 1870 and 1883, Parliament saw the introduction of a new suffrage bill every year except 1880. Women-led Victorian pressure groups, according to Martin Pugh, lobbied politicians to bring the suffrage issue to the table, successfully establishing the terms of the debate that would eventually win women the vote after World War I. The effectiveness of these women's organizations, in Pugh's account, depended upon their use of parliamentary channels that granted women influence in formal political debates.[69]

Like the journalists spearheading the campaign for women's employment, Becker also used less formal means to bring the suffrage issue into the public sphere. The mainstream press did give female suffrage limited but regular attention. However, it was women's newssheets, such as *Woman* (1872), the *Woman's Gazette* (1875–79), the *Englishwoman's Review*, and, of course, the *Women's Suffrage Journal*, that brought the issue to prominence among women in England to Scotland. In Ireland, the short-lived *Women's Advocate* (1874) published articles including "Women's Suffrage" and "Methods of Political Action."[70] Other articles, such as "Women's Suffrage vs. the *Spectator*," encouraged women to write letters to the press and MPs as well as to organize local suffrage societies. *Women's Advocate* lambasted the Irish press for not granting the "claims of women to a more positive legal status" a more "cordial recognition." Run by Mrs. T. J. Haslam with the help of her husband, the newssheet targeted a female readership while appealing to male "chivalry" to assist women in winning the vote.

Suffrage newssheets thus set out to convince women of the efficacy of participating in debates over suffrage, parliamentary or otherwise. Becker encouraged women to attend prosuffrage meetings and through the *Women's Suffrage Journal* offered directions on how to petition Parliament, gathering over three million signatures for petitions in favor of women's suffrage in the period from 1866 to 1879.[71] The paper also rallied support for a series of nine meetings at the Free Trade Hall in Manchester that succeeded in packing the largest hall in the city "from floor to ceiling with women of all ranks and occupations."[72] Manchester, a city with a long tradition of radical liberal politics, emerged under Becker's influence as a center of suffrage activity. The claims that women householders should have the same voting privileges as their male counterparts informed these early debates. Jane Rendall's study of the controversy over allowing Lily Maxwell, a woman householder mistakenly put on the voting register after the Reform Bill, to vote in the 1867 Manchester by-elections illustrates how debates over the criteria for voting within liberal voting circles affected the early women's suffrage movement in Britain. Supporters of Maxwell came to understand women's economic status as explicitly linked to her political rights.[73] For women like Becker, equal suffrage remained an essential part of liberalism's democratic promise.

Becker's early leadership provided a driving force for publicizing women's political claims during the 1870s and 1880s. Before starting the *Journal,* she started the Manchester Ladies' Literary Society in 1867. This woman-run club provided a space for its female members, excluded from male clubs due to their sex, to debate social and political issues. At a meeting of the Society held on January 30, 1867, Becker emphasized the importance of women's interest in science and read a paper by Charles Darwin that he had sent, according to Becker, along with his "good wishes for [the Society's] success." According to Becker: "The only course for the excluded person seems to be to try what can be done by forming a society of their own."[74] Manchester's ladies apparently were not ready for such a radical departure; the society failed to attract enough members after its inaugural meeting. In March of the same year, Becker tried again to mobilize women by reissuing as a pamphlet a widely read article on female suffrage in the *Contemporary Review,* asserting: "It may be denied that women have anything to do with politics; it cannot be denied that politics have a great deal to do with women."[75]

Three months later, Becker formed the Society for the Promotion of the Enfranchisement of Women in Manchester as a forum to discuss political ideas with other women. Members fortunately foresaw the difficulty of having two organizations called "SPEW" and soon changed the name to the Manchester National Society for Women's Suffrage.[76] By 1870, the committee started a suffrage publicity campaign to raise funds for the cause. Becker had undertaken national lecture tours under the aegis of the committee during 1869 with this intention but found public speaking difficult. "I am much bewildered, puzzled, unnerved and dissatisfied about my lecture, and unable to see my way clearly to mend matters" confided Becker to a close friend after her first lecture.[77] Echoing Parkes's experience on the podium ten years earlier, Becker claimed that her novelty status as a woman speaker subjected her to both heckling and insults.

After her tour, Becker directed her energies toward the more anonymous, semipublic arena of print. She started the *Manchester National Society for Women's Suffrage Journal* on March 1, 1870, as the organ of the Manchester branch of the National Society for Women's Suffrage. The predecessor to the *Women's Suffrage Journal,* this penny newssheet was the result of "long and careful" planning by Becker and Jessie Boucherett.[78] Compared to women's periodicals of the 1860s, the *Journal* had a more "newsy" sensibility. (Boucherett's long-running *Review,* by this time a quarterly paper priced at one shilling, was around half the physical size of this new paper.) Overall, the *Journal* shared a number of characteristics of 1870s newspapers: bigger, cheaper, and formatted in a multicolumn layout. Becker formed a limited liability company in 1869 and took the controlling interest, enlisting only the occasional assistance of three other women to help with the writing and editing.[79] Growing dissatisfied with the *Journal*'s limited audience in Manchester, Becker looked for an opportunity to expand the influence of her penny paper. In 1871, she affiliated the paper with the London-based National Society for Women's Suffrage, which helped expand the influence of the *Journal* beyond the circle of Manchester's radical liberal elite. Ten years later, the paper moved its permanent home to London, as it continued to grow as a "medium of communication" among members of affiliated societies in London, Edinburgh, Bristol, and Birmingham.[80]

The retitled *Women's Suffrage Journal* achieved national and international notoriety, claiming readers throughout the United Kingdom, North America, and New Zealand. Circulation grew steadily from a few thousand in the beginning to over fifteen thousand in 1874.[81] In this search for a broad readership, Becker widened its scope. In addition to publishing "full information of the progress of the movement for removing the electoral disabilities of women, accounts of public meetings and lectures, correspondence and original articles on the subject," the *Journal* "also record[ed] and discuss[ed] other questions affecting the welfare of women—such as education, employment, industrial or professional, and legislation affecting [women's] property and personal rights."[82] Published monthly, the *Journal*'s review format offered readers summaries of the latest news on women's suffrage from local branches and throughout the world. Lead articles also discussed the Married Women's Property Acts of 1874 and 1882, wife beating, child welfare, employment, and education from Becker's own female liberal perspective. In one series of articles on employment discrimination, Becker took on the Nine Hours Factory Bill, arguing that the act would limit women's ability to control her own labor.[83] Another article, "The Shocking Treatment of a Wife," challenged the light sentence given to a man accused of using his bulldog to attack his wife while brutally beating her. Publicizing such issues provided readers with a female-centered perspective on social reform unavailable to them in any other medium.

Becker encouraged an activist sensibility among readers through her coverage of social issues. In 1874, Becker increased the number of the pages to sixteen to make more room for reader comments without raising the price: "We ask the cooperation of friends in the shape of contributions of articles, reviews, correspondence, paragraphs and newspaper cuttings, suitable for publication in its columns."[84] This appeal had the intended effect of increasing circulation while promoting a belief that such reader participation would increase the *Journal*'s influence: "we trust that the large class of thoughtful women among whom it circulates will take the opportunity it affords of bringing their opinions and sentiments under the notice of the public which regards the *Journal* as the exponent of the principles and the progress of the movement for the removal of the political disabilities of women."[85] Becker's British and international readers were thus invited to use the *Journal* as their own forum to debate reform issues as both readers and writers.

Maintaining a nonprofit medium for women's politics posed special challenges. Printing five thousand copies of the *Journal* cost seventeen pounds, with an additional two pounds three shillings for every thousand after that.[86] From the beginning Becker wanted the *Journal* to support itself, despite limited revenue from issue sales and subscriptions. National Society for Women's Suffrage members, libraries, literary institutions, mechanics institutes, cooperative stores, reading rooms, and financially strapped readers were all eligible to receive the *Journal* for free. "I should certainly have sent in my subscription to the good cause," claimed one grateful reader after receiving her free copy, "but that I have gone through the greatest trials of poverty and privation."[87] All MPs also received copies at no charge, as did institutions interested in women's enfranchisement.[88] For all others, the price remained unchanged at one penny during the paper's twenty-year existence.

In spite of its low price and the limited resources of the NSWS, Becker kept the *Journal* afloat by developing a hybrid commercial model. News publications had just started to use advertising to boost profits during this period.[89] In 1874, Becker transformed the front page of the *Journal,* once reserved for editorials, into a "contents page" where article titles shared space with a host of various small advertisements.[90] By 1877, revenue from advertisers and subscriptions made the *Journal* self-supporting.[91] Advertisements included full-page ads for prominent products such as Willcox and Gibbs sewing machines, Goodall's Baking Powder, Epp's Cocoa, Whelpton's Vegetable Purifying Pills, Cash's Frillings (fabric trimmings), and "cheap" tea. The *Journal* also advertised pamphlets and other publications, although on the basis of sheer number, consumer goods ads appear to have provided the largest revenue.

The steady sale of advertisements, increasing circulation, and the support of the National Society for Women's Suffrage, as well as the participation of readers, became crucial to the success of the paper. Becker encouraged readers to view the *Journal* as their paper and the issues it covered as their issues. The "Treasurer's Report" column published subscription lists monthly, stating the name and the amount received from each subscriber. Becker went so far as to solicit prize money "offered by an anonymous donor" if the goals of the subscription drive were reached. Readers generously responded when Becker urged: "Friends of the cause are urged to endeavor to aid it by promoting the circulation of the *Journal*."[92] After receiving over eleven hundred pounds in subscription in 1873, she pressed readers to find 650 more subscribers to "place the committee in a satisfactory financial position."[93]

By the 1880s, the *Journal* provided more than, in the words of Millicent Fawcett, "a very valuable record of all that concerns the development of the women's suffrage movement."[94] Much like her Langham Place colleagues, Becker wanted to make her paper a truly all-women-run enterprise. The *Journal* had long supported the project of the WPS and wanted to replicate its success in Manchester.[95] The project ended in failure when "the thirty young women being taught the trade of typesetting were forced to retire when the local printers union threatened to 'down tools.'"[96] No printer in Manchester could break the will of the union or, as the WPS had done, circumvent it by creating a separate printing house. Though unable to replicate the WPS's success, Becker used her newssheet to encourage women's identification with a growing, female-centered social activism. Publicizing meetings, crusading against gender injustice, and familiarizing women with a political process that excluded them made up the building blocks of an extraparliamentary political culture that later came to influence the terms of the suffrage debate itself.

Reforming Agendas

As Becker's *Journal* inspired women to rally around the cause of women's suffrage, other newssheets that targeted the female activist started publication. During this period, suffrage made up part of a constellation of women-led, single-issue campaigns. This diversity proved crucial as the optimism of the 1870s faded after Parliament rejected a women's suffrage amendment to the 1884 Reform Bill.[97] (No other suffrage legislation was introduced until 1912.) Despite waning interest, the *Journal* quietly continued the campaign until Becker's death in 1890. Other reformers took up a series of social issues that helped sustain women's political culture during this period. Broadening the definition of what constituted political activity beyond direct appeals to Parliament helps explain how women continued to build networks and a culture of reform outside of the formal political system that excluded them. Thus, suffrage can be understood as an important cohesive force in the making of a female political identity, when considered in the context of other single-issue campaigns. Newssheet editors engaged readers in topics such as employment, education, poverty, and temperance. By the turn of the century, as Pugh has argued, these issues had become associated with a domestic-centered agenda in the public mind that no longer precluded women's involvement.[98] Sophia van Wingerden has argued that reformers feared being cast out into the "Never-Never Land of extra-governmental and extra-parliamentary action" when hopes of the franchise faded.[99] Evidence suggests, however, that casting larger liberal reform issues as domestic matters within the pages of women's newssheets helped fuel the development of a gendered political culture that thrived rather than faltered in an extraparliamentary arena.

Editors cultivated the belief among their female readers that they belonged to a political community that had the obligation to articulate opinions about issues relating to women's economic and social well-being. In 1874, Amelia Lewis started *Woman's Opinion* as a penny paper to represent "the social, domestic and educational interests of women." She claimed her paper would not allow the "few to answer for the many" or let "one sex answer for the other." Women should speak for themselves, and Lewis would guide them in using their intellect to "gain the conception of circumstances from their own individual reflection, not from the diluted reflection of others."[100]

Lewis's journalism career started in 1872 with the publication of *Woman*, "A Weekly Journal Embodying Female Interests from an Educational, Social and Domestic Point of View" (fig. 5). A newssheet, she believed, should serve as a voice for disenfranchised women: "Woman has had no representation as a Class, has had no public voice as a Class, has had no means of education as a Class, but has been deemed sufficiently provided for in our social system by being acted for by man." Woman had three public duties: becoming "members of society in general," advancing her "own individuality," and acting as a "sister to the other members of the sex."[101] Each weekly issue promoted women's education, married women's property, and domestic reform to an international audience that included readers in Germany, France, Russia, Sweden, Switzerland, Holland, Belgium, Spain, India, Australia, and North and South America.

The archival record offers only scant details regarding Lewis's personal history. Her journalism, however, reveals her commitment to the cause of the reform in both public and domestic matters such as the "food and fuel" movement.[102] Lewis started the *National Food and Fuel Reformer* in 1874 as a penny paper to help women best utilize household resources. Her invention, the "People's Stove," encouraged the economical use of fuel and "new

WOMAN;
THE SOCIAL REVIEW.

REPRESENTING THE EDUCATIONAL AND SOCIAL INTERESTS OF THE PEOPLE.
REGULAR CORRESPONDENTS ARE NOW RETAINED AT BERLIN, VIENNA, PARIS,
AND ROME; OTHERS ARE BEING APPOINTED ELSEWHERE.

EDITED BY AMELIA LEWIS.

REGISTERED AT THE GENERAL]   [POST-OFFICE AS A NEWSPAPER.

VOL. I.—No. 26.   LONDON: SATURDAY, JULY 20, 1872.   PRICE TWOPENCE.

CONTENTS.

FOOD FOR THE MILLION.—I.

IT is daily becoming of more importance, how we mean to procure alimentary sustenance for the bodies of our increasing millions; that we do not progress, in the ratio in which we increase, to find food for our population, is obvious. It is a fact easily to be ascertained by enquiry, of no very profound character, that a century ago men and women of the poorer classes were better fed than they *are* now, or *can* be fed now, and yet beyond the question of diseased meat, which touches by far more the richer classes, our Legislature remains perfectly unconcerned about the fact that a weakened, unhealthy mass of humanity is being reared by this insufficiency of provender. Where is it to come from? Do we rear more cattle for food? Do we cultivate more waste lands? Do we encourage the growth of wholesome and cheap vegetables? Do we push our fisheries? Do we patronize artificial methods of rearing poultry and eggs? Do we teach our poor to combine and learn new preparations of food? Do we set prizes upon prizes, not on refinement of produce, but on invention or adaptation of new mediums of supply? Nothing of the sort; the poor must either half starve, stilling the craving of their empty stomachs by alcoholic drinks, or they must get the means to buy food by surreptitious ways—or they must emigrate. But the very poor cannot emigrate, for emigration requires some means, even when assisted by Governmental and Voluntary aid. What remains therefore? The workhouse, that will be filled to overflowing should the stoppage of trade increase, and food become dearer. What means the workhouse? Depression and loss of moral vitality; heavy taxes for the middle classes, and general despondency that something is wrong somewhere. We do not, however, legislate, or we ought at least not to legislate for

smooth roads but also for the rough roads, and this want of food among the large masses of the people is a very rough road. It is the insipient enemy which, with bad housing, will eat into the vital powers of the nation, and produce such ugly sores, as will disturb the circulation of our national life-blood; it is the horrid forerunner of drunkenness, disease, riot and immorality. —want of food has upset thrones, torn asunder the ties of humanity, trampled down every sacred feeling, and has lit the torch of rebellion.

Let us not be deceived, let us look the enemy straight in the face, for he is nearing, nearing in the streets of our overcrowded capital, loudly knocking at the door of our hardy miners, tempting the pale workers in the manufacturing districts with false promises, undermining order, disturbing social combinations, and hurling threats at lazy turpitude, at incapable executive management, at want of foresight, and at that general want of sympathy, which allows the well-to-do to sit unconcerned in his arm-chair, till the hour of danger strikes, and the ugly monster has risen in the hideous shape of famine!

Let us forestall such an emergency *now*; let us combine now, at once, for grave and thorough action; not to give away food, but to bring it home to all those who labour honestly for its attainment; let us ask of the Legislature boldly a Commission that should inquire into the food supply and its stoppage. No private enterprise *can* do it; it is a step that must be taken by the Legislature itself—a step that must once for all recognise the need of millions, too dependent on the classes by whom they are employed, to act vigorously and effectively for themselves.

The opening of a market for supply is decidedly an improvement, but it touches not all classes, and though Columbia Market must be a boon for those who can go there, it will require the foresight which the Baroness Burdett Coutts possesses, multiplied to an infinite degree before we can safely lay our heads on our pillows and say, "All is well; we have sent the monster from our national door."

We trust something in the way of inquiry will be done before the House rises, and that some indications will be given, that the supply of food is as important a question as any now occupying the Commons or Lords. They need not open grannaries, as Joseph, the administrator of Egypt, did, but they ought to make those great social questions, from which we draw our very material, and through that our moral being, the subjects of the most earnest discussion and inquiry.

EDITOR.

COLUMBIA MARKET.—In relation to the market a letter has been received from Mr. Ayrton, the First Commissioner of Works, in which, after regretting his inability to accompany the deputation to the Lord Mayor, he says:—" Understanding that the Corporation of London have accepted a grant from Lady Burdett-Coutts, of Columbia Market, for the purpose of providing a fish-market, I presume the Corporation will take all the steps that may be necessary to carry out that object. Should it be shown by them that they are unable to do so, or principles in cookery" to help combat deprivation through domestic science. These ideas were carried forward in her last publication, *Health Leaves,* started in 1879.

Relatively cheap to produce and easy to distribute, newssheets allowed reformers to publicize both mainstream and experimental agendas. Editors such as Lewis used newssheets to advertise ideas and gain support for their causes. "Ignored" by the mainstream press, as Evelyn March Phillips had observed, news on women's causes found expression in small advocacy publications dedicated to general and single-issue reform. New titles published in the 1870s and 1880s provided further space to discuss women's economic status in an open forum. Increasingly, editors and contributors established their own authority on domestic issues through statistical surveys, reports on contemporary social policy, and employment listings. Such work often resulted in petitions, reports, and the formation of specialized organizations. Union journals and general employment magazines alike attempted to create new opportunities for women while agitating for better laws. Conversely, women workers themselves used newssheets to garner information on remunerative employment.

Working women began to play an increasingly important role in the women's press movement during the 1870s and 1880s. Serving both as occasional readers and writers, some did actual work for the press at organizations such as the WPS and Bale and Sons. As opportunities opened up, new employment newssheets promoted the cause. Louisa Hubbard started the *Woman's Gazette* in 1875 to help women find work: "It is not therefore from any wish to separate the interests of men and women that we devote this paper to the special need of the alter sex; but merely because it appears that the field of educated and industrial female labor is quite unprovided with any recognized advertising medium."[103] The *Gazette* published job listings for everything from wood engraving to nursing and ran advertisements (for "a moderate price") for organizations that helped women workers.

Hubbard's interest in women's employment came from working with Jessie Boucherett and Emily Davies.[104] Possessing an independent income, Hubbard chose not to marry and instead decided "to champion the cause of the unmarried woman," claiming: "from the first I refused to apologize for her existence."[105] She funded the *Gazette* and pledged any profits made from the sale of the paper to go to "the same purpose as that for which it is established—viz. the benefit of women depending on their own exertions for livelihood."[106] Although Hubbard wrote most of the content, she did publish articles on women's employment by other writers, while encouraging correspondence and advertisements from those seeking or offering work: "It is obvious that with such an outline to fill in, the editor will need all the assistance she can obtain and she therefore invites the support of all who take an interest in the cause which is so dear to her."[107]

In 1874, Emily Faithfull started a competing newssheet called *Women and Work* (1874–76) that, unlike the more narrowly focused *Gazette,* included topical news stories on factory legislation, education, and unemployment.[108] Hubbard meanwhile had exhausted both her financial resources and mental health and, at the advice of a close friend, followed Faithfull's lead by turning the *Gazette* into a more general interest paper in order to attract a wider readership. In January 1880 the *Woman's Gazette* became *Work and Leisure,* "in the vain hope that it would be more nearly self-supporting." According to her biographer, Hubbard "managed to spend more money on her own venture than would have been warranted from a commercial point of view."[109] Although the name change did not make Hubbard's journal self-supporting, *Work and Leisure* helped fill an important, social need. "There is certainly no more useful and informing periodical respecting women's work, and where to obtain employment than this gazette," claimed one organization.[110] Readers relied on Hubbard's newssheets, which were viewed as less politicized than periodicals such as the *Englishwoman's Review.* As Boucherett wrote to Hubbard, "I hope you are not thinking of giving up *Work and Leisure.* It is very useful. . . . Many people take it who would be shocked by the *Englishwoman's Review.* It is doing a good work don't give it up. You are instilling sensible ideas among a set of people who would perhaps not hear of them otherwise."[111]

As Boucherett's comment suggests, less overtly political periodicals provided opportunities for women to voice opinions that they might not feel comfortable sharing in other venues. Such publications also encouraged women to publish their own work: "I have never published a pamphlet on the subject of the training of women," remarked one contributor; "I have thought and written on it and should be very willing to send you any manuscript on a plan I was once anxious to pursue."[112] Hubbard gently encouraged readers to get involved in politics. In "What Should Women do in Elections?" Hubbard suggested that "we must all do something," including influencing male electors to make wise decisions.[113] The multifaceted ways that women used even narrowly focused newssheets illustrates how the women's press functioned as a medium of exchange that encouraged women's participation in public discourse as authors and readers.

Newssheets affiliated with specific women's organizations provided a similar forum. The *Journal of the Women's Education Union* (1873–82), founded and edited by education reformer Emily Shireff, served as a medium of communication for members of the Women's Education Union while discussing "all efforts made in favor of women's education whether connected with the Union or not and whether in our own country or abroad." Shireff hoped to "aid in arousing the public" from its "indifference" to the question of women's education.[114] She also encouraged readers to use the correspondence column to write on "any topic" relating to education "*outside the field of politics.*" In articles and editorials, Shireff repeatedly asked her audience to help make the *Journal* a "medium of correspondence" for member interests and public debate.[115]

The *British Women's Temperance Journal* (1883–92), the official organ of the British Women's Temperance Association (BWTA), shared the fervor of Shireff's newssheet. Mrs. Margaret Lucas of London helped establish the *Journal,* which replaced the *Crusade,* a small "neighborhood temperance paper," in 1883.[116] This "Popular and High-Class journal Devoted to the Position and Progress of Woman's Work in the Great Temperance Reform" was priced at one penny and solicited both letters and original articles from readers. Content focused largely on how (male) drinking affected women and family well-being. The newssheet served the over two hundred branches of the Association, in support of what the editor called "that on-marching Woman's Cause in England."[117]

To engage women in social and economic questions, women's newssheet editors looked for ways to spread the influence of specialized periodicals beyond their growing but nevertheless small list of subscribers. The attempt to increase circulation in order to achieve a greater base of readers remained a constant concern. Newssheets such as the *Women's Suffrage Journal,* the *Women's Temperance Journal,* and the *Women's Education Union Journal* relied on organizational support for promotion and even to help with production costs. Non–institutionally based newssheets such as the *Woman's Gazette, Women and Work,* and *Woman* faced serious limitations, as they often had to rely on subsidies from editors themselves rather than institutional support. Such periodicals had trouble sustaining themselves outside the commercial marketplace. In addition, the two pence price charged for the *Woman's Gazette* still remained above the means of the lower middle and working classes, effectively limiting the journal's subscribers to middle- and upper-class readers. Many women looking for employment, therefore, could only expect to occasionally purchase such newssheets or possibly gain access to them in the reading rooms of places like the Women's Protective and Provident League.

Newssheets thus often benefited from both formal and informal connections with women's organizations that supported them through member subscriptions and, in some cases, direct financial assistance. Without additional income from advertising revenues, only just beginning to take root as a substantial funding source for newspapers during this time, non–institutionally based periodicals folded as soon as editors ran out of money. However, although most newssheets sustained financial losses, many maintained a relatively stable existence as part of a woman-centered political culture. Newssheets provided a forum for the introduction and coverage of domestic issues that remained part of a wider Victorian liberal reform agenda. Through reading and supporting newssheets, reformers found themselves connected to a host of women-run networks that asserted their right to help define the nation through female-led reform programs.

Representing All Women?

As the foregoing discussion suggests, although women's newssheets claimed to represent the interests of all women, they remained firmly in the control of middle- and upper-class patrons. These women guided the direction of the women's press, effectively mediating discourse in forums that targeted an upper-middle- to lower-middle-class Anglo-European audience. Some papers, however, did focus on non-Anglo women and the working classes. Meant for consumption in the English-speaking world, colonial women's newssheets took on a voice that claimed to represent rather than directly engage with the views of colonized women. Nowhere was this more apparent than in women's periodicals on India. Reformers published two main types of newssheets about India during this period: the missionary journal and antivice paper.[118]

Started in October 1880, *India's Women* represented the Church of England Zenana Missionary Society. "The chief object of this Magazine," the editor claimed, "is to speak for the women of the Far East, whose cry for help too often falls unheeded on the ears of pre-occupied Christians of England."[119] *India's Women* had a mission: to Christianize Indian women and save them from what British women considered "unfair" Hindu laws that bound them. The Zenana Society used its newssheet both to publicize and gain support for their reform project: "Each number will contain one or more papers supplied by contributors whose personal knowledge of India and its needs will give special value to their statements, and include information, not only of India's women but also of her country, her history, religion, modes of life, etc. . . . Above all, we hope to tell the story of their turning from idols to serve the living and true God."[120] Unlike domestic-focused newssheets, missionary publications did not invite their subjects to "talk back." (The aforementioned contributors included women missionaries rather than Indian women themselves.) Such publications self-consciously spoke for Indian women regarding reform, thus revealing more about the preoccupations of evangelical British women than the Indian women they claimed to represent.

Nevertheless, evidence suggests that missionary activities had the unintended effect of encouraging the emergence of a nascent women's political consciousness among Indian women themselves. As Padma Anagol claimed of Christian missionary activity, female missionaries played a complex and important role in creating "a dynamic women's movement" during the late nineteenth century in India.[121] Another periodical, founded by the Society in April 1886, further supports Anagol's findings regarding missionary organizations. *Daybreak* addressed the "missionary student and Young people," in a more informal and less evangelical mode than *India's Women.* Priced at one penny, it was full of serial tales and newsy articles and excluded the more organization-centered information found in *India's Women.* Ultimately, these evangelical newssheets emerged as a forum for English churchwomen and Indian women converts to participate in the missionary project of the Church of England away from the authorial hand of male leaders. These newssheets can be understood as helping to facilitate the process described by Anagol regarding Indian women's early challenges to patriarchal authority within a Western Christian evangelical context.

Even considering the potential subversive feminist nature of such publications, colonial newssheets nevertheless remained firmly in the control of *British* women. They thus echoed the particular religious, political, and ethical agendas of such reformers and their organizations. During the same period the antivice campaign, led by Josephine Butler, turned its attention to India. By the mid-1860s it was clear that the British government would extend the Contagious Diseases Acts, laws that required the inspection of prostitutes in order to prevent the spread of venereal disease among soldiers, to India. This move, according to Philippa Levine, had the intention of enforcing racial and gender hierarchies in the colonial context.[122] These acts had been repealed in Britain in 1886 due to the campaigns waged by Butler in three different newssheets. Each contained information not only about the repeal campaign but also about India and Indian women.

Butler believed that advocacy journalism provided the best means of influencing British policy regarding the Contagious Diseases Acts in India.[123] The *Shield* (1870–1970) served as the main voice of the campaign to repeal the Contagious Diseases Acts in Britain, temporarily ceasing publication in 1886. When the government threatened to reinstate the acts in India, the paper started up again. Butler started the *Dawn* (1888–96) to monitor laws governing prostitutes in the colonies and on the Continent. In 1898, she started the *Storm-Bell* (1898–1900) as the special organ of her Ladies' National Association for the Abolition of State Regulation of Vice. Each of these periodicals provided a space for British women to participate in the debate over the state regulation of vice. Butler was keenly aware of the importance of print in mobilizing her campaign. She issued appeals to readers for support while making the journal more "interesting and useful" by including illustrations and commentaries independent "of the repeal issue."[124] According to Butler, the mainstream media provided little help to the campaign: "The conspiracy of silence of the press has done us this service . . . it has forced us to create a literature of our own."[125]

Colonial women's journals clearly were never intended as forums for the equal exchange of ideas between British and Indian women. (Only after World War I did journals that attempted to represent Indian women's views emerge.)[126] During the late nineteenth century, Indian women, who had literacy rates of below 2 percent, did not figure prominently as representatives of their own interests in a press that claimed to represent all women. Women's reform periodicals often cast women in the colonies as "heathens" who needed British women's help to combat "barbaric" religious laws rather than as equal partners in an emergent political discourse about the status of women.

Working-class women also often found themselves spoken for in the pages of such periodicals by women who believed that they knew the true needs of their "less fortunate sisters." In contrast to colonial newssheets, however, working-class women's voices did occasionally emerge. Even though newssheets largely remained in the control of the elite and educated middle classes, journals that claimed to represent the interests of working women did exist. This was due, in part, to improved literacy and education and increased accessibility to cheap periodicals among British women. Started in 1876 by Emma Paterson, the *Women's Union Journal* focused on improving conditions and employment opportunities for working women (fig. 6). As the official organ

THE WOMEN'S UNION JOURNAL:

THE ORGAN OF THE

WOMEN'S PROTECTIVE AND PROVIDENT LEAGUE :—

Office, *Industrial Hall, Clark's Buildings, Broad Street, Bloomsbury, W.C.*

No. 131.—Vol. XI.　　DECEMBER, 1886.　　Published Monthly. Price One Penny. Year's subscription, including postage, 1s. 6d.

MRS. PATERSON.

The readers of this journal have a right to expect from it some brief record of the life and work which have been cut short, to the deep grief of many and to the incalculable loss of many more. Brief and imperfect such a record must be in any case, and doubly so in this, for Mrs. Paterson was valued and is regretted, as a personal friend, by all who worked with her, and it is not easy to write concerning the life of a friend so recently lost.

Emma Ann Smith was born April 5th, 1848 ; a record of the family history goes back to her grandfather, Stephen Smith, born 1781. Henry Smith, Emma's father, and son of the above, was born in 1808. In 1837 he became Head Master of a School at East Ham, and in 1843 Head Master of the School attached to St. George's, Hanover Square, then situated in Belgrave Street, Pimlico ; a post which he filled with credit and success for 21 years till his death from typhoid fever, in 1864. During this interval Emma was born, and, as her exceptional ability showed itself, well and carefully educated under her father's eye. She was his constant companion ; girl friends and cousins used to laugh at her devotion to study and call her "the book-worm," but though at that age she liked books best, she had other tastes as well, and her father's boasts of Emmie's progress in German or Italian were wont to end : " and you should only hear her *whistle*, she can whistle as well as any boy !" Mr. Smith's death in 1864 left his widow and daughter unprovided for ; two unsuccessful attempts were made by the former to establish a school, in the second of which Emma took part for a short time, but she disliked teaching and after a short experience as governess to young children gave up the attempt. About 1866, she obtained more suitable employment as secretary or amanuensis to an elderly lady, who was employed as clerk by the then secretary of the Workmen's Club and Institute Union. At this time she had leisure and opportunities for more reading, of which she eagerly availed herself, and she also became to some extent familiar with the work of the Union, so that, on the strength of her experience and the recommendation of her employer, she was appointed, in July,

1867,—when still only a girl of nineteen—assistant secretary to the Union itself. One who knew her well at that time, writes *à propos* of the possible difficulties in the way of so young a woman doing the office work of a Society for men, in which men of all classes were calling constantly :—" there was a cheerful and equable presence of mind and self-respect, which made her relations with men perfectly easy, both for them and for herself. It would have been *impossible* for any man to make her a personal compliment, or to be rude." Her memory for every name, fact or date that could be useful was noticed with admiration, as only to be accounted for by her genuine interest in what was going on, and her conscientious desire to do what she undertook with the utmost possible thoroughness. No better preparation for her future life could have been imagined than this work, which brought her naturally and pleasantly into contact with the *élite* of the London workmen, in a relation which caused her "great capacity for business " to be first displayed in their service. Of the three honorary secretaries who held office with her,—Mr. Thomas Paterson, Mr. Hodgson Pratt and the Hon. Auberon Herbert—the first became her husband ; the words of the second will be found on another page, and with the third also she formed a firm and lasting friendship.

In February, 1872, after nearly five years services, she resigned her post in order to become secretary to the Women's suffrage Association, and she was then presented with an illuminated address and a gold watch by the governing body of the Union, in token of the appreciation commanded by "her practical ability and good judgment," her eagerness to extend the sphere of the Society's usefulness, without regard to the consequent increase of her own duties, and other qualities equally familiar to those who know Mrs. Paterson's later work. As secretary of the Suffrage Association, we are told* that she "fulfilled the duties of her office with great zeal and ability," and it is at this date that we must begin her life as an 'agitator ;' at least in a recent letter about the Staffordshire nail-making districts, she spoke of a visit to that county about 1871 as being made "before I was an agitator." She was married to Mr. Paterson, July 24th, 1873, and at the same time

* *Englishwoman's Review.* December, 1886. "Emma Ann Paterson."

Figure 6. The Women's Protective and Provident League organ, the *Women's Union Journal,* front page.

of the Women's Protective and Provident League,[127] the journal supported the interest of women employed in industrial trades by seeking to prevent the depression of wages, provide sickness funds, arrange registration of employment notices, and arbitrate employee–employer disputes.[128] Selling for one penny and printed by the Women's Printing Society, the *Journal* saw itself as the voice of the working woman because of its encouragement of reader participation in labor questions.

Paterson published a mix of information intended to create a sense of community among readers. The *Journal* placed reports of injustice in the printing trades, for example, next to announcements of social meetings at the League rooms. A section called "Gossip" was published alongside general interest articles on topics that included relationships between "Men and Women." In the correspondence columns, readers could respond to editorials and express opinions on information found in the paper. Published monthly, the *Journal* did not provide up-to-the-minute coverage of parliamentary decisions or current events. Rather, it included general coverage of reports of trade union meetings, the results of local school board elections, and reprints of articles in mainstream newspapers on women's employment. Readers recognized the usefulness of this mix of information and readily responded to circulation drives and appeals for funds, recognizing that the publication of the newssheet stretched the League's "small funds."[129]

The newsy and easy-to-follow format of Paterson's small penny paper soon became the envy of working men's periodicals. As one male correspondent wrote:

> When I compare the *Women's Union Journal* with most of the journals started on behalf of the workmen, the conclusion is forced upon my mind that men have wished to soar too high and as a natural consequence have overshot the mark aimed at. They must also go in for a highly paid editor, sub-editor and staff in proposition, which caused expenses to run in almost every case to enormous losses on the sales. Again they could not be content with reports and notices of meetings and authentic news especially applicable to their state and condition but they must have high-flown leading articles far beyond the grasp of the comprehension of more than two thirds of their readers.[130]

Such workmen's journals failed as "a medium of communicating with one another," something he believed Paterson's newssheet achieved. As the letter concluded, "I am glad to see the women use greater wisdom in the selection and management of their journal than the men have up to the present moment."[131]

The *Journal* survived until 1890, outliving Paterson, who died in 1886. In its place, the League published a cheaper quarterly version of the newssheet that contained accounts of meetings and information on women's industrial work. The editor justified the decision to cut cost, claiming that "women's labor receives attention in the columns of nearly all the leading papers" and that since working women "were not great readers," this new version would suffice.[132] In this scaled-down publication, "the work of the League will be placed before the public in a form showing more clearly the lines on which those working for the cause are proceeding."[133] This shift from a journal for and by working women to an informational newssheet revealed the difficulty of representing the interests of all working women in one paper. Women workers were no more a monolithic category than their middle-class counterparts. However, the fading of the *Journal* left the working-class reader with far fewer opportunities than middle-class readers to participate in female reform culture via a women's press that catered to middle-class interests.

New Directions

By 1890, most of the special interest women's newssheets started in the 1870s and 1880s faced problems related to funding, editing, and readership. These difficulties sparked a debate on the usefulness of women's newspapers as a genre. While newspapers throughout the country mourned the death of Lydia Becker and her *Woman's Suffrage Journal* in July 1890, the *Woman's Gazette*, a new general interest women's periodical started in 1888, used the occasion to call into question the usefulness of single-issue journalism. "The *Women's Suffrage Journal* will appear no more," the *Gazette* announced;

> the occasion may make us consider whether, after all, newspapers devoted to a single object are of much use. It is unlikely that any persons read them who are not already converted to the reform advocated. . . . The converted read the paper of course in a dutiful spirit, and find it rather dull, as the arguments are already well impressed on their minds. The only use of such a paper is to gather together all the facts which the active reformers require to know in order to fight with the newest weapons. But the actual fighters for a reform are few in number: far too few to make up the circulation of a good paper. Hence the circulation languishes and the paper becomes a burden on the well-wishers to the cause who are already very probably too much burdened already.[134]

The *Gazette* suggested that the best way to draw attention to a political movement was to get "reports of meetings and readable paragraphs into the columns of the general newspapers." This tactic would attract more people to the movement while avoiding the "dangers of a special organ." To the loyal readers of the *Women's Suffrage Journal*, the *Gazette* proclaimed: "We think they will find they are really better off without it."[135]

Such an assessment called into question the optimism of midcentury advocates of a free press who had touted the periodical as a democratic forum that would support reform causes. Changes ushered in during the late Victorian era demanded a reimagining of the relationship between reform campaigns and the press. New technology, new readers, and new opportunities for women combined to create a different kind of advocacy journal. The demise of the *Women's Suffrage Journal* thus marked the end of an era in women's political journalism. A more dynamic women's periodical replaced single-issue newssheets that claimed to serve the broad interests of women. Individual campaigns that had started to languish, like suffrage, would be subsumed in more generalized publications. The *Englishwoman's Review's* small suffrage section, for example, condensed information once found in Becker's *Journal* and served as the new organ for the National Society for Women's Suffrage for the next twenty years.[136] Such periodicals covered other campaigns like women's employment and education, which meanwhile had worked their way into the larger domestic liberal reform program. The legitimating of single-issue campaigns as women's issues that existed as part of the wider realm of social reform rendered the newssheet less critical as a medium to publicize these causes.

The decline of the single-issue periodical reflected more general changes in the relationship between Victorians and the press. If journalists and editors were to preserve the notion that the press represented the "Fourth Estate," they had to find new ways of appealing to a growing literate public. Rejecting the label of "dull," editors of the turn-of-the-century women's press expanded the scope of papers by broadening their political commitments. As the next chapter demonstrates, this shift mirrored trends in the British press that included the rise of mass marketing techniques pioneered by the New Journalism. Editors employed tactics used by their mainstream counterparts, hoping that by using this modern journalistic style they would better engage readers in these semi-anonymous public forums by making papers both more entertaining and less insular.

Launched the same week as Henrietta Muller's *Women's Penny Paper*, the *Gazette* itself helped usher these changes. According to the *Englishwoman's Review*,

> if the reader of this *Review* could have been told twenty years ago that two weekly penny papers dealing with the "woman question" would be issued within a week with the hope of finding adequate support they would have considered the assertion absurd beyond belief; but such is the case and moreover

the new papers are, so far as the first numbers go, amusing and interesting. The first named *Woman's Gazette* has a direct political bias and aims at being the organ of the Women's Liberal Federation. . . . Its motto is "Liberty, Justice, Humanity" and it proposes to give its attention to all questions affecting the social well-being and political position of women. The *Women's Penny Paper* contains a bright editorial . . . and a great deal of miscellaneous information, reviews, etc. Both papers will doubtless help to make woman of leisure more interested in the work of the world which goes on around them and thus accomplish more useful work.[137]

Even papers that, like the *Gazette,* served as organs of institution, it seemed, had starting pitching themselves to a broader readership. At the same time, editors remained self-consciously aware that their readers belonged to a class of women who could afford to dedicate time to political concerns. Thus, although addressing a broader agenda, these new "amusing and interesting" papers remained largely part of an elite world of female reform culture. The new woman activist, as imagined by turn-of-the-century editors, would engage in a female-centered political culture through newspapers that represented women's public commitments as part of her larger identity as citizen.

The publicizing of single-issue campaigns by women's papers anticipated a central role for the female reformer in the new century. During this period, periodicals "for and by women" transformed from newssheets into political newspapers, expanding both the purpose and scope of the women's press movement. Women's organizations certainly continued to have their own official organs, which claimed to speak for the larger interests of "womankind." As problems with this method of women-run, not-for-profit journalism emerged, editors of the 1890s put new strategies into place. They pointed to low circulation and limited support for independent causes as part of the unsuccessful journalistic practices employed by editors of single-issue newssheets. By the end of the century, women's political papers boasted a greater diversity of readers. At the same time, following the pattern of other past and present British advocacy press institutions, such periodicals kept the leadership of such periodicals in the hands of a group of the educated classes.[138] Middle- to upper-class women largely funded and edited women's newssheets while mediating the discourse articulated in their pages. This tension between market pressures and class-based agendas guided the ambition of editors to make the women's press into a gendered medium for communication. In the process, women's newspapers came to play an important role in defining the boundaries of women's political culture well into the twentieth century in terms of both issues and material practices.

3

Gendering the News
for the New Woman Activist

"Women can't write and don't want to read," press baron Lord Northcliffe declared in 1903, when the *Daily Mirror,* his newspaper written for and run by women, failed to attract a large audience after only nine months in circulation. Northcliffe's entrepreneurial spirit led him to reorganize. Replacing his female writers with an all-male staff, he successfully converted the paper into an illustrated daily targeted at a male audience still in circulation today. For publishers such as Northcliffe, the news was not a genre intended for women.

By the beginning of the new century, however, women *were* reading, writing, and making news. Unlike mainstream periodicals and ladies' magazines, women's newspapers drew readers into the world of domestic and international news stories by using rhetorical strategies that gave women a stake in those events. Such publications went a step further than the *Daily Mirror,* which reported only on general news topics by establishing themselves as authorities on woman-centered reform issues. Advocacy papers did not seek a mass audience to gain commercial legitimacy. Rather, editors believed that they held a special role as producers and distributors of knowledge directly relating to women's interests. Their purpose was decidedly different from that of Northcliffe, who had made his name and fortune running the *London Times* and creating several of Britain's first million-plus circulating dailies. As more and more women came into their own as wage earners and primary consumers of household goods and services, publishers started to recognize them as a target audience. Northcliffe tried to tap into this market with a publication called the *Women's Times* but again failed. Piquing women's interest in domestic politics and foreign news during a period when women lacked the basic tenets of citizenship, as he discovered, proved a failure when cast as a moneymaking enterprise.

Women editors thus shared Northcliffe's ambition but not his method. Cultivating reader interest in political news was important not only for its consumerist possibilities but also for pushing a female-centered reform agenda. Regardless of its actual ability to influence social policy or cultural change, women's advocacy journalism, since its inception at midcentury, represented the primary medium for publicizing women's employment, education, and legal disabilities. Specialized periodicals defined these issues as urgent social questions through ongoing exchanges between editors and a growing, dedicated audience of readers. By the 1890s, women's advocacy publications claimed significant cultural authority over topics relating to women and effectively established themselves as legitimate spaces of political and cultural discourse.

Engagement in public debates over the Woman Question led to increased prominence for those publications that contested contemporary representations of the new woman activist. Aided by changes brought on by a burgeoning Victorian press industry, the women's press found new ways to promote women's participation in public discourse. Women's newspapers, for example, provided new professional opportunities for a growing number of journalists, while encouraging readers to engage with a host of international and domestic news topics that rarely found their way into most publications that targeted women. Women's advocacy journalism thus developed into a highly visible, alternative news medium for both writers and readers. Such periodicals asserted an authoritative female voice on international and domestic issues at the turn of the century by bringing demands for reform out from the margins and into the mainstream.

The independently run women's newspapers discussed in this chapter, although still small in terms of circulation and size in comparison to their mainstream counterparts, established themselves as nationally recognized advocacy publications during the 1890s. The founding of the *Women's Penny Paper* (1888–91) by Henrietta Muller in 1888 marked a new departure in advocacy journalism. Rather than focusing on perennial political and social issues and organizational news, as newssheets had done earlier, Muller's paper reported general women's news for the woman reader. The two women-run periodicals that evolved out of the *Women's Penny Paper*, the *Woman's Herald* (1891–93) and the *Woman's Signal* (1894–99), built on Muller's vision. Margaret Shurmer Sibthorp's newspaper *Shafts* (1892–99) took press advocacy a step further by addressing working-class readers while promoting a radical, woman-centered social agenda. Registered as newspapers for sale at home and abroad, these papers represented by the most prominent women's press publications of the period and kept readers informed of happenings in Britain and the world. By expanding the purpose that had been held by a narrowly defined press that had served the interests of particular women's communities during the 1870s and 1880s, editors such as Muller and Sibthorp made possible the transformation of the single-issue newssheet into the broad-based newspaper.

The advocacy newspaper grew up alongside the newssheet, a genre that continued to appeal to small audiences during this period. Turn-of-the-century newssheets included women's employment papers, prosuffrage journals, reform (such as protemperance) publications, and trade union journals. Several dozen newssheets emerged to represent women's organizations in London alone.[1] Newssheets could not attract nearly the same size readership as women's newspapers. As suggested in chapter 2, there was a growing sentiment by the late 1880s that newssheets were far too narrow a medium to wield significant cultural influence. Women's newspaper editors responded to these concerns with bold headlines, sketches, interviews of famous women, and other eye-catching features. Simply put, editors focused on increasing circulation rather than preaching to the converted. This chapter tells the story of this new women's advocacy journal and the attempts by editors to make it into a competitive liberal reformist news medium.

A rapidly expanding periodical market helped drive the advance of women's newspapers. Market-driven practices and technical innovations pioneered during the 1870s and 1880s translated into dramatic structural changes for the periodical press manifested in the New Journalism. Developed first in the United States, "yellow journalism," as critics called it, thrived on publishing sensational narratives of heroism, scandal, and, in the case of the Spanish-American War, propaganda. Photographs replaced less sophisticated woodcuts, as bold headlines promised to grab the readers' attention. Lower production costs also accompanied these changes. The wide application of advanced mechanical printing techniques meant that newspapers could be printed cheaply and quickly, making them an affordable commodity for all classes.[2] Advertisers utilized this new medium as a space to hawk their wares while providing an invaluable source of income for periodicals. Although journalistic license to print dramatic stories as news put the credibility of many publications in question, rising circulation rates indicated the growing influence of this "new" press on both sides of the Atlantic.[3]

The women's press movement welcomed the changes ushered in by the

New Journalism as a new professionalism took hold of women's newsrooms. Editors expanded their role to include the management of news staffs, advertisers, and shareholders. They often paid contributors and had administrative support staffs. One editor employed a subeditor. Women staff writers for the first time listed their primary occupation as "journalist." This new professional journalist helped make women's newspapers more attractive to readers though her lively and often sensational articles. Through the introduction of new professional standards, the women's press moved away from its origins as largely an amateur enterprise.

Like mainstream news publications, woman's papers employed creative rhetorical and presentational strategies intended to draw in readers. Overall, these publications *looked* more like modern newspapers. Attractive in appearance, with illustrations throughout, they had grown in size and resembled tabloids rather than newssheets and literary journals, the largest measuring fourteen by ten inches. Distinct columns replaced narrative formats, and short news briefs delivered information in concise paragraphs.[4] Some of the new techniques used by editors to draw in subscribers were interviews with famous literary and political women, features that reported dramatic tales of "What women are doing around the World," and artistically rendered mastheads.[5]

Innovative business practices helped make women's advocacy journalism into a serious business enterprise. Decreasing production costs made penny papers standard by the 1890s. W. H. Smith helped make periodicals more widely available, by providing more attractive and numerous bookstalls.[6] By the turn of the century, readers could more easily buy women's newspapers from newsagents rather than from offices of organizations that published a particular title. The lowering of newspaper postal rates in 1870 further reduced the cost of delivered subscriptions.[7] Finally, more flexible incorporation laws decreased business risks and made capital more available to fledgling enterprises.[8]

Despite moves toward increased professionalism and commercialization, women's newspapers continued as an alternative medium. Politics, not profits, drove turn-of-the-century editors. At a time of increasing consolidation and corporatization of the press, women's newspapers expanded their advocacy role. This added diversity during a period that historians such as Jean Chalaby, Alan Lee, and Lucy Brown have claimed witnessed the beginning of the decline of a vibrant, contentious press culture in Britain due to increasing commercialization. The women's press continued as a critical advocacy medium in part because of the selective use of New Journalistic techniques to further a woman-centered reform agenda.

Women's newspapers thus merged the gender-based business practices of the preceding decades with new commercial models. Proprietors eagerly capitalized on innovations that led to the expansion of women-run publications. For example, all women's advocacy periodicals gave more space to advertising. They hoped to increase profits and offset expenses by showing advertisers the benefit of promoting products in periodicals targeted at the female consumer. Improved printing technology made illustrations easier to produce and advertisements more attractive. Layouts changed to a more commercial format, as the number of pages in women's newspapers grew to accommodate new advertisers. Like mainstream news publications, they mixed advertisements together on the same page as copy. This ensured high visibility; potential customers were less likely to miss an advertisement that shared space with editorial material. Announcements asked readers to mention to merchants that they had seen a particular advertisement in a women's paper in order to guarantee advertiser patronage. These new ways of doing business increased the visibility of the women's press movement. By developing innovative marketing strategies for their newspapers, editors found new ways to promote the "advancement of women" in Victorian Britain through the medium·of "their press."

Making "Women's News" for the Woman Reader

Focusing on both the quotidian aspects of women's lives and the happenings of women around the world, women's newspapers reinvented themselves at the turn of the century as conduits of general information, as well as of knowledge specifically related to women's causes. Readers came to recognize what editors called "the common interests of women" through reading the news. These newspapers thus served a dual purpose: keeping women involved with issues that affected their own lives, while at the same time encouraging the support of women's causes within the larger context of Britain, the Empire, and the world. Social reform news dominated the pages of women's newspapers. Journalists reported on domestic issues such as employment, local school board elections, and education, as well as happenings in Parliament. Current events columns introduced British women to both national and international news. Analysis of seemingly faraway international events provided one way for editors to create women's regular connection with contemporary, newsworthy events.

In general, newspapers appealed to women's interests, broadly defined, rather than to a particular political party or agenda. Some reporting dealt conservatively with social reform issues, while some presented more radical positions. This diversity encouraged readers to choose their own political and social affiliations by not tying papers to the agendas of particular women's organizations. News reporting in the women's press, like that in other news sources, however, was not neutral or objective. As Michael Schudson has argued about the American media, news and newsgathering constitutes a "cultural form" whose product translates into particular kinds of "public knowledge."[9] Newspapers thus produce information for particularized audiences. Editors published stories to keep their readers' interest while connecting them to a larger community that came to share, within the space of the women's newspaper, a common set of cultural references. News stories had the intended effect of increasing women's investment in political, social, and economic topics. Why would a woman have any interest in happenings in the Near East, for example, if she could not imagine herself as connected to that world?

One strategy used rhetoric that created heroic narratives of women who acted in very public ways against inequality. The *Signal's* "What a Woman Did: A True Story" described the bold rescue by the French consul's wife of "300 Armenian Christian" refugees, whom she led across the Turkish desert to the "Alexandrette harbor." Threatening to make an international incident out of the affair if she, her four small children, and the refugees were not granted safe passage, authorities ensured that all successfully reached their destination. The story, told with some dramatic license, ended: "If some brave woman like her were at the head of public affairs today, the Eastern question would have been solved long ago, and the six great European powers would have ceased to be the laughing stock of the world."[10] Selecting news that combined concerns about British foreign policy with the action of daring women invested readers in nontraditional arenas that were previously considered solely the domain of their fathers, husbands, and brothers. In this way, journalists asked readers to see themselves as citizens who had not only a stake in society but also an obligation to fix foreign affairs.

National news, from both London and the provinces, took on its own importance. Regular columns in the *Women's Penny Paper* included "English News," "News from the North," "Current News about Women," and "What They Are Doing in the Political World." Two related types of stories that invited readers to cast judgment dominated these pages: narratives of injustice and narratives of women's triumphs. "During the recent revision of voting lists in Leeds, the anomalous state of the law, or otherwise the muddle-headed state of the lawyers, was shown to perfection," one report claimed regarding a female rate-payer, who, as a "deserted wife," was not allowed to take part in local elections. The sympathetic and even sensational portrayal of this "abused" and "abandoned" wife demonstrated the inequality inherent in the local election policy.[11] British towns and cities emerged as sites of heroic actions by women who emerged as public actors. When the Women's Liberal Association passed over a Mrs. Bayles for the position of secretary to "make room for a gentleman" on the board, the *Women's Penny Paper* happily reported that the board eventually ignored the men's "ungallant" behavior, and, through women's influence, "Mrs. Bayles has been returned."[12] Through these storytelling devices, the news thus gave readers a sense of their own importance in public life both at home and abroad.

Building on an early principle of the women's press, newspapers provided information that expanded readers' general understanding of the world around them. The *English Woman's Journal,* the *Englishwoman's Review* and the *Victoria Magazine* had all published stories intended to widen women's reading habits beyond central topics such as employment or education.[13] By the turn of the century, newspapers drew women into discussions of current affairs by creating a role for them in potentially shaping those events. Reporting the news turned into an opportunity for telling stories intended to help women form opinions and, in some cases, mobilize. For example, the *Women's Penny Paper* dedicated a large column to the Leeds weavers in 1888 that described attempts to form a new union branch to combat oppressive working conditions.[14] Women were not mentioned at all in the article. However, the implicit assumption remained clear: the reader would and should form an opinion about and ultimately support the cause of the weaver and unionization in general.

Other articles were less subtle. "The Disease of Anarchy" put the question of the "madness" of alleged terrorist Colney Hatch before readers, claiming that the government should rule all terrorists guilty of "homicidal insanity" and place them "in a criminal lunatic asylum." The *Signal* implored readers to come out against such acts not because of their direct impact on women but rather because of their "moral" depravity and negative impact on civic life.[15] Other slanted articles on socialism, antivivisection, and temperance called for more individual forms of action. *Shafts,* for example, linked these issues to women's well-being *because* they affected society's progress. Such articles addressed women readers as concerned citizens who should voice their opinions on issues, including the security and progress of the nation.

While encouraging interest in contemporary issues, a small women's press industry brought reformers together in a growing body of networks and associations. Editors relied more and more on the financial and political resources of London in the drive to become a truly national presence. Unlike the British socialist press, which produced hundreds of small publications throughout the provinces and relied on local news for their copy, the women's press remained very much an urban phenomenon.[16] This held true in part because of the diverse types of news that they published. London, as the seat of government and political administration, provided access to domestic and colonial news for papers that could not afford the services of the early news agencies. In addition, the capital city placed women editors close to Fleet Street papers that the women's press drew on for national and international information. Newspaper distributors had their offices in this busy urban center, which also contained a greater concentration of potential advertisers.

Editors also utilized the London-based organizational networks set up by the women's press earlier in the century. Evidence suggests that editors often solicited articles from friends who lived and worked in the city. Becker's *Women's Suffrage Journal* benefited from such connections after the paper moved to London in 1881. Lady Henry Somerset used contacts to start the *Woman's Signal* in 1893, asking Francis Power Cobbe, "Will you write me an article on any subject you like? I should be very grateful and support from you would be very valuable."[17] These networks, as historians have demonstrated, made up an important part of women's associational life in London, which included interactions at political meetings, at women's clubs, and in reading rooms.[18] Friends would sometimes even refuse payment for their work to help support women's journalism.[19] This volunteer tradition grew out of the model established by Langham Place during the early days of the women's press movement.

In the midst of urban life, the women's newspaper emerged as a semipublic space for the woman reader. Reporters guided readers in discussions of current events, effectively creating a safe arena for correspondents during a period when women's public presence as workers, shoppers, philanthropists, and entertainers was still being contested. The inherent anonymity of print enabled the author to control the level of publicity brought on by the act of publishing. Some women continued to employ pen names, while others found women's periodicals a free space where publishing their name brought prestige rather than ridicule. As one *Penny Paper* correspondent remarked:

> I quite àgree with your esteemed correspondent, Miss Sara S. Hennell, that
> it is better for women to sign their names openly to whatever they write, and

I should much prefer to do so myself as I have fully the courage of my opinions. I live, however, with an aged father who shrinks from publicity either
for himself or for me and I feel it my first duty not to inflict pain on him. As
my name is quite unknown to fame it can matter little to my readers whether
they know me as Miss Jones, Brown, or Robinson.[20]

"Minerva" who signed this letter continued to be a regular "anonymous"
correspondent in the coming years. The press enabled such women to maintain and regulate their own public personae. It also provided new opportunities for women to safely connect themselves to a larger community of
readers interested in domestic and international affairs. These personal and
print-based networks, created by the evolving world of women's journalism,
enabled women to reimagine their role in turn-of-the-century Britain not
only as readers, writers, and businesswomen but also as public citizens.

Alternative Public Spaces

Why did reformers use women's newspapers to produce an alternative public
space during the late nineteenth century? One answer lies in the inability of
the commercial periodical market to represent a broad range of topics and
opinions relevant to women. To achieve the mass circulations imagined by
proprietors like Northcliffe, papers had to streamline news coverage in order
to appeal to the highest possible number of readers. Mainstream newspapers
had little room to represent women's interests, as well as those of other particular communities. A thriving advocacy press developed during this period
to provide its own version of news to constituents that included socialist,
temperance, antivice, church reform, Irish nationalist, and ethnic presses,
such as the Yiddish and the black press.[21] Together, these class-, ethnic-, and
politically based interest groups sustained the development of the British
advocacy press industry. Thus, at the same moment that increasing commercialization threatened the diversity of the press, an advocacy movement
grew up in response to create alternative discursive spaces.

Advocacy papers and the organizations that supported them played a small
but important part in maintaining a vibrant, extraparliamentary political
life in Britain. As part of this expanding constellation of advocacy journals,
women's advocacy journalism provided an opportunity for dialogue between
mainstream opinions and minority voices by acting as a new medium for
public discourse. Mainstream editors interested in debates about women, as
well as general questions regarding social reform such as vice legislation and

temperance, took news published in the women's press seriously. Florence Fenwick-Miller, editor of the *Women's Signal*, said: "I know that the influence of the paper has been very widespread indeed. Many of my brother editors have made a practice of quoting from these columns with due acknowledgement each week."[22] Such "borrowings" were not only on women's subjects; "reports of speeches at public meetings, even those made by members of Parliament in some cases, have frequently shown that the substance was gleaned from the *Signal.*"[23] The increasing visibility of such information in other papers ensured at least some familiarity by general readers with causes that advocacy periodicals promoted.

The existence of multiple spaces for public discourse, each having its own recognized sphere of influence, has forced a reevaluation by critics of the Habermas's formulation of the bourgeois public sphere.[24] Historians have found evidence of numerous thriving public spheres that survived the rise of a mass commercial media during the late nineteenth and early twentieth centuries, further challenging Habermas's historical model of the public sphere as a late eighteenth-century phenomenon.[25] The emergence, or rather continuation, of what Nancy Fraser calls these "subaltern counterpublics" despite the rise of a mass commercial press medium provided an entry point for women in the already existing cultural dialogue over political, economic, and social issues.[26] As Philip Ethington has argued about the United States, the survival of the public sphere was particularly important in the case of women, as the late nineteenth century saw their first real entry into political culture.

By the turn of the century, the women's periodical press had developed into a viable "alternative public sphere." Supporters believed that only a news medium shielded from the competitive workings of the periodical market could provide serious news for the woman reader. Women's newspapers brought readers into the dialogue over social and political issues in a regular and periodic format that sometimes challenged and often reinforced existing cultural values. This characteristic, coupled with a commitment to provide readers with a regular diet of serious news, set women's newspapers apart from commercial periodicals addressed to women.

Not all papers that claimed to represent women's viewpoints were part of this growing alternative public. "The thinking portion of Englishwomen owe you a debt of gratitude," commented one reader, "for until the *Women's Penny Paper* was published the so-called women's journals were anything but flattering to their intelligence."[27] The women's newspapers in this study sought first to inform and educate readers and only second to make a profit. Like their predecessors, editors often spent their own money to make women's newspapers a success. Domestic ladies' magazines and other commercial publications for women discussed in earlier chapters continued outside of the model of advocacy journalism: the expanding market-driven commercial press run mainly by men for women did not have as its purpose the representation of the specialized agendas of women's interest groups. "Forward, but not too fast" was the motto of *Woman* (1890–1912), a ladies' paper that distanced itself from "advanced" periodicals such as the *Women's Penny Paper*. Started as a moderate political paper, *Woman* was turned into "fashionable ladies magazine" not long after its first issue in order to achieve a mass readership. Papers such as *Woman* echoed the experience of the *Queen* during the 1860s: women's politics did not sell. The market for *domestic* women's periodicals, however, continued to grow. This "feminization of the press," as Margaret Beetham has called it, spurred male editors to find new ways to capitalize on the increasing middle-class demand for news as entertainment.[28]

The mainstream press, like the women's commercial press, failed to develop as an adequate space for political discourse, despite numerous attempts by women writers and activists to promote their own agendas in its pages. Many lamented the lack of "women's news" found in the national press. Some, however, still questioned the efficacy of specialized newspapers: "Far to be preferred over special papers for women is the healthy admixture of news concerning their interests and doings in the columns of the general press," one writer for the *Englishwoman's Review* claimed.[29] Florence Fenwick-Miller did both. In addition to editing the *Women's Signal* starting in 1895, she also published extensively in the mainstream press: "Many of the London daily newspapers . . . inserted articles on women's interests from my pen, and I have contributed also to a very large number of leading provincial journals and always had the 'Cause of Women' in view."[30] Fenwick-Miller, however, remained an exception. For many reformers, women's newspapers provided the best vehicle for the promotion of their aims and agendas. The following story of Henrietta Muller's *Women's Penny Paper* illustrates how editors created a distinct space for women's news in late Victorian Britain.

Community Building: The *Women's Penny Paper*

Henrietta Muller founded the *Women's Penny Paper* in October 1888 to help women, as she put it, learn to use their own "voice" (fig. 7). "Conducted, Written, Printed, and Published by Women," the paper invited readers into

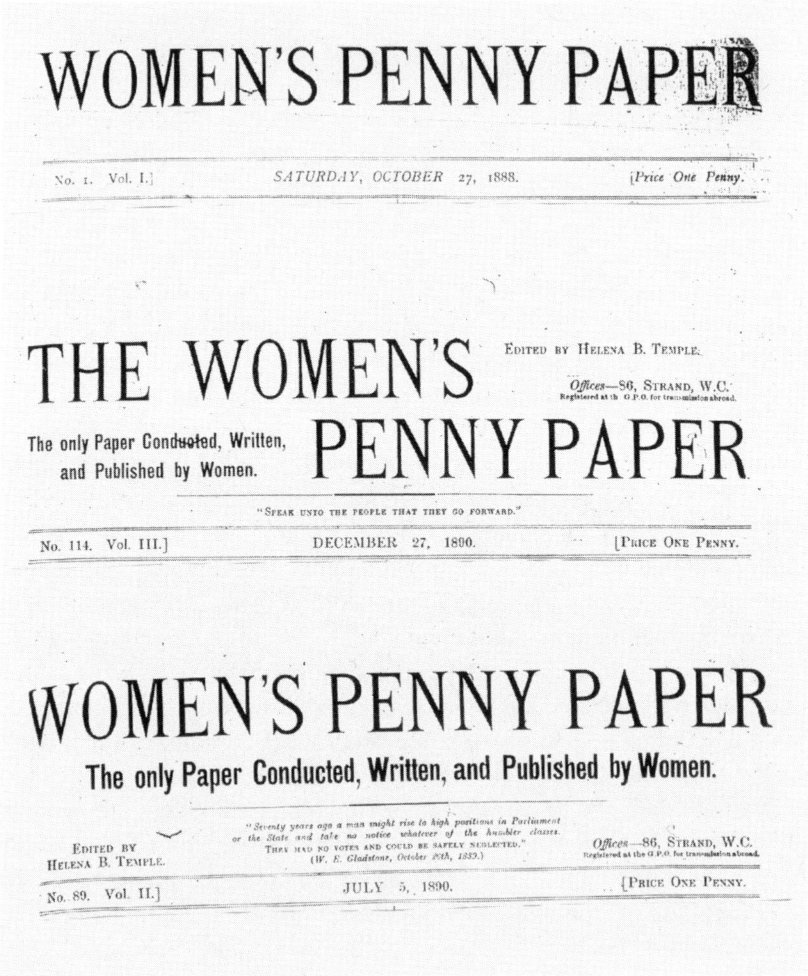

WOMEN'S PENNY PAPER

No. 1. Vol. I.] SATURDAY, OCTOBER 27, 1888. [Price One Penny.

THE WOMEN'S PENNY PAPER

Edited by Helena B. Temple.

Offices—86, Strand, W.C.
Registered at the G.P.O. for transmission abroad.

The only Paper Conducted, Written, and Published by Women.

"Speak unto the people that they go forward."

No. 114. Vol. III.] DECEMBER 27, 1890. [Price One Penny.

WOMEN'S PENNY PAPER

The only Paper Conducted, Written, and Published by Women.

Edited by Helena B. Temple.

"*Seventy years ago a man might rise to high positions in Parliament or the State and take no notice whatever of the humbler classes.* They had no votes and could be safely neglected."
(*W. E. Gladstone, October 28th, 1883.*)

Offices—86, Strand, W.C.
Registered at the G.P.O. for transmission abroad.

No. 89. Vol. II.] JULY 5, 1890. [Price One Penny.

Figure 7. Three mastheads from the *Women's Penny Paper.*

an imagined sisterhood built on a vision of female activism. Its bold headlines and lively news features provided a model for other publications eager to expand beyond the limited world of the newssheet. Muller claimed to "inaugurat[e] a new feature in journalism—and one for which a great need exists." "Although we claim for women a full share of power with all its duties, responsibilities and privileges in public and private life, and although we do so with a full sense of the gravity of our claim, we will not forget the lighter and brighter side of things, the beauty, the brightness and the fun which make the chequered lights on our way."[31] Women's papers of the past, although they "have done good" limited themselves, remaining "conservative in spirit . . . run[ning] in a mechanical way along old lines."[32] Innovation, in terms of journalistic style, form, and content rather than tradition, guided Muller's drive to capture the loyalty of the activist woman reader.

This new departure in women's journalism maintained a "progressive policy" of political objectivity. Like mainstream newspapers after the repeal of the press taxes, the *Penny Paper* looked to advertising and subscription revenues rather than subsidies from political organizations for support. Women's newspapers by the 1890s embraced the marketplace rather than special interest organizations to maintain their independence by appealing to a wide constituency of readers. As "editress," Muller aimed at providing readers of all classes, opinions, and political affiliations with cheap access to news:

> We shall endeavor to supply our readers with general English and Foreign News in such a way as to place before them the leading questions of the day in plain and concise language, so that those busy women who have not leisure to read the daily papers may so far acquaint themselves with important events of the day, as to be able to form and express their opinion upon them. Our pages will be open to all shades of opinion, to the working woman as freely as to the educated lady; to the conservative and the radical, to the Englishwoman and foreigner.[33]

Muller assumed women would both make up the majority of her reading audience and provide her with weekly subject matter: "We look to reproducing the ideas of the day in their freshest and newest form, to creating a newspaper which shall reflect the thoughts of the best women upon all the subjects that occupy their minds; we shall tell of the work of the noblest women, and represent the loves of the truest and sweetest."[34] The *Women's Penny Paper* thus set the boundaries of a particularized gender-identified community both created and reinforced through the medium of the periodical press.

A fiery and ambitious spirit, Muller led a highly visible public life. The daughter of a German *émigré* businessman, she was born in Valparaiso, Chile, in the early 1850s and later attended Girton College, where she read classics. Muller moved to London, where she remained active in political and intellectual circles throughout the late 1870s and 1880s. She helped Emma Paterson found the Women's Printing Society while still at Cambridge and involved herself with women's trade union agitation. Muller sat on the London School Board for Lambeth, founded the Society for the Return of Women as Poor Law Guardians, maintained membership in the Personal Rights Association and the National Vigilance Association, and supported the temperance cause. She also joined Karl Pearson's Men's and Women's Club and wrote regularly for the *Westminster Review*. Having a sizable personal income, Muller easily supported her political activities. In 1895 she left London to tour alone in Europe and Asia. In China, she studied "the religion of the people and position of their women." Having earlier become a theosophist, she eventually joined her friend Annie Besant in India and lived abroad until her death in 1906.[35]

The inspiration behind the *Women's Penny Paper* stemmed from Muller's political and intellectual activities in London. There she came into contact with many later contributors to her penny paper, including Elizabeth Wollstoneholme Elmy, Lady Henry Somerset, Francis Power Cobbe, and Florence Fenwick-Miller. Her membership in Pearson's Club, in particular, convinced her of the need for women to have a political space for their own ideas. Pearson started the club in 1885 as a forum for middle-class liberals, socialists, and feminists, as Judith Walkowitz put it, "to talk about sex." A "humorless" and "cold" man, Pearson assembled a group of notable women that included Olive Schreiner, Elizabeth Cobb, and Loetitia and Maria Sharpe to discuss topics relating to sexuality and race, childbearing, chastity, and prostitution.[36] Muller, dubbed a "man-hater" by Cobb and challenged intellectually and politically by Pearson, was one of the club's more radical members, advocating increased social power for women based on the "moral strength" that came from their ability to control their sexual appetites.[37] Differences between Muller's and Pearson's philosophy regarding human sexuality ultimately contributed to her decision to resign from the club in 1888.[38]

Muller's dissatisfaction, however, ran much deeper than her intellectual conflicts with its founder. She claimed that male members repeatedly "silenced" their female counterparts. "At the last meeting," Muller explained in her resignation, "it was the same old story of the man laying down the law to the woman and not seeming to recognise that she has a voice and the woman resenting in silence, and submitting in silence."[39] Anticipating Pearson's response to her decision to start her own club, she wrote: "You will say 'this is prejudice'; I will not deny it. I will merely say that in my club every woman shall find a voice and shall learn how to use it."[40] Six months later, Muller started the *Women's Penny Paper*. "Discussion" would take place in the medium of the press, with a widened constituency of participants, rather than in the more elite world of the intellectual club.

Due to the growth of women's business and intellectual networks since the founding of the *English Woman's Journal* thirty years earlier, women like Muller could imagine the possibility of women controlling all aspects of the production of a paper that represented the interests of growing constituency of educated women. Her connections with the Women's Printing Society enabled her to conceive of a paper entirely "written, edited, printed and published" by women.[41] She also ensured that women contributed most of the articles and correspondence, so as to fulfill her mandate to help women to "find" and "use" their voices. Muller had experienced the limitations of mixed-sex debates firsthand. The *Penny Paper* provided readers with a forum not simply to engage other women on the difficulties faced by their sex but to engage in Victorian public life.

Muller's was not a sex-exclusive project, however, but rather one that served first as a medium to cultivate women's engagement in public life. Like other advocacy papers, she welcomed male supporters. The correspondence section did include a small number letters from male readers. "A Man who Believes in Women" expressed concern over "male chairmen at women's meetings," claiming that placing men in such positions actually impeded the progress of such organizations.[42] Showcasing male writers opened the paper up to criticism by those in the press who questioned the legitimacy of the woman journalist. When the *St. James Gazette* pointed out that a man had written one interview for the paper, implying that a lack of qualified women writers necessitated it, Muller angrily responded: "some people would rather *not* believe that a paper can be conducted and written by women only. *The Women's Penny Paper* proves this fact, and proves it up to the hilt."[43] Such criticism ensured relegating men to essentially an auxiliary role.

The *Women's Penny Paper* provided a voice *for women* by encouraging them to utilize their press as a relatively anonymous space where they could read the news and learn about goods and services. Though correspondents could use pen names, Muller had a policy "that no communications will be inserted unless the name and address of the writer accompany every contribution" in order to privately track the identity of contributors. Muller herself used a pen name, "Henrietta B. Temple," although her status as editor was widely known.[44] Promoting this kind of "anonymous" associational life freed the woman journalist to engage in political writing that might have otherwise opened her up to censure by friends, families, and colleagues.

Muller used advertising both to raise revenue and support a larger, woman-centered reform agenda by targeting suppliers of products of interest to women. Attractive, illustrated ads mixed large and small copy to capture the reader's attention and held a more prominent place in the paper than they had in newssheets such as the *Women's Suffrage Journal.* "Ladies are shoppers, Advertise in the *Women's Penny Paper* WHICH THEY READ" appeared prominently in the advertising section.[45] By 1890, the paper dedicated three full pages of its twelve pages to advertisements. Rather than highlighting fashion, advertisements emphasized the utility of their products. "Invigorator Corsets," keenly aware of the paper's advocacy of "dress reform," advertised their corsets in the *Women's Penny Paper* as "Health Insured," offering numerous testimonials by doctors of their benefit to women's well-being.[46] Other advertisements included those for training colleges, bank accounts, books, political journals, "ventilated" refrigerators, and disinfectants.

The introduction of innovative journalistic practices further supported women's entry into public life. As Rosemary Van Arsdel has argued, women's papers played a central role in popularizing this new feature of the New Journalism.[47] The *Penny Paper* was the first to dedicate a column to interviewing famous women, including Lydia Becker, Emily Faithfull, Olive Schreiner, Barbara Bodichon, and Priscilla Bright McLaren, as well as lesser known painters, authors, and lecturers. Other papers imitated the *Penny Paper*: "It is astonishing how many newspapers and magazines have discovered that there are some notable women in the world whose lives are worth recording and whose deeds it is well to make known to others," remarked Muller. "The discovery does not date back very long and we are glad that one of our aims is thus being accomplished. The *Queen* and the *Echo* have largely introduced 'Interviews' during the last year."[48] Such publicity for the gentler sex, still looked on with suspicion by many Britons, served a larger purpose. For Muller, the "Interview" column represented

> one of the strongest weapons which the women's party possesses. Hitherto our opponents have been able to charge women with incapacity generally and specifically, they have been free to deny them powers or faculties which women undoubtedly possess, and at the same time they have been able to suppress those facts in the lives of living women which proved that they possessed them. Now the barrier of silence in being broken, every account published of a woman who has talent, or pluck, or industry, gives the lie in the most effectual way to those who deny her powers only because they fear them.[49]

This new feature had a clear purpose: to promote women's status as legitimate public figures by publicizing their achievements.

Other features helped build a print-mediated community based on commonalities of gender. The "Book Review" column solicited books "about women or books by women" including those on suffrage, employment, and education and novels with female protagonists. The classified advertisement section, "Our Bon Marche," allowed women to advertise goods and barter services, as one reader pointed out, for fees well below those rates charged in papers "published by men."[50] The paper also encouraged an entrepreneurial spirit. The paper's "patent editor" supplied a "weekly list of patents applied for by women" in the "To Women Inventors" column. An advice column, "To Women out of Work," offered suggestions to women seeking employment that ranged from advertising women's specialized skills to prospective employers to suggesting "uncrowded" professions for women to helping with trade union agitation.[51]

Such features, in addition to editorials and serialized stories, contributed to a sense of overarching female solidarity. "Your excellent paper," one reader wrote, "is a cause of so much thankfulness for what it has already done—drawing women together."[52] The periodic characteristic of the newspaper, combined with its identification as being "for and by women," served as an important link between women readers, writers, and consumers. In particular, the types of information published in women's papers helped bind women together in an imagined, gender-based community of readers.[53] According to Benedict Anderson, the emergence of print capitalism at the end of the eighteenth century played a central role in determining formation of national identities based on a common language and culture. This "fraternity" of the nation that he describes can apply as well to communities within already existing nations that identify themselves according to their mutual self-interest. By the turn of the century, the women's press produced a community that was defined not by the geographical boundaries of nation but by the culturally defined category of gender. As Kate Flint has argued, reading provided women with the possibility of a creating a community based on shared gendered experiences made possible through their interaction with texts. "Such a community," according to Flint, "may stretch far beyond the reader's immediate social world to incorporate other readers whom she may never meet in person."[54] Women's newspapers, I argue, not only connected women in this imagined community but also helped mobilize women reformers to act on their own political and cultural beliefs. The turn of the century saw the beginnings of the development of such an activist sensibility, which achieved its greatest notoriety during the opening decades of the twentieth century with the advent of the suffrage press.[55]

The *Penny Paper* encouraged reader participation in social reform by billing itself as a "thinking woman's paper."[56] Muller wrote: "The sensationalism which consists in reporting and describing terrible crimes is absolutely incompatible with our interpretation of excellence."[57] Editorials encouraged the "support of fellow sisters" in numerous causes, including antivivisection, the establishment of women's trade unions, colonial issues, the Poor Law, dress reform, and, of course, the perennial question of nontraditional employment for women. Unlike mainstream papers, the *Penny Paper* encouraged readers to act on new knowledge. The "Bible Readings" column, for example, encouraged women to "develop their faculties more fully" in order to fulfill their social and moral responsibility to society.[58] Articles on the subject of "infant marriages" in India implored readers to raise their voices "to hurry on reform in the matter." "In India," claimed Muller, "women have made a beginning and done good work, but there is much yet to do."[59] One reader, having read in the *Penny Paper* that women in the United States had started a protest over "the shocking treatment of Russian prisoners," proposed organizing support for their "suffering sisters" in Russia who were forced to live with the "inhuman horrors" of this government policy.[60] As these cases illustrated, advocacy journalism distinguished itself from its mainstream counterpart through cultivating a belief in women's power and responsibility to serve as active members of British society and to play a part in shaping contemporary events.

In creating a sense of community among readers, the paper emphasized British women's leadership in creating what it called a "Universal Sisterhood." "Our Creed" addressed the imperial duty of the woman reformer: "she who does not practise altruism, she who is not willing to share her last morsel with another, woman, she who neglects to help her Sister Woman, of whatever race, nation, or creed, and who is deaf to the cry of woman's misery; she who hears another woman slandered and does not undertake her defense as she would undertake her own defense is No True Woman."[61] By purchasing the paper, "true" women joined this international sisterhood that created a leadership role for middle-class British woman in imperial and domestic matters to "defend" their fellow "sisters." Potential "members," however, included the working class, imperial subjects and ladies alike, creating an imagined sense of inclusively that transcended class and racial boundaries. A letter signed "One of the Sufferers" encouraged readers to speak out against the low wages of "shop girls." Another reader proposed giving these women free copies of the paper in order to help the "intelligent overworked class of women to acquire knowledge necessary for their guidance in matters pertaining to woman's good."[62] Readers themselves referred to the paper as "Our Paper" in their letters, further contributing to an "insider" quality to the belief among the paper's primarily middle-class readership that it served a broad gendered community of readers.[63]

Membership in this imagined "sisterhood" required reader support with circulation. Although exact figures do not exist, evidence suggests that the paper circulated widely, achieving mention in the *Daily News,* the *Pall Mall Gazette,* the *Leeds Mercury,* the *Evening Standard,* the *Liverpool Mercury,* the *Globe,* the *Nottingham Daily Guardian,* and the *Bedfordshire Times.* Available at newsagents including Smith Bookstalls and by subscription, the paper had readers throughout the British Isles and in the United States, thanks to the efforts of readers who solicited subscriptions and manned advertising booths at places like the 1890 Edinburgh Exhibition. American women's periodicals recommended the paper to subscribers, whose letters regularly appeared in the paper.

These same readers suggested schemes for increasing the influence of the paper. One believed that order forms and limited neighborhood distribution impeded circulation among a wider class of reader: "A young lady, employed at one of the Aerated Bread Company's depots, told me she should be glad to take a copy every week but could not obtain one at any shop she passed."[64] After lending the paper to a woman who later became a subscriber, another reader proposed "that all who are now taking the *Women's Penny Paper* should do their best to introduce at least one other subscriber during this month of June." Muller responded to such suggestions by offering prize competitions for readers who brought in new subscribers. She also asked them to inform her of places "where the paper is not procurable," reminding them that in the case of advocacy journalism, "demand creates the supply."[65] Through these actions, readers assisted in the advancement of "their" paper in very direct ways.

Readers took their membership in this sisterhood seriously. Supporters assisted with distribution by ordering multiple copies of current issues and archiving old ones. Organizations such as the Young Women's Guilds kept the entire run of the paper in their reading rooms for middle-class working members to examine.[66] Other institutions provided working-class girls in regions where "the libraries are few and poor" with the *Penny Paper* in their reading rooms.[67] Subscribers also sent their own copies to friends, who then passed them along to acquaintances.[68] These "recycled" papers, however, were only on temporary loan, as the original owner expected the last reader to send the paper back to her to archive for later reference.[69] Ascribing value to periodicals as texts worthy of preservation, individual readers helped facilitate the circulation of women's papers by promoting the general influence of the paper, both among other women readers and the wider public.

Encouraging reader engagement in both the political projects and mundane affairs of the *Penny Paper* enabled Muller to build a small but dedicated community of activist readers and participants. This decision to involve readers in the journal in such direct ways paved the way for new opportunities, not only for women readers but for women writers as well. As the following section illustrates, the visibility of the *Penny Paper* also helped the professional woman writer find her voice.

GENDERING NEWS JOURNALISM

In 1890, women's demand for news not only about but also for them manifested itself in symbolic battle over the rights and abilities of the woman journalist. The *Women's Penny Paper* sparked a flurry of controversy when its editor applied "for accommodation in the press gallery of the House of Commons." Muller argued that the paper needed a female representative in the press gallery in order to better report political news relevant to women.[70] Responses from MPs, pressmen, clergymen, and prominent women were decidedly mixed, proving Muller's contention that "public opinion is intensely sensitive on the subjects of Woman and the Press."[71]

The *Penny Paper*'s application to the press gallery sparked a heated public debate regarding the fitness of women as news journalists. Over twenty-five different periodicals, including the *Times,* reported on the controversy. Many believed women had no business in the press gallery. "No room," some pressmen claimed, since more established newspapers also lacked gallery passes. Women should instead stick to what they knew, reporting only on social affairs and writing feature columns. "Lady reporters are enterprising women, but 'the Gallery' is hardly the sphere in which they would shine professionally," one source claimed.[72] Not only would women serve as a distraction in the gallery, argued opponents, but also they would ask to be "waited on," leading to an unprofessional working environment. Others asserted that women would "ruin" the profession with cheap labor. "I have no objection to women reporters as women," remarked a male reporter, "but directly if they were admitted into the gallery they would begin to undersell us. That is what happens in every trade that women touch."[73]

Supporters maintained, however, that women journalists should have some access to seats, especially when the Commons debated domestic reform issues. The *Pall Mall Gazette* asserted that determining eligibility for a seat in the gallery based solely on "the sex of the applicant" was "absurd."[74] "In no daily paper are questions of special interest and importance to women reported as fully as they certainly would be in a woman's paper," claimed Muller.

> Only women know to their better cost, how little they can learn from the reports in the Dailies of debates on their particular questions. . . . The most important of all debates for women are those on Woman's Suffrage. The longest reports of these in the *Times* or any other *Daily* are bald and uninstructive, and after reading them all that we feel is that we have learnt very little about "Our Debate." . . . Under these circumstances it is not strange that women begin to feel like reporting themselves.[75]

One *Penny Paper* reader suggested that women should don gender-neutral dress and "sneak" into the press gallery, thus proving the ease with which women could circumvent such exclusion. Although Muller seems not to have taken this advice, she responded: "We cannot tamely submit to a capricious exclusion of women reporters from the gallery of the House of Commons in these days of women journalists."[76]

After the press gallery controversy faded, the *Penny Paper* continued to advocate for the woman journalist. Discussion gradually disappeared from the press after April 1890, when Muller conceded that she could not change tradition. Despite losing the battle, the attention given to the press gallery controversy illustrates how women's newspapers encouraged journalists to expand their expertise beyond fashion and social reporting in this newly emerging profession for the woman writer. Much like her counterparts in the mainstream press, Muller employed a staff of writers, including a "corresponding editor," a "managing editor," and regular news columnists. Notable women contributors included Florence Fenwick-Miller, Lydia Becker, and Francis Power Cobbe.

This period also witnessed the beginning of attempts to organize women in the journalism profession, as was evidenced by the founding in 1895 of both the Institute of Women Journalists and the Women's Press Association. The latter was made up of "a small syndicate of trained journalist women" who would "supply literary contributions to newspapers, dealing with all subjects which may be supposed to interest women."[77] Writing in the *Penny Paper,* Cobbe described the difficulties facing women journalists and offered the following advice: women should "practice" and develop their own style and never sacrifice their principles and professionalism to an editor.[78]

As Cobbe recognized, the mainstream press, although no longer a hostile place for women journalists willing to cover nonpolitical topics, still remained a strongly sex-segregated institution. The actual number of women classified as professional journalists increased during this period. According to census figures, in 1841 only fifteen women held positions as authors, editors or journalists. By 1881 that number had risen to 660. Such growth, although significant, was still relatively small, considering that Britain saw the publication of over two thousand newspapers during this period.[79] Most women failed to earn a living by their pen. As journalist Catherine Drew remarked in a paper presented at an international press conference in 1894, "for the woman journalist the fact ought to be placed on record that English manufacturers and proprietors of journals are building up large fortunes by her labours, yet she has no share of the profits. Cooperation is confined to the labor itself, not to its results."[80] Drew informed her largely male audience of the challenges faced by women wanting to specialize as news journalists: "The great majority of women journalists are what in the medical profession would be known as 'general practitioners.' Her [the woman journalist's] knowledge, theoretical and practical, must range up and down in a gamut of subjects not included in any curriculum."[81]

Political reporting, with few exceptions, such as Francis Cobbe, remained the domain of men. Women journalists, although employed as essayists and feature writers, understood that mainstream publications had little interest in employing female reporters. The advent of the Women's Pages during this era of New Journalism did provide some women with work in the mainstream press. "The woman journalist . . . has been, in great measure, created by writing on subjects she understands in journals for her own sex," remarked Evelyn March-Phillips.[82] "One is horribly handicapped in being a woman," claimed another woman journalist:

> A man meets other men at his club; he can be out and about at all hours; he can insist without being thought bold and forward; he is not presumed to be capable of undertaking only a limited class of subjects, but is set to see anything. Mr. TP O'Connor, in one of his clever articles, tells a would-be journalist that the first essential element is to get taken on in an office in any capacity. "Go as an office-boy, if need be," he says—I quote from memory—"but get into an office anyhow." The immense difficulty a woman finds in getting into an office in any recognized capacity makes a journalistic beginning far harder for her than for a man.[83]

Such informal rules of the profession thus further prevented women's entry into the trade.

Women's publications thus provided a welcome space for those on the margins of Fleet Street. Reporting news for a female audience also opened up new employment possibilities unavailable in the mainstream press. Supported by a dedicated community of readers, women journalists found new ways to challenge their limited status as "general practitioners" in the profession. Campaigns such as the press gallery controversy led by the *Penny Paper* played no small part in publicizing the cause of the professional woman journalist and her ability to report on serious news subjects for an educated audience.

A Call to Arms: Political Activism and Women's Advocacy Newspapers

When readers picked up a copy of the *Penny Paper,* they participated in Muller's vision of promoting political activism through emphasizing women's moral and domestic duty to the nation. In 1892, Muller changed the name of the paper, "in deference to the wishes of many friends and subscribers," to the *Woman's Herald* to emphasize her "aim to herald in the New Womanhood." "Our new name," she claimed, "is thought to be more consistent with the high place which the *Women's Penny Paper* has taken." Continuing its upbeat reporting of women's social, political, and economic progress while noting general news items every week, the *Herald* maintained its predecessor's strong advocacy character: "Our policy will be in the future, as it has been in the past, to reflect truthfully and accurately every phase of woman's work and thought . . . and to promote her development in any and every direction which she herself believes to be right." According to these principles, through private introspection women would find a public role.

Muller intended what she dubbed the "New Womanhood" as a call to action and declared the paper's motto: "Speak unto the People that they go Forward." In April 1892, however, ill health forced her to retire from journalism. She sold her entire interest to the newly formed "Woman's Herald Co." Shareholder Lady Henry Somerset, *nee* Lady Isabel Somers-Cocks (1851–1912) proved a suitable choice as Muller's successor. A published novelist and essayist with a crusading sensibility, she held membership in the Women's Suffrage Society, served as president of the British Women's Temperance Association for more than twenty years, and acted as vice-president of the World Women's

Christian Temperance Union. The eldest daughter of the third Earl Somers-Cocks, she married the Lord Henry Somerset in 1872. Lord Henry's implication in the notorious Cleveland Street male prostitution scandal forced him to retire from public life. This gave his ambitious and headstrong wife the freedom to indulge her own interests on the family's sizable income without his interference.[84] Women's education advocate Christina S. Bremer, assisted Somerset. The new proprietors praised Muller for making the *Herald* one of Britain's "well established organs of public opinion" and looked for new ways to better serve what they called the "compatible interests" of women and the nation (fig. 8).[85]

The new editors envisioned a formal political role for women and affiliated the paper with the Liberal Party: "As it is the aim of the Liberal women to educate their sisters in politics, they need an organ such as the *Herald* to embody their views." Two other women's papers, the *Women's Gazette and Weekly News* (1888–91) and the *Women's National Liberal Association Quarterly Review and Report* (1895–1918), also had links to the Liberal Party and provided a voice for women working on "liberal causes." Unlike its competitors, however, the *Herald* emphasized "women' interests" over the Liberal line, refusing to turn the paper into merely a partisan "newssheet." "This widening of interests is distinctly an addition to, and not an alteration of [the paper's] former object. It will still remain the fearless and uncompromising advocate of women's question that it has ever been, nor will it hesitate to blame the Liberal Party if that Party should be untrue to its Liberalism in matter affecting women."[86] The *Herald*, in departing from the nonpartisan tradition of the women's press, encouraged readers' engagement in parliamentary political culture by promoting women's causes through the support of Liberal Party politics.

For the disenfranchised, however, Liberal Party affiliation proved too narrow a platform. Support of a broader social reform agenda had more attraction for female activists than party politics. The lack of the franchise, in many ways, shaped the informal character of women's political participation in the coming decades. After the failure of the *Women's Suffrage Journal* in 1890, the suffrage movement faced a period of rebuilding. Many activists began to embrace reforms associated with, but not directly tied to, the Liberal Party. The women's press movement helped facilitate this shift by lending publicity to campaigns for social reform during this period. Women's advocacy for a variety of Liberal-inspired reform issues thus continued to take place on the periphery, in semipublic venues such as the press. This extraparliamentary

Figure 8. Two mastheads from the *Woman's Herald*.

approach to politics provided women with a new kind of public voice in an arena that was closed to them by virtue of their sex.

Somerset's decision to discontinue affiliation with the Liberal Party also had to do with the leadership's unresponsiveness to issues such as suffrage.[87] In pursuit of her advocacy program, Somerset called for female unity to combat parliamentary apathy: "The women's cause is one whether it be Franchise, Temperance, Peace, Education, Sanitation, or whatever else it may be, the time has gone by for dealing with it piecemeal. The *Woman's Herald* will endeavour to familiarise its readers with the wider outlook, and treat every question from a standpoint common to all those who are labouring for one cause."[88] Somerset appealed to "all the most distinguished women" for assistance in creating a role for women in public life through a professionally produced and widely circulating political paper. She also hired a "subeditor," Edwin Stout, the current assistant editor of the *Review of Reviews* who had served on the *Pall Mall Gazette*.[89] Although he remained with the paper for less than a year, Somerset used his experience to help adopt New Journalism techniques, including artistically rendered mastheads depicting images of saintly political women, a new triple-column format, and increased space for advertising. Stout, a professional already established in the field, gave the paper a more credible image as a newspaper. After his departure, Somerset remarked: "all the qualities he pressed into [the paper's] service, and by which he won for it a place among the best journals of the day—these are still with us for our help and direction, given generously now as aforetime."[90] Men such as Stout thus helped lend a professionalism that moved the *Herald* away from the fringe and closer to the mainstream journalistic establishment. Through these strategies, Somerset hoped to bring together those "labouring for one cause" in an informal woman-centered reform community.

The paper depicted the ideal female activist as a worker whose moral superiority justified her inclusion in the polity. In January 1894, Somerset changed the name of the paper to the *Woman's Signal* to support her seemingly preordained mandate:

> The *Woman's Signal* will go into battle. Its mission will be to rally the multitude of earnest women who feel that they are responsible for the use of all the energy and influence which highest Power has given them, and who believe also that they will have to account, not only for any whom they may have caused to perish, but for those also whom they might have saved. Thus we shall seek to define and defend the place of woman in political life, to direct and enforce her influence among the great army of workers.[91]

Unlike papers such as the *Women's Protestant Union* (1893–1954), which crusaded for social reform through "defending Christian Protestantism," despite the use of such highly charged religious rhetoric, the *Signal* did not affiliate with any organized religion. Somerset asserted: "We shall preach, not parties, but principles; not expediency, but purity of motive and purity of practice."[92] Instead, she looked to the temperance movement for inspiration, aligning the paper with the British Women's Temperance Association. Editorials in both the *Signal* and the *Signal*'s supplement, the *Woman's Signal Budget* (1894–95), lambasted the English people as a "nation of drunkards" appeared alongside general news features in the coming years (fig. 9).[93]

The decision to focus on a particular cause rather than a broader social reform agenda converted the *Signal* into a paper intended for a highly specialized community of readers. The paper grew to a large penny paper that printed between twenty and thirty triple-column, nine-by-twelve-and-a-half-inch pages each week. Somerset and her new assistant editor, Annie Holdsworth,[94] pursued the vision of the *Signal* as a beacon of morality without regard for the bottom line, however, and the paper continued to lose money.[95] Certainly, newssheets like those of the 1870s and 1880s continued to deal with specialized issues such as vice, education, religion, and employment. Such papers survived on small, specialized audiences. In the case of the *Signal,* connecting the cause of women's social, political, and economic advancement with that of temperance proved a poor strategy for a paper that claimed to "seek to define and defend the place of woman in political life."

This type of single-issue reporting did not fit in well with the circulation-conscious era of New Journalism. After a year and a half of disastrously falling circulation rates, it looked like the *Signal* would fail. Tired of subsidizing the paper and writing most of its copy, Somerset made Florence Fenwick-Miller editor in 1895.[96] Fenwick-Miller toned down Somerset's crusading rhetoric, instead asking readers to follow her example as a public woman who, as Rosemary Van Arsdel has claimed, "worked for what she thought was right."[97] The strategy paid off, and the *Signal* grew in influence as a popular forum of public opinion. Registered as a newspaper, the *Signal* billed itself as a "progressive paper for women." Although actual circulation statistics remain difficult to verify, according to Fenwick-Miller, "in one year, more than 300,000 signals go broadcast, every one of the fifty-two numbers containing material to serve for the education of fresh minds on the Woman's cause."[98] By comparison, W. T. Stead estimated the per-issue turn-of-the-century circulation of the *Times* at thirty-five thousand and the *Westminster Gazette* at twenty thousand.[99] These figures offer a useful comparison to claims that the *Signal* had an average circulation of fifty-seven hundred copies per week. Women also continued to lend papers to one another and shared subscriptions. "I have lent it to my friends and recommend it far and near," one loyal reader claimed.[100]

Fenwick-Miller's editorship emphasized women's responsibilities to the nation through general interest stories that connected readers to "culture,

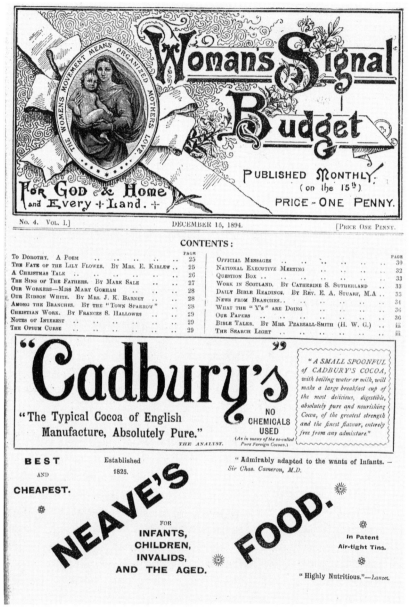

No. 4. Vol. I.]   DECEMBER 15, 1894.   [PRICE ONE PENNY.

CONTENTS:

"Cadbury's"

"The Typical Cocoa of English Manufacture, Absolutely Pure."
THE ANALYST.

NO CHEMICALS USED

(As in many of the so-called Pure Foreign Cocoas.)

"*A SMALL SPOONFUL of CADBURY'S COCOA, with boiling water or milk, will make a large breakfast cup of the most delicious, digestible, absolutely pure and nourishing Cocoa, of the greatest strength and the finest flavour, entirely free from any admixture.*"

BEST AND CHEAPEST.

Established 1825.

"Admirably adapted to the wants of Infants. — *Sir Chas. Cameron, M.D.*

NEAVE'S FOOD.

FOR INFANTS, CHILDREN, INVALIDS, AND THE AGED.

In Patent Air-tight Tins.

"Highly Nutritious."—*Lancet.*

Figure 9. *Woman's Herald* supplement: *Woman's Signal Budget,* front page.

thought, and concern for public welfare."[101] Attempting to strike a balance between information and entertainment, she supported cooking contests, published dress supplements, and offered prizes for the best readers' short stories. According to Rosemary Van Arsdel, "her goal was to make the content (of the *Signal*) different from the ordinary 'ladies paper' then in existence—more catholic and cosmopolitan—and to reflect the interest that modern women should feel in public welfare and progress."[102] The column "Signals from the Watchtower" had reports ranging from suffrage news to organizational meetings to general news on public affairs. Fenwick-Miller replaced Somerset's motto, "For God, Home and Every Land," with "A Weekly Record and Review of Woman's Work and Interests at Home and in the Wider World." The new editor intended the *Signal* to be a broad-based women's paper that she hoped "to interest and be of use to *all* women." This brand of outward-looking political journalism that imagined an expanded role for women based on their special status as moral guardians of the nation and Empire emerged as the model for the women's press of the coming century.

SHAFTS: A "RESPECTABLE" AND RADICAL MEDIUM FOR WOMEN

The move to promote an action-based politics for a broad group of women readers within the context of a general interest newspaper most clearly manifested itself in the publication of *Shafts*. Started by Margaret Shurmer Sibthorp (1851–c.1915) in November 1892 as a women's literary newspaper, *Shafts* declared as its motto "Light comes to those who dare to think" (fig. 10). A literary-minded woman with a radical political sensibility, she was born in Scotland in 1851 and married Stephen Sibthorp at age twenty-two. Before moving to London, the Sibthorps, with their two children, resided in Liverpool and later Wolverhampton, where Margaret found employment as a "writer and secretary."[103] She started *Shafts* as an "advanced" paper in London in order to provide women with "an opportunity of expressing publicly their thoughts." The masthead declared it "A Paper for Women and the Working Classes," making it the first women's advocacy periodical to explicitly address readers outside of the middle class.[104] Through the publication of *Shafts,* Sibthorp further radicalized a woman-centered social reform agenda during the turn of the century. *Shafts'* professional-style news sections, editorials, and literary articles provided an intellectual space for the

Figure 10. *Shafts,* cover page.

"new political woman" who found herself involved with reform issues that had traditionally rested outside of her purview.

Before starting *Shafts,* Sibthorp learned the newspaper business through holding a position at the *Woman's Herald.* According to her friend and later *Shafts* contributor Elizabeth Wolstenholme Elmy, Sibthorp left after disagreeing with Somerset's decision to affiliate the paper with the Liberal Party.[105] Believing that a nonparty paper would better serve women's interests, she started *Shafts* with the intention of making it the first advocacy "woman's daily paper" in Britain.[106] With the financial backing of an anonymous woman friend, Sibthorp published *Shafts* instead as a weekly newspaper until October 1899.[107] The paper, printed by the Women's Printing Society, quickly became known as a reliable news medium "for and by women."

Shafts prominently featured domestic reform topics, including prostitution, antivivisection, urban sanitary reform, prison treatment, "dangerous trades," and social purity and, like the *Herald* and *Signal,* emphasized women's moral duty to affect social change. In short, *Shafts* crusaded against social injustice, exposing "cruel[ties] practised toward Women, Children and the Poor":

> The aim of *Shafts* is to awaken thought; to induce people to ask why, to question—Is the condition of things which I see around me right and just? Is this that I have believed, spiritually, morally, socially, the truth? Am I justified in remaining content with this or that, because my grandparents and parents saw no harm in it, or is it my duty to look into my light, and if I find it but dim, to search humbly but determinedly for a truer and brighter light by which to study my daily tasks?[108]

Editorials and news articles solicited reader responses. Sibthorp also encouraged women to start new associations to combat problems including animal cruelty and unjust labor laws. As a forum for commentary on social issues, *Shafts* expected both contributors and readers to play an active role in supporting its projects.

Shafts also provided a space for dialogue on more general topics. Literary features included debates between readers and contributors over the portrayal of women in fiction. Reader letters including discussion of sex education and women's right to control family size. Sibthorp used the paper to impart knowledge about sex to girls and women alike, claiming that females had been kept in ignorance too long regarding matters that so dramatically affected their own lives. As a theosophist, Sibthorp also published reports on religion, including women's status under Islam. Sensational stories of male cruelty and women's unequal legal treatment, a by-now-familiar trope of women's papers, also appeared. These features took on a lively tone, thanks to sophisticated graphics, poetry, and numerous advertisements that lent a more conventional feel to a paper considered the most progressive women's paper on the market.

Evidence gleaned from articles and reader letters suggests that *Shafts* had a more socially radical audience than the *Signal.* Readers often expressed support of controversial topics such as female sexuality and religion. Correspondence was presented as a dialogue among correspondent, other readers, and the editor. Editorial comments also often appeared at the end of controversial letters requesting responses; for example: "I hope some of the readers of Shafts will reply to this letter; the subject is worthy of earnest thought."

Some topics covered in the correspondence section included: "Modern Fiction and the Cause of Woman," "The Married Women's Property Act," "A Woman's Health League," and "Compulsory Vaccinators to the Rescue."[109]

Sibthorp tried to reach less radical readers as well. The paper's more literary aspects drew in those seeking to discuss contemporary fiction and women's status, a unique feature of *Shafts*.[110] Sibthorp also encouraged links between *Shafts* and other more moderate papers such as the *Herald,* the *Signal,* and the *Englishwomen's Review.* The "Publications Received" column, for example, provided weekly summaries of topics in papers related to "women's interests."

To facilitate reader participation in her progressive program, Sibthorp created a model of action based on women's dual role as mothers and citizens. For politically moderate and radical-minded readers alike, the appeal of *Shafts* rested on its promotion of a woman-centered agenda. Articles, editorials, and Sibthorp's public speeches enforced her belief in "the immeasurable superiority of woman over man, and of her consequent right to rule."[111] In her writing she avoided using the masculine pronoun and argued that society would be better off if it was "mothered":

> Give your child every possible chance for health, strength[,] purity and capacity, by the care and attention you bestow but do not forget that there is other work for you, as well as home work, that this world of ours has been brought to an awful degradation, through the absence of women from the seats of Government; that until she take her place in every department of public life unhampered, the work of destruction will go on apace.[112]

Social change, therefore, would start at "home" and move to the public sphere through the work of women. The state's ability to protect the destitute thus remained contingent upon the experience of competent mothers.

Through such appeals, *Shafts* created a mode of political action that incorporated already existing notions of appropriate feminine behavior with new models of political action. The emphasis put on true womanhood and women's moral and political responsibility to the state in turn-of-the-century papers created a political voice for women that both drew upon and challenged the traditional gendered hierarchies. Periodicals such as *Shafts* and the *Women's Herald* posited politics as an interest consistent with women's traditional role as wives and mothers. This helped bring women's newspapers away from the fringe and into dialogue with existing cultural conceptions of womanhood while legitimating them as alternative spaces for the expression of minority opinion.

Telling women to take an active role in society was one thing; actually prompting them to do so, however, was quite another. Advocacy newspapers asked women readers to expand their perspective to include domestic and world events in order that they might advance the progress of the British nation as responsible citizens. Editorials, letters to the editor, and articles suggested projects ranging from starting reform societies to letter writing to participating in actual protests. For Muller's largely bourgeois female audience, many of whom actively shunned "publicity," such activities remained problematic at best. Even for papers such as *Shafts,* targeted at a broader class of reader, ideas about female respectability held strong currency.

Woman's advocacy newspapers at the turn of the century represented for readers a womanhood that both appeared modern and maintained traditional Victorian cultural values. This tension continued to be a central focus of the women's press throughout the suffrage era and beyond, as it participated in creating a respectable identity for female political activists. As the following account of the cultural debates over the identity of the "New Woman" illustrates, central to that project was the invention of a nonsubversive image for the emergent political woman.

MAKING THE "NEW WOMAN" READER INTO A SOCIAL ADVOCATE

"Without warning," the *Woman's Herald* declared in August 1893, "woman suddenly appears on the scene of man's activities, as a sort of new creation, and demands a share in the struggles, the responsibilities and the honours of the world, in which, until now, she has been a cipher." The *Herald* labeled this woman the "New Woman," and it was here, in the pages of the turn-of-the-century women's press, that she was first invented as a fictional icon to represent the political woman of the coming century.[113] This vision of the New Woman was not the mannish and overly sexualized New Woman popularized in novels and mainstream periodicals of the 1890s but a symbol of a new female political identity that promised to improve and reform English society. From 1893 to 1897, the women's press created a respectable image for political women by inventing an identity for the New Woman.

Simultaneously, the mainstream press proposed a counterimage of the New Woman as a dystopian vision of a society gone wrong. Using their own brand of print journalism, the women's press promoted a "womanly" vision of the New Woman that challenged popular perceptions of "independent" or "masculine" women, embodied in the New Woman of the mid-1890s, in an attempt to stake out a political role for women as citizens. This concluding section examines an alternative discourse of the New Woman, a discourse created by the women that the aforementioned caricatures were intended to parody.

By the 1890s, the identity of the public woman was highly contested. Eliza Lynn Linton started the debate with an article published in the *Saturday Review* in 1868 entitled "The Girl of the Period," in which she lambasted the independent woman as "a creature who dyes her hair and paints her face, whose sole aim is unbounded luxury, and whose dress is the chief object of such thought and intellect as she possesses."[114] By the 1870s and 1880s, popular journals, magazines, and novels joined Linton's outcry and lampooned politically active women as the "shrieking sisterhood," labeling them "Wild" or "Odd." Women, according to public perception, threatened to turn society on its head by appropriating male behaviors and shunning marriage.[115] *Punch* notoriously lampooned this invented woman who, for many, symbolized a real threat to the traditional British values. Caricatures of "independent women" appeared throughout the 1880s, depicting women in masculine dress and following nontraditional pursuits that included education, politics, and sports.[116]

The women writers at whom such critiques were directed used women's newspapers to manufacture their own image of the political woman. The *Herald* article "The Social Standing of the New Woman" marked the first time that the term New Woman, with the imposing capital letters, appeared in a periodical.[117] They called her the New Woman, as they believed it was on her shoulders that the future of civilized society rested. The *Herald* represented her as a reasonable and thoughtful woman who had only the best interests of the British nation at heart. In essence, the New Woman represented a utopian vision of the model social reformer. Women's newspapers represented her interest in politics and social justice not as a challenge to her dedication to the home but rather as an extension of her domestic duties.

After her introduction as a symbol of the woman reformer, the New Woman made her first appearance in the mainstream press in the spring of 1894, over six months later than in the women's press. Novelists Ouida and Sarah Grand battled out the definition of the New Woman in a series of articles in the *North American Review*. For Grand, the New Woman represented a superior breed of liberal-minded women.[118] Ouida, on the other hand, had little patience for the utopian ideals of the women's movement, labeling the New Woman an "unmitigated" and "self-important" bore who was convinced that upon her shoulders "hangs the future of the world."[119]

These two competing images fueled the New Woman debate at the turn of the century.

Journalists writing for the women's press constructed discussions of the New Woman based on her role as a model for the next century, a truly "new" and totally reconstructed woman who represented the hope for England's future, as she would take her skills as domestic manager into public life. The *Herald* anticipated her birth in the June 1893 article "Womanly Women": "a truer type of woman is springing up in our midst, combining the 'sweet, domestic grace' of the bygone days with a wide-minded interest in things outside her own immediate circle, extending her womanly influence to the world that so sadly needs the true woman's touch to keep it all that true woman would have it. The woman comes forth for the world's need."[120]

It did not take long for women's newspapers to transform the "womanly woman" in the foregoing description into the New Woman. As already noted, by August 1893, writers for the women's press had already claimed an identity for the New Woman that rested on her single-minded promotion of the advancement of women.[121] Her social standing was debated alongside articles on suffrage and the "rights of married women." The woman's press had high hopes for this invented icon, as she embodied both traditional and progressive ideals in her role as a politically engaged social reformer.

Promoting the cause of the fictional New Woman, for many women readers and writers, meant creating a public role for real women. The women's press argued on behalf of the New Woman in terms of her rights as an individual and self-fashioned domestic reformer. The New Woman, according to the *Woman's Signal*, symbolized a woman's right to education, remunerative employment, and amusements, as well as "the right to take an intelligent interest in her country's welfare and to express that interest in the way usual in democratic countries."[122] This representation of the New Women enabled reform-minded women to lay claim to a special public role for their sex not incongruous with women's traditional status as wives and mothers.[123]

Women's newspapers made it possible for readers to discuss the utopian ideal of the New Woman in a public forum. For example, Sibthorp used *Shafts* to advertise her free lectures on the New Woman. The New Woman also appeared in the "Letters to the Editor" column. A series of five rather lengthy letters on "modern fiction and the cause of woman" illustrated how readers and writers exchanged ideas and debated cultural values. The letter "Modern Fiction and the Cause of Woman" prompted heated responses that challenged the editor's suggestion that modern fiction, such as Olive Schreiner's *Story of an African Farm* and Grant Allen's *The Woman Who Did*, harmed the cause of women by portraying women as acting on their sexual drives. Others wrote in defense of the so-called Modern Woman Novels, claiming that promoting the ideal of sex equality would result in more freedom for women. Within these debates, an identity for the New Woman emerged out of the negotiations that took place in such public exchanges.

The women's periodical proved an ideal place for women to create their utopian ideal of the New Woman. Constructed as a distinctly female space, these papers promised to take their readers seriously by publishing their opinions. Although men also participated in the debate, they did so in a more limited way. "I belong to the sex which is 'unfitted' for the study of the subject to which *Shafts* is chiefly devoted [*sic*]. . . . So I read *Shafts* feeling somewhat as though I were prying into a communication meant for someone else," declared one male reader.[124] This reader's own language self-consciously cast him as an unintended participant in the debate over the modern woman. Some blamed men outright for attempts to define the New Woman themselves. One irate reader wrote: "The modern woman . . . has to bear the brunt of any foolish idea that *man*kind chooses to bring forward as her aim."[125] Signing her letter "A Modern Woman," she made it clear that women had a personal stake in defining not only the aims of the women's movement but also the identity of the players in the debate.

As both an imagined space of female community and a real vehicle for promoting dialogue, the women's press produced images of the New Woman throughout the mid-1890s. Contributors, editors, and readers, however, recognized that others also claimed an identity for the New Woman. The following verse from *Shafts* illustrates that the *Signal* could not claim the New Woman as the property of its readers alone:

> She has pondered o'er the teaching,
> She has made its truths her own;
> Grasped them in their fullest meaning,
> As "New Woman" she is known.
> 'Tis her enemies have baptised her,
> But she gladly claims the name;
> Hers it is to make a glory,
> What was meant should be a shame.[126]

The "enemy" in this verse remained none other than the mainstream press. Indeed, such periodicals played a crucial role in bringing the New Woman debate to national attention, having "baptized" her as a negative icon in popular culture.

The New Woman soon emerged as a readily recognizable figure, making her first appearance in the *Daily Telegraph*, the *Daily Chronicle*, and the *Pall Mall Gazette* in 1894. As she continued her rise in the coming years, different interests appropriated the term, giving the New Woman a host of alternative cultural meanings. A symbol of a world turned upside down, the figure of the New Woman played on the fears of a society that believed women, with their claims to sex equality and equal citizenship, had almost literally taken on a male persona. A poster used to advertise the popular 1894 play *The New Woman* encapsulated this fear. Depicting a lit cigarette in the foreground and a latchkey on the wall, this image represented the New Woman as independent in both her social practices and lifestyle. She also wore spectacles, presumably to read the books scattered about her on the floor, including such immodest and most likely invented tracts as *Naked but Not Ashamed* and *Man the Betrayer*. These symbols of secular education appear to have replaced conduct books and the more traditional symbols of Victorian womanhood. Instead of children and other symbols of the hearth and home, the New Woman chose to surround herself with subversive literature that challenged her subordinate role to that of man. In deploying such images, the mainstream press created a threatening portrait of a mannish woman who denied her natural role as wife and mother. Ultimately, the utopian vision created by the women's press translated into a dystopian nightmare for social critics writing for the mainstream press.

The New Woman debate peaked in the popular press in 1895 with the advent of the well-known caricature of the "manly" New Woman in *Punch*. This cartoon depicted two rather large, mannish-looking women sporting neckties and smoking cigarettes in the foreground. Jack, a handsome young gentleman pictured in the background, is just about to leave. When implored by the women to stay for tea, Jack wryly responds, "Oh, I'm going for a Cup of Tea in the Servants' Hall. I can't get on without female society, you know!" Society, as suggested by this scene, could not survive in an androgynous state. Men not only wanted but needed female company and would transcend class boundaries to get it. Another depiction of the New Woman explored the anxiety of what the mannish New Woman would do to sex difference. The answer to the caption "What the New Woman Will Make of the New Man!" seemed to be very bored men and discontented, mannish women. According to the mainstream press, the New Woman did not symbolize the hope for a totally reformed womanly utopia but a dreadful situation where the line between masculine and feminine behavior was almost indistinguishable.

That same year women's newspapers opened up their pages to discuss and revamp the mainstream press's New Woman. Readers made it clear that they had had enough of Mr. Punch's New Woman. A letter published in the *Signal* defined the "New Woman proper." Signing herself "A Thorough Believer in the New Woman," the author condemned "the 'Manly' New Woman of Mr. Punch" as distasteful because she "seeks to be an imitation of man in every aspect." The "real" New Woman "is pre-eminently womanly and desires to remain so. She prefers the society of her own sex to that of men, and is, as a rule, popular among women—which I think you will admit is a very good test of her womanliness."[127]

To further combat the dystopian vision of the New Woman, writers emphasized the "womanly" characteristics of the New Woman by calling upon images from the past. An article in *Shafts* entitled "Is the So-Called 'New Woman' a Modern Prodigy?" drew the link between the New Woman of the 1890s and the progressive woman of the 1770s. Quoting a description of the "modern woman" from the *Female Spectator,* a late eighteenth-century women's magazine, this author provided the New Woman with a pure and virtuous grandmother. The New Woman of the 1890s thus became merely an extension of this traditional womanhood that had had a long and respectable history.

Depictions of women's dedication to domestic duties and motherhood made up an important part of the representation of this New Womanhood. Advocating gainful employment only for unmarried women, women's newspapers encouraged women to seek joy through marriage and motherhood, claiming wage earning as no substitute for the joys of the home. Quoting the *North American Review, Shafts* agreed that "the great problem of the age" was how to "emancipate woman and preserve motherhood."[128] "More New Women" offered a solution to this dilemma: domestic training for the New Woman. A *Signal* reporter visited a cooking school that trained future New Woman. These young women joyfully took part in every stage of the process:

> Then comes the—to them—really charming process of "clearing up." Three or four girls clean knives and forks, others go into the little scullery and wash pots, pans, crockery . . . while another lays the table. But the crowning glory appeared to be to scrub the table. We are told that this is a joy that *never* fails, and, indeed, to see the energetic and very thorough manner in which work is done by little girls is quite a revelation to an outsider.[129]

Women's newspaper thus used the New Woman's commitment to the home and the British nation to defend her against the vitriolic charges of the mainstream press. The *Signal* published the following verse to rescue the term New Woman from "misuse" by her critics:

> If healthy minds and love of right,
> To you may seem a novel sight,
> If lofty purpose, strength of will,
> To cleanse the world from every ill
> Be just a little "New" dear sir,
> 'Tis right that we should make a stir.
> For God and Home and Land we fight,
> And God above defends the right.

Defining women's role as a warrior in the fight to defend the world from "every ill" elevated the New Woman to a place of importance, while harkening back to an earlier nineteenth-century vision of moral energy radiating from the home into society.[130] Unapologetic in her commitment to "God and Home and Land," this womanly New Woman justified women's claims to a public role by 1895. As the final lines of the foregoing verse resolved,

> We'll ever try the world to mend,
> And be "New Women" to the end.[131]

The women's press further extended the theme of the womanly woman in the coming years, claiming the identity of the New Women, indeed, until the end. By early 1897, the New Woman had faded as a contested icon in British culture. Lectures on the New Woman advertised in *Shafts* in late 1894 and early 1895 had stopped. Other references had to do with the New Women of other nations. Articles on "The New Woman in Turkey" and "The New Woman in Germany" were published in 1897 and 1898, respectively, having as their subject not the image of the New Woman but the progress of the women's movement in these two countries. Although turn-of-the-century women's newspapers kept their "virtuous" and respectable image until their own demise around 1900, the New Woman no longer served as a symbol for the respectable political woman. Likewise, the New Woman had all but disappeared from the popular press by 1898 and was referred to only sporadically during the early decades of the twentieth century.

Over the course of the New Woman debate, the term that had begun as an attempt to create a legitimate public identity for women emerged as a contested terrain over which competing cultural values were negotiated. The success of the women's press in controlling public perception of the image of the New Woman was inevitably limited in the face of a powerful and widely circulating mainstream press. There is some evidence, however, that the utopian vision of the New Woman entered the mainstream by the end of the debate. In 1895, *Shafts* reprinted a verse that had appeared in *Punch* that depicted the New Woman not as a man but as a self-sacrificing woman whose eyes "flamed" at "wrong or injustice." In characteristic verse, *Punch* concluded of "The Real New Woman":

> Oh, what if she never should do or should dare
> In regions by Woman untrod?
> Yet, when her step passes, men turn from dispair [*sic*],
> And trust in the world and in God.
> Oh, what if no "record" she cares to eclipse,
> Nor manners nor morals defies?
> But pain she would face with a smile on her lips,
> And Death with a light in her eyes!

Such praiseworthy depictions of the New Woman, however, were rare. "The Real New Woman" failed to counter the earlier negative images of the New Woman in the public eye. Rather, the image of the disreputable New Woman continued to dominate the debate over women's status as public actors and in many ways still shapes our perception of this cultural icon today.

Although the image-making campaign of the 1890s was largely a failure, the women's advocacy press had clearly started to take on a new function. Women's newspapers provided women with a version of the news that they could use. At the same time, editors claimed that women had the ability to influence public discourse over issues that mattered to themselves and the nation. The women's press had lost the battle over the New Woman but had in the process successfully located women's politics in the realm of respectability.[132] A new model of political action thus developed within its pages that helped to shape women's political culture during the early twentieth century, particularly in relation to the suffrage movement. As the *Women's Tribune* proclaimed in its 1906 inaugural number: "Women must speak more and more emphatically; more of them must speak; much speech is action; silence is not always golden."[133] Women's periodicals provided an important vehicle through which to bring such voices out from the margins.

From their vantage point outside of the formal structures of political life and the mainstream press establishment, women's newspapers had ample opportunity to promote domestic reform in the public sphere. Press advocacy, as the example of the women's press demonstrates, provided a means of contesting ideas and producing alternative discourses during the period when many critics began to lament what they understood as the declining diversity of the British newspaper industry. By the early twentieth century, women's press advocacy had established itself as a highly visible alternative space for women activists and journalists to engage in both reporting and news-making activities. The far-reaching implications of legitimating women's new role as social advocate, however, remained problematic at best. As the case of the suffrage press in the next chapter reveals, women's newspapers not only helped draw public attention to the Woman Question but also played an important part in shaping the role of the female political activist in public life. In this way, women's newspapers helped shape the nature of women's political culture in the new century.

4

Reforming the Nation: Suffrage Advocacy and Edwardian Political Culture

Running a women's newspaper was serious business in early twentieth-century Britain. Sophisticated production, efficient distribution, and high circulation took center stage for this new generation of Edwardian editors and journalists as they created a medium that sought both influence and prestige in the marketplace of ideas. By 1910, women's political journalism had developed into a well-established forum for political discourse. "Suffrage Newspapers," as contemporaries called them, capitalized on the publicity given to women's reform issues by turn-of-the-century advocacy journals such as the *Women's Penny Paper* and *Shafts*.[1] In addition to spreading information and providing commentary on topics that included poverty both at home and abroad, child welfare, women's employment, and legal inequality, as their predecessors had done, this bold new suffrage press called for material changes in political and economic structures. Editors focused on female enfranchisement, in particular, as a universal remedy for the ills of both women and the nation. As women's newspapers developed into propaganda tools for suffrage, they introduced a new discourse, centered on the call of "Votes for Women," that challenged women to act in the name of equal citizenship. The suffrage press thus played a key role in enabling women to participate in a wider public discussion over the future role of women as citizens, while creating a multifaceted political community for female activists.

Suffrage periodicals constituted a highly visible and, in some cases, popular news medium that boasted circulations as high as fifty thousand copies weekly during the first decades of the twentieth century. They appeared in a variety of forms throughout the British Isles, ranging from regular weeklies and monthlies to more sporadic publications. Over twenty-five different pro–

women's suffrage papers circulated before 1918 published by and for women. These national papers targeted urban and provincial bourgeois women as well as working-class women living in East London. Women's groups associated with the Church of England, the Catholic Church, labor organizations, and the international peace movement all had their own prosuffrage organs during this period.[2] The words "women" and/or "suffrage" often appeared in their titles and marked them as the voices of a highly politicized female constituency. Like the networks sustained by the smaller advocacy publications of the nineteenth century, the community of women involved in the struggle for the vote relied on suffrage papers as an invaluable medium for the exchange of ideas and information.[3]

Women's periodicals such as Becker's *Women's Suffrage Journal* had dealt with the subject of suffrage from the beginning, but the issue of votes for women had never dominated the discourse of women's political culture. This new generation of suffrage newspaper, however, had a larger, more politicized agenda. Rather than understanding the vote as part of a larger series of conditions necessary for the improvement of women's social position as papers had in the late nineteenth century, the suffrage press portrayed the vote itself as a necessary precondition to any advancement of women's status. The rhetoric of suffrage advocacy claimed that the vote would empower women to improve the nation. Political issues affecting women, promoted by earlier advocacy papers, were given a new strength when placed behind the banner of suffrage. Suffrage newspapers asked women to imagine themselves as activists who had a hand in advancing British society by promoting their own interests as voters. In foregrounding the issue of suffrage, editors encouraged readers to develop a new political consciousness that cultivated a gender-identified community built on the principles of political action.

This chapter interweaves the stories of the four most popular and influential suffrage journals published during the first decades of the twentieth century. It reveals a sophisticated network of individuals and ideas that worked together to produce a discourse that challenged the male-centered tradition of mainstream liberal ideology in the years preceding the outbreak of World War I. Despite its material prominence, historians have never critically examined the suffrage press as a cultural institution that helped sustain a network of activists excluded from formal politics by virtue of their sex. Scholars, instead, have used such periodicals to provide information about the suffrage campaigns, without taking into account their role in shaping the identity of participants and the movement itself.[4] This chapter reassesses historical accounts of women's political culture during the suffrage era by exploring how women's newspapers and women journalists produced and disseminated an alternative political discourse within an increasingly commercialized mainstream news media climate. Understanding the women's newspaper as an important cultural tool and the political woman journalist as a central actor in Edwardian Britain, I argue, reveals the complex role the women's press played in creating an institutional infrastructure that linked a diverse range of women together as suffrage advocates.

The rise of the suffrage press took place within the larger context of a changing British press establishment in the early twentieth century. As Stephen Koss has illustrated, this period witnessed the beginning of a concrete shift away from Victorian news-making practices. As seemingly limitless expansion met with the realities of a saturated market for print, the result was increased consolidation in an Edwardian marketplace that demanded both news and entertainment. Selling papers and advertising rather than catering to the needs of political parties now fully determined a paper's success. At the same time, the press began to take on a new, important cultural function: holding what Koss called "a monopoly on the commodity of propaganda." Pamphleteering and public speeches gave way to a culture that looked to newspapers for guidance on important issues. The press emerged as a primary representative of popular opinion in a way previously unimaginable to Victorian journalists, who had bound themselves to the codes of an earlier brand of partisan journalism before the repeal of the "taxes on knowledge." This change resulted, according to Koss, in making the mainstream press "the best available index to popular opinion as well as the single most convenient mechanism for guiding it." For Koss, the decline in partisan journalism, coupled with the contraction of the number of "quality" newspapers, contributed to the "fall" of a vibrant and highly contested political press culture in Britain during the first half of the twentieth century as a legitimate arena for political discourse.

Koss's assertion that "alternative mass media had not yet arisen" to challenge mainstream newspapers' claim as sole representatives of public opinion needs to be reassessed in the light of the emergence of a popular suffrage press that represented disenfranchised woman citizens.[5] A newly refashioned women's alternative press took advantage of changes in the commercial industry that expanded newspapers' cultural authority and ability to shape public opinion. Through the use of propaganda and mass marketing techniques, suffrage papers built on the foundation laid by turn-of-the-century women's newspapers as they asserted their status as the best medium to guide public opinion on subjects that they appropriated as women's issues, such as social reform, education, and political reform. Although the suffrage press was not part of the mass newspaper media along the lines of Northcliffe's enterprises, these papers did hold significant cultural authority over issues relating to women's status and political causes. Their longstanding nonpartisan status contributed to the continuation of a woman-centered political program. By capitalizing on changes brought on by a commercialized and market-driven print culture, suffrage newspapers developed into a visible medium that challenged a sex-exclusive political discourse both on a real and symbolic level.

The example of the suffrage press suggests that mainstream newspapers in this decreasingly partisan political climate thus did not have sole claim to be representatives of "public opinion." The women's press was not alone in this enterprise. According to Deian Hopkin, "every socialist group established in Britain after 1880 eventually launched its own organ" as an alternative to the mainstream "capitalist" or "class" press.[6] Much as socialist papers spoke for the interests of their constituencies in the face of a powerful commercial press establishment, women's papers represented the opinions of readers who found that the mainstream British press ignored or miscast issues of importance to women reformers. In the process, the women's press provided the vehicle for the development of a contested print-based political culture that captured the imagination of Edwardians during one of the most high-profile political campaigns of the twentieth century.

After introducing the origins of the suffrage press, this chapter turns to the making of the female political activist within the pages of the two most influential papers of the period: *Votes for Women* (1907–18) and *Common Cause* (1909–20). The next section uses the case of the *Vote* (1909–33) to discuss the proliferation of diverse agendas promoted under the banner of suffrage, while examining the problem of distribution and circulation faced by competing women's newspapers. Finally, I explore responses to the extremist newspaper the *Suffragette* (1912–15) so as to understand the growing, though ambiguous, status of the public woman in Edwardian political culture. Together, these narratives of the suffrage press reveal the important role played by alternative print media in advancing the interests of marginalized political communities during the tumultuous decades of the early twentieth century.

The Origins of the Suffrage Newspaper

The suffrage press emerged out of the new world of Edwardian liberal politics to represent women's claims to full citizenship. The rise of the Liberal Party to power at the beginning of the century symbolized for many the end of the longstanding aristocratic tradition in government and the beginning of a new democratic mandate. As Ian Fletcher has argued, a disruptive culture of politics emerged during the Edwardian period that resulted, in part, from interest groups that clamored for political recognition in the face of a Liberal Party that was ultimately reluctant to expand the boundaries of the political nation.[7] Women's suffrage advocates joined labor unionists, socialists, and Irish nationalists in challenging the legitimacy of a state that they believed marginalized their interests, despite the ruling party's purported commitment to reform.

Before suffragists entered this contested arena, the women's press was in disarray. The death of patron Jessie Boucherett threw the staid old *Englishwoman's Review* into financial crisis.[8] A new title, the *Women's Tribune,* started by Christiana, Lady Herringham, in 1906, failed to find an audience and lasted only four months. Meanwhile, the issue of women's suffrage had gained momentum and, thanks to the bold tactics of the nascent "militant" Women's Social and Political Union (WSPU), notoriety. The diverse and rapidly proliferating women's suffrage societies agreed: they needed a fresh voice to provide organizational news to members that would counter the flow of unfavorable coverage of suffrage activities by the mainstream press.

In June 1907, J. E. Francis, the radical proprietor of the Athenaeum Press, started a broad-based monthly prosuffrage periodical to "give publicity to the cause of the enfranchisement of women."[9] Francis declared the new periodical's columns "open to intelligent objectors as to warm sympathizers" of all affiliations the cause.[10] Supported by funds from the "constitutionalist" National Union of Women's Suffrage Society (NUWSS), the "militant" Women's Social and Political Union, and later the Women's Freedom League (WFL) and the Men's League for Women's Suffrage, *Women's Franchise* began as a temporary vehicle to allow the growing number of suffrage societies to place the issue of women's suffrage before the public. Francis considered this a "necessary" noncommercial venture: "any profits which there may be shall be allocated to the Societies which give their support" (fig. 11).[11]

For Francis, suffrage represented an umbrella issue that unified all prosuffrage organizations and thus should not fall victim to particular political interests. A relative newcomer to the world of suffrage politics, he did not understand the increasingly contested terrain of women's associational life. Infighting between the constitutionalist and militant factions led to battles over what the periodical covered: each organization accused Francis of granting the other too much publicity. When the WSPU wanted out, the NUWSS took over the funding of the paper, appointing its own members to the staff

Women's Franchise.

Vol. II.—No. 75.　　　THURSDAY, DECEMBER 2, 1909.　　　PRICE ONE PENNY.

Contents.

Notice to Subscribers and Contributors.

Articles containing information on the subject of Women's Suffrage should be addressed to the Editor, who will return those not considered suitable as soon as possible if a stamped addressed envelope is sent with the MS. As the paper is on a voluntary basis, and all profits go to help the cause, no payments are made for contributions.

The General Editor gives the widest possible latitude to each of the Societies represented in this Paper, and is only responsible for unsigned matter occurring in the pages devoted to general items.

'WOMEN'S FRANCHISE,'
EDITORIAL AND PUBLISHING OFFICE,
13, BREAM'S BUILDINGS, CHANCERY LANE, E.C.

THE BUDGET.—Women should note that

September 29th is the last day for claiming any benefit or relief offered by it.

INCOME-TAX RETURNS are prepared, APPEALS conducted, and OVER-PAID TAX recovered by Mrs. E. AYRES PURDIE, A.L.A.A., Certified Accountant, and at present the only woman who is entitled, under the Revenue Act of 1903, to appear on behalf of a Client before the Special Commissioners of Income-Tax.

CRAVEN　HOUSE,　KINGSWAY,　W.C.

THE Women's Labour League met during the Conference at Hull to consider various social and industrial subjects Chief among them was the question to be submitted at the Conference of the Labour Party, that the League should be eligible for affiliation to the Labour Party, but without the right to vote in the election of the Executive. Mrs. Wilson, of Halifax, protested against the restriction; she claimed affiliation on the same terms as men, or not at all, and she moved that the Women's League should express dissatisfaction with the terms proposed. Miss Smith seconded the motion. In speaking to the resolution, Miss Bondfield pointed out that the Labour Party were stretching a point in women's favour, as they were not really entitled to what was proposed until they had 5,000 members, after which declaration the motion was lost.

IN addressing the newly-formed Women's Unionist League at Southport, at its first meeting on May 23rd, the chairman Councillor R. Morris, in his opening speech, made vigorous defence of Women's Suffrage. He said he was fully persuaded that the day was not far distant when women would be granted the Parliamentary vote. When Napoleon I. was fighting the

English at Waterloo, one of his generals drew his attention to the advancing Scottish regiments in full Highland dress Napoleon is said to have exclaimed: "It is bad for us—the women are coming!" And in time to come, when the women of the country were thoroughly roused, and realized the power of the ballot box, it would mean the removal of much of the ignorance, crime, and poverty which now existed.

OUR readers will be interested to hear that the third volume of the 'Life and Work of Susan B. Antony' is now nearly completed, and will probably be ready by February 15th, which is her birthday. The volume will be even more interesting than its predecessors, for it will contain the account of Miss Antony's later achievements and of the recognition of her great work for Women's Suffrage in Europe as well as in America. The book will be on sale at the headquarters of the National American Women's Suffrage Association, Warren, Ohio, where orders can be sent in advance. The price will not exceed ·50 dols.; it is not published for profit, but "to complete the wonderful record of a life devoted to the cause of women with a singleness of purpose unmatched in the history of our movement."

Proposed New Paper.

THERE would appear to be an opening for a weekly paper appealing primarily to the increasing class of educated women who have intellectual, industrial, or public interests. The number of such women grows daily larger. 'The Englishwoman's Year-Book,' published last year, included institutions and societies of various kinds, the number of which (not counting "refuges" and "homes") amounted to some thousands. It may fairly be reckoned that each of these institutions or societies represents the co-operation of at least three women. Probably every one of these women, besides a good many others unconnected with any of these institutions are interested in many topics quite untouched by the average "woman's paper," and dealt with only very inadequately by any existing review or magazine. A reading public is thus constituted which, no doubt, would never be vast—never comparable in numbers with the public catered for by *Tit-Bits* or by the *Strand Magazine*—but which, on the other hand, would probably be very steady. The aim should be to create a review which no member of that public would willingly be without.

The proprietor of *Women's Franchise*, foreseeing from the beginning that his enterprize was but a first step that would probably need to be followed by other steps, several months ago registered the title *The Woman Citizen*. It is now hoped that money will be forthcoming to issue under that title a greatly enlarged and extended paper. Like *Women's Franchise*, the new paper will consider the right to a vote as occupying the first place in the interests of *The Woman Citizen*, and Suffrage topics will therefore receive special attention.

Although the paper will be in no sense a party organ, its general tone will be distinctly progressive. A paper that should remain neutral upon vital social questions could neither be very valuable nor very interesting.

The general aim will be to fill in the gaps left on the one hand by the so-called "women's papers," and on the other by the daily newspapers. In the former attention is mainly directed towards the frivolous, personal and material aspects of life; dress, amusements, society gossip, cookery, &c.; in the latter the interests of women are dealt with either on an inadequate scale or not at all.

Figure 11. *Women's Franchise,* front page.

and buying up most of the declining monthly circulation. Francis remained firm, claiming that after the departure of the WSPU, "on no account will we permit any person or society to dictate to us as to the exclusion of other people from using our pages."[12] Unable in the end to satisfy any society, the paper limped along for another two years, publishing its final issue in September 1909, after the NUWSS and the newly formed offshoot of the WSPU, the WFL, pulled out of the project.[13]

Despite its failure, *Women's Franchise* reminded the burgeoning suffrage organizations of the power of controlling the press. Each group served distinct communities of activists with their own agendas. This led to the rise of a diverse suffrage press that promoted the cause of suffrage to the wider public using multiple propaganda tactics. To reach politicians and the public, suffrage groups started independent organs to promote particularized agendas. In other words, although they all agreed on the importance of the vote, each organization used the issue differently to push their own political projects, which included social reform, education, employment, and international feminist politics, among others. The women's press served as a lifeline for female activists, who relied on suffrage newspapers to keep them informed. Having its own paper also meant that an organization could use the press as a way to recruit members as well as for propaganda and publicity.

The suffrage press thus emerged as its own genre of advocacy newspaper, dedicated to serving the needs of a new radicalized women's political culture that needed its own voice. As editor Evelyn Sharp chastised the *Daily Chronicle* in 1907:

> I am sorry you feel you cannot take up a definite position on the suffrage question, after all. . . . However, if you send round reporters to get news of the movement as you tell me you are doing in your letter that is all to the good—as long as they get correct news. The one suffragist who gained admittance to Mr. Sydney Buxton's meeting on Friday evening did not, for instance, jump upon her chair or shout at the top of her voice. She stood up and very quietly said one sentence in reply to an incorrect statement made by the speaker on the platform. The rest was uproar; but not of her making. You see, I know, because I was the suffragist.[14]

Inaccurate and inconsistent reporting coupled with negative coverage of events led suffrage organizations to believe that they each required their own separate national medium to cover the progress of these growing societies.[15]

This new generation of women's advocacy newspapers emerged as prominent voices of the disenfranchised woman citizen. Through extraparliamentary activities, such women took a new interest in government policy making. Suffrage rose to prominence as the hook upon which to hang all other women's issues, a virtual panacea for the past and present ills of women. Each newspaper, however, had its own political agenda and published propaganda that linked the granting of the vote to women with such things as a decline in venereal disease, better health care for children, provisions for widows, and public safety. Thus, even a seemingly single-issue campaign like the vote had embedded within it a set of highly contested issues that remained a crucial part of a constantly evolving dialogue about women's status in prewar Britain. Prosuffrage organizations, although they did not speak with one voice nevertheless developed a very real sense of community among both leaders and the rank and file. Through the medium of the suffrage newspaper, a multifaceted and vibrant women's press culture emerged to serve the needs of this expanding political movement. Having an independent advocacy paper enabled organizations to promote their own ideal for women's advancement to their largely female constituencies, while supporting the larger cause of women's enfranchisement in the face of a recalcitrant liberal state.

The Birth of the New Suffrage Press

Advocacy journalism emerged during the Edwardian period as a theater for radical political life, which found itself increasingly tied to the marketplace. Starting a suffrage newspaper required a number of financial and business-related resources that were largely provided through institutional support from women's organizations. First and foremost, organizations had to raise capital. The formation of joint stock companies remained the preferred method of raising funds; supporters bought shares in newly formed corporations that started to handle the publishing of that groups' newspaper. Weekly periodicals required a minimum initial outlay of capital of two thousand pounds, twice what it had cost to start the *English Woman's Journal* sixty years earlier.[16] Printing costs, followed by other "journalistic and establishment expenses," ranked as a periodical's largest expenditures. Starting with two thousand pounds of capital required a circulation of at least thirty-five thousand for a penny weekly to make a profit.[17] Production costs grew considerably beyond those of the Victorian era, as suffrage papers mimicked mainstream weeklies by employing larger full-time staffs and, at times, paying contributors. Sophisticated layouts and photographs, used extensively throughout the press by 1910, further increased expenses.[18]

These rising production costs challenged suffrage organizations to rethink earlier models of advocacy journalism before starting a paper. All newspapers published during this period faced an increasingly competitive marketplace, forcing many periodicals to consolidate production costs. By 1910, three companies controlled over a third of the circulation of morning dailies.[19] Advocacy journalism had a built-in flexibility that shielded it from the trend toward such cost cutting and consolidation. Through subsidies, donations, and volunteer workers, these papers had the freedom to promote agendas outside mainstream public opinion without having to worry about alienating potential corporate supporters.

At the same time, the changing world of print made the suffrage press more conscious of the importance of succeeding in the marketplace. Increasingly, the suffrage press embraced the sensibility of the commercial mainstream press. During this period, according to D. L. LeMahieu, a belief that "profitability measured public support" gained credence in the mainstream press. If a paper did not pay its own way, Northcliffe proclaimed, it "can not be said to represent any substantial section of the people."[20] Seeking influence as a forum for public opinion, suffrage newspapers focused on making both news *and* profits by increasing space dedicated to advertising and using more aggressive sales drives. Unlike the mainstream press, however, suffrage organizations used any income to further propaganda work rather than to benefit individual investors.

Suffrage organizations thus turned press advocacy into a business. Started as independent institutions that had shareholders and advisory boards, suffrage newspapers remained separate entities from their respective organizations. This practice protected members from concerns with business liabilities that plagued earlier women's advocacy journals run directly by individuals or institutions. Organizations instead informally offered fledgling papers extensive institutional resources, such as providing volunteers to sell papers at home and abroad. Although with varying degrees of success, suffrage organizations maintained separate institutional functions between themselves and the newspapers that supported their viewpoints.

The development of this increasingly professionalized yet highly partisan news medium resulted in the production of a more sophisticated and commercially driven women's advocacy periodical. Suffrage newspapers were large, measuring over twice the size of their earliest predecessors. The first women's periodical, the *English Woman's Journal,* was the size of a quarto-sized book, measuring eight and a quarter by five and a quarter inches. Suffrage papers averaged over thirteen by nine inches in size. Their tabloid-size sheets and multipaged, bold-faced format dwarfed even women's periodicals of the 1890s by comparison. Bold headlines, large fonts, political cartoons, and photographs grabbed the reader's attention, as editors attempted to capture a mass reader base. Pages had multiple columns with lead stories set in layouts that mimicked the high-circulation daily papers of the new century. Other

Edwardian advocacy periodicals similarly adopted techniques used by the mainstream press. According to Chris Waters, socialist papers adopted new features, such as sporting pages and women's columns, which were found in papers such as the *Daily Mail* and *Express,* "to boost circulation figures and thus attract advertising revenue."[21]

Suffrage papers welcomed the trend of attracting aggressive, high-revenue advertisements that targeted the female consumer. Advertisements took over more and more space in the most popular suffrage periodicals, pushing a variety of domestic products for women.[22] These products ranged from ready-to-wear fashion to household furniture and appliances (fig. 12). As D. L. LeMahieu has argued, the continued pursuit of profit, coupled with the rise of the department store, ensured that "newspapers and advertising became inextricably linked."[23] The women's press could not afford to be left behind. Advertising sponsors funded the propaganda used to garner support for the cause that suffrage advocates claimed would fulfill the liberal demo-cratic promise. Regardless of the paper's message, many advertisers gladly used such periodicals to target their largely middle- to upper-middle-class audience.[24] Such support remained essential to providing revenue to expand the influence of the suffrage press.

Despite these changes in format and business practices, suffrage newspa-pers continued to be published not only for but also primarily by women. According to suffrage leaders, women had a responsibility to represent them-selves to the public through the press. "The great need of this time is for women to learn to stand and to act alone," Christabel Pankhurst claimed, after the male-run radical newspaper the *Daily Herald* offered to serve as the voice of the WSPU. "It comes to this. The men must paddle their canoe, and we must paddle ours."[25] Such sentiments echoed the ideal of women-run enterprises. In reality, suffrage advocacy often necessitated the cooperation of male readers, writers, and politicians, as these papers elbowed their way into the highly contested world of Edwardian political culture.

Political Propaganda and the Making of the Suffrage Advocate

The two most popular suffrage papers, the WSPU's "militant" *Votes for Wom-en* and the NUWSS's "constitutionalist" *Common Cause,* shared an interest in informing the woman reader of her role as political citizen, an identity invented for readers within the pages of the suffrage press. Editorials and lead articles addressed women as potential activists who could change the

THOMPSON'S
OF TOTTENHAM COURT ROAD. LTD.
"Right in the heart of Furnitureland."

We have refitted the whole of our basement as Furniture Showrooms, and here one may find every possible range of Furniture from Jacobean to the very latest in Office fittings. Our Value for Money system holds as good in our Furniture Dept. as in every other. Write for a catalogue.

Reproduction of Fine Oak Jacobean Dresser, fitted four Cupboards and two Drawers. Brass or oxydised handles. Polished Dark Brown Antique Colour, 5 ft. wide, 6 ft. 9 ins. high, back to front, 1 ft. 10 ins. **£7 7s. 0d.**

Everything for the home.
163-170 TOTTENHAM COURT RD. LONDON.W.

J. S. GREGG,
GLOVE, HOSE and VEIL SPECIALIST.

TERMS STRICTLY CASH.

Gloves sent on Approval.

3/11 and 4/6 per pair.

Best Paris Kid Glove & Suede (Four Button) with points, in Black and Self, the Newest Shades. Two Button Pique. Kid, all Shades 2 6

Note.—All Gloves offered by J. S. GREGG are brought direct from the Manufacturer, and every pair guaranteed to wear.

First Floor : **91, New Bond Street, LONDON, W.**
Catalogue Post Free on application.

As supplied to H.M. the Queen.

WRIGHT'S PATENT (No. 28,293),
A NOVELTY FOR XMAS, NEW YEAR, WEDDING and BIRTHDAY PRESENTS.

The brown earthenware tea-pot is the recognised best tea-maker. WRIGHT'S PATENT is a perforated Silver Casement, beautifully designed, made in two parts, which fits the brown tea-pot, and is fixed by four screws.

"WRIGHT'S PATENT," Old Bond Street (Corner of Piccadilly) Over Stewart's Tea Rooms. Telegrams : "Rightinfit, London." 'Phone : 1196 Gerrard)

'The Conqueror' Skirt

The best Skirt yet invented for bicycling, walking, climbing, games, and all forms of out-door exercise.

Suffragists will find it specially useful for out-door Speaking.

The Skirt is divided, yet can be worn anywhere without this fact being detected, because of the *loose*, detachable apron in front, which, while hiding the division, does not interfere at all with the freedom. The apron can at any moment be removed entirely if required.

A model Skirt will be sent on demand for inspection, postage free. We strongly advise a trial of this most useful addition to women's attire.

Skirts can be made to measure :

PRICE - - ONE GUINEA for the Making.
Material can be supplied if desired extra.

TAYLOR & BLAKE,
101, STATION STREET, BIRMINGHAM.

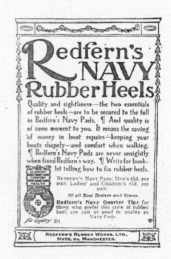

Redfern's NAVY Rubber Heels

Quality and sightliness—the two essentials of rubber heels—are to be secured to the full in Redfern's Navy Pads. ¶ And quality is of some moment to you. It means the saving of money in boot repairs—keeping your boots shapely—and comfort when walking. ¶ Redfern's Navy Pads are never unsightly when fixed Redfern's way. ¶ Write for booklet telling how to fix rubber heels.

REDFERN'S NAVY PADS: Men's 6½d. per pair, Ladies' and Children's 4½d. per pair.

Of all Boot Dealers and Stores.

Redfern's Navy Quarter Tips for those who prefer this style of rubber heel, are just as good in quality as Navy Pads.

REDFERN'S RUBBER WORKS, LTD., HYDE, Nr. MANCHESTER.

Figure 12. Suffrage newspaper advertisements.

terms of political debate through acting on knowledge acquired from suffrage newspapers. This helped create for readers a romantic vision of the woman as activist. At the same time, the familiar images of the "unruly" suffragette and "respectable" suffragist emerged as a popular dualism to represent the extremes of Edwardian feminism. When taken together, these representations reveal the ambiguous identity of the female activist as public woman. If, as Barbara Green claims, "feminist identities are discursively produced" through "reiteration," the suffrage press developed as an important vehicle in the process of defining the modern political woman.[26] As the juxtaposition of these two papers illustrates, the women's advocacy press emerged as a powerful producer not only of ideas but also of particularized political identities, both radical and conservative, that played a role in shifting status of the public woman in prewar Britain.

When Emmeline Pethick-Lawrence first read the "startling account" of the arrest of a group of women who disturbed a 1905 election meeting in Manchester by "shrieking something about 'Votes for Women,'" she was traveling in South Africa with her husband, Frederick. The Pethick-Lawrences, as longtime supporters of radical causes, made immediate plans to meet these women upon their return and hear their side of the story, believing "that accounts of current events in the newspapers had to be read with discrimination."[27] The leadership of the WSPU quickly initiated Emmeline into its ranks in the spring of 1906. Not long afterward, the organization drew in Frederick as a supporter, first as a donor and then as legal counsel for imprisoned suffragettes. His most striking contribution, however, was lending his expertise as a previous proprietor and editor of the radical political paper the *Echo,* to help his wife start *Votes for Women.*[28] As the new voice of the radical WSPU, *Votes for Women* little resembled the tame *Women's Franchise* (see fig. 13).

The paper solicited a particular brand of activist reader: "To the brave women today who are fighting for freedom; to the noble women who all down the ages kept the flag flying and looked forward to this day without seeing it: to all women all over the world of whatever race or creed or calling, whether they be with us or against us in this fight, we dedicate this paper."[29] *Votes for Women* encouraged women "freedom fighters" to engage in protests that often involved physical confrontations with police and the destruction of property. In this way it emerged as a radical woman's voice that promoted militant politics to readers and the wider British public.

With practical business training still unavailable to most women, *Votes for Women* capitalized on Frederick's business skills to further its agenda.

VOTES FOR WOMEN

EDITED BY FREDERICK AND EMMELINE PETHICK LAWRENCE

VOL. VII. (New Series), No. 322.　　　　FRIDAY, MAY 8, 1914.　　　　Price 1d. Weekly (Post Free)

THE BUDGET

A PATRIOT.

Mr. Lloyd George, instead of removing the admitted grievance of married women in respect to income tax, has made it very much more serious by his new Budget. *(See page 485.)*

CONTENTS

DEDICATION

To the brave women who to-day are fighting for freedom, to the noble women who all down the ages kept the flag flying and looked forward to this day without seeing it, to all women all over the world, of whatever race, or creed, or calling, whether they be with us or against us in this fight, we dedicate this paper.

THE OUTLOOK

Lord Selborne's Bill for Woman Suffrage was debated in the House of Lords on Tuesday and Wednesday last. The division on the second reading was taken on Wednesday, just before we went to press, and resulted in a majority of 44 against the Bill. From these figures it will be seen that though the Bill was defeated, there is a considerable body of opinion among the Peers in favour of the enfranchisement of women. And the minority would probably be converted into a majority in the event of a Bill being sent up by the Commons.

Support from the Bishops

The feature of the debate on Tuesday was the powerful defence of the measure delivered by the Bishops of London and Oxford. The Bishop of London, who declared himself a convert to woman

suffrage, asked the grave question whether opponents of the measure wished to have a second Ulster on their hands in the shape of a womanhood in revolt. Which was the wiser course, he said, to allow all these women to smart under a sense of injustice or to try to remove the grievance while there was yet time? After all, women were a more law-abiding sex than men. Referring to his own Bill for raising the age of consent, he said that if he had the votes of a million women behind him he would feel sure of carrying it into law.

Why Not Remove the Injustice?

The Bishop of Oxford made a spirited defence of the women taking part in the suffrage campaign. First putting aside the militants, he said that he did not believe there existed in the world a body of human beings more capable, better instructed, better equipped as voters, or nobler than was to be found in the body of women who in this country were now foremost in demanding this reform. He could conceive no principle of statecraft which justified them in withholding the vote from women. Turning to militancy, he asked by what spirit of logic they could make their violence an excuse for denying just that very element of justice which was the only thing that accounted for the violence. Where they found violence which was accompanied by a claim for justice, there was only one way to suppress violence, and that was to grant the claim for justice.

Lord Selborne Defends His Measure

Lord Selborne himself, who introduced the Bill, made a careful and moderate speech, claiming for

the Bill that it would add to the stability of the State. From his knowledge of other parts of the Empire, and of the conditions at home, he was profoundly impressed with the high sense of patriotism of women. He spoke strongly of the methods adopted by those in the House of Commons, who, posing as the friends of woman suffrage, had succeeded in torpedoing the Conciliation Bill.

Lord Curzon's Opposition

Lord Curzon delivered the principal attack. His arguments may be summarised as follows: (1) Woman suffrage would be injurious to the social relations of the sexes. (2) It would weaken the prestige of the country in the eyes of the world. (3) There is no agreement between suffragists as to the character of the Bill to be passed. (4) The present Bill for enfranchising one million women would lead subsequently to the enfranchisement of many million, and also to women M.P.s and Ministers of State. (5) The present militancy raises a doubt as to the fitness of the female temperament and character for the discharge of political functions. (6) Women, owing partly to their physiological functions, and partly to qualities inseparable from their sex, are not the possessors of that class of gift which is required for the Government of the State.

Our Reply to His Arguments

Our answer to these time-worn shibboleths of the anti-suffragists may be given shortly as follows: (1) is negatived by the experience of Australia, New Zealand, and all the countries where women already vote; it is found that the relation between the sexes

Figure 13. *Votes for Women*, front page.

Frederick recognized his auxiliary role in this "woman's medium" from the beginning: "I did not at first deem it my business to take any active part in the struggle. The day had gone by when 'ladies' expected 'gentlemen' to be kind enough to tell them how to get the vote. This was a campaign organized by women and executed by women who were out to show the stuff they were made of."[30] He realized however, that "there was a danger that by the very exuberance of its growth the movement would outrun its own coordination. There was a need for what is today called 'planning' on the business side."[31] In the early years of the suffrage movement, as Angela John reminds us, the financial and legal knowledge and status of men such as Frederick Pethick-Lawrence proved invaluable.[32] As he worked in cooperation with Emmeline, his newspaper experience helped make *Votes for Women* into a well-run professional organization and formidable news medium (see fig. 14). Frederick carefully positioned himself in the background as a business partner to Emmeline. As he described his sometimes anonymous role in *Votes for Women:* "My wife and I were joint editors. She signed her contributions to its columns, while I wrote the unsigned notes of the week and some of the leading articles."[33] Thus, Frederick quietly pushed the paper to prominence as a medium for women by playing an auxiliary role.

Figure 14. WSPU editorial office, May 1913. © Museum of London.

The Pethick-Lawrences determined a political strategy that would make *Votes for Women* self-supporting. Frederick had watched the *Echo* go under despite his pouring of large sums of money into the publication. The survival of *Votes for Women* depended on its ability to support itself so it would not drain funds needed to support other propaganda activities. After starting it as a threepenny monthly, the Pethick-Lawrences converted the paper within six months into an affordable penny weekly. Since sales of the paper alone did not cover production costs, the proprietors looked for other ways to raise revenue, sending members of the WSPU out into the street to solicit advertisers for the paper.[34] Consumer goods, rather than the ads for books, literature, and training schools for women that had dominated earlier women's papers, took center stage. Oxford Street merchants supported the paper, along with purveyors of soaps, beverages, and a host of "cures" for all kinds of ailments. According to Frederick, readers "made a practice of doing all their shopping with firms who advertised in its columns," thus ensuring advertisers' continued support of the paper.[35] In 1909, the Pethick-Lawrences declared success and handed the paper over to the WSPU as a profitable publication. They continued to serve as joint editors until October 1912,[36] when the Pankhurst leadership questioned their dedication to extreme militancy and forced them out of the WSPU.[37]

The paper's unbridled consumerism served another purpose: it literally made political activism fashionable. *Votes for Women* brought advertisers and readers together on the basis of their mutual interest, although for very different reasons, in women's suffrage. Advertisements and endorsements published in the paper reminded the middle- and upper-class female consumers that made up the majority of the suffragette movement to buy goods from merchants who supported their paper. Erika Rappaport has revealed the important relationship that developed between women's domestic magazines and advertisers in helping constitute the female consumer during this period.[38] For suffrage newspapers, creating a relationship between merchants and readers remained crucial for their survival. They thus led women to believe that they could directly help the movement by adjusting their customer loyalties. Merchants catered to the needs of suffragettes as a matter of good business, recognizing them as a target audience for quality, ready-made goods. Department stores such as Selfridges and Liberty sold WSPU clothing and paraphernalia and dedicated shop windows to their display. Editorials told readers where to purchase items that featured the official suffragette colors: purple, white, and green. One company even designed a bicycle in the WSPU tricolor.[39] Such "support" of suffrage brought female shoppers into their stores, where merchants assumed that they would buy more than just suffrage costumes and banners. In constituting women as shoppers, the WSPU thus enlisted consumer culture in the service of suffrage.

This mutually beneficial consumer relationship contributed to the visibility of women's suffrage on the major retail streets of London, while providing activists with mass-produced items that they could use for propaganda. Prosuffrage consumer goods also helped hold the movement together. As Margaret Finnegan has argued about American suffrage paraphernalia used in the United States campaign during this time, prosuffrage consumerism functioned to keep the suffrage movement "alive," as these products served as symbolic material reminders to participants of the importance of their cause, especially in times when success seemed elusive.[40] The loyalty of British suffrage advocates was reinforced through the emblematic consumer goods that they bought from Oxford Street merchants to visually represent and memorialize their movement. In garnering the support of a relatively affluent class of women, the suffrage movement on both sides of the Atlantic perpetuated itself, in part, through a reliance on the spending habits and shopping patterns of women who wanted to see themselves as participants in an unfolding political drama. *Votes for Women* thus provided a space for the movement to manipulate aspects of the growing consumer economy for its own political purposes.

A growing network of women activists supported this project during the 1910s (figs. 15, 16). As Emmeline observed, "*Votes for Women* had a sensational career. From its foundation . . . as a small monthly magazine, it had become by 1909 a widely read woman's weekly newspaper with a circulation of nearly 30,000 and a large advertisement revenue."[41] At its peak, the paper had a weekly circulation of nearly fifty thousand.[42] Although *Votes for Women* held the highest circulation of any women's advocacy title, it never came close to rivaling the million-plus circulations of the most popular daily papers. Brian Harrison's study of what he calls "pressure-group periodicals" maintains that the historical significance of reforming periodicals, however, rests in their ability to target influential audiences, or "opinion-formers." Suffrage newspapers did precisely that by appealing to a constituency of women who remained active in British cultural and political life as social reformers and philanthropists. Suffrage papers also distributed free copies to MPs and most mainstream press editors. According to Harrison, factors such as the number of different periodicals published to support a cause, rather than the circulation of one particular title, should be used to determine influence. When taken together, suffrage papers support these findings, maintaining a growing national presence as a press medium for and by women.[43]

Figure 15. Packing of
Votes for Women,
Clements Inn.
© Museum of London.

Figure 16. Selling *Votes
for Women.* © Museum
of London.

To increase its visibility, the WSPU established a separate publishing arm in the summer of 1908: the Women's Press. Elizabeth Knight, a WSPU member, ran the press that supported the publication and sales of all literature, postcards, and clothing bearing WSPU colors and emblems.[44] Sales were brisk, as receipts more than tripled in its first year of operation, jumping from two thousand pounds in 1908 to over seven thousand pounds in 1909.[45] In 1910, the Women's Press took over publication of *Votes for Women* and moved out of the WSPU offices at 4 Clements Inn to a new location at the top of Charing Cross Road, where the business of publishing and sales took place over the next several years.[46] A large "Votes for Women" clock prominently adorned the top of the storefront, ensuring that even if Londoners did not actually buy the paper, they could not ignore its presence as a prominent advocacy medium for women.

The Union, however, wanted its propaganda both seen *and* read. Leaders of the WSPU called *Votes for Women* the best link "between the public and the union" and believed it the most effective means of shaping public opinion. Influencing a largely apathetic British public and reluctant Liberal government remained the key to raising the status of women's suffrage as a serious political issue. The mainstream press had failed to adequately represent the suffrage cause, according to WSPU leaders. In the midst of the Conciliation Bill controversy, which promised but eventually failed to grant women the vote, Christabel Pankhurst complained:

> The manner in which the Press boycotts all our Constitutional work and distorts and misrepresents our militant action is proving to be a most serious hindrance to the progress of our work because the great mass of intelligent and thinking people who really want to understand the whole question, can find no means of getting the necessary information. There is no way out of the difficulty save that of increasing the circulation of our paper, *Votes for Women*. It must be brought to the notice of an increasingly large public, because in its columns alone can the truth about our agitation be found.[47]

Votes for Women acted as both a center of information and a watchdog over any "misrepresentations" of the movement printed by the mainstream press.[48] Distributed by W. H. Smith and John Menzies, the paper appeared on the newsstands every Thursday and sold alongside the most influential papers of the day.[49]

Women constituted the paper's biggest group of supporters by far. Readers loved the bold and sensational reporting. Political cartoons mocking government policies adorned the front page of every issue, while headlines announced the government's latest atrocity against suffragettes. Pictures of protests regularly appeared alongside narratives of heroic actions of women agitators, adding to the shocking, propagandistic character of the publication. Readers also found straight talk about women's politics: "All the news of the Woman's movement will be found each week in *Votes for Women*," one advertisement claimed. The publication of what it called the "'hot' news of what had happened, was happening, or was planned to happen in the immediate future" was unusual for a weekly journal.[50] The suffrage press thus expanded the scope of the innovations of earlier women's periodicals that pioneered efforts to bring serious news to women readers. Readers came to expect news that put women in the center of current political debates while questioning Liberal government policies that failed to recognize women's demands. The paper also featured political commentary and letters to the editor columns to "give to its contributors a free hand, in order to state their view of the position of affairs."[51] *Votes for Women* thus drew in a particular kind of woman reader: bold and unapologetic in her support of the women's movement and eager to state her opinions.

A community of readers invested in the movement grew up alongside those who regularly participated in the activities of the Union. Articles asked readers to join as active members of the larger suffrage community by taking part in rallies and attending meetings. In the case of the June 1908 "Votes for Women" demonstration in Hyde Park, the paper coordinated transportation efforts for a small fee.[52] For those unable to participate in the activities of the Union, *Votes for Women* contained full reports of all major activities in both London and the provinces. Editorials allowed readers to "hear" the voices of leaders such as Christabel and Emmeline Pankhurst who challenged basic assumptions regarding women's public role. *Votes for Woman* had a powerful radicalizing potential for readers. As one subscriber remembered, "with regard to what led me into the Suffrage Movement, I may say that I was born a Suffragette, and that it was reading 'Votes for Women' which made me see that it was my duty to take an active part in the movement from the beginning."[53]

Following in the footsteps of its late nineteenth-century predecessors, the suffrage press developed a number of innovative journalistic practices. *Votes for Women* joined other suffrage papers in featuring exclusive news stories not covered in mainstream newspapers that chronicled injustices suffered by women. Emmeline Pethick-Lawrence's introduction of investigative reporting encouraged the mobilization of women readers. In one instance, Emmeline discovered a working-class mother who had had her children taken away from her on the charge of neglect. After probing further into the case, she discovered that the state had failed to call witnesses who would have testified "accurately" as to the childrens' condition. Emmeline mounted her own investigation and found that this "poor widowed mother" had locked her children in the basement to avoid the school officers and Poor Law authorities' taking her children away from her. Once the House of Commons heard Emmeline's story, they released the woman to the care of a "special commissioner" from *Votes for Women*. Emmeline investigated the case "not only in order that an individual wrong must be righted, but also to show that nothing less than a national pension to allow widows to bring up their children decently could stop the cruel suffering at present inflicted on mother and children alike."[54] *Votes for Women* drew attention to other similar police court cases, "urging widows' pensions as a solution to kindred problems." By marrying propaganda-style techniques with investigative reporting, Emmeline Pethick-Lawrence drew attention to the middle-class woman's role in leading reforms that would address the everyday concerns of women who had been denied their citizenship rights.

This method of reporting was a variation on the "human interest story" genre made popular by the daily press. Instead of focusing on the lives of powerful elites, newspapers engaged readers by telling often dramatic and formulaic tales of the common man. As LeMahieu has argued, these stories brought in readers by "underscoring the significance of commonplace events" and appealing to the "emotions of private life."[55] Suffrage papers took the human interest story a step beyond a prurient interest in private affairs. By focusing on the social injustice inflicted upon the lives of the "common woman," these stories implicitly linked women together in a female-centered vision of political reform. The heart-wrenching tales that portrayed all women as victims of an unfair system intended to stir readers to action. The solution was always the same: "Women's votes . . . would give the political urge necessary to carry this reform."[56] Dramatic news stories, mediated by *Votes for Women* reporters, drew readers together in a common concern for righting the wrongs of woman.

The paper thus fulfilled two equally important and related functions for readers. First, it illustrated the need for the vote through sensational stories and propaganda. It also provided readers with important information about the movement. The paper solicited writers who supported the ideals of the Pankhursts and would write polemical articles on women's rights as citizens. "I gather from your last book . . . that you are a Suffragette," read one appeal. "Will you write something for [*Votes for Women*]? The kind of sketch

I have in mind is an argument for the Vote, as your books are."[57] Even news articles used rhetoric that placed women at the center of political life. Editors carefully selected international and national news stories that highlighted women's unequal status. Unlike similar stories published in turn-of-the-century women's papers, however, these news items specifically highlighted the unfair treatment of women and always offered the franchise as a solution.

Votes for Women clearly spurred readers to take an activist role in British political life through protests and other propaganda efforts. Vandalism, and later political violence, became the favored mode of protest advocated in its pages. However, many more women read the paper than participated in militant action. These readers joined an imagined community of radicals who willingly rejected Victorian definitions of propriety in favor of public identities as activists for women's causes. Although never as numerous as those belonging to the constitutionalist wing of the movement, suffragettes maintained a powerful symbolic presence in prewar Britain.[58] Militancy on its own certainly did not win women the vote and, according to Martin Pugh, may actually have hindered its progress.[59] What it did do was to provide a highly visible arena for women to see other women acting in very public ways as a special interest group for the first time.

Votes for Women played a crucial role both in creating an informed community of women radicals and in directing their activities. "At the present time when the ordinary National Press is closing down its columns more and more against suffrage news, boycotting peaceful propaganda and distorting militant action, no one can understand aright what is going on who is not a regular reader of our paper."[60] Readers and contributors alike relied on the paper as the representative of a radical women's voice in prewar politics. *Votes for Women* grew in popularity during this period and became bolder in its presentation of revolutionary ideas, especially in its unrelenting criticism of the Liberal Party. The sensational stories and propagandistic rhetoric facilitated the creation of the image of the radicalized public woman willing to be seen fighting for the cause in the streets. Eventually, more radical newspapers such as the *Suffragette* would build on this imagining and threaten to upset the established political order by mobilizing women to act against the state.

As the WSPU gained increasing notoriety by using *Votes for Women* to orchestrate protests and mobilize activists, other suffrage organizations came to realize that effective media propaganda remained the bread and butter of women's political culture in Edwardian Britain.[61] A year and half after *Votes for Women* hit the newsstands, a quieter and more measured voice emerged in the alternative press. The "constitutionalist" National Union of Women's Suffrage Societies, with its Victorian sensibilities, rejected the high-profile militant propaganda of the WSPU and what it saw as the gross commercialism of *Votes for Women*. After the demise of *Women's Franchise,* members proposed to start "an organ in the first instance to cater for our own Members, to publish their news as well as to have other features."[62] The NUWSS decided to shelve the proposed two-page weekly called the *Coming Citizen* when "friends in Manchester" came up with the capital necessary for creating a general interest suffrage paper to serve as the voice of moderate suffragist women.[63] Run independently from the NUWSS, the new paper nevertheless maintained both financial and organizational connections. In 1909, members founded the Common Cause Publishing Company in Manchester as a limited liability company, with two thousand pounds in capital issued in one-pound shares, complete with a shareholder-elected executive committee and paid editorial staff.

The NUWSS wanted its *Common Cause* newspaper to represent "women's opinion" on a broad range of issues, including, but not limited to, suffrage. "A paper giving the Woman's point of view was necessary," they claimed; "we could have the man's point of view in all others." The political radicalism of *Votes for Women,* according to the NUWSS, failed to represent the opinions of the majority of "law-abiding women" who advocated for constitutional change. *Common Cause* evoked a wide-ranging mandate that included an internationalist feminist agenda: "We wished to have an organ of the feminist movement throughout the world. We had need of foreign news, and we believed there was room for such a journal of general information of the Women's movement at home and abroad."[64] Information, rather than sensational stories and dramatic political cartoons, dominated *Common Cause* in its claim to represent the broad interests of "womankind"(fig. 17).

In many ways, the paper appropriated the style of late nineteenth-century women's advocacy journals. Subtitled "The Organ of the Women's Movement for Reform," the paper had a two-column layout and segmented paragraphs that expressed its no-frills style. This simple early format included a plain masthead with only the name of the paper, date, and one-penny price printed at the top. Sixteen pages in length, the paper published both foreign and domestic weekly news alongside information about the societies related to the organization. Serious in its presentation of news and somber in appearance, the paper appealed to the educated woman reader who sought to have a voice in contemporary British politics. "Women do not ask for the vote mainly because they want to govern, but because they want not to be misgoverned," read one editorial. "Their lives are determined by the state,"

The Common Cause.

The Organ of the Women's Movement for Reform.

VOL. I. No. 28.   Registered as a Newspaper.   OCTOBER 21, 1909.   ONE PENNY.

The News of the Week.

The Contentment of the People.

One Mr. William Jones, M.P., has been making surely one of the strangest of all the strange speeches we are now hearing. "No Government in our history," says this representative of the male electors, "has been so sympathetic to the grievances of all classes of the community." Ah, but women do not constitute a class; they are in all classes, and therefore they can expect no sympathy for their grievances. "Leaders of all organisations that spell progress have been allowed free access not merely to the officers of the various departments of State, but straight to the Cabinet Ministers who direct those departments." We rub our eyes. Have we somehow missed it? When did the Prime Minister receive the women Suffragists? "The kernel of the Budget was social reform. It was not the swollen battalions or the big navies that made an empire, but the comfort, the happiness, and the contentment of its people." But the women are not content; there is, we know it, "passionate discontent" among them. Women are not "the people." We know they cannot be, for Mr. Jones went on to say "the only people who have complained are the very rich, the landed interests, the brewing interests," and this wonderful gentleman added the amazing remark: "Not a single deputation has gone from the workers of the community either to Mr. Asquith or to Mr. Lloyd-George." There is, we know, a portion of the retina called "the blind spot"; Mr. Jones, M.P., must surely contrive to turn that portion of his eye on to the patient women of the Freedom League, as he passes in and out of the gates at Westminster. Two weeks ago they completed an aggregate of 10,000 hours of waiting. This deputation has in truth "gone," but it has not yet "returned."

Deputation to Lord Pentland.

On October 13 a deputation from the Glasgow and West of Scotland Association for Women's Suffrage was received by Lord Pentland at the Central Hotel, Glasgow. Mrs. Hunter, who is the active hon. secretary, spoke of the great increase in the demand for the enfranchisement of women, and after submitting evidence of this, she urged Lord Pentland to use his influence with the Government to include Women's Suffrage in the promised Reform Bill, and to urge upon Mr. Asquith to receive a deputation from the association when he visited Glasgow to receive the freedom of the city. Councillor Pratt supported her, and declared that his work in local government led him to recognise the value of women in dealing with social problems.

Lord Pentland, in reply, complimented the deputation on the sincerity and moderation of their remarks and the singular appropriateness of all they had said. On behalf of himself and his colleagues he said they were very watchful of public opinion on this and other matters, and they were very much alive to all that was going on—he was afraid necessarily—in connection with that subject. He was not sure—he would if he could—but he was not sure that he could say anything at that moment to further the desires which they had laid before him. He was very willing to put himself at their disposal in order that they might meet and exchange their sentiments on the particular situation, and while he did not think he could undertake to carry out to the full the desires which they had expressed about the Reform Bill and the opportunity that Mr. Asquith might have when he came to the city, he said very willingly that he would convey both requests to Mr. Asquith and his colleagues and his own vivid impression of the earnestness with which they had put forward their views.

County Councillor Ballantyne, in thanking Lord Pentland for receiving the deputation, expressed the hope that no accidental circumstances would per-

Photo., Elliott and Fry.

MRS. HENRY FAWCETT, LL.D.

Figure 17. *Common Cause*, front page.

yet "the laws are not always what the women approve—they are by no means what they would be if the women's voices were heard."[65] Reviews of books and a sizable correspondence section helped engage readers and writers with relevant contemporary topics and ideas in an open forum.

The *Common Cause* represented the NUWSS's constitutionalist stance: favoring change through legitimate channels of government over the militant strategies and sensationalism represented in the pages of *Votes for Women.* Cultivating a cooperative and humanitarian rather than a separatist ideology,[66] the paper appealed to readers who supported the idea that women's special role as wives and mothers provided her with the legitimate authority to have a voice in social reform. The tone of the paper from the very beginning echoed that of the women's press of the late Victorian era:

> The women's demand for the vote is more than the mere demand to effect reformative legislation. . . . It is also the demand that the mother-half of humanity should be given its proper place: that the preserver and producer of life, the maker of men, should be as highly honoured as the destroyer of life, the maker of things: that the affectional [*sic*] woman-nature intent upon the conservation of the home and the race, should have its due representation beside the more extreme and appetitive male nature.[67]

Common Cause appropriated the ideology of motherhood and reform politics first articulated in the women's press during the New Woman debate in order to advance women's status as legitimate political subjects. The type of female activist cultivated in the pages of *Common Cause* remained the ultimate respectable radical: a public woman who claimed her place as a political actor on the basis of her private role as wife and mother.

The rhetoric of *Common Cause* embraced a moderate, "law-abiding" program to promote political change and addressed women as informed citizens while teaching them the "arts and customs of politics."[68] "We don't want to score; we don't want to conquer; we want to understand . . . believing in the ultimate victory of right, not might, we advocate peaceful penetration and constitutional action," proclaimed the inaugural number.[69] The editor sought to keep readers up to date on current events to counter popular perceptions that women remained "politically incompetent."[70] Mobilization would come through the education of potential women activists, the public, and, most important, elected officials. Although claiming nonparty status, the paper supported individual members of the Liberal Party, despite the government's overall poor support of women's suffrage, and expressed frustration over WSPU efforts to break up political meetings. Unlike the WSPU with its pursuit of an "anti-Liberal election policy," the NUWSS supported whichever candidate best stood behind the issue of women's suffrage.[71] Thus, the paper provided suffragists interested in working within the boundaries of the party system with a political voice, despite their disenfranchised status.

Common Cause cultivated a community of readers seeking an alternative to both the more radical *Votes for Women* and the mainstream press in general. The paper's first editor, Helena Swanick,[72] like Emmeline Pethick-Lawrence, was introduced to the suffrage movement after reading about Christabel Pankhurst's and Annie Kenney's protest at the 1905 Liberal Party meeting. Swanick, a Girton graduate and frequent contributor to the *Manchester Guardian,* however, objected to WSPU methods and decided to join the constitutionalist movement rather than the militants. As editor, she created a successful advocacy medium for women who shared the organizations' ideals. The title "Common Cause," according to Swanick, linked women's cause with man's struggle for the first time: "The bother with the mass of the Press of the country is that it does not recognize that human questions like war, or the birth-rate, or tariffs, or a miners' eight-hour day, have quite as much to do with women as with men." Women's issues were lost in a web of commercial interests, she claimed, and "ultra-mannish papers . . . scarcely print anything rational about women, palming off on them, as women's interests, the fashion drawings and chatter which are the recognized way of promoting commercial interests of men."[73] *Common Cause,* she pledged, would offer women the opportunity to engage in rational public discourse. In the face of an increasingly homogenized commercial press culture, Swanick shaped the suffrage newspaper into an important site of both social and political criticism.

For Swanick, the serious woman reader deserved a newspaper that did not pander to the demands of Britain's emergent commercial media culture. *Common Cause* thus, in some ways, looked backward to its nineteenth-century predecessors to provide a model of an informative paper for and by women that flatly rejected the sensationalism of *Votes for Women* in favor of factual reports and evenhanded editorials. As the editor of a paper for "educated women" that included all classes "educated in the ways of life and humanity," Swanick refused to make the paper a "pale copy" of its counterpart published by the WSPU, who ran what some referred to as "the popular paper." "I saw no paper doing what I wanted the *Common Cause* to do," Swanick claimed, "and it seemed to me far better to give the paper a character of its own than to adopt processes by which other papers with other ideals succeeded." Swanick realized the difficulty of her stance: "A newspaper cannot have it all ways, and if it eschews sensationalism it will have to wait for success. Such success has seemed to me worth waiting for."[74]

The demands of the marketplace soon made Swanick rethink her decision to "eschew" the sensationalism of modern commercial journalism. The nineteenth-century model of the small-scale, editor-supported, specialized advocacy paper had given way to a more professionalized media culture that placed greater financial and creative demands on papers and their editors. Financial loses led to heavy subsidies during the first year from the NUWSS, who urged members to support the paper: "It is a valuable asset of our work, but in so far as it is not made to pay its way, the cost of maintaining it must come on to the funds at Headquarter, and this necessarily implies that less money will be available for organization and political work throughout the country."[75] The NUWSS issued two thousand additional new company shares at one pound each during the summer of 1910 and continued to subsidize the paper in varying degrees. Members also supported *Common Cause* but insisted that the Company find a way to support it through sales and advertising revenue.[76]

Ever conscious of its role as an advocacy newspaper for and by women, *Common Cause* continued to approach the demands of the market with caution through the use of modest presentation strategies. To prevent *Common Cause* from draining the NUWSS's limited resources, Swanick solicited more advertisers, touting the paper as "an excellent advertising medium" for products targeted at women. Illustrated ads placed prominently together on one page replaced more sober copy within six months of the first issue. Swanick, however, pledged that *Common Cause* would not completely embrace modern advertising practice. When one advertiser suggested that if he ran ads for clothing and cosmetics, she might "do something to help us" by pushing the products in the editorials of the paper, she flatly turned him down. Unlike *Votes for Women*, where a strong tie developed between advertisers who stocked suffrage paraphernalia and the paper, *Common Cause* distanced itself from endorsing particular goods and services and instead solicited advertisers who provided "food for the body or the mind."[77]

In the midst of this retooling, some at the NUWSS began to criticize Swanick's modest changes as having gone too far. Those members on the board of the Common Cause Publishing Company, demanded both that *Common Cause* achieve the high circulation of *Votes for Women* while maintaining their paper as a respectable news medium untainted by sensationalism that focused on the distribution of information on and about women's social status and political activities. Members loudly protested when Swanick altered this mandate in order to make the paper more attractive to a wider audience of women readers.

Many in the NUWSS resisted Swanick's modest attempts to update the paper in terms of its format and content, favoring a more nineteenth-century newssheet style for the paper. Soliciting advertisers did not sit well with some. As Swanick recalled:

> We used to derive a considerable income from drapers' and milliners' advertisements . . . a delegate to one of our Council meetings averred that, if we would only abandon these advertisements she was "quite sure" the increase in our circulation would more than make good our loss. When I asked her whether she would guarantee an extra sale of 5,000 copies for every page of advertisement scrapped . . . she was staggered. . . . If only she had been as free with her money as with her advice![78]

Swanick also came head to head with the committee regarding editorial content: "The *Common Cause* was excessively ballasted with unreadable matter, reports of societies, committee and council meetings, appeals for money and the like."[79] Unlike *Votes for Women*, which stirred up publicity through reporting on controversial subjects in every issue, *Common Cause* remained committed to its constitutionalist principles, not wanting to keep "score" or "conquer" its rivals.[80] By contrast, the militants often criticized the NUWSS in their pages. They also disrupted peaceful prosuffrage protests, effectively undercutting many of the constitutionalists' propaganda efforts. For Swanick, the NUWSS's refusal to use the paper to publicly criticize even the most extreme acts of their militant counterparts affected both the prestige and popularity of the constitutionalist cause.[81]

The committee eventually came to understand that if *Common Cause* wanted to increase circulation and become self-supporting, it had to provide readers with light and interesting reading alongside political reporting.[82] Although sensationalist reporting never found its way into the paper, by the time Swanick left in 1912, *Common Cause* had begun to make a successful transition from a sober-looking informational advocacy newssheet into one that published photographs, excerpts from famous women novelists, and political cartoons. According to NUWSS statistics, circulation grew to as many as twenty-three thousand copies per week.[83] By giving readers more variety, entertaining features, and serious news, the paper transformed itself into an effective advocacy news medium capable of reaching a wide audience of potential political activists. *Common Cause* could never claim status as "the popular paper," a moniker claimed by *Votes for Women*. However, it did gain prominence through its own measured and careful reporting of women's politics and news, emerging as one of the most important women's newspapers of the Edwardian era.

Votes for Women and *Common Cause* contributed to the expansion of a gender-based political culture by casting women as public actors, whether militant or constitutionalist, while encouraging them to have a voice in political affairs. The reliance on propaganda and mass marketing techniques increased not only the circulation but also the relevance of women's newspapers as an alternative medium for the exchange of diverse ideas about women's status in Britain. Whether through the sensationalist reporting of *Votes for Women* or the more tempered analysis of the *Common Cause,* suffrage newspapers sent a powerful message to readers: activism required engagement with print culture to both acquire knowledge and affect change. The suffrage press, through its manipulation of modern print media practices, created a new type of idealized female activist who claimed a place for herself as a legitimate participant in the public sphere.

Selling the *Vote*

Women's entry into Edwardian political culture found its clearest articulation in the rise of a diverse suffrage culture. Understanding how different suffrage organizations worked in tandem, if not in cooperation, to shape public opinion and parliamentary decision-making has emerged as part of a revisionist interpretation of the movement.[84] The suffrage culture that developed during this period relied on its own press for publicity and communication. In addition to the relatively popular and well-funded *Votes for Women* and *Common Cause,* a number of smaller periodicals entered the market to support their associated organizations. These included Sylvia Pankhurst's *Woman's Dreadnought* (1914–24), a socialist paper targeted at working class women of the East End; the *Independent Suffragette* (1916–18), the organ of an offshoot of the WSPU; the *Liberal Women's Review* (1914), which protested the Liberal government's position on suffrage; the *Church League for Women's Suffrage* (1912–17), published for prosuffrage Church of England members, and the *Catholic Suffragist* (1915–18); the organ of the Catholic Women's Suffrage society; and at least a dozen others. These papers ranged from long-running newspapers to multiple-issue journals and represented an array of opinions on how to win the franchise and what benefits it would bring to women and the nation. Smaller organizations fed on the publicity generated by the propaganda of the WSPU and NUWSS that kept the issue of suffrage before the public. Together they maintained suffrage as a live political issue. As the following story of the small-circulation but long-running *Vote* newspaper demonstrates, suffrage journalism challenged female activists to see themselves as participants in liberal reform politics.

Published by the Women's Freedom League, the *Vote* represented the views of a militant group founded on democratic principles that had split from the more autocratic WSPU in September 1907. After the failure of *Women's Franchise,* the WFL used its limited funds to start a circular called the *Women's Freedom League Temporary News Sheet* (1909), similar in scope to the NUWSS's *Coming Citizen.* Without its own public voice, however, the WFL realized that its participation in suffrage debates would be severely limited. In August 1909 they began the Minerva Publishing Company as a limited liability company, hoping to raise two thousand pounds of capital to publish the *Vote.* With only 365 pounds having been raised through share sales, one member remarked: "Many felt that this position was an impossible one, and indeed we all considered it bad finance, but it was an absolute necessity to the work of the Women's Freedom League, indeed to its very existence, to have this paper."[85] Though a well-respected periodical noted for its stand on women's employment, education, legal reform, and prostitution, the *Vote* never achieved the circulation of *Common Cause* or *Votes for Women.* The paper averaged two thousand copies weekly, a considerable number of which the WFL required member branches to purchase. Sober in both content and appearance, the paper represented a "constitutionalist militant" perspective that often placed it politically between the more radical WSPU and the conservative-minded NUWSS (fig. 18).[86]

Smaller papers like the *Vote* thrived, in part, by integrating nineteenth-century business models with the realities of the new marketplace. The paper survived for the next twenty years through creative management strategies and the help of individual members. Minerva solicited printing orders from outside of the WFL to subsidize the *Vote.* Vertically integrating the publishing and production of the paper through the Company, however, failed to make the *Vote* self-supporting, forcing Dr. Elizabeth Knight to subsidize the paper. As women's newssheet editors had discovered, patronage enabled them to concentrate on propaganda efforts rather than having to rely on advertisers and issue sales for funding.[87]

The *Vote* asked readers to help place the issue of granting women the franchise before the public, claiming that "there is no subject of greater national importance."[88] The League believed in its "special duty" to provide a

THE VOTE

FOR WOMEN'S FREEDOM.

EDITED BY CICELY HAMILTON AND MARION HOLMES.

The Organ of the Women's Freedom League.

No. 1—PRELIMINARY. WEDNESDAY, SEPTEMBER 8, 1909. [REGISTERED AT THE GENERAL POST OFFICE AS A NEWSPAPER.] ONE PENNY.

Contents.

Notice to Subscribers and Contributors.

Articles containing information on the subject of Women's Suffrage should be addressed to the Editor, who will return those not considered suitable as soon as possible if a stamped addressed envelope is sent with the MS. As the paper is on a voluntary basis, and all profits go to help the cause, no payments are made for contributions.

The General Editor gives the widest possible latitude to each of the Societies represented in this Paper, and is only responsible for unsigned matter occurring in the pages devoted to general items.

THE BUDGET.—Women should note that September 29th is the last day for claiming any benefit or relief offered by it.

INCOME-TAX RETURNS are prepared, APPEALS conducted, and OVER-PAID TAX recovered by Mrs. E. AYRES PURDIE, A.L.A.A., Certified Accountant, the present the only woman who is entitled, under the Revenue Act of 1903, to appear on behalf of a Client before the Special Commissioners of Income-Tax

CRAVEN HOUSE, KINGSWAY, W.C.

Proposed New Paper.

THERE would appear to be an opening for a weekly paper appealing primarily to the increasing class of educated women who have intellectual, industrial, or public interests. The number of such women grows daily larger. 'The Englishwoman's Year-Book,' published last year, included institutions and societies of various kinds, the number of which (not counting "refuges" and "homes") amounted to . It may fairly be reckoned that each of these institutions or societies represents the co-operation of at least three women. Probably every one of these women, besides a good many others unconnected with any of these institutions are interested in many topics quite untouched by the average "woman's paper," and dealt with only very inadequately by any existing review or magazine. A reading public is thus constituted which, no doubt, would never be vast—never comparable in numbers with the public catered for by *Tit-Bits* or by the *Strand Magazine*—but which, on the other hand, would probably be very steady. The aim should be to create a review which no member of that public would willingly be without.

The proprietor of *Women's Franchise*, forseeing from the beginning that his enterprize was but a first step that would probably need to be followed by other steps, several months ago registered the title *The Woman Citizen*. It is now proposed to issue under that title a greatly enlarged and extended paper. Like *Women's Franchise*, the new paper will consider the right to a vote as occupying the first place in the interests of *The Woman Citizen*, and Suffrage topics will therefore receive special attention.

Although the paper will be in no sense a party organ, general tone will be distinctly progressive. A paper that should remain neutral upon vital social questions, could neither be very valuable nor very interesting.

The general aim will be to fill in the gaps left on the one hand by the so-called "women's papers," and on the other by the daily newspapers. In the former attention is mainly directed towards the frivolous, personal and material aspects of life : dress, amusements, society gossip, cookery, &c.; in the latter the interests of women are dealt with either on an inadequate scale or not at all.

Figure 18. The *Vote*, front page.

fresh perspective on the question of women's franchise while publicizing the movement and drawing in converts: "We call our organ the *Vote* because we hope and believe that through its pages the public . . . will come to understand what the Parliamentary Franchise means to us women. . . . To us the vote is not a mere shibboleth, a party cry. It is a thing of deep significance. In every issue of our paper different sides of this will be brought forward."[89] The *Vote* served the political ideals of the members of the league while influencing public opinion on the importance of women's suffrage.

In representing the constitutional militant point of view, the paper served those women who were unsatisfied with the other major suffrage societies.[90] "We are convinced the *Vote* will fill a long-felt want" claimed the editor, who maintained that its "nonparty" status would appeal to politically minded women alienated by the rhetoric and tactics of either the constitutionalists or the militants.[91] Though suffrage papers were unified in their desire to win women the vote, each one pushed particularized agendas that often transcended the larger issue of the vote. The *Vote* drew working-class and lower-middle-class readers into its ranks by pushing a decidedly socialist viewpoint and crusading for the poor. This commitment included reporting on issues such as child welfare and lobbying for the hiring of women police. The paper dedicated four extra pages in one issue, for example, to chronicling "the facts concerning the cruel outrages on little children." Features such as the "Women in Industry" column championed the cause of the downtrodden, in Britain and the wider world. To keep readers abreast of major social and economic issues, the paper gave summaries of current events as they related to women's role in the nation. By focusing on issues that received limited coverage in other papers, the *Vote* contributed to the diversity of opinions that surrounded the suffrage issue.

A sensitivity to class issues as they related to gender shaped the paper throughout its publication. Charlotte Despard, the paper's first editor and leader of the WFL, was a dedicated socialist and supporter of the Labour Party who tirelessly promoted the *Vote* as a voice for women who believed in militancy but rejected the autocratic character of WSPU.[92] Born into privilege, she married Maximilian Despard, a wealthy businessman with a radical sensibility. After her husband's death in 1890, she retreated to a simple manner of living, wearing her widow's mantilla and "sensible" dress during the rest of her life. Despard used her wealth and status to help the poor, living for many years in Battersea. For many, she represented a heroic figure who had learned the language of sacrifice. Her vision, in many ways, shaped the direction of the paper. Working-class women who had left the WSPU, such as Hannah Mitchell, found themselves drawn to the WFL because of Despard's attempts to defend the interests of poor and working-class members to the middle-class leadership of the organization.[93] For example, when the newspaper committee proposed to raise the price of the *Vote* from one penny to two, Despard supported protests from working-class members and convinced leaders to keep the price low for their benefit.[94]

Although the *Vote* could not compete with the popular *Votes for Women* or the more sober but still well-known *Common Cause,* the paper provided an important alternative socialist vision of female activism for its readers. Together these papers created a complex identity for the female activist that resists easy categorization as either "rebellious" or "law-abiding." In the case of the *Vote,* reader dedication remained crucial in determining its success in pushing its vision of political activism in the face of what one member called the paper's "miserable circulation." Members took over distribution from apathetic newsagents by buying extra copies for local reading rooms, women's college common rooms, and free libraries throughout Britain. Some made it habit to leave their already read copies on trains and buses for other potential readers. The *Vote,* thanks to the efforts of members, found itself on the doorsteps of MPs and other politicians. The *Vote* even traveled with members on vacation who distributed it abroad. The difficulties with circulation and competition with other papers helped make the *Vote* into a rallying point for members, whose dedication to the paper created a sense of unity and purpose. Through their efforts, the *Vote* emerged as a public voice for and by women who shared its particular vision of the direction of the suffrage movement.

Taking Suffrage News to the Streets

As the example of the *Vote* suggests, despite its growing professionalism and the employment of popular press techniques, the women's press remained a grassroots medium that relied heavily on the support of volunteers for its success. This brand of "activist membership" historically had thrived in other reform movements that enlisted members to promote their particular agendas to the British public. Publishing a periodical provided one important means of creating connections between members and the public while engaging them in the happenings of the organization. During this period, for example, the British Women's Temperance Association's *Wings* (1892–1925) and the Social Purity Alliance and the Moral Reform Union's *Pioneer* (1886–1918) joined other groups that included socialist and working-class organizations, along with numerous religious and ethnic societies, in publishing their own papers through member support.[95]

Asking members to participate in the production and distribution of such publications often proved a highly effective strategy in cementing links within reform movements. As Brian Harrison has argued, selling papers gave members "something worthwhile to do," while allowing the rank and file to "let off steam" over "the slow pace of legislative change" that plagued political movements.[96] Volunteering to sell papers, however, provided more than a safety valve for pent-up frustration. In the case of the suffrage press, this activity helped create a sense of community and common purpose among a new generation of female political activists who volunteered to sell papers in the streets, at meetings, and abroad. The spectacle of selling papers on the street while creating a vehicle for community building also helped produce a modern identity for the female reformer that was marked by her ambiguous relationship to public space.

Suffrage organizations drew upon a British radical political tradition that had long utilized the town center for speeches and propaganda distribution. Sylvia Pankhurst described the WSPU's modern expression of this political idiom:

> Our members at once volunteered to sell [*Votes for Women*] in the streets and were soon turning themselves into sandwich women and parading about with its contents [hanging] from their shoulders, riding, on horseback through Piccadilly with its posters hanging from the saddle, selling it from . . . buses and carriages, canvassing for subscribers and advertisers for it and evolving a hundred and one devices to increase its sale. As a result of these efforts both its size and circulation increased rapidly.[97]

Votes for Women soon deployed a sizable brigade of sellers throughout Britain via the WSPU's Women's Press office.[98] "Suffragette buses" paraded through the streets of London on publication day with signs and "megahorns" announcing that week's lead news story and leaving sellers off at pitches throughout the city. This volunteer force played a central role in getting the latest suffrage news out to sympathizers and detractors: "On rivers, lochs, on sea beaches, wherever holiday crowds foregathered, up would go a little banner and a girlish figure in holiday garb would rise and . . . offer copies of the paper, *Votes for Women,* for sale, taking names and addresses from those who wished to hear more about the movement."[99] It also served to create a visible public role for the female activist by granting her an invaluable role as a propagandist for the movement.

Other suffrage organizations followed the WSPU in using street selling to push the boundaries of acceptable public behavior for women by casting it as a duty performed by women members. After the failure of less energetic circulation schemes, the NUWSS encouraged members to form the "Common Cause selling Corps" to sell the paper on the street.[100] Those who had been inactive in the organization's campaigns were urged to view joining

the corps as "an opportunity for service": "Members of the NU are beginning to realize the great importance of street selling and sellers are coming
forward well; but of course we want a very great many more so as to have
the NU colors and the Common Cause in all parts of London. For this will
bring home the movement to people the importance of the movement in
a way that nothing else can."[101] Such appeals strongly influenced members.
Some women went against their parents' wishes that they not appear in public hawking suffrage propaganda, volunteering to sell papers in Hyde Park
on Sundays.[102] Like their counterparts in the WSPU, the NUWSS initiated
competitions and gave awards to those members and branches who sold the
most papers. The corps sellers did not disappoint. Goals were placed as high
as five thousand copies for some issues by the *Common Cause* circulation
manager and accounted for a large percentage of total sales.[103] Street selling
thus proved the most effective means of both mobilizing an activist mentality
among members and spreading propaganda.

Street selling soon developed as the lifeblood of the WFL's propaganda effort. Without it, they claimed, it would be impossible to "spread our news and
our information and educate public opinion. . . . That is why the *Vote* is kept
running; if it does not reach the public and does not educate, then there is no
need to keep it going."[104] Despard inspired members to sell "their" paper by
claiming that "in every town where we have a branch there should be a brigade
of sellers, there should be amongst the Branches . . . a friendly competition as
to which can sell the greatest number of copies."[105] This dedicated volunteer
force played a particularly important role for smaller papers such as the *Vote:*
"We want heaps more volunteers to sell the *Vote* at public meetings. . . . We
cannot spend money on advertising."[106] *Vote* sellers were rewarded for their
service by not having any other job in order that they might concentrate on
the task of selling as many copies of the paper as possible.

To encourage member activism, the WFL created a bold new street-selling unit called the "Vote Brigade" in 1913. The organization's handbook,
"Ye Doomsday Book of Ye 'Vote' Brigade" codified street-selling rules while
creating a legitimate arena for women's political activity. The booklet praised
"Rebel Women" of the "Vote Brigade" for "ventur[ing] out in all weather
and at all hours, without profit or gain except the profit accorded to all those
who have been the instruments of showing the Sacred Flame of Freedom
to a Fellow and the Captain of Ye Vote Brigade."[107] They held the first rally
at WFL headquarters, where leaders issued guidelines for when and where
members would sell all unsold copies of the *Vote* to "the few who posses
freedom of thought and some little brain." Branches encouraged members

to sell in their own neighborhoods so that "even if the paper did not sell it would be always seen everywhere. And up and down the country we would be confronted by the *Vote* [*sic*]."[108] This new brigade offered prize competitions for shares in Minerva and organized "selling rallies" and poster parades to help make the paper more visible, particularly in London. Through serving on street-selling brigades, women willingly made their private commitment to suffrage public by taking to the streets to support their paper.

Through the use of such distribution techniques, suffrage newspaper commanded presence as a well-recognized voice of the women's movement. The British public also "read" the *Vote, Votes for Women,* and *Common Cause* on sandwich boards, posters, and advertisements paraded by members on the streets whether they bought the paper or not.[109] This visibility particularly helped papers with smaller readership, such as the *Vote.* As Andro Linklater has argued, the *Vote* came to represent "woman's point of view": the Commons quoted from its pages and mainstream journalists used it as a source for information on topics related to women. Prominent Tories, Irish Republicans, and MPs from the Labor and Liberal parties all had praise for the *Vote.*[110] By taking their message to the streets, members of the WFL demonstrated that a publication with a small circulation could command a voice in politics by advertising the issues that it determined were central to women's interests. These included agitation for women police, socialist politics, and the representation of the demands of Irish women. The use of popular journalistic techniques to promote these issues led to an increased visibility to the suffrage cause in general. In their own particularity, these papers facilitated the growth of a diverse extraparliamentary suffrage culture.

The sale of suffrage newspapers on the streets of major urban centers thus served a dual role: it boosted the actual sale of papers while giving the movement increased visibility through encouraging women's public service. Street selling, the NUWSS leadership convinced its members, would help "to build up a really important piece of propaganda work, one that appeals to people who are not reached by the more direct methods of meetings and speeches."[111] Hired hands not only failed to present a "respectable" image to the public but also did not sell enough papers, often dumping extra copies rather than bringing them back at the end of the day. Men hired to carry sandwich boards would often sit down on the job. "We were appalled to find that men and boys were alike in their desire to get something for nothing," remarked Maude Royden, a former seller and editor of the *Common Cause.* "When we got over the shock, we laughed and did the work ourselves."[112]

Women who faithfully sold the paper continually confronted skeptics, a move that forced them to defend their stance in public. Royden described the job of the street saleswoman: "Carrying a sandwich-board is really a vile job. You cease to feel human when you do it for long. Giving handbills is not much fun either. Selling a newspaper is no joke." Royden, however, recognized the importance of this duty and praised those who carried it out: "There is a great deal to be said for doing a job which you have decided must be done. This was the great strength of the Women's Suffrage movement as I knew it."[113] Such hands-on participation personally invested members in the cause by showing their willingness to put fears aside and face potentially uncomfortable and even dangerous situations. For example, the risk of being arrested for obstruction deterred women from selling propaganda on city sidewalks, forcing suffrage advocates to walk in the street while carrying signs and hawking their papers. The willingness to suffer humiliation revealed the intense dedication that paper selling inspired among members who wanted to make their organization's voice heard.

To mediate the potential dangers faced by street sellers, the suffrage press tightly regulated the image of the political-public woman that their papers created. The WFL and the NUWSS, in particular, struggled with the issue of respectability by enforcing strict dress codes and producing positive images of suffrage advocates in their pages. In a possibly not-so-subtle jibe at the more ostentatious WSPU, the WFL asked members not make spectacles of themselves by overdoing their advertisement of the union: "Brigaders [sic] are requested not to wear short green skirts, white socks, and yellow boots, nor to indulge in the extremes of fashion such as wearing the hat hanging on one ear with a skirt slit up back and front and at the sides, even if the words 'The Vote' are printed in yellow on a green underskirt."[114] *Common Cause* newspaper stewards stressed uniformity and neatness in appearance for their sellers. Mediating a respectable image for women sellers developed as a key strategy in melding the image of the public woman with that of private citizen.

Through their protest activities and especially through the sale of suffrage literature, middle-class women claimed a political presence on the streets almost overnight. Such public "performances," as Barbara Green has called them, helped blur the lines between public action and private duty.[115] The romantic image of the street seller who easily navigated public space as a private citizen presented in suffrage papers often failed to meet up with harsh realities of street selling and demonstrated the limitation of what Judith Walkowitz has called women's "urban freedom."[116] The image of the self-sacrificing activist had been formulated ideologically through the pages of the women's press and practically through her experience on the street. In the articulation of this contested identity, some women came to embrace the status of political activist, a role traditionally considered outside of the purview of respectable female behavior.

This new form of women's protest created a special problem for the British government. Masculine notions of citizenship embedded in the Ancient Constitution and reified in modern British political life largely had determined Liberal responses to "unwomanly" political protests. Suffrage advocates engaged in what Jon Lawrence has called a "politics of disruption" that characterized prewar British political culture and experienced constant humiliation and physical injury at the hands of police for actions ranging from picketing to vandalism.[117] The government continued to work out what constituted an appropriate expression of dissent by these newly made women rebels. Through the use of press propaganda, suffragists attempted to establish the legitimacy of women's political action by creating a doctrine of inclusion based on the freeborn rights of English *women*. Edwardian Britons were witnessing the coming of age of the modern female political subject who drew on a radical tradition of street politics to bolster her citizenship claims. In the process, traditional gender hierarchies remained a crucial factor in determining both government policy and public reaction to militant protests that claimed a kinship with other male-run British radical movements.

Politics, Publicity, and the State:
The Case of the *Suffragette* Newspaper

"Raided!" read the headline of the new and extreme radical voice of the WSPU, the *Suffragette,* on May 2, 1913.[118] The British government had kept a close watch on this voice of militant suffragism for several months before they took their final dramatic action to stop its publication. Prior to raiding its offices, the government had unsuccessfully tried a number of tactics to curb the militant suffragette protests. Searching the offices of the WSPU and smashing the type of a forthcoming issue represented the final step in the state's campaign to put a stop to the thousands of pounds of damage to public and private property that they claimed the *Suffragette* persuaded its readers to commit. Why the government decided to prosecute the *Suffragette* for inciting these crimes emerged as part of a battle over establishing the boundaries of what constituted legitimate political discourse. Radical suffrage papers emerged as an incendiary political medium that linked women's protests in what Ian Fletcher has called a "chain of equivalence" with a larger culture of prewar political dissent that challenged the credibility of the Liberal government's commitment to democratic reform.[119] Over the course of events connected with the prosecution of the *Suffragette,* the issue of press freedom took center stage in justifying the call for political inclusion by female activists whose militant protests represented a real and symbolic threat to public order.

From the beginning, suffrage advocates used the rhetoric of the "freedom of the press" to stake their citizenship claims. Having its roots in both liberal thought and radical political culture, journalists had argued for the liberty of printers to publish material critical of the establishment in political tracts, the courts, and the streets since the inception of the periodical press.[120] By the time of the *Suffragette* controversy, the government had not taken the dramatic action of closing down a newspaper for over seventy years. Eliminating the "taxes on knowledge" in the 1850s paved the way for a free press that remained largely unregulated during the second half of the nineteenth century. The government seemed to have solved the problem of the incendiary journalist by expanding the boundaries of acceptable political discourse. Communist, socialist, and other radical newspapers went virtually untouched by government regulation during this period and enjoyed relative autonomy. The underground radical journals of the beginning of the century gave way to the reformist advocacy journals of the second half of the nineteenth and early twentieth centuries.

The women's press had never engaged in a "politics of disruption" before the advent of suffrage militancy. In the year preceding the trial of the *Suffragette,* the WSPU stepped up its campaign against the Liberal government in the name of votes for women. The philosophy of political violence had its roots in the radical political culture of the 1830s, when men had justified the destruction of public and private property to protest their disenfranchisement.[121] "The argument of the stone, that time-honoured political weapon, is the argument I am going to use!" declared Emmeline Pankhurst to a group of cheering supporters in 1912.[122] Antisuffragists refused to recognize women's political demands on the basis of the English radical tradition. When comparing suffrage campaigns with those that preceded the nineteenth-century Reform Bills, one MP asserted: "In the case of the Suffrage demand, there has not been the kind of popular sentimental uprising which accounted for the burning of the Nottingham Castle in 1832 or the breaking down of Hyde Park railing in 1867. There has been no great ebullition of popular feeling."[123]

To explain the movement's support, another claimed that "large numbers of emotional females" acted under the influence of propaganda rather than from any justifiable political position.[124] Opponents used this argument to diminish the legitimacy of women's citizenship claims by discrediting them as legitimate political actors. Protests perpetrated by women on women's behalf thus fell outside of the realm of a "traditional popular politics" that posited a masculine model of political action. These "unwomanly" and "unladylike" demands for citizenship prompted violent and highly sexualized responses that called into question women's public presence. As ardent antisuffragists reportedly shouted to suffragette marchers, "You ought to be beaten and dragged round Trafalgar Square by the hair of your head."[125]

Despite widespread critiques of militancy, the WSPU continued to use the press to promote violence. On March 5, 1912, the government undertook its first raid of the WSPU and *Votes for Women,* confiscating documents and wielding arrest warrants for those in charge. The police "ransacked" the office "in a determined effort to secure evidence of conspiracy," claimed Emmeline Pankhurst upon her arrest. "They went through every desk, file, and cabinet, taking away with them two cab loads of books and papers," including minute books, receipts, and many personal items.[126] Christabel Pankhurst, a key figure in the Union, however, evaded capture and fled to Paris. Government officials searched for Christabel while trying to stop *Votes for Women* from circulating in Britain by intimidating printers into censoring large sections of the paper.

In Paris, Christabel continued to run the WSPU and direct *Votes for Women* from afar. A letter written to acting London editor Evelyn Sharp revealed how much militancy relied on media spectacle for its strength. "The government never strikes at us without strengthening us," claimed Christabel, who encouraged the publicity surrounding her escape. "I understand that Mr. Bodkin [the prosecutor] has been quoting from our militant utterances—mine especially. What more do we want at present! . . . In writing my things, I shall be guided by the cards which the enemy play [*sic*] in the trial. . . . I feel the tide is turning in our favor now that we are getting out of the stormy atmosphere that is always created by new militant developments." According to Christabel their newspaper would best further the Union's goals: "it is for the time being . . . possible to produce a really militant paper without giving the enemy any handle which he can seize."[127]

Leaders of the WSPU used the trial that followed this first raid as an opportunity to link militancy to oppositional politics. According to Cheryl Jorgensen-Earp, Emmeline Pankhurst argued that militants should be seen "not as criminals but as political activists" who, like their male radical pre-decessors, were "willing to suffer for the cause of political reform."[128] The WSPU used its propaganda machine to capitalize on publicity offered by the trial. Supporters read the following response to the conspiracy charges against their leaders: "the real issue before the Court was the right of the disenfran-chised to employ, upon the total failure of peaceful methods, methods of militancy involving defiance of the law."[129] The jury, although it convicted the defendants, called for the government to "exercise the utmost clemency and leniency," while taking "into consideration the undoubtedly pure motives which underlie the agitation that has led to this trouble."[130] In casting suf-fragettes as political actors with a radical pedigree, the WSPU cast militancy as an extreme though legitimate time-tested mode of dissent.

Christabel represented herself as a "political exile" to justify the publication of the "really militant paper" that she had imagined earlier. The split of the moderate wing of the militant movement from the Pankhursts during this same period provided the practical motivation for starting the *Suffragette*. Completely unrestrained in its politics, the new paper took risks that the more moderate *Votes for Women* would not. In January 1913, the *Suffragette* promoted a heightened campaign centered on the destruction of public and private property. Suffragettes destroyed a jewel case at the Tower of London, cut telephone and telegraph wires between London and Glasgow, burned an orchid house at Kew Gardens, smashed windows, set railway carriages on fire, and burned prosuffrage slogans onto putting greens.[131] By April 1913, no end was in sight to the violence, making the *Suffragette* newspaper a target of prosecution by the Liberal government. One official recommended the following course of action: "I would suggest for your consideration whether the time has not come for the publishers and printers of this paper, and for the Union, to be prosecuted for illegal conspiracy."[132]

The decision to close down the information center of a political movement challenged the principle of a free, unfettered press that had existed in practice since the beginning of the second half of the nineteenth century. The weekly paper had done very well in the months preceding the April raid, expanding its copy to fill twenty pages and significantly increasing the number of adver-tisements.[133] The *Manchester Guardian* reported the government's position: "That organ must be put a stop to as a continued danger to society in dissemi-nating literature of that kind and writings of that kind."[134] During the raid, police arrested the assistant editor, general secretary and manager, financial secretary, business manager, and advertisement editor. They searched and then released the other women present in the office at the time. Meanwhile, detectives surprised the printers of the *Suffragette* and "seized all the copy that was being set up for that day's issue." Only Christabel's lead article was spared, as it had not yet arrived at the printers.

In open defiance, the paper was printed anyway, with the banner headline "Raided!" printed across the top in an attenuated form, and according to one source, it "enjoyed a particularly brisk sale."[135] The temporary editorial staff sent a copy of the contraband paper to the Home Office, with the following handwritten note addressed to the secretary:

In spite of being RAIDED!! We openly publish our paper and defy you and your so called English government, whom are [not fit] to hold the [title] of [men]. Please show this to all your colleagues with the complements of the WSP Union [who will] never be suppressed or [subject] to slavery. Free speech is *not* allowed but public opinion cannot be squashed by the police.[136]

Frustrated with the results of the raid, the government started a campaign of harassment against printers who defied orders from the Home Office not to print the *Suffragette*. The government made their strategy clear:

Difficult as it may be to inflict punishment on the women who are conducting the movement, the same considerations do not apply to the printers. . . . It should be made clear that even if the full sentences imposed on all the women cannot be carried out, those who, for their own profit, assist them in their campaign are also liable to punishment and will in fact be punished. If printers were deterred from publishing incitements to violence, the movement itself would be hampered not a little.[137]

Using a broad definition of "incitement to commit a crime," police arrested printer after printer on conspiracy charges for publishing the *Suffragette* and even alerted custom authorities to watch for copies coming in from abroad that might include "inflammatory material." Potential printers received the official warning: "If there is any printer who can be found after this warning to print and publish the literature of these women associated with the WSPU, he might find himself in a very awkward position as an 'aider and abettor' of these persons in carrying out their objects."[138]

These activities both shocked and infuriated the mainstream press establishment, who challenged the Liberal government's action. Although the militant suffrage press consistently ridiculed and embarrassed Liberal candidates who did not support women's suffrage in its pages (a campaign that historians have seen as moderately effective in getting such candidates voted out of office), left-leaning journalists came to its aid after the raid. In general, the press did not support the tactics of the WSPU. Nevertheless, they could not defend the total censorship of a newspaper, however incendiary it proved. The National Labor Press in Manchester took over the printing of the *Suffragette* after the arrest of the first printer. The police immediately arrested the manager for failing to heed the government's warning. In his defense, he claimed that he had "read every line of it and could assure [the government] that it was innocuous."[139]

The consequent imprisonment of the printer was called "ill-judged" by the *Nation,* and a lead article the *Manchester Guardian* challenged the government's right to suppress the paper. It was one thing to confiscate a copy of a paper containing libelous or indecent material, but it was another to close a paper down, as it appeared the government had attempted to do.[140] *Newspaper World* printed an article claiming that it believed that the *Suffragette* could indeed be printed within the limits of the law and that the government should allow it to do so.[141] Even the more moderate rival paper *Votes for Women* condemned the raid: "The latest act of coercion adopted by the Government against the revolutionary section of the suffragists is perhaps the stupidest thing they have done yet."[142] In the wake of the raid, Bernard Shaw quipped that the home secretary must have been deluded into "believing himself to be the Tsar of Russia."[143]

Despite these criticisms, the government continued its policy of harassment in order to stop suffragettes from using radical women's advocacy papers as tools of propaganda for militant protest against the state. According to Ian Fletcher, in the face of increasing trade union agitation and Irish nationalism, the government came to understand the figure of the "insubordinate suffragette" as a larger "symptom of popular disorder."[144] This meant that to justify what many viewed as its antiliberal position, the Liberal government had to claim that it was not limiting the freedom of the press but preventing criminal activity. Over and over again, officials asserted that they would not prosecute those who published and printed the *Suffragette* "unless after its publication it was found to contain incitements to the commission of crime or the destruction of property." Police, however, went after the distributors of the *Suffragette* and its sellers, ensuring that no mainstream bookseller would carry the paper.

The government's repressive policies only strengthened the resolve of the WSPU. It continued to publish the *Suffragette* underground while heightening the terror campaign against public and private property (figs. 19, 20, 21, 22, 23).[145] They employed the Scottish Newspaper Company to publish the paper, away from the direct hands of London authorities, and members of

"The Suffragette," December 19, 1913.   Registered at the G.P.O. as a Newspaper.

The Suffragette

Edited by Christabel Pankhurst.

The Official Organ of the
Women's Social and Political Union.

No. 62—Vol. II.   FRIDAY, DECEMBER 19, 1913.   Price 1d. Weekly (Post Free) 1½d.

BRUTE FORCE.

The Government's Only Weapon.

Figure 19. The *Suffragette,* front page.

Figure 20. *Suffragette* office, May 1913. © Museum of London.

Figure 21. Suffragette selling a copy of *Suffragette*.

Figure 22. Suffragettes in poster parade, July 13, 1914. © Museum of London.

Figure 23. Women reading the *Suffragette*.

the WSPU continued to sell the paper in the streets. The paper commemo-
rated the week of the raid as "Suffragette Week," to "to celebrate the defeat
of the Government's attempt to suppress the *Suffragette* and to win a greater
number of readers."[146] Such actions resulted in increasing the circulation of
the *Suffragette* after the raid to unprecedented levels, making it, according
to its own estimates, "the largest suffrage paper in the world."[147]

The radical suffrage newspaper emerged out of this struggle as an important site of contestation in women's struggle for citizenship. Suffragists
drew on historical precedent while inventing their own brand of advocacy
journalism that legitimated the claims of a female-centered political community based on liberal ideals. As a medium of exchange between its members
and the public, the *Suffragette* presented an alternative political agenda while
pushing the limits of public discourse. In the process, the paper challenged
the gendered boundaries of the political nation through helping to fuel a
culture of disorder that harkened back to an earlier radical tradition.

For early twentieth-century female radicals, controlling the press meant
the ability to mediate a powerful set of discourses regarding women's status
as political actors. As Helena Swanick claimed, "it will be impossible for
any future historian to write an adequate account of the Suffrage movement by reference only to the public press. The censorship was extreme and
grotesque."[148] Shutting down one small but highly visible paper continued
to be a controversial method employed by Liberals to curb violent political
protest by suffragettes.

The campaign ultimately achieved limited success by effectively reasserting
government control over certain kinds of political discourse. Brian Harrison
and Martin Pugh have gone as far as to argue that the publicity generated
by papers such as the *Suffragette* ultimately had no real political impact at
all. Coverage of militant incidents in the press merely brought notoriety, not
influence. Although the radical propaganda of the paper did not single-handedly change British attitudes about the female political activist, the *Suffragette*
controversy suggests that political historians have overlooked the role of
advocacy journalism in potentially shaping how women used the press to
legitimate a public role for themselves within the liberal tradition. In the end,
this radical challenge in the constitutional idiom contributed to the crisis of
credibility eventually faced by the Liberal government.[149] Through repressive measures aimed at silencing the voice of the suffragettes, authorities
ensured that militancy had a limited impact on changing women's citizenship status. What the government did not count on during the controversy
over the *Suffragette* newspaper was the liberal response to the protection of

that time-tested ancient right of Englishmen and now, Englishwomen: the freedom of the press, an ideal that the radical female activist used to assert a legitimate place for herself as a political actor in British society.

Ironically, it was another type of state-sponsored violence that finally silenced the *Suffragette*. Not long after the beginning of World War I, a new paper called *Britannia* replaced the *Suffragette* as the jingoistic and extreme patriotic voice of the WSPU.[150] All militant activities ceased in order to support the program of the war. Through this publication, the government's once most ardent critics would prove themselves the state's most loyal supporters, a move credited by Nicoletta Gullace as helping to break down the masculine bias behind liberal ideals regarding citizenship claims during the war.[151] In order to challenge the government's denial of women's status as citizens, the WSPU remained dedicated to the political principles and stability of the British nation. These once-violent radicals truly believed that theirs was a legitimate popular voice that supported rather than undermined the foundations of the state. Suffragettes claimed this status as political actors well before the granting of the franchise. As these newly politicized female activists understood their place in British political culture, the freedom of their alternative press was not a privilege but their birthright.

5

Strategies of Dissent:
Women's Wartime Political Journalism

World War I has traditionally served as a major dividing line in histories of women's political culture. The literature largely has represented the dramatic story of the ending of the militant suffragette struggle after the firing of the first shots of the war as ushering in a period of muted pragmatism on the part of female activists.[1] Historians have depicted feminism after 1918, when women with established residence over age thirty were granted the franchise, as a political movement that clung to the equal suffrage issue in an attempt to prevent fragmentation.[2] The story of the women's press during and after the war complicates this narrative by revealing the important role played by women's newspapers in developing a multifaceted female public identity through the continued representation of women as political actors within their pages. Feminism did not quietly fade from prominence, as many historians have argued, but rather began to focus through print media-driven campaigns more directly on cultural and intellectual critiques that challenged broader social values regarding the status of women.

This stance, in many ways, echoed the reforming spirit of the women's press dating back to the Victorian era. Women's political culture maintained its historical nonparty character in order to advocate for changes that would culturally and politically benefit women. As the story of the women's press demonstrates, women's politics had always existed outside of the fray of formal political structures, in part due to its very nature as a movement for and by the disenfranchised, and in part by design. Even the campaign for the vote largely rejected the use of the formal British party system and instead relied on propaganda focused broadly on government policies that reinforced prevailing cultural attitudes about women's citizenship. The NUWSS dropped its nonparty status to cooperate with the Labour Party, starting in 1912, but, as Martin Pugh argues, this caused a great deal of conflict within the organization, as many considered it simply "a marriage of convenience" that had little real impact on the future activities of the organization.[3] For women activists, experience with broken promises from party elites had proven that a nonpartisan stance was beneficial. In attempting to explain the ambivalent relationship of women to the formal British party structure, historians have primarily focused on why women did not successfully sustain their own "Women's Party" or join traditional political party structures after the granting of the franchise.[4] These institutions, I argue, had not historically served their interests, and it remained, for many, questionable that they would after the obtaining of the vote.

The following two chapters attempt to shift the terms of the debate on women's political participation from one focused on their successes and failures in the party system to one centered on the less formal political structures traditionally relied on by female activists to gain access to the public sphere. By the 1920s, women activists had modified the extraparliamentary form of political culture that they had invented during the Victorian era to continue their agitation for both full citizenship and social reform. This nonparty approach, however, remained increasingly difficult to justify after almost eight and a half million women came to hold the privileges of full citizenship. These same women also faced, with the rise of a truly mass media, an array of news sources that vied for their loyalty. The question of who actually represented the voice of British women in politics emerged as a key issue that informed the nature of women's political culture, starting during the war and continuing through the 1920s and 1930s.

Feminists attempted to maintain a gender-based community during and after the war by using their own brand of print journalism to bring a woman-centered social agenda into mainstream political discourse. This chapter and the one that follows speak to the difficulties faced in trying to create a unified movement based on new assumptions about women's political and cultural authority as citizens who had served the state during the crisis of World War I. As Nicoletta Gullace has argued, feminist organizations played a crucial role in renegotiating the boundaries of a masculine-biased definition of liberal citizenship through proving their willingness to "do their bit" as patriots to help win the war.[5] Women's newspapers, first through publishing wartime propaganda directed at women and later through the development of a feminist minority discourse, invented a world that continued to place the woman activist at the center of political and social change.

The Suffrage Advocate Goes to War

"We must keep alive ideas and ideals during the war, and no paper conducted by men will put forth women's view as women themselves will. We are one half the nation: we must be heard," declared the editor of *Common Cause* on August 14, 1914.[6] During World War I, women's newspapers employed new strategies to bring women's citizenship claims and calls for social reform into public discourse. Reliance on readers, staff members, and volunteers enabled suffrage papers to continue as the voice of the politically mobilized woman during the conflict. This support helped circulation of suffrage papers hold steady during much of the war, despite wartime economic and social dislocations. *Common Cause* reported only a "slight decline" in "revenue from weekly sales and from advertisement," and the *Vote* successfully increased circulation through street-selling brigades.[7] Members of other organizations, such as the Church League for Women's Suffrage, helped maintain their paper's circulation, despite facing what they called "special difficulties arising out of war conditions."[8] The *Suffragette* changed its name to *Britannia,* emerging as a prowar publication that represented the new jingoistic nationalist-feminist position of the WSPU.[9]

The crisis of war, as suggested by the Pankhurst's pronationalist wartime turn, however, had transformed women's politics. In two of the major prewar publications, suffrage no longer took center stage. Rather, these newspapers dedicated themselves to proving women as worthy of citizenship because of their war work. *Common Cause* pledged to suspend "ordinary political propaganda" and did so until 1916. *Britannia,* dedicated almost entirely to promoting suffragette support of the war, claimed as its motto "For King, For Country, For Freedom." The *Vote* continued to agitate for women's suffrage during the conflict, although, like the WSPU, it suspended all militant activities after the government released suffragette prisoners. The Pethick-Lawrences' *Votes for Women* maintained an ambivalent stance toward the war while continuing to support the suffrage campaign. New wartime suffrage papers also emerged, including the *Suffragette News Sheet* (1916), *Independent Suffragette* (1916–18), and *Catholic Suffragist* (1915–18). Despite the pressures of war, the publication of such titles suggests a conscious attempt on the part of suffrage advocates to keep the debate over women's political representation alive in wartime political discourse.[10]

Whether agitating for women's greater involvement in the war effort or suffrage, women's newspapers played an important role in promoting a vibrant women's political culture based on an ethic of public service. The women's press depicted the political woman activist in a new public role: war worker. Propaganda campaigns in women's newspapers told readers that women could help win the war without firing a shot.

This tactic gained ground with feminists who believed that women should earn their citizenship through showing their commitment to national service. As Nicoletta Gullace has shown, "organized feminists were able to take control of the discourse, drama, and spectacle of war to serve their own ends and further the campaign for female citizenship," through undermining the link between male service and citizenship that had historically stood in the way of women's suffrage claims.[11] Women had used this argument as early as 1907, when Mabel St. Clair Stobart founded the Women's Convoy Corps, according to Jenny Gould, "to allow women to demonstrate that they were capable of taking a real share in national defense."[12] "Women! Your Country Needs You!" Millicent Fawcett declared in a bold *Common Cause* headline. "Let us show ourselves worthy of Citizenship whether our claim to it be recognised or not."[13] The war, according to many suffrage leaders, provided a perfect opportunity for women to prove this dedication. Suffrage press propaganda, as Susan Kingsley Kent has demonstrated, encouraged women to "strengthen the Home Front" through engaging in activities that initially included knitting clothing for soldiers and, later, in industrial labor such as munitions work.[14]

Wartime propaganda served another strategy: it depicted an activist political identity for women in the midst of a conflict that cast them as auxiliary workers. Although patriotism certainly played a large part in motivating women to support the war, suffrage organizations worked hard to connect those efforts to the cause of votes for women. Even periodicals such as *Common Cause* and *Britannia* that pledged to put the war first continued to discuss suffrage in their pages. Articles that appealed to women to help in the war effort regularly depicted war work as necessary to furthering the suffrage cause. *Common Cause,* for example, defined women's involvement in the war on its masthead as an opportunity to prove that suffrage demands were "for duties rather than rights" and that "their ideal is the service of humanity." By 1916, as Sandra Holton has demonstrated, after the issue of votes for military men arose in the Commons, outright campaigning for the vote reemerged.[15] The Pankhursts, although refusing to openly campaign for suffrage until after the war, expressed the opinion in *Britannia* that it would be a "wonderful thing" if women were granted the vote during the war. Emmeline believed, according to her daughter Sylvia, that after enfranchisement, "women would work with greater energy, enthusiasm, and patriotism for the security of their native land."[16]

Women's newspapers thus maintained the question of women's political and cultural status as a live issue throughout the war by promoting a model of tactical cooperation between readers and the government. Maintaining this balance between political advocacy and public service proved important during a period of increased government surveillance of the media. During the war, all branches of the press had to adapt to changes that regulated political reporting. The government set up a regulatory system that relied first on "voluntary censorship" on the part of newspaper editors and later on varying degrees of direct censorship from the War Office.[17] Many in the press complained of any restriction on press freedom but in the end willingly cooperated with the government during the crisis. Protests of the sort made in favor of the *Suffragette* newspaper in 1913 gave way to compliance with new stringent news guidelines. The British government applied pressure to newspaper editors whose cooperation, they believed, remained essential in shaping public opinion and maintaining "national solidarity." "The general tendency in the press," Koss has claimed during the war, "was one of submission."[18] News publications became the eyes and ears of the nation at the front and wielded significant power over garnering the support of the nation for the war effort at home. Through regular pressure placed on editors, the government made such "voluntary" compliance mandatory.[19]

Other material challenges also confronted the wartime media. All periodicals had to deal with the rising cost of newsprint and printing supplies, as the British economy readied itself for war. Fleet Street faced impending labor shortages as the government called up male journalists and printers for war service. Lost revenue from advertisers affected by the economic restrictions placed on consumers during the war contributed further to the financial uncertainty faced by publications, including the *Times,* the *Daily Telegraph,* the *Daily Chronicle,* and the *Westminster Gazette.*[20] Although the *Times* maintained its prewar size, the war forced the paper to raise its price from one penny at the beginning of the war to three pence by March 1918. Other papers also faced price increases along with size reductions, and many dropped popular features, such as fiction and photo essays, for lack of space.[21] The press thus had to maneuver government controls while facing increased economic hardships brought on by wartime restrictions.

These changes in media practices had important implications for the women's press. For papers such as *Britannia,* censorship posed a real threat. Despite the paper's fervent support for the war, the government generally viewed *Britannia* as a subversive influence, no doubt due to its connection with its radical predecessor and its vocal criticism of government war policy. The War Office ignored the paper for the first couple of months of publication but began to worry when Christabel Pankhurst openly "accused [Sir Edward Grey] of treachery in regard to the Balkan campaign" in the December 10, 1915, issue of *Britannia.* Under the jurisdiction of regulation 27 of the Defense of the Realm Act, which prohibited the publication of "statements likely to prejudice His Majesty's relations with Foreign Powers," the police raided the premises of *Britannia* on December 16 and seized a copy of a forthcoming issue. This first raid resulted in sending *Britannia* underground but did not silence its attacks against members of the government, including Asquith himself. By February, the government tracked down the paper's place of publication, at the new suffragette headquarters in Mecklenburgh Square, and seized "the type, paper, and several copies of *Britannia.*"[22]

Britannia was not alone. Papers that overstepped the bounds of the gentleman's agreement of "voluntarily cooperation" found themselves similarly treated. In September 1915, DORA had been amended to ease the prosecution of noncompliant papers:

> The Press Bureau with the consent of the Secretary of State, may issue instruction prohibiting the publication without lawful authority in any newspaper, periodical, book, circular, or other printed publication, or any information statements, reports, letters of other matter of such classes or descriptions . . . which appears to the Press Bureau to be prejudicial to the public safety or defense of the Realm.[23]

Radical publications that pursued an antigovernment stance, such as the socialist and pacifist press, risked falling out of favor with the wartime Press Bureau. Thirty-five socialist and pacifist papers that did not submit copy for approval by the Bureau found themselves taken off the government's list of approved papers in 1915.[24] The same year, the National Labour Press had its premises raided twice.

The political climate had clearly changed since the war declaration and required suffrage organizations to shift tactics. Criticizing government officials, something most suffrage papers had regularly done with varying degrees of effectiveness before the war, made them fair game of the Press Bureau. The government could thus restrict freedom of speech in a way that had been considered unacceptable before the war heightened concerns about national security. The government watched the activities of suffrage organizations, which faced increasing pressure to support the official wartime policy or risk being silenced.

The war, in many ways, altered the tenor of the political criticism once engaged in by the emboldened Edwardian female activist. Most women's organizations had to balance concerns over national security with politics. After participating in an international women-led peace protest on the eve of the war, Millicent Fawcett received the following note from Lord Robert Cecil:

> Permit me to express my great regret that you should have thought it right not only to take part in the "peace" meeting last night but also to have allowed the organization of the National Union to be used for its promotion. Action of that kind will undoubtedly make it very difficult for friends of Women's Suffrage in both the Unionist and Ministerial parties. Even to me the action seems so unreasonable under the circumstances as to shake my belief in the fitness of Women to deal with great Imperial questions and I can only console myself by the belief that in this matter the National Union do not represent the opinions of their fellow country women.[25]

Officials clearly recognized the importance of enlisting the cooperation of suffrage organizations in the war effort and resorted to threats when leaders fell out of line. Women's newspapers remained a crucial tool in helping to mobilize the home front, and their compliance became mandatory. The publication of the "International Manifesto of Women" was the last sign of war protest that appeared in the major suffrage newspapers. The August 14, 1914, editions of the *Common Cause* and the *Vote* announced each paper's full cooperation with the government to their readers.

Due to the war, women's papers had to find ways of casting women's politics in a different, more diplomatic key. The suffrage press did more than simply maneuver the restrictions of government press policy to provide propaganda for suffrage during the war; it maintained its commitment to function as a woman-run news medium by finding new ways to represent women and focus public attention on a woman-centered political agenda. Keeping any paper afloat during wartime required perseverance as well as resources. Suffrage organizations supported their newspapers "as a valuable means of recording the activities of women" during the war and "to keep in touch with the public and with each other."[26] *Common Cause* maintained its size and its low price, despite rising costs associated with wartime shortages, through the dedication of NUWSS members, who were "urged not to relax their efforts for pushing the paper," and the financial support of the Common Cause Publishing Company.[27] The WFL's "urgent desire" to maintain the circulation of the *Vote* meant keeping the suffrage issue before the public. It also provided "the link between all members and the one means by which the entire League can be kept in touch with vital decision plans."[28] Like *Common Cause*, the *Vote*, although reducing its size from around fifteen to eight pages, avoided difficulties faced by male-run publications, in part by having its own female-run publishing house that remained unaffected by conscription.

Having a press for and by *women* took on an important material and economic meaning during wartime. Specifically, it provided an important medium for coordinating efforts to help not only the war effort but also the women most affected by the war at home. Each week the columns of women's papers were full of descriptions of women's work for the war and appeals for further aid that carried such titles as "How to Help," "Notes from Headquarters," "What Our Societies Are Doing," "The Suffrage Societies and the National Crisis," and "What Other Women Are Doing." Most significant were the organizations supported and, in many cases, set up by women's suffrage societies almost immediately following the war declaration to help coordinate women's war work. *Common Cause* reported on the NUWSS's setting up of a registry of volunteers, hospital units sponsored at the front, and the Women's Service Bureau; the *Vote* on the WFL's Women's Suffrage National Aid Corps; *Britannia* on the "conscription" of women into industrial work for the war; and *Votes for Women* on the United Suffragists' support of the Women's Emergency Corps. The weekly chronicling of all women's activities, big or small, demonstrated to the public and the woman reader the goal of women's propaganda during the war: "Above all, we want to emphasize the vital part which women have to play in a crisis like the present."[29] Through their detailed recording of women's war work, women's newspapers represented the woman activist as the ideal citizen through her commitment to the war and its victims at home.

The activities promoted in the women's press created a highly visible state-sponsored cultural role for women. As the first private institution to mobilize women for war work, the suffrage press published work records for each major suffrage society in order to avoid overlap. First and foremost, women's organizations wanted to publicize the woman activist's loyalty to the nation by coordinating women's war work. As *Common Cause* noted, "it is essential that work should be linked up with national organization, so as to avoid overlapping on the one hand and neglect on the other."[30] To facilitate such coordination, the NUWSS requested local branches to send news of their activities to help those displaced by the war to the local press. *Common Cause* advertised the NUWSS's Active Service League, while the *Vote* directed WFL branch organizations to send out letters to mayors in London and the provinces and to the provosts in Scotland in order to better promote its schemes for community relief. Even independently minded *Britannia,* at the request of Lloyd George, agreed to publicize a street demonstration in support of women's entry into the munitions factories in order to help with the impending labor shortage. The women's press thus provided an important institutional infrastructure for women's home-front mobilization.

Women's newspapers assumed a direct role in representing the needs of the nation to readers, while functioning as the voice for activist women during the war. Editor Ellen Garrett linked citizenship with service by making the case for keeping in touch with the course of women's war work through *Common Cause:* "It is the duty of every woman, worthy of the name of Briton to GIVE THE MOST EFFICIENT HELP to the nation at this terrible crisis, and WE KNOW ALL ARE WILLING TO HELP, but the problem often is to choose THE BEST WAY. *The Common Cause will tell you.* The paper exists now with one aim, 'how best to help women sustain the vital energies of the nation.'"[31] Women would "nourish" the nation through their indefatigable efforts. As Sandra Holton has argued, promoting women's war work can be seen in and of itself as a strategy for keeping the movement together after the suspension of "ordinary political propaganda."[32] Such activities certainly helped strengthen women's associational ties while encouraging them to remain engaged in politics. The press, as Garrett's comments illustrate, served an important role in cultivating the connections described by Holton by playing on familiar tropes of feminine service. Women would not risk "desexing" themselves through war work but rather would fulfill their much-needed role as "helpers": "The Societies of the National Union are responding in magnificent style to the national need, and it is good to know that all their 52,000 members may now consider themselves members of the 'Active Service League' and work together to promote the common cause of the whole human family at this calamitous time."[33]

The government pushed women to enter into auxiliary military service as well,[34] but it was through suffrage press propaganda that many women found themselves first introduced to the idea of war work as a patriotic duty for women. Immediately after the war declaration, the women's press filled its pages with patriotic appeals, such as "Your Country Needs You," and proclaimed, "Every Woman Must Play Her Part!" One cartoon in the *Common Cause* depicted a soldier and a nurse below a caption that read: "Mobilization! Not Only These Two, But ALL Can Help." Through this propaganda effort, women's newspapers helped mobilize an already existing community of activist women while encouraging others to play a part in the war effort.

Continuing to agitate for the women's franchise during the war, the *Vote* offered a more overtly politicized role for its readers than did *Common Cause.* In its first wartime issue, the paper informed readers that supporting women's franchise continued to be the best way of serving the nation's interests. Although reduced in size, this number quickly sold out, leading the staff at the *Vote* to conclude: "this is the time when women must insist on their right to direct power in the State and that never again must they be voiceless in the face of such a calamity as the war now raging."[35] Appeals to help in the war effort did figure prominently, but unlike *Common Cause*, the *Vote* remained most concerned with waging an effective propaganda campaign in support of women's larger social and cultural interests. Polemical articles against the government's attempts to reinstate the Contagious Diseases Acts during war, for example, reinforced the *Vote*'s status as a forum for women's political discourse. Asquith himself recognized and used the *Vote* as a forum to state his official opinion on the matter and, according to his secretary, concerned women could "read full particulars of the Prime Minister's position on the question in 'The Vote.'"[36] As a recognized political voice for women, the paper often took on such a watchdog role over war policies that affected women and children. The campaign to raise government pay to soldiers' and sailors' wives was particularly forceful. "Mothers Don't Count" read one dramatic headline.[37] Other issues taken on by the *Vote* during the war included the fight for women's maternity centers.[38]

Advocacy journalism thus continued to provide a political voice for women during a time of national crisis, through a strategy of cooperation with the government that bound activists together in common pursuits *as women,* whether through war work or the advocacy of women's interests, broadly defined. The disruptions of the war, however, had a profound impact on shaping the future course of women's political culture. During this period, a more cautious female activist emerged who already began to engage in the tactics of the interwar "prudent revolutionary" feminists described by Brian Harrison.[39] Her role in "sustain[ing] the vital energies of the nation" recalled the rhetoric of Victorian women's political culture that capitalized on women's role as wives and mothers as a justification for their "intrusion" into public life as New Women. The woman activist of World War I, however, remained keenly aware of limitations imposed both by censorship and her auxiliary status as war worker. As the following discussion illustrates, dissenting wartime voices further threatened to upset the underlying fragility of a movement that relied on its own print-based propaganda to sustain the powerful illusion of consensus.

Alternative Discourses

As prowar suffrage papers made the case for women's citizenship based on national service, other papers used to war to create a forum for internationalist and democratic dissent. Despite tightening government controls over the media, pacifist, socialist, and women's organizations defiantly challenged state mandates. Their journals represented the alternative viewpoint of women whose opinions were marginalized by jingoistic prowar suffrage discourse. A culture of dissent had emerged at the inception of the women's press movement, but it was during the war that such voices found their clearest articulation in female-run publications. Such periodicals spoke for women outside of mainstream British women's political culture. In many ways, the war served to further expose the political and class divisions inherent to this wide-ranging movement. Two papers published in London during the war challenged the nationalist and class-based character of other women's organizations: the pacifist *Jus Suffragii* (1906–29) and the working-class *Woman's Dreadnought* (1914–24). The reasons for these two controversial women-run publications continuing to publish internationalist and antiwar propaganda, in the midst of increasing government pressure on dissenting viewpoints, reveal the range of opinions represented within the women's advocacy press as it provided a forum for the articulation of marginalized political discourse.

The British public generally supported the war and sought out newspapers that published stories about patriotism, national service, and wartime heroics. Northcliffe's decision to push his fervent prowar nationalism in the pages of his publications helped boost both circulation and profits.[40] Periodicals that used this strategy, including *Britannia* and *Common Cause,* had little trouble attracting an audience. Pacifism, however, remained a difficult issue for feminists during the war.[41] Millicent Fawcett tried to limit dissent within the ranks of the NUWSS through promoting women's war work, but two factions within the Union, the Manchester and North Eastern Federation, emerged to challenge the prowar policy promoted so strongly in the pages of *Common Cause.* Several prominent NUWSS members resigned from the organization, including the paper's current editor, Maude Royden, who had shown her early support for the internationalist movement by writing for *Jus Suffragii*. Previous editor Helena Swanick resigned her position on the executive committee as a result of the organization's stance on the war. Swanick eventually joined the Union of Democratic Control, where she later served as editor of the organization's paper, *Foreign Affairs*.

In creating these divisions, the war offered new opportunities for dissenting women's political organizations. *Jus Suffragii*, or "the right to vote," pushed an alternative internationalist agenda to attract readers by using a by-now-familiar rhetorical tactic: they tied women's interests to the cause of peace much in the same way prowar papers had linked the advancement of women with nationalist dedication to the war effort. Columnists argued that women should not support the war, as it dramatically hindered the political and social advancement of all women beyond Britain's national borders. Although the popularity of the war marginalized pacifist views, it also enabled leaders to recast feminism, as Leila Rupp has shown, in an internationalist key during the interwar years.[42] The *Woman's Dreadnought* similarly challenged the largely class-based bias of Edwardian feminism by discussing the war in its weekly columns as a tragedy for working-class women, who were exploited by the government in the factories while their husbands were sent away to fight.

Members of these political communities used women's newspapers as the most effective—and in the case of the international feminist movement limited by the constraints of war, the only—way to communicate with one another during the wartime crisis. The conflict interrupted the developing prewar internationalism of many British feminist organizations by limiting contact between members of belligerent states. This break in communication was most clearly illustrated after the NUWSS executive committee voted against sending members to the International Congress of Women held in The Hague. The NUWSS supported the international organization but decided that members should not associate themselves with a conference that favored pacifism. The passport system introduced during the war acted as a further impediment to the international feminist movement. Pacifists such as the Pethick-Lawrences, for example, experienced difficulties traveling abroad to international meetings because of wartime travel restrictions.[43]

The war made internationalist women realize that they would have to use caution in advocating for the protection of the needs of "all women," regardless of national origin. *Jus Suffragii* editor Mary Sheepshanks declared the paper "neutral" when it came to war-related issues. The paper, however,

published articles on how the horrors of war had affected women in belligerent countries and even went as far as to set up relief organizations funded
by readers to assist women in Germany and Austria. The mainstream press
quickly condemned the paper's stance on the war. According to Sheepshanks,
"our relief work has roused the evil sprit of the Daily Press and I have had to
open a special file for 'anonymous abuse.'"[44] As Sheepshanks discovered, her
transnational feminist politics remained in the eyes of many an irresponsible
political act on the part of unpatriotic women.

Mary Sheepshanks had long associated herself with radical political causes
and considered herself, according to Sybil Oldfield, "a citizen of the world"
rather than Great Britain.[45] Born into poverty as the eldest girl of seventeen
children on the outskirts of Liverpool in 1872, she attended one of the first
state-sponsored girls' high schools established after the Education Act. After
graduating from Newnham College, Cambridge, Sheepshanks went into social work and served in some of the poorest areas of London. Her involvement
in the suffrage movement was inspired by her friendship with John Bright's
granddaughter, Dr. Hilda Clark. She joined the internationalist branch of
suffragists, which led to her subsequent involvement with the International
Women's Suffrage Alliance in 1908.

Jus Suffragii began in 1906 as an international suffrage journal with socialist
leanings that reflected Sheepshanks's own political convictions (fig. 24). The
International Women's Suffrage Alliance published it monthly in both English and French for fourpence, four francs, or four marks. It claimed a wide
international circulation concentrated primarily in Europe and America.
Under Sheepshanks's watch, *Jus Suffragii* immediately began to campaign
for peace after the first declarations of war. Although a significant number
of women supported the pacifist movement from the beginning, pacifist
views were marginalized during the war in Britain.[46] Sheepshanks herself
was the victim of censure among her prowar suffrage friends for publishing
the opinions of "enemy" women. The prestigious Lyceum Club in London
banned her from the organization in 1916 after she read a telegram aloud
from German women expressing their support of women's efforts to win
the franchise. Her own brother refused to speak to Sheepshanks after reading of the Lyceum's action against his "unpatriotic" sister.[47] As the voice for
a women's suffrage organization that had refused to support the war, *Jus
Suffragii* relied on a highly dedicated community of readers and volunteers
who risked public and private censure in preaching the message of women's
advancement through international cooperation.

Female pacifists thus largely understood women's citizenship in interna-

JUS SUFFRAGII

MONTHLY ORGAN OF THE

INTERNATIONAL WOMAN SUFFRAGE ALLIANCE.

PRICE PER YEAR, 4 SHILLINGS; 4 MARKS; 5 FRANCS; 2½ FLORINS; 5 KRONER; $1.

Volume 7. No. 11.   AUGUST 1, 1913.

THE ASSEMBLY OF THE PROVINCE OF KWANTUNG IN WHICH NINE CHINESE WOMEN SERVED.

The Canton Assembly.

When the Chinese Revolutionists had won their point and had overthrown the Manchus, they turned their attention to the reform of their Government. The Manchus, in tardy recognition of the growing democratic sentiment in the country, had established Parliaments called Assemblies in each Province. The Revolutionists retained their Assemblies but declared for new elections. As no national law-making body yet existed, and no constitution had been adopted, each Province was granted authority by the Provisional Government to conduct the first election as it liked. The Revolutionary Society of the Province of Kwantung, whose capital is Canton, decided to set aside ten seats for women and to allow the women of the Province to elect these women members. This was done, and ten women were duly elected. One resigned because she went abroad for study; the others served. They were all well educated, highly respected women. Several were the wives of pro-

minent merchants, and two were head mistresses of girls' schools. The above view presents a portion of the Canton Assembly and six of the women members. Men and women in South China dress similarly, both wearing loose trousers and long coats. The dress is exceedingly hygienic and comfortable and as worn by the Chinese women is artistic and becoming. These Chinese women not infrequently spoke in the discussions of the Assembly and manifested a remarkable aptitude for deliberative procedure. Many Chinese women revealed a truly great talent for public speaking and were among the most successful propagandists in the first revolution.

Now a second revolution is in progress, being directed against the Republican Government. Apparently it has been initiated by the same people and is supported by the same Provinces as the first one. Canton, Nanking, and Shanghai were leaders in the first as they are leaders in the second. The North and the South have never been in close sympathy and understanding, and it has long been predicted by foreigners that two Governments would eventually develop out of the old Empire. The

Figure 24. *Jus Suffragii*, front page.

tional rather than national terms. Rather than believing that the war would liberate British women through proof of their service to the nation like its prowar counterparts, *Jus Suffragii* asserted that the war threatened to oppress women throughout the world and promoted a program of international cooperation among Western women. The International Women's Suffrage Alliance maintained that war represented the greatest infringement on women's liberties and fought to end hostilities in the name of women's freedom. Linking pacifism to women's advancement, *Jus Suffragii* filled its pages with articles advocating the improved care of children, equal divorce laws, education, illegitimacy laws, temperance, and the legal status of women throughout the world. This internationalist agenda challenged suffrage advocates to see women's political liberty as a problem that transcended national boundaries.

This international sisterhood asked women activists to see themselves as world citizens. At Christmas 1915, one hundred British women pacifists signed the following "open letter" addressed to the readers of *Jus Suffragii*.

> Sisters,
> Some of us wish to send you a word at this sad Christmastide, though we can but speak through the press. . . . Those of us who wished and still wish for peace may surely offer a solemn greeting to such of you as feel as we do. Do not let us forget our very anguish unites us, that we are passing together through the same experiences of pain and grief. . . . Can we sit still and let the helpless die in their thousands, as die they must—unless we rouse ourselves in the name of humanity to save them? There is but one way to do this. We must all urge that peace be made.
> We are yours in this Sisterhood of sorrow.[48]

Jus Suffragii provided the most effective means of unifying female pacifists during of war. Although their propaganda had little impact on ending World War I, the paper continued to be an important voice for internationalist women. As one New Zealand supporter wrote in 1919: "What has been the abiding bow of promise on four years of cloud and storm? Not creed, not art, not science, not socialism—all these have failed. But the thin gold link of our International Suffrage Press has held us all together in one high sisterhood—British, Germans, French, Hungarians, Latins, Slavs, and Teutons."[49]

In the end, the pressures of war strengthened *Jus Suffragii*'s status as a forum for an internationalist feminist politics led by Western women. Promoting this wartime sisterhood proved difficult in the midst of European state-sponsored censorship. Printed in London, each issue had to be reviewed for its content, making reporting of international news difficult. Sheepshanks thus relied on readers "in neutral countries to furnish news and articles, especially news of women's doings in Germany and Austria."[50] In addition, the war interfered with the regular business of subscriptions and sales, requiring financial support from readers, particularly from American members of the International Suffrage Alliance. Such support was essential in keeping the movement and its internationally circulating political medium alive during the war.[51] "*Jus Suffragii,*" claimed the *Irish Citizen,* "was never so useful as now to the Suffragists of all countries as a medium of intercommunication."[52] The tenacity of advocacy journalists in articulating controversial opinions during the war thus proved crucial in sustaining the voice of the internationalist female political activist in the face of growing internal and external political challenges.

Wartime print culture sustained other marginalized communities as well, revealing not only the political but also the class divisions among activist women. Working-class women saw the emergence of the first political periodical solely dedicated to representing their opinions during the months just preceding the war. Started by Sylvia Pankhurst in March 1914, the *Woman's Dreadnought* declared itself a voice for "working women": "the chief duty of the *Dreadnought* will be to deal with the franchise question from the working woman's point of view, and to report the activities of the votes for women movement in East London. Nevertheless, the paper will not fail to review the whole field of the women's emancipation movement."[53] The *Dreadnought* was born out of a schism between Sylvia and her sister Christabel and mother Emmeline. Sylvia had coordinated the East End branches of the WSPU from the beginning years of the organization and remained a firm believer in adult suffrage, a stance that supported the full enfranchisement of all women over the age of twenty-one without property qualifications. This position placed her on the fringes of the militant suffragette movement. In January 1914, Christabel and Emmeline, who did not support the adult suffrage position, tried to quell Sylvia's activities by expelling her and the East London Federation from the WSPU.[54]

The question of the legitimacy of working-class representation in the women's movement drove this conflict. Concerned by the impact the severance of political ties with her family would have on her organization, Sylvia changed the name to the East London Federation of the Suffragettes and continued to lead the agitation for suffrage in the name of working-class women. Friends who joined Sylvia after the split encouraged her to start a paper to express the viewpoint of the women the new organization claimed to represent.[55]

"The *Suffragette*," Sylvia claimed, "gave little attention to the special needs of women such as ours. Obviously we required an organ, and now that we had been cut off from the WSPU, we were free to publish one. . . . It was my earnest desire that it should be a medium through which working women, however unlettered, might express themselves, and find their interests defended."[56] The *Dreadnought* did not necessarily emerge as the unmediated voice of the working-class woman. Sylvia carefully "corrected and arranged" manuscripts submitted to the *Dreadnought*, using her editorial prerogative to create a paper "to be as far as possible written from life."[57] "Volunteer working women reporters" were employed to go into neighborhoods and investigate the actual conditions of life in the East End and, according to Sylvia, "produced far truer accounts than any Fleet Street journalist as they knew what to ask and how to win the confidence of the sufferers."[58]

To reach working-class readers, the *Dreadnought* modified traditional advocacy journalism business practices. Sylvia intended for advertising to completely support the costs of the paper, allowing her to give it away for free. When advertising support failed to materialize, the paper solicited donations and went on sale for a halfpenny, half the price of the average paper at the time.[59] Eventually, the burden of funding fell on the shoulders of one of Sylvia's most faithful supporters, Norah Smyth, who gave the paper most of her inheritance.

The *Dreadnought* started out as little more than a propaganda sheet along the lines of those published by provincial Independent Labour Party branches. Sylvia soon transformed the paper into a four-page weekly measuring eighteen by twenty-four inches. In its form as a working-class women's newspaper rather than propaganda sheet, members aggressively sold the *Dreadnought* throughout the East End; some were supported in numbers by their husbands, who defended them against harassment by the police. Although official figures do not exist, one historian estimated circulation at eight thousand weekly, most of which street sellers distributed in London.[60] Members also engaged in propaganda campaigns, much like those of other prosuffrage organizations, by chalking streets and displaying banners and parasols that promoted the *Dreadnought*.[61]

Increasing government concerns regarding the ability of the press to shape public opinion immediately placed the paper in the middle of controversy. Fearing arrest, publisher J. E. Francis, who had started *Women's Franchise* and had later published the *Suffragette*, angered Silvia by censoring an account of the force-feeding of a jailed suffragette.[62] The paper continued to court controversy; the day the inaugural number went on sale, a demonstration held by the East London Federation in Trafalgar Square ended in a riot that landed Sylvia back in prison.[63] She secretly edited the paper from her cell, claiming: "There would be no sleep strike in prison till what I had set myself to write for the *Dreadnought* had been completed." She welcomed what she called the "heavy burden" of her clandestine editorship: "What that paper meant to me!" she later remarked, and credited the paper with "sav[ing] her life" while in prison by giving her something to do to help sustain her marginalized movement.[64]

The war, however, provided the *Dreadnought* and the women it represented with the greatest challenge. Sylvia insisted on representing the needs of under-represented working-class women while refusing to support the war effort as had her sister and mother in *Britannia*. Subtly expressed at first in the pages of the *Dreadnought,* this antiwar sentiment developed fully in 1915, when the first signs of dissatisfaction with the war emerged in public debate.[65] Sylvia's biographer Barbara Winslow characterized the *Dreadnought* as "arguably the most influential anti-war newspaper in England."[66] Sylvia's activism and her paper's growing reputation led to a public repudiation by her mother. In a telegraph sent from America and released to the press, Emmeline condemned a rally held in Trafalgar Square for adult suffrage and against conscription. The cable read: "Strongly repudiate and condemn Sylvia's foolish and unpatriotic conduct. Regret I cannot prevent use of name. Make this public."[67]

This incident represented more than the simple manifestation of a family feud among three strong-willed political activists. Both Emmeline and Christabel continued to be ardent critics of Sylvia's work throughout the war because they believed that it divided the cause. In 1917, they attempted to unify women's politics under the banner of prowar politics by announcing in *Britannia* the formation of the "Women's Party." Although the short-lived organization never came to hold significant influence, it revealed an important rift in women's political culture. The Women's Party would stamp out the kinds of dissent raised by Sylvia's propaganda, according to a speech delivered by Christabel at Queen's Hall in November 1917: "We believe that it is imperative to form a women's party in these days when certain influences are seeking to herd women voters into the wrong political camps."[68] This power struggle continued throughout the war. Even before the vote had been secured, suffrage, once considered a great unifying force among women's organizations, now threatened to permanently divide women's political culture.

Throughout the war years, this battle over who would speak for women, whether working, middle, or upper class, continued to be waged within women's advocacy newspapers. The *Dreadnought* followed its own path, refusing to participate in the ardent nationalist feminism supported by the rest of Sylvia Pankhurst's family, and publishing passionate articles that unified the political and economic cause of the woman worker during war. Columns warned readers that they should carefully watch the everyday workings of the war machine, which threatened to exploit women workers while denying them citizenship. Such articles challenged readers to demand the recognition of women as workers and citizens during the war. "A Minimum Wage for Women" argued that the government should provide better pay to women war workers: "Let us demand that the standard of women's wages be raised immediately. Let us band ourselves together to insist on a minimum wage for women."[69] "Exposés," such as "The Sweating Scandal," uncovered the unfair wages being paid to women employed in War Office contracts: "Women, those of you who are organizing workrooms, do not shelter yourselves behind the sweating practiced by other people—pluck out the beam from thine own eyes!"[70]

These critiques magnified more muted challenges issued in other papers, such as the *Vote* and women's factory newspapers published during the war. With titles such as *Shell Magazine, Bombshell,* and *Shell Clippings,* these newspapers, according to Claire Culleton, "articulat[ed] the dangers of factory work" while "chronicling the dangers and unfair practices" endemic to wartime work.[71] As products of the factory environment and thus linked closely to the government war machine, these papers could not take on such issues with the same kind of fervor as antiestablishment papers such as the *Dreadnought.* In this way, the paper acted as a medium to articulate working women's concerns regarding war policy in a public forum. To bring about change, the *Dreadnought* made clear to its readers, working women would have to challenge state-mandated policies through political action.

Dedicated to both working women's economic interests and the goal of ending the war, the paper increased its influence as a national rather than strictly East End publication, with a circulation of ten thousand copies weekly.[72] Although the material needs of working-class women took first priority, the *Dreadnought* continued suffrage advocacy as well. In June 1914, Sylvia arranged a well-publicized deputation made up of six working women to put their case before the prime minister. Thousands gathered to hear the result of this unprecedented meeting that marked the first time Asquith had ever granted a suffrage deputation of any persuasion an audience.[73] Five months after the initial meeting, Sylvia published her "One Woman, One Vote" campaign in the *Dreadnought* in order to insist that working women no longer be "left out in the cold." The government should recognize demands for equal representation, she claimed, despite the current crisis. The paper published a letter sent on behalf of readers to Asquith to remind him of his earlier promise to include the women of the East End in any franchise bill, as their involvement in the war effort revealed how much they "urgently need the protection of political power."[74]

Although Asquith remained unconvinced on the issue of adult suffrage and refused to grant another deputation, the *Dreadnought*'s campaign revealed the growth of gendered public voice that had developed within the working classes during the war. The *Dreadnought* served as an advocate for working women by offering a democratic critique of the elitism of the suffrage movement. In mobilizing the working-class reader on the issue of women's war work, some of the most dangerous kinds having been taken up by the working classes, the paper illustrated the important contributions of working-class women to the nation. The injustices chronicled by the *Dreadnought* galvanized the movement that Sylvia had started in the prewar years to fulfill what she understood as feminism's obligation to the working class.[75]

In the end, the war brought the female political activist to prominence by providing new opportunities for her to engage in public discourse. Women activists used the advocacy press to strategically engage in a variety of tactics to sustain a diverse extraparliamentary political culture. As the popularity of old and the growth of new titles illustrated, women's newspapers supported alternative political voices while carefully maneuvering around formal and informal censorship. But the war, while acting as a catalyst for change, had taken its toll by revealing deep fissures in women's political culture. Much of this division stemmed from the underlying motivations behind the varying positions taken by suffrage organizations on the war and suffrage. Interwar political activists would face the reality of a divided feminist movement that could no longer maintain unity based solely on the imagined solidarity of the prewar suffrage era. It was in the pages of the women's press after World War I that such differences were contemplated and negotiated.

6

The New Feminist Reader and the Remaking of Women's Political Culture after World War I

I suppose there is nothing more irritating to a feminist than the average "Woman's Page" of a newspaper. . . . Women's interests today are as wide as the world . . . and it is nearly as foolish to assume that all women are interested in recipes as to assume that all men are interested in what to plant after wheat or the latest formula for artificial manure.

—Letter to *Time and Tide,* 1927

For the politically minded woman reader, the postwar era posed new challenges. The winning of the franchise for women over age thirty after the war left some activists wondering to what extent a feminist-identified agenda would enter mainstream discourse in the face of an expanding media industry that came to have increasing cultural and political power after the war. The sustained development of a female-centered political culture within the pages of the women's press resulted in the subsequent transformation of the women's press by the 1920s into an influential intellectual and cultural space for the activist reader. At the same time, divisions brought on by the war revealed cracks in the crumbling façade of a movement that professed to unify all women under the banner of the vote. The emergence of a feminism based on protecting women based on their inherent sexual difference challenged the more equality-oriented rights discourse of the prewar era. During the interwar years, previous Edwardian concerns about political equality increasingly came to share the stage with a range of social reform issues that came to define women's political activism.

Understanding the needs of the new feminist reader remained difficult at best. "Feminism" itself emerged as a highly contested term within the framework of the postwar political landscape, with multiple interests attempting to define its meaning. Historians have described the division as arising between "new" and "old," or "equality," feminism.[1] "New" feminism, as pioneered by one of the first female MPs, Eleanor Rathbone, encouraged women to embrace their special role as wives and mothers in their demands for reform. This ideology advocated "family allowances" and other welfare programs linked to women's domestic identity as a panacea for their needs. "Old" feminists rejected the idea that society should make separate allowance for men and women based on sex-defined differences and pursued the cause of equality for women before the law. As Harold Smith has pointed out, many feminist organizations of the interwar period counted both "new" and "old" feminists among their members.

These divisions, however, often caused difficulties. Susan Kent described the conflict in the following terms: "To 'old' feminists, espousing a strictly egalitarian position, 'new' feminist arguments reminded them of nothing so much as the antifeminist arguments marshaled in the nineteenth and early twentieth centuries to deny women equality with men."[2] By 1917, this split had already emerged in organizations such as the NUWSS, dividing members into two distinct camps.[3] The militant ranks faced the additional stress of seeing some of their own become disillusioned with liberal democracy altogether and embrace fascism.[4] These divisions underscored one of the main issues that determined the course of women's political culture during the interwar period: how could women's organizations effectively address the disparate voices that all claimed to speak for feminism?

This ideological conflict, according to historian Cheryl Law, proved a strength rather than a weakness of the interwar women's movement, which grew in terms of a diverse commitment to social and political issues.[5] Legislative gains that came from both "old" and "new" feminist ideals were made on a number of fronts that included the equalization of divorce laws and protections for unmarried mothers and children in 1923, children's guardianship acts and pensions for widows and orphans in 1925, and, of course, equal suffrage in 1928—all of which resulted from lobbying by women's organizations that also supported the candidature of female MPs during this period. The emphasis on what some have called "welfare feminism," focused on everyday issues that affected women, Law argues, should not be dismissed as taking the teeth out of a vigorous feminist movement but rather as its ultimate fulfillment.[6] Women's political culture had relied on the link between liberal reform and women's role as social guardians, or "mothers," to make the case for women's political inclusion since the Victorian era. It was during the 1920s that social reform campaigns found clearest articulation by women's organizations, which—after the initial franchise victory—adapted their extraparliamentary brand of politics to new political circumstance.

One of the most accessible means of developing reform agendas still remained the alternative press. The interwar years marked a crucial decade in the transformation of the British media. With one foot in the Victorian past and one in the future of today's news-making practices, Britain had started to show signs of the rise of a mass media culture. The founding of the BBC in 1922 and the rise of radio as a news medium offered the public new choices. Simultaneously, newspaper readership steadily rose from 3.1 million in 1918 to 10.6 million in 1939, as more and more power became consolidated in the hands of Lord Northcliffe, his two brothers, Lord Rothermere and Lester Harmsworth, and Lord Beaverbrook.[7] As James Curran and J. Seaton have argued, despite claims by press barons that they represented "the voice of the people," this consolidation instead produced a powerful elite interested in conserving the status quo.[8] The alternative press found itself caught in the middle of these changes. Earlier in the century, radical papers—such as the *Daily Citizen* and *Daily Herald,* both started in 1912—though popular with readers, had failed to attract the mass audiences and advertising support necessary to sustain themselves as commercial publications. The success of advocacy papers thus continued to rely on politically engaged constituencies and dedicated editors to push reforming agendas.[9]

For women's political papers, this changing cultural and intellectual climate created both problems and new opportunities. The period between the wars witnessed the continued expansion of women's role as primary household consumers. Advertisers wanted to find ways of attracting female consumers and expanded their reach into multiple media arenas.[10] As women's education and interest in politics after the granting of the vote increasingly mirrored those of their male counterparts, newspapers began to target them as readers. Mainstream publications that combined entertainment and news aggressively courted the serious-minded woman reader and provided her with a wide variety of choices. Northcliffe had pioneered this shift as early as the turn of the century by providing numerous new features in the daily press targeted at a female audience. In order to give women a reason to pick up daily papers, Northcliffe placed serious financial news next to sensational stories, as he had done when trying to start the *Daily Mirror* as a women's paper at the turn of the century.[11] His competitors in the quality press followed suit and by the interwar years had succeeding in drawing in women as readers. The *Westminster Gazette,* for example, touted itself as the paper for the "educated woman," and other periodicals such as the *Times* soon followed suit.[12]

In addition to competition from popular dailies and the quality press, the women's press faced challenges from both radio and domestic magazines. As radio listening was an activity first confined to the home, before the advent of the transistor in the 1950s, women found themselves the target of early broadcasters that built schedules tailored to the pace of domestic life.[13] During the same period, domestic magazines had grown both more attractive and popular, taking advantage of color layouts and improved publishing techniques that developed after the war. As Martin Pugh has argued, their popularity increased in part due to improved living standards and money brought in from advertisers interested in selling consumer goods to women. According to his estimates, by the late 1930s, "five out of every six women in Britain read at least one woman's magazine each week, and many read three or four."[14]

Although this audience most likely differed in terms of demographics from those that bought women's political papers, these statistics suggest that more and more choices faced the woman reader of this period and competed for her loyalty. Rather than dismiss domestic magazines as products of a growing consumer economy centered on the home, scholars have argued that these periodicals did serve a mixed function. In addition to acting as conduits of domesticity, they challenged women to think about political and cultural issues that affected them in their daily lives within the "problem pages" and letters to the editor columns.[15] Though largely prescriptive in terms of social behavior, most papers did offer practical advice for coping with interwar society, rendering domestic magazines both a popular and useful medium for an increasing number of British women.[16]

Despite internal and external challenges, the extraparliamentary brand of activism supported in the pages of women's newspapers for almost seventy years continued to have a place in British political life. After women with established residence over age thirty won the franchise with the passage of the 1918 Representative of the People Bill, however, suffrage papers faced a choice: to broaden their field of reporting beyond political propaganda or close down. The pioneering *Votes for Women* chose the latter and ceased publication once the suffrage victory appeared imminent in 1918, as did *Britannia.* The editor and driving force behind *Jus Suffragii,* Mary Sheepshanks, resigned from her post in 1918 after the suffrage victories in Britain, North America, Scandinavia, Germany, and parts of eastern Europe in order to focus on postwar humanitarian issues.[17] A relative newcomer, the *Woman's*

Dreadnought changed its name late in the war to the *Workers' Dreadnought* and emerged as a communist advocacy paper. Other papers such as the *Church League for Women's Suffrage* changed their names. Instead of focusing on the vote, the newly named *Church Militant* shifted its emphasis and campaigned for women's ordination in the church after 1918.

As the wry commentary from *Time and Tide* that opened this chapter suggests, the commercial media's one-size-fits-all approach to journalism did not satisfy many female activists' desire for news. The *Common Cause* and the *Vote* continued their commitment to the ideal of a press for and by women by continuing to cover the franchise issue. They, too, adjusted their focus, however, to educating the new woman voter while continuing to agitate for equal suffrage. As a voice for the newly enfranchised woman voter and her disenfranchised sisters, supporters of interwar periodicals had a daunting task ahead of them. If these publications were to survive, they had to increase their appeal to readers who possessed a newly formulated political sensibility that resulted from the partial enfranchisement of women.

New Directions: The Feminist Weekly Review

Women's papers that continued during the interwar years hoped both to compete with other periodicals and gain influence in political and cultural life by producing a new genre of publication for the female reader: the weekly review. The political weekly, in this era of growing commercialism and competition, held a special place in the hierarchy of British media. Influential weeklies such as the *New Statesman,* the *Spectator,* and the *Westminster Gazette* could never expect to reach the circulation of the popular dailies and rather measured success through attracting a discriminating and politically minded public. According to Stephen Koss, by the 1920s, weeklies "appropriated many of the critical functions of the political press."[18] This "golden age" of the political weekly paper enabled such publications to enjoy widespread respect among both supporters and detractors and commanded real influence over British political culture. Up through the early 1960s, these "journals of opinion" served as a vital space for writers to make their political and literary reputations.[19] The major weeklies, however, only dealt with questions relating to women tacitly, if at all. Women were also nearly nonexistent on their staffs. One historian characterized the *New Statesman* as a paper "written by men, for men."[20] Women's weeklies took a slightly different form from male-run reviews: continuing to operate at arm's length from party politics, while emphasizing their role as intellectual and cultural spaces for news. Within the pages of the women-run review, women activists could launch critiques of society in a reasoned out public sphere that did not necessarily relate to the everyday intrigues of parliamentary politics.

The NUWSS and the WFL in particular found the weekly review a useful medium to unify and provide practical information for feminist constituencies after the war. Their papers helped meet the needs of a newly enfranchised female public by providing a forum for broadly addressing women's political questions in a semianonymous space. After the war, the NUWSS expanded its scope beyond the single-issue franchise campaign by changing its name to National Union of Societies for Equal Citizenship (NUSEC). *Common Cause* reflected this spirit and emerged as the *Woman's Leader,* a title that asserted its role as a critical guide for the woman reader (fig. 25). As one NUSEC member remarked, the need to provide useful information for the new female voter was immediately felt: "Soon after the passing of the representation of the people act into law, questions began pouring into the office from women asking whether they were qualified to vote." The *Leader* developed a regular "Questions and Answers" columns to deal with such inquires.[21]

Editors promised readers a paper twice the size of the old one, "full of new life," with new literary features and political essays.[22] This strategy involved drawing the support of women journalists and "well-known names" in the literary business to contribute articles "of special interests to feminists."[23] The NUWSS had tried a similar tactic when they started a literary review, along the lines of the *Nineteenth Century* and the *Contemporary Review,* called the *Englishwoman* in 1909, for members who wanted a serious forum to discuss feminist issues in greater depth.[24] By 1921 the paper had folded, leaving the *Leader* to combine the literary and political side of social critique into one periodical.

The *Woman's Leader* thus targeted the politically minded woman reader while emphasizing both literary and cultural perspectives. Each week readers expected political opinion pieces and essays dealing with contemporary issues from both the "old" and "new" feminist perspectives. "All who are interested in matters concerning both women and children find this weekly paper indispensable," one enthusiastic board member claimed.[25] Loosely associated with NUSEC, the *Leader*'s independent board members looked for ways to make the paper "cease to be the organ of one particular society."[26] Reviews in the mainstream press called the *Leader* "an invaluable medium of broadcasting the most recent information about Bills before Parliament," claiming that "it is not difficult to trace the extent of [the *Leader*'s] influence

THE

WOMAN'S LEADER

IN POLITICS   IN LITERATURE AND ART

IN THE HOME   IN LOCAL GOVERNMENT

IN INDUSTRY   IN THE PROFESSIONS

AND

THE COMMON CAUSE

Vol. XII.   No. 37.   FRIDAY, OCTOBER, 15, 1920.   Price 3d.
Registered as a Newspaper.

Contents :

THE COMMON CAUSE PUBLISHING CO. LTD., 62, OXFORD STREET, LONDON, W.1,

and all Bookstalls and Newsagents.

Figure 25. *Woman's Leader,* front page.

in the Press Cutting from different parts of the country received at Head-quarters."[27] Readers also liked the new paper, driving a "very great" demand for the first five issues that resulted in readers having to order advance copies from their newsagents.[28] During the 1920s, the board continued to seek to increase the paper's moderate circulation to support its development as a mainstream review focused on issues of particular interest to women.

Similarly, the *Vote* adapted the review format to provide a broad-based, accessible forum for women interested in politics and social reform. The WFL doggedly pursued the granting of full enfranchisement for women, while offering readers international reporting and columns dedicated to national happenings relating to women (fig. 26). The *Vote* published more opinion pieces, essays, and political cartoons than in the past and started a new current events feature focused on France, Germany, and Scandinavian countries. Female contributors wrote articles such as "When I am MP" and "Where Is Equal Franchise?" to engage in the wider political debate on equal citizenship.[29] Each week this woman-run and -financed paper featured a "typical woman" and maintained its commitment to publishing news that women could use. The *Vote* made it clear that it provided information for women outside of the intellectual elite. Priced at one penny, it was the cheapest of the women's papers of this period and prided itself on maintaining a working-class readership.

The paper distinguished itself by focusing on political news rather than literary features. As one reader explained, "I have seen people put down the 'Common Cause' and take up the 'Vote.' The 'Vote' has more news in a nutshell than any other paper." In other papers, the reader did not "get all the tiny details of what is being done by women."[30] This "newsy" quality of the *Vote* made it an important source of information for busy men and women. Although it was still considered a "women's paper," men also read the *Vote* during the 1920s: "I have frequently heard men say that there are so many newspapers and periodicals to read that they get very embarrassed, and they often get a good summary in the 'Vote' each week that keeps them very well informed on political matters."[31] The paper also had subscribers abroad, many of them English nationals. Although circulation remained relatively small throughout the 1920s, the *Vote* built a reputation as a well-respected political paper.[32]

A shifting periodicals market, combined with changes in the strategies of the women's movement, helped make the weekly review into an integral part of women's political culture. The women's review provided a medium to connect activists to larger issues that remained an integral part of gendered

WHAT IRISH WOMEN WANT !

THE VOTE

THE ORGAN OF THE WOMEN'S FREEDOM LEAGUE.
NON-PARTY.

Vol. XXX. No. 1,003.   ONE PENNY.   FRIDAY, JANUARY 11, 1929.

OBJECTS : To use the power of the Parliamentary vote, now won for Women upon equal terms with men, to elect women to Parliament, and upon other public bodies; to establish equality of rights and opportunities between the sexes ; and to promote the social and industrial well-being of the community.

PRINCIPAL CONTENTS.

THE POSITION OF WOMEN IN IRELAND.
SOME GRIEVANCES AND A MORAL.
By H. SHEEHY SKEFFINGTON, M.A. (Member of Dublin County Council).

Equal Franchise.

The present year will see all Ireland on the same equal footing as to voting. Though in the Free State women have voted since 1921 on the same terms as men, in Northern Ireland (the Six County area) they were, as in Great Britain, allowed the vote only on attaining the age of thirty. Now that Great Britain has moved, Northern Ireland has swung into line. The newly-enfranchised women are already presenting a problem to the male politicians, for it seems that, in certain areas, where the political balance is delicately adjusted, notably in the counties of Fermanagh and Tyrone, the younger women will vote Nationalist or Labour, and may thus cost the Conservatives a few seats. If this should happen it will be but a just return, for the Unionists of the north-east corner have usually been anti-suffragists of the deepest dye!

Jury Service.

To balance the slight advantage which the women in the Free State area hitherto possessed, comes the special disability they suffer under, as contrasted with their sisters in the Six County area. In Southern Ireland women were deprived by the late Mr. Kevin O'Higgins, Minister for Justice, of their right to sit on juries, on the plea that women "did not like" jury service, and that it was indelicate to force them to act. When the various women's societies and other bodies interested in citizenship, child welfare, and the like, protested, vigorously lobbying Members in both Houses on the question, a sop was thrown to them in the form of a "voluntary panel." Women (and men, did they so desire) being asked to send in their names to the sheriff if they were desirous of serving on juries. Some women (not a large number, it is true, because many objected on principle to the discrimination; and others, though prepared to take their turn if called upon, could not, if they were working under employers, claim to get off for a service not required by law) sent in their names over a year ago, but nothing has been heard since of the voluntary panel, which does not seem to have materialised. As far as one can gather, in the North of Ireland, as in Great Britain, the jury service for women is well maintained and has proved a success.

Judiciary and Police.

There are, so far, no women judges in the Free State or in Northern Ireland, though there is an increasing number of women barristers and solicitors. There is a woman probation officer in the Children's Court in Dublin, though the presiding magistrate is a man. There are no women police, though women act in the detective and secret service force, in a few cases, having, however, no power of arrest. In the Bridewells (or temporary prisons) policemen are in charge, having access to the cells where women prisoners are kept, the so-called "matrons" of such places being merely cleaners or charwomen without authority or status.

Justices of the Peace exist only in Northern Ireland. In the Free State paid magistrates take their place, the newly-created Peace Commissioners being largely honorary officials for the administration of oaths and the like minor offices. Of these there are several hundred men, but not, I believe, more than a dozen women, if there are even so many. I know personally of only one. All are supporters of the Government, such appointments being made on party lines.

Married Women.

In the Civil Service, the teaching profession and in all government appointments, women are usually paid less than men—sometimes for the same, sometimes for more onerous work. They are excluded from many of the higher Civil Service posts, and they are invariably dismissed when they "lapse" into marriage. Only National teachers are exceptions to this rule, because they have a powerful trades-union and are employed directly by managers and not by the Government. Of late, the rate of pay offered to nurses for Government and hotel appointments is so low that there is a shortage of qualified nurses, many emigrating to the U.S.A. or to Great Britain, where pay is higher and opportunities of advancement in their profession wider. Go a year for a qualified nurse or midwife is no unusual offer! It is not surprising, therefore, that many local bodies have had no applications in answer to their advertisements for trained, qualified nurses. "This must keep Irish." Irish nurses, through their union, are politically on strike against such conditions.

Figure 26. The *Vote,* front page.

critiques of social, economic, and political life in Britain after World War I by integrating the call of universal womanhood suffrage with "new" and "old" feminist critiques. Women's organizational culture, which had traditionally relied on print media as a mouthpiece for particularized agendas, however, faced a changing political landscape that challenged the priorities of a movement predicated on a gender-identified political culture.

1928: The Women's Political Press at a Crossroads

The headline of the April 6, 1928, issue of the *Vote* read "Equal Franchise Victory: Our Splendid Majority." The passage of the second reading of the Representation of the People Act the previous week, by a vote of 387 to 10, had promised to enfranchise 5,000,000 women. "Ten Men against 5,000,000 Women," the *Vote* smugly declared.[33] The *Woman's Leader* also dedicated sizable space to informing readers of the extent of the new law and spent subsequent issues predicting what this new status would mean for women. The *Vote* immediately announced a new program that included fighting for more women MPs, women's admission into the House of Lords, and the sweeping pledge to fight for "full equality of women with men EVERYWHERE in National and International life."[34]

The suffrage victory had serious implications for women's political culture and the periodicals that had helped sustain it by predicating their radical reform programs on legislative equality for women. The market for women's political periodicals slowly contracted during the 1920s, as potential readers no longer seemed satisfied with the propaganda periodical of the war and prewar eras. As we have seen, postwar women's newspapers increased their appeal beyond women's suffrage, while attempting to draw in both male and female readers. The year 1928 posed new challenges. The *Vote* and the *Woman's Leader* could no longer sustain themselves as small, subsidized reviews linked to specific party organizations as they had done during their time as single-issue publications. These equality-oriented papers had to adjust to the new circumstances of their success: women now had legal recognition as full citizens. On what grounds should women reformers continue their advocacy campaigns?

As the falling circulations of these two papers during the 1920s suggested, women had started to tire of the old-style campaign periodical. No longer would readers endure the didactic, propagandistic type of article that was meant to stir women to action. Women had numerous other options when selecting political news, including "quality press" papers that now vied for their loyalty. Suffrage periodicals had failed to capture the newly enfranchised woman reader, even after switching to the new review format. Pushing a feminism weighted toward "equality" over "difference," these papers mirrored the politics of the organizations that supported them. As Susan Kent has argued, the predominance of "new" feminism during this period helped erode the power of the equality-oriented feminism of the prewar era.[35] By the late 1920s, the equality feminist position had faded from prominence. The decline of the WFL and NUSEC during these years reflected this changing political climate. Despite attempts to broaden their appeal, papers such as the *Woman's Leader* and the *Vote* continued as voices of their respective affiliated organizations and thus spoke to a narrower and narrower constituency of women.

The failure of the *Vote* and the *Woman's Leader* did not happen overnight. Serious weaknesses in the infrastructure of both papers, which also involved the perennial issue of funding, took time to take shape fully. Neither paper had ever turned a profit or broken even. This meant continued dependency on the organizations that had started them, as well as donations from members. Both the Common Cause Publishing Company, publishers of the *Woman's Leader,* and the Minerva Publishing Company, publishers of the *Vote,* failed as independent businesses, which they had set out to become after the war. By the late 1920s, both of these joint stock companies had ceased to exist as a meaningful business entity, leaving both papers in a precarious financial situation. As the general market for periodicals grew more competitive and papers became more elaborate and therefore more expensive to produce, women's organizations had to face the reality that they could no longer subsidize papers that by the late 1920s had reverted to serving as institutional newssheets.

For almost seventy-five years, women's organizational culture had depended on advocacy journalism. The inverse also proved true. As NUSEC reported in 1928, "the relations between the *Woman's Leader* and the National Union are so close that the welfare of one reacts on the other." In 1929, the paper reminded members again "how much the success of the work of the National Union depends upon its own particular publication the *Woman's Leader,*" announced a price increase of two pence, and appealed for "a third guarantee fund of 500 pounds."[36] More serious problems faced the *Vote*. For many readers, the paper had long ceased to inspire political activism. Even before 1928, readers had complained that women's reviews focused too narrowly on the suffrage question. "We do not care to be seen reading a paper called the *Vote*," claimed one WFL member. Another agreed that the name

"is unfortunate for the semi-converted; The *Vote* to most of us is only a record of our aims. Plenty of people who are in sympathy with our aims will
not look into the paper because of the name." Many on the board, however,
believed that the name served as the best way to advertise the nature of the
work for women's equality that the WFL performed.[37] The paper, however,
failed to garner the attention of the "unconverted" reader, as was evidenced
by its reliance on street rather than newsstand sales. With its financial future
guaranteed by Dr. Elizabeth Knight, the WFL put aside commercial considerations until their patron's untimely death in a road accident in November
1933. In the *Vote*'s place, the League published a newssheet that remained
little more than a bulletin, with hardly any circulation outside of the WFL
(fig. 27).[38] Although the *Women's Freedom League Bulletin* (1934–61) maintained limited political influence as an advocacy paper up through the early
1960s, ideological and material challenges prevented the paper from reaching
mainstream public that it so desired to influence through its pages.

As the organizational culture embodied by the WFL and NUSEC declined,
new institutions with different priorities and infrastructure took their place.
NUSEC sought subsidies for the paper from the newly formed National
Union of Townswomen's Guilds by offering it a four-page supplement in
the first issue of each month starting in 1930. Editors anticipated circulation
to "rise steadily as the Guilds grow in number and increase membership."[39]
Although the Guilds did continue to grow, their work did not require a weekly
paper for propaganda purposes. In 1932, NUSEC handed the *Leader* over to
the Townswomen's Guilds, who then transformed it into an organizational
newsletter, the *Townswoman* (1933–) that also included articles on household
tasks and the care of pets.

After the granting of the franchise, the long-established link between
women's political institutions and advocacy journalism as a vehicle to support women's activism had weakened. Although equality-oriented feminist
periodicals had a strong and loyal following among members, their appeal
dwindled in the face of "new feminist" critiques of society. Many considered
both the papers and the institutions that supported them to be too narrowly
focused on formal political questions such as suffrage. In addition, organizations such as the Townswomen's Guild and the related Women's Institutes
came to dominate women's associational life in the 1930s. As Maggie Morgan
has argued about the Women's Institute movement, women's activism increasingly came to be centered firmly within the domestic sphere. Concerns
over the domestic economic crisis during the early 1930s drove much of this
new activist sensibility. Organizations that did not speak to this agenda had

CARRY ON?

THE WOMEN'S FREEDOM LEAGUE

BULLETIN

Friday, November 24th   Price 2d.

[4, 0]

OURSELVES

It is with great regret that we find ourselves in the position of having to suspend our paper "The Vote". We hope this will not be for long, but in the meantime we are issuing The Women's Freedom League Bulletin which we hope will be of interest to our readers.

Our aim is to give a summary of the achievements of women at home and abroad, the parliamentary questions and answers and parliamentary notes of special interest to women, and news of Women's Freedom League activities. We cannot hope that this Bulletin will in any sense fill the place of "The Vote". We only want to continue it until we are able to re-issue our paper.

WOMEN AT HOME AND ABROAD

Woman Chairman of Children's Court
Lady Braybrooke has been appointed chairman of the Children's Court at Saffron Walden.

Inner Temple's Award to a Woman
The Inner Temple announces that a Yarborough-Anderson Scholarship of £100 a year for three years has been awarded to Miss C.H. Alexander, of St. Hugh's College, Oxford.

Firm of Women Solicitors
Miss Madge E. Anderson, LL.B., of Glasgow, who had a distinguished University career - her record was eight "firsts" - and was the first woman in Great Britain to be qualified to act as a Land Agent, having her claim for recognition upheld by the Court of Session in Edinburgh after the passing of the Sex Disqualification (Removal) Act, is coming South to take up practice in London after twelve years as a qualified lawyer with a Glasgow firm. The present partners of the firm of Solicitors she joins are both women - Miss B.H. Davey, LL.B., formerly barrister-at-law, and Miss Berthen, M.A. All three partners have been associated with the Soroptimist movement in Great Britain.

Women as XDeacons
By 16 votes to 14 Duns Presbytery has approved of the admission of women to the diaconate, as recommended by the Presbytery's Business Committee.

Woman Postmaster Protest
"The Observer" tells us that the decision of the Post Office authorities to appoint a woman postmaster for Lossiemouth, the Prime Minister's native town, has called forth an unexpected protest. The local Town Council have lodged an objection with the Post Office on the ground that the proposal to appoint a woman as postmaster is "degrading" to a town of the size and importance of Lossiemouth.

No Votes for Frenchwomen?
By 175 votes to 118, the French Senate has refused to grant a date for a discussion of women's suffrage.

First Woman Customs Expert in France
For the first time in France a woman has been appointed Customs Expert for the valuation and determination of the origin of carpets and tapestry.

Norwegian Woman Doctor's Appointment
Dr. Inga Saeves, author of scientific treatises on skin and venereal diseases, who took up practice as a specialist in venereal diseases in Oslo in 1921, has been appointed head of the section at Ulleval Sykehuset in Oslo where patients suffering from venereal diseases are treated.

Figure 27. *Women's Freedom League Bulletin,* front page.

difficulty gaining a significant audience after 1930, whereas membership in the Townswomen's Guild's and Women's Institutes grew to over 250,000 members. The activism of women involved in these organizations thus focused on the everyday aspects of women's experience rather than on the more public realm of social reform.[40] Although organizations such as the Townswomen's Guild did have their own newsletters, such publications had turned increasingly inward, functioning primarily as internally circulating documents.[41]

The alternative visions of female activism made available to women after the war had reconfigured the nature of interwar female associational life. The "old" suffrage press thus, in many ways, fought a losing battle to continue as a propaganda machine for equal rights. In addition, internal organizational conflicts prevented the *Woman's Leader* and the *Vote* from capturing a significant audience after the franchise victory. During the 1920s, the traditional connection between women's political organizations and the advocacy press began to wane, as they increasingly lost touch with the needs of this newly enfranchised constituency. These changes opened up the possibility for a competing vision of women's political culture to enter interwar British political life.

Time and Tide Wait for No Man

While the *Woman's Leader* and the *Vote* were competing to attract the reform-minded female reader, an independent women's political and cultural review hit the newsstands. *Time and Tide* first appeared in 1920 and claimed as its motto "Time and Tide Wait for No Man." This women-run periodical employed some of the best feminist and modernist writers of the period and exercised significant influence over women's political culture during the 1920s (fig. 28).[42] Despite its focus on feminism, the paper's founder, Lady Rhondda, did not want to create a periodical *only* for women that produced propaganda to support women's causes. Rather, she intended *Time and Tide* to be a feminist weekly review that would compete with the likes of the *Spectator,* the *New Statesman,* and the *Nation. Time and Tide* looked to transform women's press advocacy from a space of political propaganda into an arena of intellectual public discourse for the newly enfranchised female reader. Within its pages emerged a distinctive minority political voice, based on a nonparty feminist line, that challenged culturally constructed gendered conceptions of work, politics, and economics.

The following story of *Time and Tide*'s rise and fall as an independent po-

Vol. 1. No. 3. [REGISTERED AT THE G.P.O.] **FRIDAY, MAY 28, 1920.** WEEKLY. **Price 4d.** BY POST 4½D.

CONTENTS.

" WHO GOES HOME " sounds no more for ten days. The lobbies slumber except when broken by the tread of curious visitors during regulation hours. The smoke-rooms are silent. Doors are unguarded except by police. The whips crack no more. Committee rooms are desolate, and scattered to the four quarters of the kingdom, and far beyond it, the parties go. Government Departments breathe. Ministers flit no longer to and fro behind the Speaker's Chair. The absence of the Prime Minister is no more to be noted where all are absent. Ten days of surcease for all, and then back to business—to that kaleidoscope of event and happening, that converging centre of world affairs, that at times wakes the dullest and drowsiest member to a sense of its extraordinary place in the shaping of human destiny.

THE CONGRESS of the Royal Institute of Public Health met last week at Brussels under the Presidency of Lord Sandhurst. The Congress, the first to be held since the war (the last one was held in Paris seven years ago) may be said to mark an epoch in the development of medical research and its application to modern conditions. The Sections of most general interest to the layman were perhaps those of State Medicine and Municipal Hygiene. Infant and maternity welfare work was the subject of addresses in several of the Sections and also aroused considerable interest amongst the general public, both Belgian and English. One of the interesting features of the Congress was the strong divergence of opinions which showed itself on a number of the problems of the day. In this connection the discussion which followed Lady Barrett's paper on Ante-Natal Care was particularly enlightening as showing a definite and profound cleavage of opinion amongst those present on the fundamental issues underlying the question of the exact functions and status of Nursery Schools.

A CURIOUS EXAMPLE of the entirely false impression that may be created by stories that gain currency without any apparent justification is provided in the actual value of the English estate of the late Czar of Russia, which was revealed in an affidavit just filed in the Principal Probate Registry in London by his sister, the Grand Duchess Zenia Alexandrovna of Russia. In asking leave to presume death, she states that this only amounts to the sum of £500, whereas again and again it has been rumoured, with such determination that most people had come to believe the story, that Nicholas II., in order to protect himself and his immediate relations against the danger of confiscation in the event of a revolutionary upheaval, had privately invested vast sums in foreign securities, principally British. This turns out to be mere supposition, and the affidavit once and for all disposes of this myth. It appears to have had about as much reason and truth in it as a previous story which had Russia also for a background. We refer to the incident of the Russian troops that were seen marching about this country, on their way to the Western front at the beginning of the war, and who were apparently seen by those who insisted that they knew what they were talking about.

THE DIFFICULTIES and complications which arise in dealing with and amending modern legislation is often lost sight of by the mass of public opinion, which only sees the direct effect of certain apparent evils and fails to observe the indirect currents which are often baffling to those who are charged with the responsibility of governing countries. The new Rent Bill, the provisions of which have just been made public, provides an example, so does the Agriculture Bill. For instance, the former provides for the return of all premiums exacted by landlords since March 25 last. This

Figure 28. *Time and Tide*, front page.

litical weekly for women during the 1920s marks a final chapter in the history of the early twentieth-century women's press movement. Under Rhondda's leadership, this nonpartisan women's review developed into a well-regarded publication that approached news from a feminist perspective. Though limited in its general appeal (the paper never targeted a "mass" audience), *Time and Tide* established a reputation as an influential British political opinion paper. In many ways, the paper represented the best hope for a widely circulating, influential women's advocacy publication. Rhondda's insistence on a paper in the "equal rights" feminist tradition, however, limited the paper's appeal in the face of new feminist critiques. Ultimately, this independent weekly shared the same fate as those papers that concentrated on suffrage. Shifts in women's political culture and the periodicals and broadcasting market prevented *Time and Tide* from realizing its potential as a weekly review for and by women beyond the late 1920s. By the mid-1930s, these changes worked together to challenge the efficacy of advocacy journalism as a vehicle for sustaining feminist reform campaigns.

The intellectual feminist review had its origins in the publication of the *Freewoman: A Weekly Feminist Review* in 1911. Unsatisfied with the coverage of women's issues in *Votes for Women* and the mainstream press, disillusioned WSPU member Dora Marsden and her supporters started the paper to encourage readers to debate radical issues in the letters to the editor column and in the newly formed "Freewoman Discussion Circle." They intended the paper to be a weekly supplement to the *Vote,* but the *Freewoman*'s explicit discussion of sexual issues, including male and female homosexuality, led the WFL to reject the paper.[43] Maude Royden called it a "nauseous publication," and the first issue of the paper so offended Millicent Fawcett that she was reported to have torn it up into small pieces.[44] According to one-time contributor Rebecca West, "The 'Freewoman' mentioned sex loudly and clearly and repeatedly and in the worst possible taste."[45] Elitist in appeal, Marsden called the relatively high price of threepence purposeful: "we are not proposing writing for women whose highest journalistic needs are realised by a penny."[46]

Radical feminist journalism thus held only marginal appeal to feminist or mainstream audiences in the prewar era. The *Freewoman*'s elitism, coupled with bold articles on sexuality, led to the alienation of less radical supporters and ultimately to its downfall. By February 1912, the paper was losing twenty pounds a week under Marsden's increasingly inconsistent leadership, and a ban by distributor W. H. Smith that fall nearly guaranteed its collapse.[47] Outside investors brought the paper new life as a modernist literary paper with a feminist sensibility called the *New Freewoman* in July 1913, for sale at the increased price of sixpence. Having turned more and more toward modernism, Marsden, investors, and a group of modernist writers transformed the paper again. The *Egoist* emerged in 1914 as a foremost literary publication, with contributions from notable writers, including Ezra Pound, James Joyce, and D. H. Lawrence.[48]

Like Marsden, Rhondda started her paper in response to a growing frustration with the limits of both mainstream and advocacy journalism. *Time and Tide,* however, would follow its own path. In *Time and Tide,* Rhondda envisioned a weekly paper that would publicize women's demands for equality while influencing public opinion on cultural and economic issues from a feminist perspective. Simply put, her ambition was to start a periodical that would give educated women an influential public voice. "There is much work to do!" proclaimed Rhondda of her new paper. "The more one sees the more one feels the need for such a paper to form a rallying point for sensible women."[49] She surrounded herself with a group of like-minded journalists, playwrights, novelists, essayists, and previous editors of women's political journals, most of whom refused payment for their contributions.[50]

Rhondda believed that the mainstream press worked against women's interests by turning public opinion against feminism. Six months before starting *Time and Tide,* she organized a delegation that approached all major British news publications regarding the coverage of women's issues. The *Sunday Herald* defended itself by citing lack of space, but, as one delegate responded, there was a sizable amount of "space reserved for reporting a beauty competition."[51] The paper reserved more serious criticism for the apparent backlash against women workers after the war. "It has been forcibly and repeatedly bought to my notice," wrote Rhondda to one delegate, "that the attitude of the Press toward women and women's work is having not only a very detrimental effect upon their present position, but is actually conducive to their return to dependent and even sweated conditions."[52] The delegation cited the press's labeling of female government workers as "Whitehall Flappers" while disparaging the contributions of educated women to the post–World War I economy. Such press commentaries, they claimed, turned public opinion against women workers and led the government "to get rid of women as quickly as possible, without reference either to the expedience or injustice of the methods employed."[53]

Women's advocacy papers, in Rhondda's opinion, failed to adequately counter the one-sidedness of mainstream press coverage by focusing too narrowly on the vote as a constitutional fix that would single-handedly improve women's status.[54] A board member of the *Common Cause,* she resigned in early 1920 after having criticized both the way the organization ran the paper and its narrow propagandist slant.[55]

Rhondda chose *Time and Tide*'s weekly review format deliberately. In an era when periodicals exercised significant power over public opinion, she understood that the weekly review held particular status, as it reached a highly educated and politically active public. Editors of widely circulating daily journals, Rhondda claimed, had to "play for safety and avoid experiments, dealing only with comparatively few subjects—the subjects that form a common factor of interest to the million readers of his paper."[56] Alternatively,

> the Weekly Review, the paper which is trying not merely to talk but to think— requires if it is to be fully alive and to take advantage of all its possibilities, an intimacy of relationship between public and paper which is quite a peculiar thing, a kind of building up an organic whole so that it does come to represent the approximate point of view of its public whether they are writers or reader. Only so can it be effectively one of the opinion makers of the world.[57]

As a *feminist* weekly review, Rhondda imagined *Time and Tide* as an alternative medium of public discourse that challenged the monopoly on political ideas held by the mainstream press. Unlike the *Vote* and the *Woman's Leader,* *Time and Tide* focused on a broad intellectual and political program that reached beyond the provincial boundaries of women's political culture.

Throughout the 1920s, *Time and Tide*'s reputation grew among educated men and women as a feminist weekly of political and cultural affairs. Circulation reached a respectable level for a weekly review during this time, ranging between twelve and fifteen thousand copies weekly.[58] In addition to London intellectuals and the ruling elite, reportedly including Bernard Shaw and the Duke of York, the review cultivated a wide range of male and female readers throughout England and the world.[59] One provincial lady "told of remote country districts where Lady Rhondda's paper was read and discussed in many a cottage."[60] The review also courted readers in the British Commonwealth as they "constitut[ed] a public of whom we are proud and from whom we value suggestions."[61] "I can assure you," wrote one loyal South African reader, "that *Time and Tide* would be the last paper I should care to drop, not only because of my appreciation that it is *really* a woman's paper—but for all it and its foundress stand for in the world of womankind."[62] Another enthusiastic reader remarked, "*Time and Tide* tells us what women think and not what they wear."[63] Readers particularly liked the paper's opinion sections and voted the "Review of the Week," a segment that discussed current events, and the "Leaders," or feature articles, the "most valuable" features. The weekly review of books also ranked high.

Loyal readers proclaimed its feminism as "just right" and asked "to be guided as to opinions" even further.[64]

Rhondda recognized that in its quest to serve as an effective public forum for women's ideas, the paper also needed to reach a broad audience that included male readers. Men, according to their letters and comments, constituted some of the review's most loyal subscribers. "I do not know any other paper which succeeds in making me read so much as *Time and Tide*," claimed one zealous male supporter who praised the "extraordinary sobriety" of this "woman's paper." "I buy a great many papers every day and I find I have read all of them in ten minutes. . . . Perhaps the time will come, and that time will be Utopia, when there will only be *Time and Tide* to read."[65]

Despite her desire to attract equally enthusiastic male and female readers, Rhondda carefully maintained women's direct control over the review throughout the 1920s. *Time and Tide* intended to give its mainly middle- and upper-class women readers a forum, while promoting their social and political interests: "Educated (more or less) women haven't a rallying point or a mouthpiece," one board member claimed on the eve of *Time and Tide*'s birth. "And I'm glad this reproach to us is about to be removed."[66] Rhondda quickly rejected one member's suggestion for a male editor for the paper. "Could a man *possibly* run the paper?" asked Rhondda. "He would most certainly want to run all of us!"[67] Although the paper welcomed and even courted men as contributors and readers, Rhondda wanted to maintain *Time and Tide* as a woman's political review where writers and readers could boldly express political opinions.

As a nonpartisan review, *Time and Tide* offered, in its political commentary, what it defined as a "feminist" perspective that supported humanistic egalitarianism over party politics. Unlike suffrage papers' halfhearted and eventually futile attempts to selectively endorse politicians on the basis of their parties' support of particular issues, *Time and Tide* invented its own idealized egalitarian feminist platform. As Rhondda told her board, "I am anxious to outline a definite domestic policy in *Time and Tide* which an ideal party would adopt and press before everything else. We should include temperance, education, health, and the Six Points [a specific list of reforms to benefit women] and should, I hope, appeal to many women. I want them to have some sort of programme to test their MPs by at the general election."[68] The review addressed women as political actors who had an interest in all matters of state policy. An article entitled "Women and Public Affairs" concluded: "Woman, if she will give free play to her higher nature, has that within her which can raise public affairs into a clearer atmosphere."[69] Other articles included critiques of legislation such as the nondiscrimination Sex Disqualification (Removal) Act.[70] In casting "woman" as a universal category, the review also praised Indian women's activism as a means of guaranteeing their country's "future peace and safety." Revealing a liberal imperial bias, credit for feminist thinking among India's women was given to the British education system. *Time and Tide* addressed educated British women and, to a more limited and complicated extent, educated Indian women as a minority community who had a duty to shape social policy in their respective countries.

When readers picked up *Time and Tide* during the 1920s, they could expect features that included those on both the literary cutting edge and the radical extreme. Essays, theater reviews, and poetry by prominent feminist modernist writers that included Rebecca West, Cicely Hamilton, and Elizabeth Robins appeared regularly. In 1928, Virginia Woolf published a short story, "The Sun and the Fish," in *Time and Tide.* Cicely Hamilton's "The Backwash of Feminism" deplored the "retreat" of feminism after the partial enfranchisement of women and the "revival of the cult of femininity."[71] In another fiery piece, Rebecca West proclaimed, while urging women to lead independent lives, "I am an old fashioned feminist. I believe in the sex-war. I am, to use an expression that for some reason that I never understand is used as a reproach, anti-man."[72] Such dramatic statements often elicited strong responses, both positive and negative, from readers who had come to appreciate *Time and Tide* as an alternative forum to mainstream political discourse.

In addition to publishing radical opinion pieces, *Time and Tide* pursued Rhondda's early agenda of questioning the limits of mainstream press coverage. The press, according to the review's first editorial, "teach[es] us nothing about the women of the day," an oversight *Time and Tide* sought to correct.[73] Highlighting important and lesser known public women, in what often amounted to hagiographic essays (a feature pioneered by turn-of-the-century women's advocacy newspapers) in the "Personal Sketches" column, revealed to readers the important role that women currently played in society. This popular column made it possible for readers to imagine themselves as part of a community of women already actively engaged in public work. The paper also treated traditional "men's topics," including a "Financial Page," which provided information in plain language on investments and business news. A series of articles that critically analyzed the "national debt" further encouraged women to form opinions on the state of the economy.

Rhondda believed that her audience wanted a different type of medium that took both women readers and women's concerns seriously. The critical success of *Time and Tide* as a weekly review revealed the existence of a small but growing group of educated women readers who would pay for "hard" news. *Time and Tide*'s "Notes from Paris" feature, for example, dealt with politics and cultural life, not fashion.[74] Women readers also demanded news that directly related to their social and economic status, something *Time and Tide* continued to do throughout the 1920s by publishing articles on universal enfranchisement, equal divorce laws, health care, women's employment, and education. *Time and Tide* thus provided in-depth coverage of issues outside of mainstream political discourse.

One of the review's important contributions to women's intellectual and political life during this period was its critical examination of contemporary media practices. The mainstream periodical had gradually developed as one whose purpose was to both amuse and inform. The weekly review also followed this pattern, though differently from the daily press. Periodicals such the *Spectator,* the *New Statesman,* and the *Nation* balanced news stories with opinion pieces and literary reviews that provided thought-provoking entertainment for readers. *Time and Tide* set out to amuse and inform readers by taking on what it considered the anti-intellectual practices of the daily press by satirizing one of its most popular features: the women's page. Such pages, according to their critics, failed to recognize the diverse interests of the modern woman. Instead, they drew upon a Victorian bourgeois ideology that maintained that women had no stake in contemporary issues, even those that directly affected them, such as employment, the economy, and education. In a series of articles and letters, *Time and Tide* took on assumptions behind features that rejected a modern sensibility among women and men. "Modern women need a forum," the review concluded; "a clearing house for the exchange of ideas, a meeting place where they can learn of each other's experiments and benefit by each others conclusions."[75] *Time and Tide* challenged the mainstream press to adopt a new modern sensibility that spoke to the practical and intellectual interests of the women they claimed to address.

To highlight what the paper considered the ridiculous extremes of the women's pages, *Time and Tide* introduced the "Men's Page." This satire of fashion, advice columns, and household tips addressed the "modes, manners, and morals" of the gentleman. Complete with clearly invented letters from men to their "agony aunt column," the men's page turned frivolous journalism targeted to women on its head. Much to the delight of *Time and Tide*'s female readers, these letters from the new "meeker sex" addressed men's question regarding how to dress on a budget while looking smart.[76] One desperate "male reader" claiming to be the husband of a new lady MP wrote seeking fashion advice: "HELP!" his letter exclaimed, "I am very tall, very thin with straw-colored hair, rather decent blue eyes, and a coffee-colored complexion" and "am exceedingly anxious to help my wife by making a gracious Host at the political dinners which she is planning."[77] *Time and Tide*'s adoption of this ironic mode to critique the women's pages not only amused readers but also provided a powerful commentary on contemporary journalistic practices.

The "new" women's page, according to this critique, should take on a serious social function. *Time and Tide* called for the immediate reform of the women's page. In this new idealized scheme, such pages would provide educated women with information that did not revolve solely around hearth and home. Male readers of the women's page would also benefit, argued one "correspondent" to the Men's Page: "No one is so bewildered by this modern woman's revolution as the average husband. If he could turn once a week to the Woman's Page and find there scores of women stirred by the same unnatural discontent that seem to be threatening his own home comfort, he should certainly be intrigued. He might even begin to understand."[78] Rather than simply chronicling tales of domestic pursuits and answering questions in the "problem pages," these features, in *Time and Tide*'s critique, had a responsibility to move beyond mere entertainment. This new approach to female-targeted journalism paired commercial interests with a larger social function.

One of the reasons *Time and Tide* took on the women's page clearly had to do with the overwhelming popularity of the feature in mainstream publications. Perceived competition from dailies and women's magazines played into Rhondda's concerns with sustaining an audience for a serious-minded women's review. Women's pages successfully targeted women as readers who might not have picked up a daily paper without the promise of features that spoke to questions of fashion, cookery, and society news. Women, as editors like Northcliffe eventually discovered, would pay for a newspaper that catered to their interests while providing general news features. *Time and Tide* asked readers to examine the women's pages in a more critical way. Through its "Men's Page" satire, the review not only critiqued this practice but also attempted to capitalize on a successful feature in order to capture potential readers who might be convinced to purchase *Time and Tide* for both entertainment and news.

Time and Tide used the issue of the women's page as a platform to demonstrate the degree to which women's professional status and taste for news reading had developed. Readers of *Time and Tide* described in their letters changes in the women's pages in papers such as the *Manchester Guardian* and the *Yorkshire Post,* where they discovered "the old Woman's Editor, who in [his] shirt sleeves [is] chewing tobacco while composing descriptions of toilettes . . . has been replaced by a professional woman, probably an experienced journalist." Advertisements attempting to lure women readers to buy newspapers such as the *Sunday Times* and the *Westminster Gazette* also appeared in *Time and Tide.* One advertisement proclaimed: "Every Intelligent Man and Woman should read the *Sunday Times,*" because of the paper's coverage of "political news, foreign and domestic, articles on music, sport," and especially "its special feature for women under the title of 'A Woman's Corner' conducted by a well-known writer."[79] Although elements of the Victorian-era woman's page continued as popular features in the mainstream press, by the mid-1920s it became harder to assume, as Emily Davies had observed in the 1860s, that women had little interest in the news. The women's pages certainly continued to attract women readers, drawing them away from more serious news publications. *Time and Tide,* however, found ways to critique the success of its competitors and draw in readers by exposing the gendered assumptions that drove much of the British press.

Educated women during the 1920s not only purchased newspapers for themselves but also, as in the case of *Time and Tide,* the *Vote,* and the *Woman's Leader,* found them owned and operated by women who believed in the power of the news to facilitate a public voice for women through the spread of information. The feminist weekly review thus provided women with a space to engage in debates over accepted cultural values, while it challenged the mainstream press to see them as serious consumers of news and ideas. "At last women are beginning to express the real woman's point of view," Frederick Pethick-Lawrence asserted in 1926, "so different from the old man-dominated point of view they expressed before."[80] Women readers and writers, despite challenges faced from an increasingly dominant commercial mainstream media, found in the weekly review a useful medium through which to critique British political culture and traditional social values.

Taking Feminism into the Mainstream

As the *Vote* and the *Women's Leader* slowly faded from prominence after 1928, *Time and Tide* continued to grow in terms of both influence and circulation.

Free from many of the structural problems that had historically plagued other women's publications, Rhondda's paper took its place among the most prestigious political weeklies of the 1930s, 1940s, and 1950s. *Time and Tide* called itself an "independent non-party" weekly and remained beholden to no single feminist or other political organization. Rhondda herself owned 90 percent of the paper and in 1926 took over as editor, a position she held until her death in 1958.[81] In this capacity, she dedicated her time and personal fortune to making the paper a success. Rhondda's many influential friends and associates, a number of whom wrote for or were on staff at *Time and Tide,* provided the paper with a prestigious following, both in and outside feminist circles. The staff and shareholders of the paper, still made up mainly of women, sought to balance the paper's coverage of political and cultural life through publishing political commentary, essays, and reviews by promising and established writers.

The *Time and Tide* of the 1930s and after, however, cultivated a new sensibility. Feminism took a backseat to a broad-based cultural critique of society that was devoid of much of the fiery polemics of the 1920s. This move was self-conscious on the part of Rhondda, who believed that as a paper targeted specifically at a women's audience, *Time and Tide* would go the way of the many advocacy papers that had come before it. As a dedicated feminist and a shrewd businesswoman, she steadily moved the paper more in the direction of a mainstream review publication. Looking back on the history of *Time and Tide,* Rhondda recalled that she had intended her periodical to be a prominent political medium:

> Since I was a small child I had always wanted to edit, and indeed at the age of twelve I produced a slightly irregular monthly magazine. By the time I was in my early twenties I knew that it was a weekly review that I wanted to edit and I knew why. A first-class weekly review, as I saw it then and still see it today, is read by comparatively few people, but they are the people who count, the people of influence, the people who make the universities, the people who teach the young, the people who make the laws and the people who administer them. The good weekly review is in fact amongst the unacknowledged legislators.[82]

Rhondda recognized that as a feminist review the paper would only achieve limited influence. *Time and Tide* gradually started to hire men and by the 1950s counted equal numbers of men and women on its staff. Rhondda grew concerned that having too many female bylines and topics relating to women would, as she wrote to early *Time and Tide* contributor Virginia

Woolf, "soon kill the paper."[83] To serve as an effective critical voice, *Time and Tide* needed to reach beyond a strictly feminist readership. The paper thus attempted something other advocacy papers had never before imagined. Under Rhondda's leaders, *Time and Tide* sought to compete with some of the best known and widely circulating British reviews of the day.

Why did Rhondda find it necessary to institute these changes starting in the mid-1930s? Changes in the structure of British media had profound effects on advocacy journalism as a political vehicle. As the press found itself concentrated in fewer and fewer hands from 1914 to 1950, despite witnessing an increase in the total number of news readers, fewer and fewer titles survived in the face of increased competition. The corporatization of the news industry and rising costs associated with running a periodical during this period helped facilitate these changes.[84] A nonpartisan feminist political review could not compete with other more broadly based reviews such as the *Spectator* or the *Nation*. Rhondda's new business strategy points to the realities of both the new media market and the problems of the advocacy press model. It simply cost too much by the 1930s to run a paper on the old lines of earlier advocacy journals. The possibility of audience specialization, a hallmark of advocacy journalism, became increasingly untenable in this new competitive climate.

This shift had a profound affect on political culture in Britain. Special interest groups that had relied on cheap print for advocacy purposes had to scale back their enterprises. Organizations like the WFL and the Townswomen's Guilds, for example, employed the old inexpensive newssheet format popular with women's papers during the 1870s and 1880s to provide information to members. The possibility of launching a mass propaganda campaign from relatively small amateur publications remained highly unlikely.

Time and Tide maintained itself as a vigilant advocate for social change that never fully distanced itself from its feminist origins. Kingsley Martin, editor of the *New Statesman and Nation,* believed that the paper during the 1930s was well on its way to becoming Britain's leading weekly review, a sentiment shared by the *Times,* the *Manchester Guardian,* and the *Daily Telegraph*.[85] One critic commented "that such weekly journals as *Time and Tide* were more important than ever, now that everywhere empty minded men were jumping up and dictating to their betters, Hitler, for instance telling a man like Einstein what to think."[86] Although it remains difficult to quantify the paper's actual influence, it did continue to expand its reader base. Even during World War II, when the costs of producing a weekly soared because of paper shortages and the short supply of workers, *Time and Tide* not only continued publication uninterrupted but also witnessed an increase in its circulation, which peaked during the late 1950s at fifty thousand.[87] During this period, the paper covered Rhondda's unsuccessful fight to assume her father's title as a woman and sit in the House of Lords. Although by the mid-1930s *Time and Tide* no longer constituted solely a weekly feminist review, the motivation that had inspired Rhondda to start the paper—to move beyond a constitutional fix to solve women's inequality—remained. Articles that focused on changing cultural attitudes toward women's and children's causes, for example, still appeared in its pages, as did debates over contraception. The paper's tone assumed that it was women's responsibility along with men to help resolve broad social questions.

Long after the paper distanced itself from its more radical origins, many continued to remember it for its fiery polemics. "People took it for granted at first that the journal was designed for feminist propaganda," claimed the *Manchester Guardian* in 1958, "but, though eminent workers in the feminist movement were involved on the board of the directors, Lady Rhondda intended it to be, and made it a journal that exerted a considerable influence."[88] Rhondda reminded readers of the *Daily Telegraph* in a 1941 interview of her paper's broad interest and audience. As her interviewer summed it up, "she has round her a brilliant staff of writers. Half of them, as she has pointed out to those who would call it a feminist paper, are men."[89]

Despite self-conscious limitations on the number of female staff members, *Time and Tide* continued to have a sizable number of women represented on the board and in the editorial rooms when compared to other weekly and daily papers. Rhondda included women and women's voices in mainstream political debates through *Time and Tide* and took risks on then lesser known women authors such as Winifred Holtby, Virginia Woolf, and Vera Brittain. In her later years, Rhondda was noted for promoting women in the professions, particularly journalism. In her own life example, she had proven that women could succeed in business, having served as director of over forty companies. *Time and Tide*, however, remained her most enduring accomplishment. Although plagued with financial difficulties in its final years, *Time and Tide* proved to exert a steady influence on British political culture. After her death in 1958, countless obituaries remembered Rhondda for her accomplishments in multiple arenas of public life. Her successful melding of feminist politics with a mainstream political sensibility as an editor and journalist, however, left the most lasting impression on her reading public: "Whatever may be the ultimate fate of *Time and Tide* it will always be remembered as the personal creation of a woman who sought not only to raise the public and professional functions of her sex, but also to offer to thinking people in grasping world opinions uncontaminated by sectarian prejudice."[90]

Without the dedicated support of its founder, *Time and Tide* soon faded from prominence. At the time of her death, *Time and Tide* was in serious debt. Rhondda had spent around five hundred pounds a week of her own money to support the paper. All the money from her estate went to paying off its creditors. A successful appeal to readers for funds guaranteed *Time and Tide*'s future for a time, although the paper continued to decline until 1963, when it merged with another troubled paper, *John O'London's Weekly*.[91] *Time and Tide*, however, was remembered, not only as Rhondda's legacy but also as a testament to the potential power of alternative journalism as a political medium. Representing women's voices and political agendas within the pages of a mainstream political weekly review was *Time and Tide*'s most notable radical departure as a political weekly review, long after the paper had ceased to represent a strictly feminist perspective. By placing her paper into the vanguard of British political culture, Rhondda had set out to prove that indeed, as its early motto claimed, *Time and Tide* "waited for no man."

The combination of changes in news-making practices and women's political culture in Britain during the interwar years helped bring an end to women's advocacy journalism as it had operated during the previous seventy-five years. World War I had helped to rupture the continuities of Edwardian political life, where women had once found empowerment through bold public expressions of political dissent. The more muted responses of female activists during the interwar years had their origins in a conflict that asked citizens to join together to support the state against a common enemy. However, this new world of media and politics did not mark the end of either the woman journalist or women's political activism. As the example of Rhondda and her weekly review has suggested, the interwar years ushered in the possibility for new opportunities to question traditional gender hierarchies. How that critique played out in the coming decades had as much to do with the intellectual and institutional foundations set down by early female activists as it did with the political and social challenges that lay ahead. The story of the rise and fall of the women's press as a political institution constitutes an important defining chapter in the history of the making of the female activist in modern Britain.

Gender, Journalism, and the Female Political Subject

> On a chilly Friday in late February, 1970, I dressed carefully in a mini–sweater dress, long black leather boots and an ankle-length black and white herring-bone coat. I was preparing to go to my first ever political conference—the "Women's Weekend" being held at Ruskin College, Oxford. I had heard about the conference from a new friend, Audrey Battersby, who had moved down the road. . . . After the conference, a newsletter was produced, in order to keep groups of women all over the country in touch with each other.
>
> —Michelene Wandor, *Once a Feminist*

Michelene Wandor's description of her early days in the female liberation movement offers a highly individualized snapshot of late twentieth-century women's grassroots politics. Venturing to Oxford at the suggestion of a neighbor, she found herself associated for the first time with a feminist network of like-minded women. The community she came into contact with intended to continue the dialogue started at the conference well beyond the "Women's Weekend." "There was also a small group of women who met in London, in order to find a way of publishing some of the papers," recalled Wandor. "The groups' enthusiasm waned, but mine didn't; I took the file of papers, and asked people to write other articles, which I then edited into *The Body Politic*, the first anthology of British Women's Liberation writings." After the first flush of excitement wore off, Wandor found that the movement needed leadership to maintain its momentum. It also required a medium for communication. In 1971, Wandor, a one-time poetry editor for the British entertainment weekly *Time Out*, decided to organize another conference that laid the necessary groundwork for the publication of the radical feminist magazine *Spare Rib* (fig. 29).[1]

Figure 29. *Spare Rib,* cover page.

Spare Rib came out of the London-based underground press movement of the 1960s. This "amorphous movement," in the words of Germaine Greer, tested the boundaries of British cultural and political life. Radical periodicals that followed this program such as *IT, OZ,* and *Frendz* developed as what *Spare Rib* editor Marsha Rowe called "an authentic voice" for 1960s youth culture as "an alternative outlet" to the mass media. The development of cheap printing techniques for setting type and publishing photographs made it possible for this radical new press to emerge, despite the growing influence of large media conglomerates over periodical production and distribution during the second half of the twentieth century. New offset lithographic techniques enabled editors of alternative papers to experiment with color and layout, giving underground periodicals an eye-catching appearance that complemented their bold politics.[2]

The particularities of fashion aside, Wandor's self-representation of the making of her activist identity during the 1970s in many ways echoed early narratives of the women's press movement. From Bessie Parkes in the late 1850s to Lady Rhondda in the 1920s, women had published advocacy papers to discuss women's status and mobilize their constituencies in the name of political reform. Mirroring the achievements of the late nineteenth- and early twentieth-century women's press movement, hundreds of feminist newssheets, journals, and magazines were published in Britain in the late 1960s through the early 1980s.[3]

The years in between had been difficult for the alternative press. By the mid-1930s, the number of advocacy publications produced for and by women slowed down. With the demise of *Time and Tide* as a feminist weekly, a Victorian style of political advocacy concerned with women's representation as citizen subjects gave way to a more muted feminist pragmatism focused on the quotidian aspects of women's lives. The *Women's Freedom League Bulletin* (1934–61), as an amateur-style newssheet, stood virtually alone as a general feminist paper. This period—referred to as the "lean decades" by one bibliographer—witnessed the starting and stopping of only a handful of feminist publications.[4] The *Woman's National Newspaper* (1938), for example, tried three different incarnations in one year before giving up in failure. The period did see the rise of a number of organizational newssheets concerned with imperial and international questions, published both in the colony and the metropole, that included *Bulletin of the Indian Women's Movement* (1934–51), *Women in Kenya* (1944–57), *East Africa Women's League* (1953–56), and *Black Sash* (1956–). Most, however, were published for circulation only within their affiliated organizations.

Changes in the periodicals market, coupled with the rise of politicized associational networks, made a newly refashioned feminist press a reality during the 1970s. The modern movement for women's liberation had returned to print as a forum for political dialogue. By the time *Spare Rib* hit the newsstands in 1972, the male-dominated youth culture of the 1960s had already begun to frustrate some feminists. The small number of women who worked on underground papers soon found themselves marginalized by a movement that, for all of its rhetoric about freedom, upheld traditional gendered hierarchies. It took a total of three meetings, including the initial one called by Wandor for women radicals, to decide to start a national feminist magazine. Rowe described the purpose of this new publication: "We wanted to produce something which would reach out to women and which would also use and test our own capabilities." Although not the first periodical of the women's liberation movement—the periodical *Shrew* (1967–78) claimed that distinction in the late 1960s—*Spare Rib* emerged as one of the most distinctive and largest-circulation feminist publications of the period, averaging twenty-seven thousand copies per issue at its peak. Forming a limited liability company with only two thousand pounds capital, a group of feminist women journalists published *Spare Rib* from its first issue in June 1972 until February 1993.[5]

Spare Rib prided itself in the collective nature of its organization, the radical tone of its articles, and its ambivalent relationship to advertisers and advertising. Initially arranged on the business level as a hierarchy because of the lack of experience of many of its early founders, *Spare Rib* soon took the form of a collective wherein editorial duties were shared equally among the staff. The editors decided that the periodical would not rely on advertising revenue or "complementary copy" (articles written by magazine staff that pushed products of advertising clients) for support, as women's domestic magazines did, but rather on subscribers. Articles on subjects such as female sexuality, women and disability, education, religion, women and the professions, and women in the arts made up the magazine's eclectic collection of news. The most prominent topic in *Spare Rib*, however, was women's relationship to paid and unpaid labor. Although the context had changed, this focus harkened back to the *English Woman's Journal*, which had started the women's press movement with its discussion of women's employment. Much in the spirit of *Time and Tide*, *Spare Rib* also satirized social convention with its regular "Man's Page," which critiqued the women's pages while attempting to draw men into a dialogue about traditional gender roles.

Spare Rib shared another characteristic with its nineteenth- and early twentieth-century predecessors: financial insecurity. As a not-for-profit publication, *Spare Rib* relied on revenue from issue sales and a limited number of advertisements. The periodical had over twenty-five thousand subscribers and claimed an actual readership, based on its estimate of shared readership, of almost ninety thousand. One-time collective member Marcel Farry said: "it's very important for the magazine to be as accessible as possible . . . we don't want ideas to reach only a small number of women."[6] Despite these lofty goals and its long publication history, for many its final years tell the story of steady decline in terms of the quality of its content. In describing the end of *Spare Rib,* Paul Anderson of the *New Statesman* wondered how the periodical lasted as long as it did, claiming "low quality" articles were responsible for the periodical's death "after a drawn out illness." In Anderson's opinion, the periodical had lost its radical edge when it tried to broaden its base by appealing to a public interested in sensational stories rather than feminist politics.[7] Others, such as Loretta Loach, took a different view, claiming that despite its less radical edge during the 1980s, it nevertheless represented a "vehicle for struggle and change."[8] These contradictory perceptions of *Spare Rib* revealed the persistent difficulties that faced radical publications eager to strike a balance between market forces and political radicalism in the modern capitalist marketplace.

Although the history of 1970s feminism and its press is beyond the scope of this book, the story of *Spare Rib* is emblematic of a number of themes explored in the preceding chapters. The remarkable similarity between the narratives of nineteenth- and late twentieth-century advocacy journalism begs the question of why modern political movements found the alternative press a useful medium for the mobilization of their constituencies. Much of the reason rests with structural changes in the British periodical market. Starting in the 1850s, the end of the "taxes on knowledge" and the new incorporation laws opened up the possibility of starting a periodical cheaply and with limited risk. Improved technology and literacy made print the primary vehicle for information during the second half of the nineteenth century.

These shifts, coupled with the rise of an activist feminist movement, made advocacy journalism into a viable forum for the expression of an alternative political vision. Women's political culture relied on advocacy publications for both propaganda and to keep members in touch with one another. Changes in journalism, coupled with competition from media such as radio during the mid-1930s and, later, television, challenged the ability of advocacy journalism to maintain itself as a viable alternative political medium. By the 1970s, the structural and political conditions necessary for a return to print by radical organizations made it possible to revive a political culture that relied upon grassroots communication mediums and female associational life.

Changes in media technology accompanied the rise of ideological shifts that posited women as liberal political subjects. The women's press movement thus both shaped and was shaped by the contours of British liberal reform culture. Women's associational networks and their affiliated papers contributed to the rise of a distinctive women's political culture during the second half of the nineteenth century that culminated in the struggle for the vote. Much has been made in recent years of the importance of "ideology" and "discourse" in determining women's responses to cultural, political, and economic phenomenon. The institutions that have historically supported and promoted particular ideologies, however, have generated less attention. Advocacy journalism created a sustainable infrastructure that women placed in the service of a host of ideological programs, encompassing social, economic, and political reforms from the left and the right. Inventing a woman-run news industry was thus as much about creating sustainable institutions and structures that could be used by women to publicize ideas as it was about propagating a particular ideology or set of principles. Understanding how and why these institutions came about refocuses our attention on the everyday and sometimes mundane arenas that made the work of ideology possible. By problematizing the role of the media in modern democratic societies and through exploring the intellectual and institutional structures of the women's press movement, I hope this book has demonstrated the very real continuities that have historically driven modern women's political culture in Britain. — ✕ + Spare Rib into mainstream ..

From the beginning, the women's press understood itself as a national, and to a lesser extent international, movement. This is why I have referred to the papers in this study as "British" rather by their place of origin. Certainly, most of these papers were started in England or, more specifically, London. Editors of women's papers, however, understood their project as expanding beyond the parochial boundaries of traditional English radicalism. Women like Margaret Cousins, for example, claimed that reading *Votes for Women* in Ireland made her feel "so much one of them" that it inspired her to become involved in "the freeing of world womanhood from the shackles, unjustices, inequalities ... women suffered."[9] She started the Irish Women's Franchise League in 1908 and later helped inspire the feminist movement in India. This attempt to understand women's inequality as a worldwide problem was reflected in the universalizing tone of many women's journals. As early as 1869, Josephine Butler began discussing the need for cooperation between women in Britain and Europe with the ultimately failed launch of *Nowadays*. Although these ideas found their clearest articulation during the interwar years, they were part of an early dialogue that posited "woman" as a universal category for the first time, with all of the problematic meanings that have come to be embedded in that project. Thus, by the early twentieth century, it might be more appropriate to understand the women's press movement within a larger international rather than British context.

The voices relied upon in this book have admittedly mainly come from the strongest advocates of the women's press movement themselves: the publishers, editors, writers, and readers of women's periodicals. These women believed that the press provided a useful vehicle to facilitate their entry into public life. In this way, they echoed the sentiments of their male contemporaries, who understood the repeal of the taxes on knowledge as creating a press that represented public opinion, which they called the "Fourth Estate." Scholars such as George Boyce have called this concept a "myth," a useful fiction for journalists bent on justifying their participation in what was then a relatively low-status profession.[10] Regardless of their motivation, it is clear that many journalists built their careers around a belief that newspapers *were* there to serve as the court of public opinion. The women whose stories have been told in this book held similar beliefs about the transformative potential of the press. Whether they actually changed British society or not remains a secondary consideration when we consider how this belief in the power of the press to lend them a voice affected their self-representation in the public sphere. Appropriating issues of employment, education, social reform, and political representation as women's issues, the women's press offered participants a chance to engage in contemporary debates about modern gender identity.

Whether or not print journalism had the power to facilitate social change, the women's press movement did, in the end, radically reconfigure the female activist's understanding of her status as a political actor. Women's understanding of their own relationship to print, therefore, has remained a central part of my analysis in this study. A particular kind of female political activist has emerged in this book who believed that through her connection to the women's advocacy press and its associated institutions she could, despite her disenfranchised status, play a legitimate role in modern British political culture. The women's press movement, in addition to facilitating the development of an activist political identity, provided real opportunities for members that were often denied them in mainstream culture, including employment and self-representation. Historically, the alternative press has served as a space where political ideologies have found their earliest articulation. Women readers, writers, and editors remained part of a larger cultural process, wherein print journalism helped provide a forum for women to articulate the nature of their relationship to the Victorian liberal reform project.

Women's advocacy journalism, it is important to note, was not always necessarily subversive, often conserving the established gender order through deploying traditional cultural tropes for readers. Many so-called women's agendas found their way into a mainstream reform agenda through attention given to them through their conservative treatment in the women's press. At the same time, the women's press continued to occupy a space outside of the mainstream where women created their own political culture within the pages of their press. This dual function was what in part enabled women's advocacy journalism to survive as a medium: remaining on the margins allowed for the more important business of catering to reader interests that did not necessarily coincide with mainstream political preoccupations. As a disenfranchised community, women used advocacy papers to create a specialized forum for political discourse.

Starting in the 1850s, middle-class female activists built the intellectual and institutional foundations of this new woman-centered associational life that looked to unite its participants along gender rather than class lines. The question of women's political equality certainly provided an important thread that united the women's press. A diverse reform agenda, however, continued to be the hallmark of this extraparliamentary political culture, run by and for women since the beginning, and provided a strong foundation for the women's movement in Britain. Even during the suffrage battles, women's organizations dealt with a constellation of issues that often related only tangentially to the vote.

Historians have debated whether the competing interests embodied in the women's movement proved a strength or weakness. This is especially true in accounts of interwar feminism that have tried to explain the impact of the split between "old" and "new" feminism during the 1920s and 1930s. Did the emergence of these new discourses fragment the movement, as Martin Pugh has argued, or did they strengthen it, as Cheryl Law has suggested? Challenges to established doctrine such as egalitarian feminism did not necessarily signify a decline but rather represented the expansion of a varied political arena for women. Examining the associational networks and institutional structures that gave the movement its continuity, as this book has done, can help historians understand the variety of elements that held this sometimes divided movement together.

The alternative press during the late nineteenth and early twentieth centuries thus had the potential to allow special interest groups to take advantage of available technology and print-based media structures for the expression of diverse political agendas. This case study of the women's press, then, can help provide insights into the rise of other political movements. Shifts in the women's press happened within the larger context of changing media practices that understood political reporting as a hindrance to circulation. Media critics have long lamented the "depoliticization" of the mainstream press that started as early as the second half of the nineteenth century. By the 1920s, the changes brought on by the New Journalism's drive for high circulation and profits had affected even the most venerable of publications. Periodicals, after the Northcliffe revolution, had an obligation to both entertain and inform. Political news increasingly competed for space with other items, such as advertisements and human-interest stories. According to Jean Chalaby, whereas parliamentary reporting dominated nineteenth-century publications, by 1927, "home news on politics, economic and social affairs" constituted only 14 percent of the total news space in the *Times*. As might be expected, for other newspapers this figure was even lower.[11]

The connection between newspapers and parliamentary politics continued to weaken during this period, as periodicals ceased to serve as organs of particular political organizations. By the turn of the century, print media had taken on a broader, less partisan, and, some have said, less rigorous, political function. Women's advocacy periodicals continued to be an important alternative voice in this process of contraction and consolidation. The women's press faced new challenges and opportunities as it began to embrace the weekly review format during the twentieth century, in order to offer political and cultural critiques of interwar British society. Those periodicals that continued to rely on old methods of political propaganda and reporting, such as the suffrage press, simply could not sustain themselves in this new climate.

In its narrowest sense, this book has been the story of a series of failed experiments. The inability of advocacy journalism to succeed in the marketplace has historically ensured the limited success of papers that represent radical ideas, from the Unstamped to the Chartist to the Labour and the women's press. Concern over the limited audience for alternative publications has grown in recent years. Part of the problem is the high cost associated with publishing a periodical in today's market. The launch of the "internationalist, socialist, feminist, and green" monthly *Red Pepper* in 1994, for example, required the raising of 135,000 pounds in capital, and it was estimated that twelve thousand subscribers would be needed for the magazine to break even. Some have estimated costs at a great deal higher, claiming that it should have spent another 135,000 pounds for promotion, in order to raise the needed number of subscribers.[12] In a postmillennium periodical market dominated by a smaller and smaller number of big titles, the reality continues to be that most alternative newspapers cannot make it on their own unless they are the pet projects of wealthy editors. Conventional print remains a largely unaffordable option, leaving the alternative press to find more accessible forums for communication such as the cheap, at present, electronic media.

Advocacy journalism was born during the second half of the nineteenth century as a result of a small group of women taking advantage of economic and technological opportunities that made print journalism into a viable option for the expression of ideas. Part of what enabled the alternative British press tradition to survive through to the twentieth century was its dynamic character. The mode of political dissent continues to change, depending upon its historical context. Due to its relatively low cost, the Internet has the potential to serve as a new medium to expand accessibility to mainstream political discourse. Although the medium is different—that is, it is now electronic rather than printed—the potential for the media to provide a vehicle for radical critiques of social, political, and economic life still remains. How it is used is up to a new generation of reformers in search of a medium for community building and political expression.

Bibliography of British Women's Advocacy Periodicals

The following list provides information on advocacy periodicals published from the 1850s to the 1930s. Information on frequency, starting price, place of publication, editor(s), affiliation and title changes is provided when available. To help researchers locate these titles, library (L) and/or microfilm (MF) information is included at the end of each entry. Although this list is comprehensive to date, new research will certainly continue to add to its contents in coming years.

Abbreviations

d	penny
s	shilling
AM	Adam Matthew Publications, England
ATLA	American Theological Library Association, Evanston, Illinois
B	Bodleian Library, Oxford University
BL	British Library, London
BM	British Museum Microfilm Service, London
C	British Library Newspaper collection, Colindale Avenue, London NW9
D	Datamics, Inc., New York, New York
GC	Gerritsen Collection of Women's History (Microfilming Corp of America)
H	Harvester Microfilm, Brighton, England
IDC	Inter Documentation Company, Leiden, Netherlands
IWM	Imperial War Museum, London
LC	Library of Congress, Washington, D.C.
RP	Research Publications, New Haven, Conn.

TUC   Trades Union Congress Library, London
UM   University Microfilms International, Ann Arbor, Michigan
WL   Women's Library, London
WMP   World Microfilm Publications, London

Periodicals

Alexandra Magazine (1864–65). Monthly; 6d; London; ed. Susannah Meredith; continued as *Englishwoman's Review* (L: B; MF: GC).

Association Notes (1906–20). Irregular; organ of Federation of Women Clerks; continued by *Opportunity* (L: WL).

Barmaid (1891–92). Weekly; 1d; London (MF: H).

Birth Control News (1922–46). Monthly; London; ed. Dr. Marie Stopes (MF: D).

Bombshell (1917–?). 4d; organ of National Projectile Factory Workers (L: IWM).

Britannia (1915–18). Weekly; 1d; London; ed. Christabel Pankhurst; organ of the Women's Social and Political Union (L: WL, C; MF: LC).

British Women's Temperance Journal (1886–92). Monthly; London; organ of the British Women's Temperance Union; continued by *Wings* (L: BL).

British Workwoman (1863–96). Monthly; London (L: BL; MF: H).

Business Girl (1912). Monthly; 1d; London; ed. Helen Houston; organ of Institution of Shorthand Typists (L: C; MF: H).

Cardonald News (1916–19). Weekly; Glasgow; organ of National Filling Factory Workers (L: IWM).

Carry On (1916). 1d; Newcastle-on-Tyne; organ of Armstrong Munitions Workers (L: IWM).

Catholic Citizen (1918–?). Monthly; 1d; London; organ of the Catholic Women's Suffrage Society (L: BL, WL; MF: H).

Catholic Suffragist (1915–18). Monthly; 1d; London; continued by *Catholic Citizen* (L: BL, WL; MF: H).

Central and East of England Society for Women's Suffrage (1891–1900). Monthly; London; organ of National Society for Women's Suffrage (MF: GC).

Church League for Women's Suffrage (1912–17). Monthly; 1d; London; continued by *Church Militant* (L: C, WL; M: H).

Church Militant (1918–24). Monthly; 2d; London (L: C, WL; MF: H).

Churchwoman (1895–1903). Weekly; London (L: C).

Coming Day (1916–20). Monthly; London; organ of the Free Church League for Women's Suffrage (L: C, WL; MF: H).

Common Cause (1909–20). Weekly; 1d; Manchester/London; organ of the National Union of Women's Suffrage Societies; continued by *Woman's Leader* (L: C, WL; MF: RP).

Conservative and Unionist Women's Franchise Review (1909–16). Quarterly; 2d; London; organ of the Conservative and Unionist Women's Franchise Association (L: C, WL; MF: H).

Conservative Woman (1921–29). Monthly; 3d; Leeds; ed. Blanche L. Leigh (L: BL; MF: H).

Daughter (1897). Weekly; London (L: C).

Daybreak (1886–1918). Monthly; London; organ of Church of England Zenana Missionary Society (L: BL; MF: AM).

Domestic Servants' Advertiser (1913–?). Weekly; 1d; London; (MF: H).

Dornock Souvenir Magazine (1916–19). Organ of H. M. Factory Workers (L: University of Tulsa).

English Churchwoman (1912–37). Monthly; London (L: C).

Englishwoman (1909–21). Monthly; London; ed. Elisina Grant Richards (L: BL, WL; MF: GC).

English Woman's Journal (1858–64). Monthly; 1s; London; ed. Bessie Parkes; continued by *Alexandra Magazine* (L: B, WL; MF: RP).

Englishwoman's Review (1866–1910). Quarterly; 1s; London; eds.: 1866–82, J. Boucherett; 1883–89, C. A. Biggs; 1890–Jan. 1893, H. Blackburn and A. M. Mackenzie; Apr. 1903–July 1910, A. M. Mackenzie (L: BL, B, WL; MF: GC).

Enterprise Magazine (1912–13). Monthly; London; organ of Enterprise Club Limited for Women Clerks (L: BL; MF: H).

Federation News (1921–24). Monthly; 1/2d; London; ed. Grace Newbould; organ of the Women's National Liberal Federation; continued by *Liberal Women's News* (L: BL; MF: H).

Female Missionary Intelligencer (1854–99). Monthly; Dublin/London; organ of Society for Promotion of Female Education in China, Africa, and the East (L: BL).

Female Servants Union News (1892). Monthly; London; ed. Mrs. M. J. Sales (MF: H).

Free Church Suffrage Times (1913–15). Monthly; London; organ of Free Church League for Women's Suffrage; continued as *Coming Day* (L: C, WL; MF: H).

Freewoman (1911–12). Weekly; 3d; London; ed. Dora Marsden; continued as *New Freewoman* (L: C, WL; MF: RP).

Friendly Leaves (1876–1917). Monthly; London; ed. M. E. Townsend; organ of Girls Friendly Society of the Church of England (L: BL).

Friendly Work (1883–1917). Monthly, then quarterly; London; another organ of Girls Friendly Society (L: BL).

Friend of Women's Suffrage (1913–14). Quarterly; 1/2d; London; organ of National Union of Women's Suffrage Societies (L: BL; MF: H).

Gatherer (1882–83). Monthly; ed. Mrs. Rawlinson Ford (L: WL).

Girls' Friendly Society Associates Journal (1880–?). Monthly; London (L: BL).

Go Forward (1891–1908). Monthly; London; organ of YWCA (L: BL).

The Helpmeet (1891–1900). Paisley, Scotland; organ of Free Church of Scotland (L: BL).

Humanity (1913–14). Monthly; 1d; London; Organ of British Federation for the Emancipation of Sweated Women (L: BL; MF: H).

Imperial Colonist (1902–27). Monthly; London; organ of British Women's Emigration Association (L: BL).

Independent Suffragette (1916–18). Monthly; 1d; London; organ of Independent Women's Social and Political Union; (L: C, WL; M: H).

Indian Female Evangelist (1872–93). Quarterly; organ of Indian Female Normal School and Instruction Society (L: BL; MF: AM).

India's Women (1881–1957). Monthly; London; organ of Church of England Zenana Missionary Society (L: BL; MF: UM).

Iris (1892). Monthly; 4d; organ of Women's Progressive Society; not found, mentioned in both Beetham, *Magazine of Her Own,* and Doughan and Sanchez, *Feminist Periodicals.*

Irish Schoolmistress (1891–?). Weekly; 1d; Dublin; ed. Mrs. Alice O'Byrne (MF: H).

Journal (1893). Monthly; 1/2d; London; eds. Mrs. Ward Poole, Miss Forham, Miss Shilston; organ of British Women's Temperance Union (L: C, WL; MF: H).

Journal of the Association of Women Teachers (1892–95). Monthly; 3d; London (L: BL; MF: H).

Journal of the Workhouse Visiting Society (1859–65). Fortnightly; 6d; London; ed. Louisa Twining (L: BL).

Jus Suffragii (1906–29). Rotterdam, then London; eds. Martina Kramers, Mary Sheepshanks, Margery Corbett Ashby; organ of International Woman Suffrage Alliance (L: WL; MF: GC).

Kettledrum (1869). Monthly; London; continued by *Now-a-Days* (L: BL; MF: H).

Labour Woman (1913–71). Monthly; 1d; London; eds. Marion Phillips, Betty Lockwood (L: C; MF: H).

League Leaflet (1911–13). Monthly; London; ed. Margaret MacDonald; organ of Women's Labour League; continued by *Labour Woman* (L: C; MF: H).

Liberal Women's News (1924–36). Monthly; 1 1/2d; London; ed. Grace Newbould; organ of the Women's National Liberal Federation (L: BL, WL; MF: H).

Liberal Women's Review (1914). Monthly; London; ed. Mary Somerville; organ of Liberal Women's Suffrage Union (L: WL).

Link (1888). Weekly; London; ed. Annie Besant (L: C; MF: BM).

Modern Woman (1915–16). Weekly; London; 2d; ed. Mary Fraser (L: C; MF: H).

Monthly News of the Conservative Women's Reform Association (1914–24). Monthly; London (L: C; MF: H).

Mothers in Council (1890–?). London; ed. Charlotte Yonge (L: BL).

National Council of Women Occasional Paper (1919–22). Irregular; London (MF: GC).

National Council of Women Tracts (1898–1902). Monthly; 1d; London (MF: GC).

National Union of Women Workers Occasional Paper (1896–1918). Irregular; London; continued by *National Council of Women* (MF: GC).

New Citizen (1920–21). Weekly; London; organ of National Women Citizens' Association (L: C).

New Freewoman (1913). Semimonthly; London; ed. Dora Marsden; continued by *Egoist* (L: C, WL; MF: LC).

Now-a-Days (1869). Monthly; London; not found, mentioned in Doughan.

Nurses Journal (1891–1918). Monthly; London (L: C).

Nursing Times (1905–?). London; organ of Royal College of Nursing (L: C).

Only Way (1909–10). Edinburgh; organ of Edinburgh University Women's Suffrage Society (L: WL).

Opportunity (1921–40). London; organ of Federation of Women Civil Servants (L: C).

Our Paper (1883–1911). Monthly; London; organ of Church of England Women's Help Society; continued by *English Churchwoman* (L: C).

Our Sisters in Other Lands (1879–1937). Quarterly; London; organ of Women's Missionary Association of the Presbyterian Church of England (L: BL).

Personal Rights Journal (1881–1903). Monthly; 1d; London; (L: C, WL; MF: H).

Pioneer (1887–92). Monthly; London; organ of Social Purity Alliance and Moral Reform Union (L: WL; MF: IDC).

Protestant Woman (1894–95). Monthly; London; organ of Women's Protestant Union (L: C).

Queen (1861–1970). Weekly; 6d; London; (L: C; MF: RP).

Rose, Shamrock, and Thistle (1862–65). Monthly; 1s; Edinburgh; ed. Mary Anne Thomson (MF: UMI).

Schoolmistress (1881–1935). Weekly; 1d; London; (L: C; MF: BM).

Scottish Women's Liberal Federation (1899–1900). Monthly; Glasgow (MF: GC).

Scottish Women's Temperance News (1897–1972). Monthly; Edinburgh (L: C).

Shafts (1892–99). Frequency varies; 3d; London; ed. Margaret Shurmer Sibthorp (L: C, WL; MF: H).

Shell Clippings (1916–?). Organ of Bootle Munition Factory (L: IWM).

Shell Magazine: Leeds; organ of Employees of the National Ordinance Factory (L: University of Tulsa).

Shield (1870–1970). Frequency varies; London; eds. Josephine Butler, Alison Neilans, Margaret Schwartz; organ of the Anti–Contagious Disease Acts Association (L: BL, WL; MF: IDC).

Sisters (1895–98). Monthly; 1d; London; ed. Mrs. Hooper (MF: GC).

Storm Bell (1898–1900). Monthly; London; ed. Josephine Butler; organ of Ladies National Association for the Abolition of State Vice (L: WL; MF: IDC).

Stri-Dharma (1919–36). Monthly; Madras, India; eds. Margaret Cousins, D. Jinjarajadasa, Malati Patwardhan, Muthulakshmi Reddy; organ of Women's Indian Association (L: WL, Stanford University).

Suffragette (1912–15). Weekly; 1d; London; ed. Christabel Pankhurst; organ of Women's Social and Political Union (L: C, WL; MF: LC).

Suffragette News Sheet (1916). Monthly; 1d; London; organ of "Suffragettes of the WSPU" (MF: H).

Taxette (1920–23). Monthly; 2d; London; eds. D. Rogozin, Rose J. Florence, Dorothy C. Kelly; organ of Association of Temporary Women Tax Clerks (L: C; MF: H).

Threefold Core (1891–96). Quarterly; organ of National Union of Women Workers; continued by *Occasional Paper* (L: Girton College Archive, Cambridge University; MF: H).

Time and Tide (1920–66). Weekly; 4d; London; ed. Lady Rhondda (L: C; MF: BL).

Townswoman (1933–). Monthly; organ of the National Union of Townswomen's Guilds (L: WL).

Victoria Magazine (1863–80). Monthly; 1s; London; ed. Emily Faithfull (L: Bodleian).

Victoria Times (1873). Weekly; London (L: C).

Vote (1909–33). Weekly; London; ed. Charlotte Despard; organ of Women's Freedom League (L: C, WL; MF: BM).

Votes for Women (1907–18). Weekly; London; eds. Emmeline and F. W. Pethick-Lawrence; organ of Women's Social and Political Union (L: C, WL; MF: LC).

Waverley Journal (1856–58). Biweekly; 4d; Glasgow; (L: C; MF: H).

White Ribbon (1896–1925). Monthly; London; organ of National British Women's Temperance Association (L: C).

Wings (1892–1925). Monthly; organ of British Women's Temperance Association (L: BL).

Woman (1872). Weekly; 2d; London; ed. Amelia Lewis (L: C; MF: H).

Woman (1887). Weekly; 2d; London; (MF: H).

Woman (1890–1912). Weekly; London (MF: H).

Woman at Home (1893–1917). Monthly; London; 6d; ed. Annie S. Swan (L: BL).

Woman Clerk (1919–31). Monthly; 2d; organ of Association of Women Clerks and Secretaries (L: C; MF: H).

Woman Engineer (1919–?). Quarterly; London; organ of Women's Engineering Society (L: BL, WL).

Woman Freemason (1925–75). Irregular (L: BL).

Woman Journalist (1910–?). Quarterly; London; ed. Mrs. Pat Garrod; organ of Society of Women Writers and Journalists (L: BL; MF: H).

Woman Teacher (1919–61). Frequency varies; 1d; London; organ of National Union of Women Teachers (MF: H).

Woman Worker (1907–21). Monthly; 1d; London; ed. Mary Macarthur; organ of National Federation of Women Workers (L: C; MF: BL).

Woman Worker [An-bean-oibre] (1928). Dublin (L: C).

Woman Worker (1926–27). Monthly; 1d; London; organ of Communist Party of Great Britain; continued by *Working Woman* (L: C; MF: H).

Woman Worker for Every Woman (1908–10). Weekly; 1d; London (MF: WMP).

Woman's Advocate (1874). Irregular; Dublin; ed. T. J. Haslam (L: BL; MF: H).

Woman's Agricultural Times (1899–1906). Reading; ed. countess of Warwick (L: BL).

Woman's Dreadnought (1914–24). London; weekly; organ of East London Federation of Suffragettes; continued by *Worker's Dreadnought* (L: C, WL; MF: BL).

Woman's Gazette (1875–79). Monthly; London; ed. Lousia Hubbard; continued by *Work and Leisure* (L: BL, WL; MF: GC).

Woman's Guild: Life and Work (1890–1928). Monthly; Edinburgh; organ of Church of Scotland (MF: ATLA).

Woman's Herald (1891–93). Weekly; 1d; London; eds. Helena Temple [Henrietta Muller], Mrs. Frank Morrison, Christina Bremner, Lady Henry Somerset; continued by *Woman's Signal* (L: C, WL; MF: AM).

Woman's Leader (1920–32). Weekly; 3d; London; organ of National Union of Societies for Equal Citizenship (L: C, WL; MF: RP).

Woman's Opinion (1874). Weekly; 1d; London; ed. Amelia Lewis (L: C; MF: H).

Woman's Opinion (1915–16). Weekly; 2d; London; organ of Citizens of the World Movement (L: BL; MF: H).

Woman's Signal (1894–99). Weekly; 1d; London; eds. Lady Henry Somerset, Annie Holdsworth and Florence Fenwick-Miller (L: C/WL; MF: H).

Woman's Signal Budget (1894–95). Monthly; 1d; London; ed. Lady Henry Somerset (L: WL; MF: H).

Woman's Work in Heathen Lands (1883–?). Quarterly; Paisley; 1d; organ of Free Church of Scotland (MF: RP).

Woman's Work in the Great Harvest Field (1872–94). Monthly; London; 4d (L: BL).

Woman's World (1868). Monthly; London; ed. Charles Jones; continued by *Kettledrum* (L: BL; MF: H).

Women and Work (1874–76). 1d; London; Weekly; ed. Emily Faithfull (L: C; MF: H).

Women and Progress (1906–7). Weekly; 1d; London; (L: C, WL; MF: H).

Women in the Mission Field (1899–1903). Monthly; 1d; London; (L: BL).

Women Folk (1908–10). Weekly; 1d; London; ed. Winifred Blatchford (L: C; MF: H).

Women Workers (1891–1924). Quarterly; Birmingham; organ of Birmingham Ladies' Union of Workers (L: Birmingham Public Library; MF: RP).

Women's Charter Review (1913). Ed. Lady Laura McLaren (L: WL).

Women's Education Union Journal (1873–82). Monthly; 6d; London; eds. Emily Shireff, George C. T. Bartley (L: BL; MF: H).

Women's Employment (1900–1974). Monthly; 1 1/2d; London; ed. M. Fuge (L: C, WL).

Women's Farm and Garden Association (1900–1976). Varied; Colchester, Essex (L: BL).

Women's Franchise (1907–11). Weekly; London; ed. J. E. Francis (L: C, WL; MF: H).

Women's Freedom League Bulletin (1934–61). Weekly; 2d (L: WL).

Women's Freedom League Temporary New Sheet (1909). Weekly; continued by *Vote* (L: WL).

Women's Gazette and Weekly News (1888–91). Monthly; 1d; Manchester; organ of Women's Liberal Federation (L: C; MF: H).

Women's Industrial News (1895–1919). Quarterly; 3d; London; organ of Women's Industrial Council (L: C/WL; MF: H).

Women's International League (1916–52). Monthly; London; organ of Women's International League for Peace and Freedom (L: BL).

Women's Labour News (1900–1904). Manchester; eds. Esther Roper, Eva Gore-Booth; mentioned in Doughan.

Women's Liberal Magazine (1920). Monthly; 2d; London; ed. Lucy Masterman (L: BL; MF: H).

Women's Local Government News (1921–25). Monthly; organ of Women's Local Government Society (L: WL).

Women's National Liberal Association (1895–1918). Quarterly; London; organ of Women's National Liberal Association; continued by *Women's Liberal Magazine* (L: BL; MF: UM).

Women's Penny Paper (1888–91). Weekly; 1d; London; ed. Helena Temple [Henrietta Muller]; continued by *Woman's Herald* (L: C, WL; MF: AM).

Women's Protestant Union (1893). Monthly; East Grinstead, West Sussex (L: C).

Women's Suffrage (1907). Monthly; London (L: C).

Women's Suffrage News (1894). Monthly; ed. A. B. Louis; mentioned in Doughan.

Women's Suffrage Record (1903–6). Monthly; ed. Edith Palliser (L: C).

Women's Trades Union Review (1891–1918). Quarterly; 4d; London; ed. Gertrude Tuckwell (L: WL, TUC).

Women's Tribune (1906). Weekly; 2d; London; Continued by *Women and Progress* (L: C, WL; MF: H).

Women's Union Journal (1876–90). Quarterly; London; ed. Emma Paterson; organ of Women's Protective and Provident League; continued by *Women's Trades Union Review* (L: WL, TUC).

Work and Leisure (1880–93). Monthly; London; ed. Louisa Hubbard (L: C, WL; MF: UM).

Worker's Paper of Young Women's Help Society (1892–94). Quarterly; mentioned in Beetham.

Working Gentlewomen's Journal (1906–10). Monthly; London; 2d (MF: H).

Working Woman (1927–29). Monthly; London; organ of Communist Party of Great Britain (L: C).

Zenana Missionary Herald (1893–95). Monthly; London; organ of Women's Missionary Association (L: BL).

Notes

Introduction

1. Diary of Jessie Anthony, Anthony Family Papers, Huntington Library.

2. The term *New Journalism* refers to the commercialized techniques and sensationalist style of reporting employed by press barons such as Pulitzer, Hearst, and Harmsworth during the late nineteenth century on both sides of the Atlantic. See Michael Emery and Edwin Emery, eds., "New Journalism," in *The Press and America* (Boston: Allyn and Bacon, 1996), 171–209; R. A. Scott-James, "The Crisis in London Journalism," *English Review*, April 1912, 85–98; and Sydney Brooks, "The American Yellow Press," *Living Age*, January 13, 1912, 67–76 (reprinted from *Fortnightly Review*).

3. Flint, *Woman Reader*; Levine, *Feminist Lives in Victorian England*; Rendall, *Equal or Different*.

4. Habermas, *Structural Transformation of the Public Sphere*.

5. Levine, "Humanising Influences," 294.

6. The *English Woman's Journal* printed these examples starting in the late 1850s.

7. Flint, *Woman Reader*, 234–49.

8. Rubenstein, *Before the Suffragettes*.

9. Holton, *Suffrage Days*; Holton and Purvis, *Votes for Women*.

10. Sophia A. van Wingerden, *The Women's Suffrage Movement in Britain, 1866–1928* (New York: St. Martin's Press, 1999).

11. Vickery, *Women, Privilege and Power*, 2–4, 20.

12. "Considering the State of U.S. Women's History," 151–52.

13. Pugh, *Women and the Women's Movement in Britain*; Holton, *Suffrage Days*; van Wingerden, *Women's Suffrage Movement in Britain*; Smith, *British Feminism in the Twentieth Century*; Rosen, *Rise Up Women*; Roger Fulford, *Votes for Women* (London: Faber and Faber, 1958).

14. Hunt draws on Foucaultian analysis in defining political culture in *Politics, Culture, and Class in the French Revolution* (Berkeley: University of California Press, 1984), 56 n. 9.

15. See Jane Rendall, "A Moral Engine," in *Equal or Different* (Oxford: Blackwell, 1987); Van Arsdel, "Mrs. Florence Fenwick Miller and the Woman's Signal," 107–18; and Spender, *Time and Tide Wait for No Man.*

16. See Vicinus, *Independent Women,* Ellen Jordan, *The Women's Movement and Women's Employment in Nineteenth-Century Britain* (New York: Routledge, 1999), and Holcombe, *Victorian Ladies at Work.*

17. Levine, *Feminist Lives;* Rappaport, *Shopping for Pleasure.*

18. See Dorothy Thompson, *The Chartists: Popular Politics in the Industrial Revolution* (New York: Pantheon Books, 1984), and Hollis, *Pauper Press.*

19. See Deian Hopkin, "The Socialist Press in Britain, 1890–1910," and Peter Roger Mountjoy, "The Working Class Press and Working Class Conservatism," both in Boyce, Curran, and Wingate, *Newspaper History;* William Fishman, "Morris Winchevsky's London Yiddish Newspaper" (Oxford: Oxford Center for Postgraduate Hebrew Studies Lecture, 1985); and Benjamin, *Black Press in Britain.*

20. See Lee, *Origins of the Popular Press,* for the period 1850–1914, and Graham Murdock and Peter Golding, "1914–1976," in Boyce, Curran, and Wingate, *Newspaper History,* 130–48, for the later period.

21. Brown, *Victorian News and Newspapers,* 276. Jean Chalaby, *The Invention of Journalism* (London: Macmillan, 1998), 2. Chalaby has further argued that the commercialization of the mainstream press started not with the New Journalism but with the press tax repeals at midcentury.

22. Flint, *Woman Reader,* 42.

23. Tickner, *Spectacle of Women,* 14.

24. Barbara Onslow, *Women of the Press in Nineteenth-Century Britain* (New York: St. Martin's Press, 2000), 17–35.

25. Gallagher, *Nobody's Story;* Merriman, *Godiva's Ride;* Turner, *Living by the Pen.*

26. Brown, *Victorian News and Newspapers,* 77.

27. See her critique of the commercial aspects of militancy in "The Militant Suffrage Movement," an article reprinted in McPhee and FitzGerald, *Non-Violent Militant,* 185–93, and Barbara Green's analysis in *Spectacular Confessions,* 89–93.

28. Kathryn Shevelow attributes this relative absence of journalists to literary critics' overemphasis on the novel. Her pioneering study *Women and Print Culture* makes a convincing case for including women's periodicals and journalists in the canon of women's literature.

29. Gullace, *"Blood of Our Sons,"* 9–10.

30. Koss, *Rise and Fall of the Political Press,* 2:497–98, 681–82.

31. Holton, *Suffrage Days,* and Harold Smith, *The British Women's Suffrage Cam-*

paign (London: Longman, 1998), have traced the origins of the women's suffrage campaign to the Victorian era.

Chapter 1. Making Women Their Business

1. Parkes and Bodichon published in periodicals during the 1840s, including *Hastings, St. Leonards Gazette,* and the *Birmingham Post.* Bessie Rayner Parkes to Barbara Leigh Smith Bodichon, May 27, 184[7], Parkes Papers, Girton College Archive.

2. Incorporation proceedings for the English Woman's Journal, Limited, were held on February 12, 1858. The company was set up with a nominal capital of one thousand pounds divided into two hundred shares of five pounds each. Bessie Parkes, Matilda Hayes, Maria Rye, and Anne Leigh Smith, listing their occupations as "spinster," took the first shares. Smith purchased the controlling interest for her married sister, who could not own property.

3. Watts, *Gender, Power, and the Unitarians in England;* the 1851 census counted 50,000 Unitarians, 490,000 Methodists, 165,000 Congregationalists, and 15,345 Quakers, 4. On women in the Unitarian movement, see Gleadle, *Early Feminists.*

4. Parkes's father was Joseph Parkes, and her maternal great-grandfather was Joseph Priestley. Bodichon's grandfather, William Smith, and her father, Benjamin Smith, both had distinguished parliamentary careers. Pam Hirsch, *Barbara Leigh Smith Bodichon, 1827–91: Feminist, Artist and Rebel* (London: Pimlico, 1999), vii, 30–34.

5. Taylor, *Eve and the New Jerusalem.*

6. The radical Unstamped press of the early nineteenth century, though intended for working-class readership, was led by middle-class elites such as Richard Cobden and Richard Carlile. Hollis, *Pauper Press,* pt. 3.

7. Parkes corresponded regularly with Jameson before her death in 1860 regarding the direction taken by the women's press movement. Anna Jameson to Bessie Rayner Parkes, August 2, 1857, March 2, 1858, July 3, 1858, Parkes Papers.

8. Holcombe, *Victorian Ladies at Work,* 7–10.

9. Hall, McClelland, and Rendall, *Defining the Victorian Nation,* 34.

10. Jane Rendall, "John Stuart Mill, Liberal Politics, and the Movements for Women's Suffrage, 1865–1873," in Vickery, *Women, Privilege, and Power,* 182.

11. Rendall, "John Stuart Mill," 177.

12. Vickery, *Women, Privilege, and Power,* 4.

13. Koss, *Rise and Fall of the Political Press in Britain,* vol. 1; Lee, *Origins of the Popular Press.*

14. Hollis, *Pauper Press;* James Epstein, "Narrating Liberties Defense: T. J. Wooler and the Law," in *Radical Expression.*

15. Wilson, *First with the News,* 26, 46–47.

16. Parkes, *Essays on Women's Work,* 168.

17. The latter included several Irish and left-wing political publications. Marie-Louise Legg, *Newspapers and Nationalism: The Irish Provincial Press, 1850–1892* (Dublin:

Four Courts Press, 1999); Deian Hopkin, "The Left Wing Press and the New Journalism," in Joel H. Wiener, ed., *Papers for the Millions: The New Journalism in Britain, 1850s–1914* (New York: Greenwood Press, 1988), 225–42; Stanley Harrison, *Poor Men's Guardians: A Record of the Struggles for a Democratic Newspaper Press, 1763–1973* (London: Lawrence and Wishart, 1974).

18. Lee, *Origins of the Popular Press,* 21–36.

19. T. Carlyle quoted in George Boyce, "The Fourth Estate: The Reappraisal of a Concept," in Boyce, Curran, and Wingate, *Newspaper History from the Seventeenth Century to the Present Day,* 19–20. Boyce claims that the nineteenth-century press made such assertions "to establish its credentials in the eyes of politicians and the public."

20. Margaret Beetham in *Magazine of Her Own,* and Cynthia White in *Women's Magazine.* See also Vann and Van Arsdel, *Victorian Periodicals and Victorian Society,* and Koss, *Rise and Fall of the Political Press in Britain,* vol. 1. Beetham argues that although "women's magazines opened up new opportunities" for women, "economic and editorial power was still retained almost entirely by metropolitan, middle-class men," 129–30.

21. Beetham, *Magazine of Her Own,* 17.

22. Shevelow, *Women and Print Culture,* 21.

23. Shevelow includes periodicals written by women for women such as Eliza Haywood's *Female Spectator* (1744–46).

24. Shevelow, *Women and Print Culture,* 10.

25. Adburgham, *Women in Print,* and White, *Women's Magazines.*

26. Beetham, *Magazine of Her Own,* 2.

27. Palmegiano, *Women and British Periodicals,* xvi, xxxvi.

28. Palmegiano, *Women and British Periodicals,* xvi, xxxvi. Palmegiano lists periodicals that covered topics relating to women before 1860.

29. Koss, *Rise and Fall of the Political Press in Britain,* 1:416.

30. Koss, *Rise and Fall of the Political Press in Britain,* 1:416. Bennett, as quoted by Koss, 1:416.

31. Kathleen E. McCrone, "National Association," 45; Lawrence Goldman, "Social Science Association," 96. The NAPSS was disbanded in 1886.

32. Goldman, "Social Science Association," 123.

33. Jameson "venture[ed] to place this new edition under the auspices of the Society for the Promotion of Social Science" by addressing then president Lord John Russell in a preface of a new edition of *Sisters of Charity and The Communion of Labour* in 1859.

34. McCrone, "National Association," 64.

35. Parkes to Bodichon, October 19, 1859, Parkes Papers.

36. *Saturday Review,* June 14, 1862, and *Blackwood's,* October 1861, as quoted in Worzala, "Langham Place Circle," 183, and Yeo, *Contest for Social Science,* 129.

37. The idea for SPEW was first discussed during the October 1859 NAPSS conference in Bradford. Worzala, "Langham Place Circle," 189.

38. "The Uses of a Special Periodical," *Alexandra,* September 1864, 258.

39. Minute books, January 1860, Papers of the Society for Promoting the Employment of Women, Girton College Archive (hereafter cited as SPTW Papers). Information on SPEW comes from the Society's minute books and annual reports, SPTW Papers. The organization still functions as the Society for Promoting the Training of Women. See Michelle Elizabeth Tusan, "'Not the Ordinary Victorian Charity': The Society for Promoting the Employment of Women Archive," *History Workshop Journal* 49 (Spring 2000), 221–30.

40. Incorporation under the Companies' Acts of 1856 and 1857 followed soon after member dues would no longer cover costs. Boucherett supported SPEW as primary shareholder until her death in 1905.

41. Lord Shaftsbury was president until his death in 1885. Gladstone, Sir Page Wood, and the Oxford bishops were among the first vice presidents. George Hastings, who had advised Parkes on incorporating the *English Woman's Journal,* was also an active member. SPEW maintained its independence because of its separate administrative function. Two main committees ran SPEW: the General Committee, initially appointed by the NAPSS, and the Managing Committee, appointed by the General Committee. SPEW had its own bank account, and subscribers paid separately to join the organization: ten shillings per year or five pounds for a lifetime membership.

42. Levine, *Feminist Lives.*

43. Kathryn Gleadle, *British Women in the Nineteenth Century* (New York: Palgrave, 2001), 77.

44. Parkes, *Essays on Women's Work,* 61.

45. Bessie Rayner Parkes to Mary Merryweather, [?], 1857, Parkes Papers.

46. Parkes, *Essays on Women's Work,* 61. See also "Review of the Last Six Years," *English Woman's Journal,* February 1, 1864, 364. Jameson also supported starting a new journal.

47. Lee, *Origins of the Popular Press,* 50–51.

48. Blackburn, *Women's Suffrage.* A woman of independent means from a well-established French Protestant family, Boucherett was the last survivor of the Willingham family. She was educated at a "noted ladies school" and described by her contemporaries as a strong individualist.

49. "The Uses of a Special Periodical," *Alexandra,* September 1864, 258.

50. "The Reviewer Reviewed," *English Woman's Journal,* May 1858, 204.

51. Davies, as quoted in Worzala, "Langham Place Circle," 325.

52. Anderson, *Imagined Communities.*

53. Flint, *Woman Reader,* 42.

54. Flint, *Woman Reader,* 162.

55. "Open Council," *English Woman's Journal,* November 1860, 215.

56. "Open Council," 215.

57. "Notices of the Press," *English Woman's Journal,* September 1858, 73.

58. "Notices of the Press," 73.

59. *English Woman's Journal,* October 1860, 142; Parkes to Bodichon, January 5, 1858, January 8, 1860, Parkes Papers.

60. Beetham, *Magazine of Her Own,* 59.

61. Beetham, *Magazine of Her Own,* 142–53.

62. Emily Davies to Nannie, January 2, 1863, Bodichon Papers, Girton College Archive.

63. Bessie Rayner Parkes to Barbara Leigh Smith, [?], 1862, Bodichon Papers.

64. Beetham, *Magazine of Her Own,* 96.

65. "Open Council," *English Woman's Journal,* February 1859, 427.

66. "Passing Events," *English Woman's Journal,* May 1858, 213.

67. "Passing Events," *English Woman's Journal,* August 1860, 431.

68. Parkes, *Essays on Women's Work,* 62–63.

69. Parkes quoted in Emily Davies to Barbara Leigh Smith Bodichon, January 14, 1863, Bodichon Papers.

70. "A Few Words to Our Friends and Subscribers," *English Woman's Journal,* September 1858, 70.

71. "A Few Words to our Friends and Subscribers," 70.

72. "General Notices: Industrial Employments for Women," *Scotsman,* October 4, 1860.

73. Jessie Boucherett in Stanton, *Woman Question in Europe,* 259.

74. Felicity Hunt, "Opportunities Lost and Gained," in John, *Unequal Opportunities,* 87.

75. *Scottish Typographical Circular,* November 1860, 277; September 1862, 149.

76. *Scottish Typographical Circular,* November 1860, 244.

77. Sonya Rose, *Limited Livelihoods: Gender and Class in Nineteenth-Century England* (Berkeley: University of California Press, 1991), 7–11.

78. Sally Alexander, *Becoming a Woman and Other Essays in Nineteenth to Twentieth-Century Feminist History* (New York: New York University Press, 1995), 15–17.

79. Hunt, "Opportunities Lost and Gained," 88–89. Cynthia Cockburn, *Brothers: Male Dominance and Technical Change* (London: Pluto Press, 1983).

80. Parkes to Bodichon, January 5, 1858, Emily Davies to Barbara Leigh Smith Bodichon, January 1863, Bodichon Papers.

81. *Scottish Typographical Circular,* June 1860, 271.

82. "Victoria Press," *Queen,* December 7, 1861, 261.

83. "Women Printers and Editors," *Englishwoman's Review,* September 1876, 390.

84. "Victoria Press," *English Woman's Journal,* October 1860, 122–24.

85. *Victoria Magazine,* March 29, 1871, 148.

86. On royal patronage see Prochaska, *Royal Bounty.*

87. Minutes, General Committee, March 1860, SPTW Papers.

88. See also "Women Compositors," *English Woman's Journal,* September 1861, 38.

89. *Scotsman,* October 4, 1862.

90. *Rose, Shamrock, and Thistle,* May 1862, 1–4; October 1862, 481–86; May 1864, preface. See also Reynolds, *Britannica's Typesetters,* 32.

91. 1861/1862, *Edinburgh Post Office Directory,* xlii; 1862/1863, xliii.

92. *Scottish Typographical Circular,* May 3, 1862, 138–39.

93. "A Word to the Three Kingdoms," *Rose, Shamrock, and Thistle,* May 1862, 2–3.

94. Davies to Bodichon, January 1863, December 23, 1863, Bodichon Papers.

95. Memorandum of Association of the English Woman's Journal Company, Ltd., Public Records Office.

96. Parkes to Bodichon, April 1, 1862, Bodichon Papers.

97. Lee, *Origins of the Popular Press,* 55, 57, 71–72, 79.

98. "The Uses of a Special Periodical," *Alexandra,* September 1865, 258.

99. Parkes to Bodichon, April 17, 1864, Bodichon Papers.

100. Lloyd, *Susanna Meredith,* 4.

101. "The Uses of a Special Periodical," *Alexandra,* September 1864, 257.

102. Parkes to Merryweather, November 30, 1864, Parkes Papers.

103. See Emily Davies, "Family Chronicle," unpublished autobiography, 1864, Davies Papers, Girton College Archive, and Fredeman's account of the incident in "Emily Faithfull and the Victoria Press," 143–45.

104. Minutes, General Committee, March 27, 1866, SPTW Papers.

105. "The Work We Have to Do," *Englishwoman's Review,* October 1866, 5.

106. *Englishwoman's Review Supplement,* April 1867, 197–98.

107. See Hall, McClelland, and Rendall, *Defining the Victorian Nation;* Sophia A. van Wingerden, *The Women's Suffrage Movement in Britain, 1866–1928* (New York: St. Martin's 1999); and June Purvis and Sandra Stanley Holton, eds., *Votes for Women* (London: Routledge, 2000).

108. Minutes, General Committee, March 27, 1866, SPTW Papers.

109. Boucherett left five hundred pounds to the *Englishwoman's Review* and two hundred pounds to then editor, Antoinette McKenzie. Thanks to Elizabeth Crawford for this information.

110. Davies to Bodichon, March 12, 1863, Bodichon Papers.

111. *Illustrated London News* quoted in *Victoria,* "Notices of the Press," November 1867, 70. Davies, "Family Chronicle," 289.

112. Davies, "Family Chronicle," 289.

113. Davies, "Family Chronicle," 337, 348–49.

114. Anne Clough in the North of England Council for the Education of women influenced Butler's interest in the subject of women's advancement. In 1868, Butler published *The Education and Employment of Women* (London: Macmillan, 1868).

115. It was described as a periodical "Dedicated to Women (although by no means

intended for their exclusive perusal)"; content consisted mainly of light essays, stories, and poetry.

116. "Woman's World," *Atlas,* December 4, 1868; "Kettledrum," *Atlas,* December 24, 1868.

117. "Kettledrum," *Kettledrum,* January 1869, 2.

118. "Kettledrum," *Kettledrum,* January 1869, 2.

119. "Kettledrum," *Kettledrum,* June 1869, 388.

120. Josephine Butler to Madame Troubnikoff, April 1869, Butler Collection, University of Liverpool Library.

121. *Englishwoman's Review* quoted in Doughan and Sanchez, *Feminist Periodicals,* 4.

122. No copies of *Now-a-Days* appear to have survived. Butler's new interest in getting the 1869 Contagious Diseases Acts repealed most likely played a role its failure.

123. "Future Plans," *Englishwoman's Review,* January 1870, 1.

124. "Future Plans," 4.

125. Davies, "Family Chronicle," 348–49.

Chapter 2. Building Networks

1. "Popular Literature—The Periodical Press," *Blackwood's,* February 1859, 181.

2. Lee, *Origins of the Popular Press,* 71–72. By 1878, the price of the faster, more efficient press machines declined dramatically, significantly lowering the production cost of small-run periodicals. Paper prices steadily fell starting in the 1870s. Brown, *Victorian News and Newspapers* , 8–9, 12.

3. Lee, *Origins of the Popular Press,* 49; Brown, *Victorian News and Newspapers,* 16.

4. Lee, *Origins of the Popular Press,* 81. See also Aled Jones, *Powers of the Press,* 71–72, 80, for trends in the mainstream press and Doughan and Sanchez, *Feminist Periodicals,* for a catalogue of women's newspapers published during this period.

5. Cranfield, *Press and Society,* 216. Cranfield also cites compulsory elementary schooling legislation of 1876 and 1880 and the raising of the leaving age from school to eleven in 1893 and fourteen in 1900.

6. Raymond Williams, "The Press and Popular Culture: An Historical Perspective," in Boyce, Curran, and Wingate, *Newspaper History,* 42.

7. Beetham, *Magazine of Her Own,* 80–94.

8. Vicinus, *Independent Women,* 121–62.

9. Levine, *Feminist Lives in Victorian England,* 67–69.

10. Brewer, *Party Ideology and Popular Politics at the Accession of George III,* and Steve Pincus, "'Coffee Politicians Does Create,'" 807–34, describe the coffeehouse as site of male sociability and political discussion.

11. My research has not found any publishing houses linked directly to women's social clubs.

12. Koss, *Rise and Fall of the Political Press,* 1:3–4.

13. "Women's Newspapers: A Sketch of the Periodical Literature Devoted to the Woman Question," *Englishwoman's Review,* October 15, 1878, 434.

14. "Women's Newspapers," 434.

15. "Women's Newspapers," 440.

16. *Defining the Victorian Nation,* 29.

17. See Walkowitz, *Prostitution and Victorian Society,* on the anti–Contagious Diseases Acts campaigns; Holton, *Suffrage Days,* on nineteenth-century suffrage agitation; and Martha Vicinus, *Independent Women,* on women's employment and education.

18. A brief survey of topics relating to women in *Poole's Index* and the *Times* and *Guardian* newspapers during the 1870s and 1880s reveals the minimal space allotted to women's involvement in social reform campaigns. Women's suffrage, however, did receive press coverage during the 1867 Reform Bill debates. Rendall, "The Citizenship of Women," in Hall, McClelland, and Rendall, *Defining the Victorian Nation,* 138.

19. Evelyn March Phillips, "Women's Newspapers," and "The Reform Act of 1867," *Fortnightly Review* 56, n.s. (November 1894), 669–70.

20. Anderson, *Imagined Communities,* 35–36.

21. Pugh, *The March of Women,* 3.

22. Rendall, "Citizenship of Women," 129.

23. Lydia Becker, for example, sold at her office "A Reply to the Protest which appeared in *the Nineteenth Century Review*" (June 1889), a reprint of a response in the *Manchester Guardian* to an antisuffrage article.

24. Paterson announced that a circulating library "has been formed at the office of the women's protective and provident league" in the first issue of the *Women's Union Journal* and regularly advertised the free use of the League's rooms for members.

25. Wilde quotations are from letters from Wilde to Wemyss Reid of September 5, 1887 and April [?], 1887, Wilde Collection, Clarke Library; Beetham quotation is from Beetham, *Magazine of Her Own,* 1.

26. The *Englishwoman's Review,* the *Women's Suffrage Journal,* and the *Women's Union Journal* all had these columns.

27. I have located twenty major newssheet titles that had significant circulation during this period. Numerous other smaller newssheets existed as pamphlet-type publications and served a far more localized community of readers.

28. Brown, *Victorian News and Newspapers,* 16.

29. Brown, *Victorian News and Newspapers,* 13.

30. Holcombe, *Victorian Ladies at Work,* 196.

31. Jordan, *Women's Movement and Women's Employment in Nineteenth-Century Britain,* 5. The 1851 census listed 56.5 percent of women as employed. In 1911, that number rose to 65.3.

32. Jordan, *Women's Movement and Women's Employment in Nineteenth-Century Britain,* 24.

33. Jordan, *Women's Movement and Women's Employment in Nineteenth-Century Britain,* 169–73.

34. Goldman, "Social Science Association," 99.

35. Antoinette Mackenzie, "Letter from the Editor," *Englishwoman's Review,* April 1910, 110.

36. Minutes, General Committee, October 9 and 28, 1892, SPTW Papers. Trade organizations often avoided the word "union" in their titles. The Women's Protective and Provident League, for example, did this "to appease the wealthy supporters" upon whom the society was largely dependent for its survival. Coates, "Things That They Have Wrought," 36.

37. Minutes, Managing Committee, December 14, 1870, SPTW Papers.

38. Minutes, General Committee, April 28, 1876, SPTW Papers.

39. *Englishwoman's Review,* January 15, 1886, 539.

40. The Women's Industrial Council, the Royal Statistical Society, the Royal Economic Society, and the Hutchinson Trustees commissioned the study.

41. Felicity Hunt, "Opportunities Lost and Gained," in John, *Unequal Opportunities,* 82.

42. Jordan, *Women's Movement and Women's Employment in Nineteenth-Century Britain,* 42–61.

43. Sally Alexander, *Becoming a Woman* (New York: New York University Press, 1995), 15–17.

44. "The Problem of Woman-Power," *Time and Tide,* May 15, 1925, 469.

45. MacDonald, *Women in the Printing Trades,* viii.

46. Burrett, *Full Point,* 1.

47. Parkes, *Essays on Woman's Work,* 143.

48. Parkes, *Essays on Woman's Work,* 168–69.

49. By 1878, the Society had dropped "cooperative" from its title, although it maintained the same cooperative principles in its dealings with shareholders and employees until at least 1906, when it reverted from a public company to one held in private hands.

50. Lady Dilke quoting Paterson in the *Fortnightly Review,* May 1889, 852. This passage quoted in "Emma Anne Paterson," in *Dictionary of Labor Biography,* edited by Joyce Bellamy and James A. Schmiechen (London: Kelly, 1979), 5:167.

51. Coates, "Things That They Have Wrought," 36n.

52. "Women Printers and Editors," *Englishwoman's Review,* September 1876, 390.

53. Managing Committee Report, May 12, 1876, SPTW Papers.

54. "Women's Printing Society," entry in L. M. Hubbard, ed., *Englishwoman's Yearbook and Directory,* vol. 18 (London: F. Kirby, 1899).

55. "Mrs. Paterson," *Women's Union Journal,* December 1886, 115.

56. "A Women's Printing Society," *British Printer,* October/November 1908, 231. Women performed all aspects of print work, "with the exception of machine work." The four kinds of print work included: "1) Composition (setting up the type, includ-

ing correction) 2) Proof Reading 3) Imposition (making up into pages and placing in the iron frame or chase) and 4) Machine work."

57. "The Battle of Life: How Women Face It: Sometimes by Printing. Why Not Oftener?" *Home Chat*, October 26, 1901, 325.

58. "Battle of Life," 326.

59. "Ladies at Case: A Few Words about the WPS," *Print*, July 15, 1896, 1.

60. The *Times* published the annual business reports of the WPS from 1895 to 1905.

61. Publications included: *Home Chat*, the *Queen, British and Colonial Printer and Stationer,* and the *Englishwoman's Review.*

62. Stewart Headlam, "The Women's Printing Society," *Church Reformer,* June 1890, 141.

63. *Selected Testimonials,* pamphlet printed by the Women's Printing Society, 1887–88.

64. The Victoria Press closed its doors in 1882, although Faithfull had ceased to be involved with the enterprise during the late 1860s.

65. Stanton as quoted in Walker Rumble, "Strategies of Shopfloor Inclusion: The Gender Politics of Augusta Lewis and Women's Typographical Union No. 1, 1868–1872," *Printing History* 18, 1 (March 1998), 18.

66. Kelly, *Lydia Becker and the Cause,* 11–12.

67. Minutes, General Committee, November 16, 1870, SPTW Papers. The *Englishwoman's Review* published a summary of Becker's paper read at the British Association for the Advancement of Science, October 1868, 48–55.

68. Pugh, *March of Women,* 14–19.

69. Pugh, *March of Women,* 33–59.

70. *Woman's Advocate,* April/July 1874.

71. Sophia A. van Wingerden, *The Women's Suffrage Movement in Britain, 1866–1928* (New York: St. Martin's Press, 1999), 23.

72. Blackburn, *Women's Suffrage,* 168.

73. Jane Rendall, "Who Was Lily Maxwell?" in *Votes for Women,* edited by June Purvis and Sandra Stanley Holton (London: Routledge, 2000), 77.

74. Address delivered by Becker at the opening of the Manchester Ladies' Literary Society, Girton College Archives; Blackburn, *Women's Suffrage,* 33.

75. Lydia Becker, "Female Suffrage," *Contemporary Review* 4 (March 1867), 307–16.

76. Kelly, *Lydia Becker,* 18.

77. Kelly, *Lydia Becker,* 28.

78. Blackburn, *Women's Suffrage,* 101.

79. Caroline Asserts Biggs, Helen Blackburn, and Francis Power Cobbe were the only other contributors to the *Women's Suffrage Journal.* Parker, "Lydia Becker." Biggs also edited one issue of the *Journal* when Becker visited Canada in 1884.

80. *Manchester National Society for Women's Suffrage Journal,* March 1, 1870, 1.

81. Parker, "Lydia Becker," 5.

82. *Women's Suffrage Journal,* April 1877, 63.

83. *Women's Suffrage Journal,* August 1873, 130.

84. "Review of Progress," *Women's Suffrage Journal,* January 1, 1874, 1.

85. "Review of Progress," 1.

86. Kelly, *Lydia Becker,* 40.

87. E. Fletcher to Lydia Ernestine Becker, March 25, 1878, SPTW Papers.

88. Kelly, *Lydia Becker,* 40.

89. Lee, *Origins of the Popular Press,* 87.

90. Lee, *Origins of the Popular Press,* 87.

91. Annual Report of the Women's Suffrage Society, 1878, as quoted by Parker, "Lydia Becker," 12.

92. "The Women's Suffrage Journal," *Women's Suffrage Journal,* April 2, 1877, 63.

93. *Women's Suffrage Journal,* October 1, 1873. Becker contributed financially to the *Journal,* although she did not have enough money to subsidize the paper completely on her own.

94. Fawcett quoted in Stanton, *Woman Question,* 89.

95. "Women Compositors," *Women's Suffrage Journal,* October 1, 1878, 173.

96. *Women's Suffrage Journal,* April 1886, as quoted in Parker, "Lydia Becker."

97. Van Wingerden, *Women's Suffrage Movement in Britain,* 55–69.

98. Pugh, *March of Women,* 69.

99. Van Wingerden, *Women's Suffrage Movement in Britain,* 68.

100. *Woman's Opinion,* January 24, 1874, 1.

101. "Editorial Address," *Woman,* Jan 27, 1872, 2.

102. *Woman's Opinion,* March 14, 1874, 56, 64.

103. Hubbard, "The Woman's Gazette," *Woman's Gazette,* October 1875, 4.

104. Jessie Boucherett to Louisa Hubbard, October 2, 18[?]; Davies to Hubbard, November 27, 1874, Autograph Letter Collection, Women's Library.

105. Pratt, *Woman's Work for Women* , 6.

106. L. M. Hubbard, "The Woman's Gazette," *Woman's Gazette,* October 1875, 2.

107. Writers included Mary Merryweather. It appears that contributors were not paid.

108. Emily Faithfull to Alsager Hill, April 23, 1874, Autograph Letter Collection, Women's Library.

109. Pratt, *Woman's Work for Women,* 6.

110. "To Our Readers," *Friendly Work,* January 1883, 2.

111. Boucherett to Hubbard, October 2, 18[?], Autograph Letter Collection, Women's Library.

112. Mary Merryweather to Hubbard, September 22, 1874, Autograph Letter Collection, Women's Library.

113. Hubbard, "What Should Women Do in Elections?" *Work and Leisure,* July 1886, 169–71.

114. "Preface," *Journal of the Women's Education Union,* January 1873, 1–2.

115. "Preface," *Journal of the Women's Education Union,* January 1873, 4.

116. "The BWT Journal: A Sketch of Its History," *British Women's Temperance Journal* 19, 2 (February 1892), 20–21.

117. *British Women's Temperance Journal* 4, 37 (January 1886), 2.

118. Other women's newspapers that published information about India and Indian women included: the *English Woman's Journal,* the *Woman's Penny Paper,* the *Woman's Signal,* the *Women's Educational Journal,* and the *Englishwoman's Review.* The *Review* published over thirty feature articles on Indian women from 1868 to 1910. Burton, *Burdens of History,* 104.

119. "Preface to Volume 11, 1891," *India's Women,* January 1891, 1.

120. "To Our Friends," *India's Women,* October 1880, 7–8.

121. Padma Anagol, "Indian Christian Women and Indigenous Feminism, c. 1850–c. 1920," in Midgley, 79–103.

122. Philippa Levine, *Prostitution, Race and Politics: Policing Venereal Disease in the British Empire* (New York: Routledge, 2003), 119.

123. Josephine Butler to Mrs. Priestman, April 1891, Autograph Letter Collection, Women's Library.

124. Butler to Priestman, April 1891.

125. Josephine Butler, *Personal Reminiscences of a Great Crusade* (London: H. Marshall, 1896), 402, as quoted in Brian Harrison, "Press and Pressure Groups in Modern Britain," in Shattock and Wolff, *Victorian Periodical Press,* 284.

126. *Stri Dharma* ("justice for women" in Sanskrit; 1919–36) was the most notable of these, publishing articles in English, Tamil, Telugu, and Hindi. See Michelle Tusan, "Writing *Stri Dharma*: International Feminism, Nationalist Politics, and Women's Press Advocacy in Late Colonial India," *Women's History Review* 12: 4 (2003), 623–49, for more information.

127. "Women's Protective and Provident League: Report of Conference," *Women's Union Journal,* June 1886, 68.

128. "Notices of Books," *Woman's Gazette,* May 1876, 124.

129. Such appeals were made periodically by the *Women's Union Journal:* "The Year 1888," (January 1889); "The Journal" (January 1884); "Our Prospects" (February 1884); "Correspondence" (January 1880); "Notice to Subscribers" (August 1890).

130. "Correspondence," *Women's Union Journal,* December 1880, 141.

131. "Correspondence," *Women's Union Journal,* December 1880, 141.

132. "Editorial," *Women's Union Journal,* December 1890, 58.

133. "Editorial," *Women's Union Journal,* December 1890, 58.

134. "The Women's Suffrage Journal," *Woman's Gazette,* September 13, 1890, 68.

135. "Women's Suffrage Journal," 69.

136. Despite this scathing critique, many readers were very concerned about what would replace the *Journal.* Haslam to Helen Blackburn, November 12, 1890, Helen Blackburn Collection, Girton College. Over thirty national and provincial papers as well in some American papers published notices of Becker's death.

137. "Notices of Books and Magazines," *Englishwoman's Review,* November 1888, 497.

138. This was a pattern that occurred with other advocacy press institutions as well. See Deian Hopkin, "The Socialist Press in Britain, 1890–1910," in Boyce, Curran, and Wingate, *Newspaper History,* 294–306.

Chapter 3. Gendering the News for the New Woman Activist

An earlier version of the section herein entitled "Making the 'New Woman' Reader into a Social Advocate" was published as "Inventing the Woman: Print Culture and Identity Politics during the Fin de Siecle," *Victorian Periodicals Review* (Summer 1998), 169–82.

1. New titles included *Threefold Cord* (1891–96), *Women Workers* (1891–1924), *Women's Trade Union Review* (1891–1918), *Central and East of England Society for Women's Suffrage* (1891–1900), *Female Servants Union News* (1892), *Iris* (1892), and the *Journal of the University Association of Women Teachers Quarterly* (1892–95).

2. Printing technology made rapid advances during the last decades of the nineteenth century. New monotype and linotype typesetting machines played a major role in this transformation. Richard E. Huss, *The Development of Printers' Mechanical Typesetting Methods, 1822–1925* (Charlottesville: University Press of Virginia, 1973), 3–24.

3. Michael Emery and Edwin Emery, eds., "The New Journalism," in *The Press and America* (Boston: 1996), 171–209.

4. The *Women's Suffrage Journal* (1870–90) was the first women's periodical to use a two-column format.

5. By the 1890s, it was not unusual to see two-, three-, and even four-column formats for women's newspapers, though the quarterly *Englishwoman's Review* still used a single-column format, maintaining its more literary style.

6. Wilson, *First with the News,* 155–80; Clear, *The Story of W. H. Smith and Son,* 83–85, 133–43.

7. Lee, *Origins of the Popular Press in England,* 61.

8. Cooke, *Corporation, Trust, and Company,* 173–78.

9. Schudson, *The Power of the News,* 1–16.

10. "What a Woman Did: A True Story," *Woman's Signal,* May 27, 1897, 5.

11. *Women's Penny Paper,* November 3, 1888, 3.

12. *Women's Penny Paper,* December 1, 1888, 3.

13. Flint, *Woman Reader,* 151.

14. "Leeds Weavers," *Woman's Penny Paper,* November 3, 1888, 3.

15. "The Disease of Anarchy," *Woman's Signal,* December 28, 1893, 2.

16. Deian Hopkin, "The Socialist Press in Britain, 1890–1910," in Boyce, Curran, and Wingate, *Newspaper History,* 294–97.

17. Lady Henry Somerset to Francis Power Cobbe, February 14, 1893, Frances Power Cobbe Correspondence, 1855–1904, Huntington Library.

18. Vicinus, *Independent Women;* Levine, *Feminist Lives in Victorian England.*

19. Cobbe had refused payment for an article for the *Women's Suffrage Journal.* Lydia Becker to Frances Power Cobbe, October 6, 1877, Cobbe Correspondence.

20. "Shall We Sign Our Letters?" *Woman's Penny Paper,* March 9, 1889, 7.

21. Deian Hopkin, "The Socialist Press in Britain, 1890–1910," in Boyce, Curran, and Wingate, *Newspaper History,* 294–97; William Fishman, "Morris Winchevsky's London Yiddish Newspaper" (Oxford: Oxford Center for Postgraduate Hebrew Studies Lecture, 1985); Benjamin, *Black Press in Britain;* Legg, *Newspapers and Nationalism.*

22. *Woman's Signal,* March 23, 1899, 184.

23. *Woman's Signal,* March 23, 1899, 184.

24. Habermas himself has amended his earlier formulation of the public sphere, saying: "It is wrong to speak of one single public," and claiming that we must take into account "the coexistence of competing public spheres" as well as "the dynamics of those processes of communication that are excluded from the dominant public sphere." "Further Reflections on the Public Sphere," in Calhoun, *Habermas and the Public Sphere,* 424–25.

25. For a discussion of various "historical publics," see Calhoun, *Habermas and the Public Sphere,* pt. 2.

26. Fraser, "Rethinking the Public Sphere," in Calhoun, *Habermas and the Public Sphere,* 109–42.

27. "Correspondence," *Women's Penny Paper,* August 2, 1890, 487.

28. Doughan and Sanchez, *Feminist Periodicals,* 12. Beetham, *Magazine of Her Own.* See also Kate Jackson, *George Newnes and the New Journalism, 1880–1910* (Aldershot, England: Ashgate, 2001), 215.

29. "Women's Enterprises," *Englishwoman's Review,* January 15, 1895, 54.

30. Fenwick-Miller, "An Uncommon Girlhood," unpublished autobiography, Florence Fenwick Miller Collection, 1854–1935, Wellcome Institute, 4.

31. "Our Policy," *Women's Penny Paper,* October 27, 1888, 1.

32. "Our Policy," 1.

33. "Our Policy," 1.

34. "Our Policy," 1.

35. See Girton College, *Girton College Register,* 1948; Lucy Bland, *Banishing the Beast,* 164–68; and Walkowitz, *City of Dreadful Delight,* 66, 105, 141.

36. Walkowitz, *City of Dreadful Delight,* 135–44, 146.

37. Walkowitz, *City of Dreadful Delight,* 152.

38. The Club lasted until June 1889. As Pearson explained, "the problem with which it [the club] has dealt are problems which can't be solved by 'opinion' but only by real scientific research, and this is just what the individual members cannot find the time to give." Quoted in Bland, *Banishing the Beast,* 41.

39. Muller quoted in Bland, *Banishing the Beast*, 31.

40. Bland, *Banishing the Beast*, 46.

41. Due to increased costs, Muller was forced to stop using the Women's Printing Society two years after starting the paper. The masthead was changed to read: "The only Paper Conducted, Written, and Published by Women," dropping the word "Printed" from the title. "Correspondence—'Our Paper,'" *Women's Penny Paper*, June 21, 1890, 416.

42. "Correspondence," *Women's Penny Paper*, October 27, 1888, 7.

43. "The *St. James' Gazette* on the *Women's Penny Paper*," *Women's Penny Paper*, April 26, 1890, 318.

44. Elizabeth Wolstenholme Elmy and Harriette Emily Colenso referred to Muller as the editor in their letters, Elmy Papers, British Library. Thanks to Jeff Guy for sharing his research on Colenso and Muller with me.

45. "Advertisements," *Women's Penny Paper*, November 3, 1888, 8.

46. "Advertisements," *Women's Penny Paper*, November 22, 1890, 78.

47. Rosemary Van Arsdel, "Women's Periodicals and the New Journalism," in *Papers for the Millions*, edited by Joel H. Wiener (New York: Greenwood Press), 243–56.

48. "Editorials: Our Interviews," *Women's Penny Paper*, December 21, 1889, 102.

49. "Editorials: Our Interviews," 102.

50. "Correspondence," *Women's Penny Paper*, December 1, 1888, 8.

51. "Correspondence," *Women's Penny Paper*, see for example the column of June 21, 1890, 413, and April 12, 1890, 297.

52. "Correspondence," *Women's Penny Paper*, June 7, 1890, 392.

53. Anderson, *Imagined Communities*.

54. Flint, *Woman Reader*, 42.

55. See chapter 4 for a complete discussion of the suffrage press.

56. "What Our Contemporaries Say of Us," *Women's Penny Paper*, December 1, 1888, 7.

57. "Our Policy," *Women's Penny Paper*, October 27, 1888, 1.

58. "Correspondence," *Women's Penny Paper*, October 27, 1888, 5; November 24, 1888, 7; and June 21, 1890, 416.

59. "A Year's Progress," *Women's Penny Paper*, December 29, 1888, 4.

60. "Correspondence," *Women's Penny Paper*, March 15, 1890, 247.

61. "Our Creed," *Women's Penny Paper*, August 9, 1890, 498.

62. "Correspondence," *Women's Penny Paper*, July 26, 1890, 476, and June 21, 1890, 416.

63. *Women's Penny Paper*, August 2, 1890, 487; June 21, 1890, 416.

64. Some working-class women regularly published letters in the paper. *Women's Penny Paper*, August 2, 1890, 487; June 21, 1890, 416.

65. "Editorial," *Women's Penny Paper*, March 22, 1890, 258.

66. "Young Women's Guilds," *Women's Penny Paper*, March 22, 1890, 261.

67. "Our Girls," *Women's Penny Paper*, April 12, 1890, 295.

68. Elizabeth Wolstenholme Elmy to Harriet McIlquham, March 17, 1889, Elmy Papers.

69. The most complete source of evidence detailing this practice is found in the correspondence of Elizabeth Wolstenholme Elmy, held in the British Library's Additional Manuscripts collection. Her letters indicate that she both passed on her own personal issues as well as regularly borrowed those of her friends.

70. "Women in the Press Gallery," *Women's Penny Paper*, March 22, 1890, 258.

71. "Women in the Press Gallery," 258.

72. "Opinions of the Press: Newcastle Weekly Chronicle," *Women's Penny Paper*, March 29, 1890, 271.

73. "Opinions of the Press Gallery," 261.

74. "Women in the Reporters' Gallery: Opinions of the Press," *Women's Penny Paper*, March 22, 1890, 259.

75. "Women in the Reporters' Gallery," 259.

76. "Women in the Reporters' Gallery," 260.

77. "Passing Notes," *Englishwoman's Review*, January 15, 1895, 54.

78. Francis Power Cobbe, "Journalism as a Profession for Women," *Women's Penny Paper*, November 3, 1888, 5.

79. Brown, *Victorian News and Newspapers*, 246–47.

80. "Record of Events: Excerpts from 'Women as Journalists,' a paper given by Miss Catherine Drew at the First International Conference of the Press at Antwerp," *Englishwoman's Review*, October 15, 1894, 250.

81. "Record of Events: Excerpts from 'Women as Journalists,'" 248–49.

82. Evelyn March-Phillips, "Women's Newspapers," *Fortnightly Review* 56, n.s. (November 1894), 665.

83. Charlotte O'Conor, "The Experiences of a Woman Journalist," *Blackwood's*, June 1893, 831.

84. Van Arsdel, "Mrs. Florence Fenwick-Miller," 117.

85. "Change in Ownership of the 'Herald,'" *Women's Penny Paper*, April 30, 1892, 1.

86. "Change in Ownership of the 'Herald,'" 1.

87. Pugh, *March of Women*, 120–23.

88. "Our Policy," *Woman's Herald*, February 3, 1893, 1.

89. Somerset to Cobbe, February 14, 1893, Cobbe Correspondence.

90. "Ring in the New," *Woman's Signal*, December 28, 1893, 2.

91. "Ring out the Old," *Woman's Herald*, December 21, 1893, 2.

92. "Ring out the Old," 2.

93. "Ring out the Old," 2. Somerset started the *Woman's Signal Budget* as a supplement to the *Woman's Signal* in July 1894 to provide propaganda for the temperance campaign. Somerset's hope was not that the *Budget* would replace the *Signal* but "that the *Budget* shall go where goes the *Signal*." *Woman's Signal Budget*, July 1894, 1.

94. "Interview: Annie E. Holdsworth," *Woman's Signal,* June 20, 1895.

95. Van Arsdel, "Mrs. Florence Fenwick-Miller," 109.

96. Florence Fenwick-Miller (1854–1935) had been involved in politics and journalism since her youth. In 1876 she was elected to the London School Board and served three terms. She was a columnist for the *Illustrated London News* from 1886 to 1918 and edited an English-language journal circulated in the colonies called *Outward Bound.* Van Arsdel, "Mrs. Florence Fenwick-Miller," 117 n. 3.

97. Van Arsdel, "Mrs. Florence Fenwick-Miller," 110.

98. *Woman's Signal,* October 6, 1898, 216, as quoted in Van Arsdel, "Mrs. Florence Fenwick-Miller," 115.

99. W. T. Stead, *Review of Reviews,* December 1904, 30, 604–5, as cited in Koss, *Rise and Fall of the Political Press in Britain,* 2:1.

100. *Woman's Signal,* February 28, 1895, 140.

101. *Woman's Signal,* February 28, 1895, 140.

102. Van Arsdel, "Mrs. Florence Fenwick-Miller," 109.

103. Thanks to Lesley Hall for sharing drafts of her *Oxford Dictionary of National Biography* entry for Sibthorp. See also Norman Brady, "*Shafts* and the Quest for a New Morality," M.A. thesis, University of Warwick, 1978.

104. The paper carried two other mottoes during its eight-year existence: "A Paper for Women and the Working Classes" and "A Monthly Magazine for Progressive Thought."

105. Elmy to McIlquham, May 18, 1892, Elmy Papers.

106. *Shafts,* May/June 1898, as quoted in Hall, *Oxford Dictionary of National Biography,* s.v., "Margaret Shurmer Sibthorp."

107. *Shafts* started as a weekly from November 1892 until February 1893. It turned into a monthly, a bimonthly, and then a quarterly before its demise in 1899. Elmy to McIlquham, July 31, 1897; February 3, 1905, Elmy Papers; and Hall, *Oxford Dictionary of National Biography,* s.v. "Margaret Shurmer Sibthorp."

108. "What the Editor Means," *Shafts,* January 1897, 1.

109. "Correspondence," *Shafts,* May 1895; July 1895; and December 1895.

110. Flint, *Woman Reader,* 151–54.

111. Elmy quoting Sibthorp to McIlquham, December 13, 1896, Elmy Papers.

112. "On Behalf of the Little Ones," *Shafts,* January/February 1895, 372.

113. "The Social Standing of the New Woman," *Woman's Herald,* August 17, 1893, 410.

114. *Saturday Review* 25 (1868), 339–40.

115. There is a vast literature on the New Woman. See Ann Ardis, *New Women, New Novels: Feminism and Early Modernism* (New Brunswick, N.J.: Rutgers University Press, 1990), chap. 1; Cunningham, introduction to *New Woman and the Victorian Novel;* and Beetham, *Magazine of Her Own,* 115–30. The New Woman novel is analyzed in these accounts as evidence of turn-of-the-century anxiety over gender and women's knowledge of their own sexuality. Others maintain that the New Woman

challenged social mores. See Elaine Showalter, *Sexual Anarchy,* chap. 3; Flint, *Woman Reader,* 294–316; and Angelique Richardson and Chris Willis, eds., *The New Woman in Fact and Fiction: Fin-de-Siècle Feminisms* (New York: Palgrave, 2001), vii–xvi.

116. See "A Rising Genius," May 11, 1878, 210; "Sporting," August 27, 1881; and "The Political Lady Cricketers," May 28, 1892.

117. "The Social Standing of the New Woman," *Woman's Herald,* August 17, 1893, 410. The year 1893 also saw the publication of Sarah Grand's novel *The Heavenly Twins,* where the term "new woman" is first used, though without the distinguishing capital letters.

118. Women's newspapers favorably reviewed Grand's work during the 1890s and published articles on her life and work.

119. Jordan, "Christening of the New Woman," 19–21. Jordan claims this exchange first introduced the term "New Woman" but makes no mention of the *Herald* article "The Social Standing of the New Woman," which appears to be the truly first capitalized use of the term.

120. "Womanly Women," *Woman's Herald,* June 15, 1893, 268.

121. "The Social Standing of the 'New Woman,'" *Woman's Herald,* August 17, 1893, 410.

122. "Social Standing of the 'New Woman,'" 410.

123. "Social Standing of the 'New Woman,'" and "Womanly Women."

124. "Letters to the Editor," *Shafts,* July 1895, 63.

125. "Letters to the Editor," *Shafts,* July 1895, 63.

126. "The New Woman," *Shafts,* January/February 1895, 378.

127. "The New Woman," *Times of India,* as quoted in the *Woman's Signal,* December 26, 1895, 407.

128. *North American Review,* as quoted in *Shafts,* February 1897, 68.

129. "More New Women," *Woman's Signal,* February 27, 1897, 118.

130. Mrs. Ellis articulated this idea in 1843 in *The Mothers of England: Their Influence and Responsibility.*

131. *Woman's Signal,* January 10, 1895, 26.

132. These images of political women can be seen as predecessors to the "respectable radicals" of the interwar years discussed by Harrison in *Prudent Revolutionaries.*

133. "The Women's Tribune," *Women's Tribune,* May 18, 1906, 1.

Chapter 4. Reforming the Nation

1. See chapter 3.

2. Doughan and Sanchez, *Feminist Periodicals,* 24–41.

3. A small antisuffrage press also emerged during this period that included the monthly *Anti-Suffrage Review,* run by the Ward family. Harrison, *Separate Spheres,* 119, 141, 151, 156, 175–76, 223.

4. Holton, *Suffrage Days;* Rosen, *Rise Up Women.*

5. Koss, *Rise and Fall of the Political Press in Britain,* 2:2, 9.

6. Deian Hopkin, "The Socialist Press in Britain, 1890–1910," in Boyce, Curran, and Wingate, *Newspaper History,* 295–98. Hopkin has identified over four hundred explicitly socialist titles published during this period.

7. Ian Christopher Fletcher, "'Prosecutions . . . are Always Risky Business,'" 254–55.

8. See chapter 1.

9. *Women's Franchise,* October 3, 1907, 1.

10. *Women's Franchise,* June 27, 1907, 1.

11. *Women's Franchise,* June 27, 1907, 1.

12. *Women's Franchise,* October 3, 1907, 1.

13. In September 1907, a group led by Teresa Billington Grieg and Charlotte Despard left the WSPU in protest of the "anticonstitutional" nature of the organization. They formed the Woman's Freedom League and started publishing their own organizational material in *Women's Franchise.* When Francis refused to take sides in the split, the WSPU pulled its support and started its own periodical, *Votes for Women,* in October. Pankhurst, *Suffragette Movement.* See hereafter for further discussion of *Votes for Women.*

14. Evelyn Sharp to Mr. Donald, December 2, 1907, Nevinson Collection, Bodleian Library.

15. Second Annual Report, WSPU, 1907, Universal Decimal (UDC) Pamphlets, Women's Library.

16. This was a relatively low sum when compared to the cost of starting a daily paper, which continued to be a financial impossibility for the women's advocacy press. According to D. L. LeMahieu, in 1850 the cost of starting a daily newspaper was twenty-five thousand pounds; by 1900 that figure grew to five hundred thousand pounds. *Culture for Democracy,* 12.

17. "On Starting a Penny Weekly," *Bookman,* February 1892, 175. Evidence from the business records of women's papers supports these estimates.

18. White, *Women's Magazines,* 60–63.

19. LeMahieu, *Culture for Democracy ,* 12.

20. Lord Northcliffe quoted by LeMahieu. LeMahieu asserts that this attitude was found in popular and quality periodicals, including the *Observer* and the *Westminster Gazette. Culture for Democracy,* 18–19.

21. Waters, *British Socialists and the Politics of Popular Culture,* 180–81.

22. Brian Harrison's sampling of *Votes for Women* found advertisements took up on average 14 percent in 1908, 34 percent in 1909, 40 percent in 1910, 32 percent in 1911, and 35 percent in 1932. "Press and Pressure Group in Modern Britain," in Shattock and Wolff, *Victorian Periodical Press,* 282.

23. LeMahieu, *Culture for Democracy,* 34–35.

24. Oxford Street merchants continued to support the WSPU even after it heightened its campaign of violence against property. A Waring and Gillow advertisement

for fine linens and fabrics in the April 10, 1914, issue of the *Suffragette*, for example, stated in bold that they were "assured by the Proprietors of this paper that as regular advertisers in its columns we shall receive substantial response to this announcement" and asked shoppers to mention seeing the advertisement in the *Suffragette*. See hereafter for a discussion of the *Suffragette*.

25. Christabel Pankhurst to editor of *Daily Herald*, August 7, 1913, Additional Manuscripts Collection purchased from Dr. Andrew Rosen, British Library.

26. Green, *Spectacular Confessions*, 7.

27. Emmeline Pethick-Lawrence, *My Part in a Changing World*, 142.

28. The *Echo* was founded in the 1860s by Passmore Edwards as the first halfpenny evening paper in London. Frederick bought the paper in order to criticize the Boer War and ran it as a radical literary paper until 1905. F. W. Pethick-Lawrence, *Fate Has Been Kind* , 57–58, and Emmeline Pethick-Lawrence, *My Part in a Changing World*, 124, 131, 140–41.

29. Emmeline Pethick-Lawrence, *My Part in a Changing World*, 180.

30. F. W. Pethick-Lawrence, *Fate Has Been Kind*, 71.

31. F. W. Pethick-Lawrence, *Fate Has Been Kind*, 761.

32. Angela John, "The Privilege of Power: Suffrage Women and the Issue of Men's Support," in Vickery, *Women, Privilege and Power*, 228, 240–41.

33. F. W. Pethick-Lawrence, *Fate Has Been Kind*, 76.

34. Pankhurst, *Suffragette*, 174.

35. F. W. Pethick-Lawrence, *Fate Has Been Kind*, 77.

36. Details on the Pethick-Lawrence/Pankhurst split can be found in Rosen, *Rise Up Women*, 173–79. For a contemporary account of the incident see Pankhurst, *Suffragette Movement*, 411–15.

37. F. W. Pethick-Lawrence, *Fate Has Been Kind*, 98–100; Emmeline Pethick-Lawrence, *My Part in a Changing World*, 280–85.

38. Rappaport, *Shopping for Pleasure*, 111–15.

39. Atkinson, *Suffragettes in Purple, White, and Green*, 27.

40. Finnegan, *Selling Suffrage*, 115.

41. Emmeline Pethick-Lawrence, *My Part in a Changing World*, 213. No official circulation figures exist except those cited by the editors and in WSPU reports.

42. Sylvia Pankhurst claimed circulation rose from sixteen thousand in 1909 to forty thousand in 1910, *Suffragette Movement*, 223. Frederick Pethick-Lawrence provided the fifty thousand figure, *Fate Has Been Kind*, 86.

43. Harrison, "Press and Pressure Groups in Modern Britain," 276–77.

44. Stanley, *Life and Death of Emily Wilding Davison* , 87–89.

45. Third Annual Report, 1908, Fourth Annual Report, 1909, WSPU, UDC Pamphlets.

46. Stanley, *Life and Death of Emily Wilding Davison* , 89.

47. Christabel Pankhurst to Mrs. Badley, April 3, 1911, Autograph Letter Collection, Women's Library.

48. Other reform organizations also charged that the mainstream press distorted their claims. Harrison, "Press and Pressure Groups in Modern Britain," 274–75.

49. Diane Atkinson, *The Suffragettes in Pictures* (London: Museum of London, 1996), 53.

50. F. W. Pethick-Lawrence, *Fate Has Been Kind,* 76.

51. F. W. Pethick-Lawrence, recorded in *The Trial of the Suffragette Leaders* (London: Women's Press, 1912), 54.

52. The fee charged by the WSPU was 11 pence, return.

53. C. L. Collier to Miss Bright, December 6, 1929, Suffragette Fellowship Collection, Museum of London.

54. Emmeline Pethick-Lawrence, *My Part in a Changing World,* 300–301.

55. LeMahieu, *Culture for Democracy,* 22–26.

56. LeMahieu, *Culture for Democracy,* 301.

57. Evelyn Sharp to Miss M. P. Willcocks, June 21, 1912, Devon Record Office, Exeter, England. Angela John is currently editing Sharp's diaries (forthcoming from Day Books).

58. Estimated branch numbers for the major suffrage organizations in 1913 were as follows: NUWSS, 460; WSPU, 90; WFL 61. Pugh, *March of Women,* 255.

59. Pugh, *March of Women,* 212.

60. Fifth Annual Report, WSPU, 1910, UDC Pamphlets.

61. By June 1909, militancy was well underway. See Kent, *Sex and Suffrage in Britain* and Rosen, *Rise Up Women,* for a detailed description of the WSPU's major campaigns.

62. The NUWSS gave over 150 pounds to *Women's Franchise* that would now be used for their own paper. They ended their limited liability agreement with Francis after he gave space to the Women's Freedom League, claiming that "it was incompatible with the National Union's manifesto to Members of Parliament to continue to share a paper with a militant society." While pledging to contribute articles to *Women's Franchise* after starting their own organ, the pulling of funds effectively ensured its collapse some months later. Special Meeting of the Executive Committee, July 13, 1907, Papers of the National Union of Women's Suffrage Societies, Women's Library (hereafter NUWSS Papers); Annual Council Meeting, January 27, 1909, NUWSS Papers; Circular letter, December 18, 1908, Papers of the London Society for Women's Suffrage, Women's Library (hereafter LSWS Papers).

63. Margaret Ashton provided most of the funds. Swanick, *I Have Been Young,* 207.

64. Sub-committee Report, 1909, NUWSS Papers.

65. "Our Point of View," *Common Cause,* April 15, 1909, 3.

66. Hume, *National Union of Women's Suffrage Societies,* 99.

67. "Our Point of View," 3.

68. "Our Point of View," 3.

69. "Our Point of View," 3.

70. "Our Point of View," 3.

71. Hume, *National Union of Women's Suffrage Societies,* 66.

72. Swanick's salary was two hundred pounds a year. She had a small staff, including a manager, a subeditor, an advertisement canvasser, and an office girl ("boys proving too unreliable"). The paper moved to London in 1911. Swanick, *I Have Been Young,* 208.

73. Swanick, *I Have Been Young,* 230–31.

74. Swanick, *I Have Been Young,* 229–30.

75. Annual Council Meeting, January 27, 1909, NUWSS Papers.

76. Even though the Common Cause Publishing Company remained separate from the NUWSS, the organization's reports regularly included subsidies for the paper in its list of expenses as it considered the paper to be a necessary part of its work. The NUWSS paid the paper's liabilities through subsidies and the sale of company shares to members. By 1915, the NUWSS assumed almost all financial responsible for the paper. Executive Committee reports, January 18 and June 20, 1912, March 4 and July 15, 1915, and Common Cause Publishing Company Balance Sheets, 1915 and 1916, NUWSS Papers.

77. Common Cause Publishing Company balance sheets, NUWSS papers, 195–96.

78. Swanick, *I Have Been Young,* 225.

79. Swanick, *I Have Been Young,* 229.

80. Hume, *National Union of Women's Suffrage Societies,* 106.

81. Swanick, *I Have Been Young,* 222–23.

82. According the Chris Waters, socialist papers faced a similar problem and resisted "cater[ing] to workers' recreational interests" as long as they could. By 1911, socialist papers reluctantly included lighter fare to draw in readers. *British Socialists and the Politics of Popular Culture,* 180–81.

83. Circulation ranged from around six thousand to twenty-three thousand copies per week throughout the paper's life. The largest circulation came during 1913 and 1914, during NUWSS-funded circulation drives and heavily promoted street sales. Minutes, Executive Committee, October 15, 1913, July 31, 1913, March 5, 1914, December 7, 1916, NUWSS Papers.

84. Pugh, *March of Women;* Sandra Holton, *Suffrage Days;* Laura Nym Mayhall, "Defining Militancy: Radical Protest, the Constitutional Idiom, and Women's Suffrage in Britain, 1908–1909," *Journal of British Studies* 39, 3 (July 2000), 340–71.

85. Fifth Annual Conference Report, January 29, 1910, 9, Papers of the Women's Freedom League, Women's Library (hereafter WFL Papers).

86. Doughan and Sanchez, *Feminist Periodicals,* 29–30. The high cost of illustrations contributed to the paper's dull appearance. Not until 1926 did the *Vote* use pictures on the front page. Annual Conference Report, April 24, 1926, 32, WFL Papers.

87. Members were reminded "that they would have no '*Votes*' at all" were it not for Dr. Knight, who contributed "hundreds of pounds a year" to the paper by the

1920s. Having had previous experience with the WSPU, she helped shape the paper's content while maintaining the final say on financial decisions. Reports, April 25, 1925, 18, and April 24, 1926, 30–32, WFL Papers.

88. Reports, April 25, 1925, 18, and April 24, 1926, 30–32, WFL Papers.

89. C. Despard, "Welcome," *Vote*, October 30, 1909.

90. Though actual reader identity is hard to determine, advertisements suggest a reader with more progressive tastes who was slightly less affluent than the readers of *Votes for Women* or the *Common Cause*. Fewer luxury items were advertised, while clothing and consumer goods ads emphasized "value" as well as quality. Vegetarian products were also advertised regularly, alongside "progressive" items such as bicycles. The paper also promoted "for and by women" goods and services, such as a woman-run bank.

91. "What We Think," *Vote*, October 30, 1909.

92. Other editors included Cicely Hamilton, Marion Holmes, and Mrs. T. O'Conner. Despard, however, remained the paper's major influence, both during and after her tenure.

93. See Mulvihill, *Charlotte Despard*, and Linklater, *An Unhusbanded Life*.

94. Annual Report, April 25, 1925, 19, WFL Papers.

95. Waters, *British Socialists and the Politics of Popular Culture;* Hopkin, "Socialist Press in Britain"; Peter Roger Mountjoy, "The Working Class Press and Working Class Conservatism," in Boyce, Curran, and Wingate, *Newspaper History;* Benjamin, *Black Press in Britain;* and Vann and Van Arsdel, *Victorian Periodicals and Victorian Society.*

96. Harrison, "Press and Pressure Groups in Modern Britain," 280.

97. Pankhurst, *Suffragette*, 283.

98. According the Atkinson, "half the rooms [of the Women's Press] were devoted to organizing the selling of *Votes for Women* throughout the United Kingdom, dispatching it abroad and distributing other propaganda material." *Suffragettes in the Purple, White, and Green*, 37.

99. Emmeline Pethick-Lawrence, *My Part in a Changing World*, 191.

100. The NUWSS first attempted to lure new subscribers in February 1909 by distributing modest circulars. By December of the same year the NUWSS organized the Selling Corps for the *Common Cause*. H. M. Swanick to NUWSS, February 27, 1909, "Private and Confidential" letter to NUWSS, December 14, 1909, NUWSS Papers.

101. Message to *Common Cause* Sellers, Committee meeting, undated, NUWSS Papers.

102. Philippa Fawcett suggested this move to compete with *Votes for Women* sales at the Park. Philippa Fawcett to Miss Gosse, July 6, 1914, Autograph Letter Collection, Women's Library.

103. Ellen Walsh to Miss Strachey, June 4, 1910, Autograph Letter Collection, Women's Library.

104. Annual Report, April 25, 1925, 21, WFL Papers.

105. President's address, WFL Conference, 1910, WFL Papers.

106. Vote Sales Report, in Annual Report, April 30, 1929, 31, WFL Papers.

107. "Ye Doomsday Book of Ye Vote Brigade: 1913–1914," WFL Papers.

108. "Ye Doomsday Book of Ye Vote Brigade."

109. Evidence from annual reports claims that street sales could range from the low hundreds to around a thousand. *Votes for Women* and the *Common Cause* typically sold several thousand papers a week using this method.

110. Linklater, *Unhusbanded Life,* 248.

111. Instructions to *Common Cause* Sellers, Reports, March 16, [1914?], NUWSS Papers.

112. Maude Royden, "Bid Me Discourse," unpublished autobiography, Royden Papers, Women's Library.

113. Maude Royden, "Bid Me Discourse."

114. "Ye Doomsday Book of Ye Vote Brigade."

115. Green, *Spectacular Confessions,* 14.

116. Walkowitz, "Going Public," *Representations* 62 (Spring 1998), 17. DiCenzo has argued that the romantic representation of street selling by suffrage organizations meant that "individual needs were subsumed within those of the cause," further problematizing women's entry into "a hostile public sphere." "Gutter Politics," 28–29.

117. Jon Lawrence, "Contesting the Male Polity: The Suffragettes and the Politics of Disruption in Edwardian Britain," in Vickery, *Women, Privilege and Power,* 216.

118. The *Suffragette* was formed after the Pankhursts' split with the Pethick-Lawrences. The Pethick-Lawrences took *Votes for Women* with them and ran it as an independent suffrage paper, out of which grew the Votes for Women Fellowship. In 1914, they joined the United Suffragists, a moderate group "composed of distinguished men and women," and ran *Votes for Women* as its new organ until the passage of the first women's franchise bill in 1918, when the paper closed down. Emmeline Pethick-Lawrence, *My Part in a Changing World,* 281–87, 302–3.

119. Ian Fletcher, "Prosecutions,'" 255.

120. Lee, *Origins of the Popular Press in England,* 21–42.

121. Raeburn, *Suffragette View,* 54. Mayhall connects the militant tradition with early radical discourse in "Defining Militancy," 342–45.

122. As quoted in Pankhurst, *Life of Emmeline Pankhurst,* 104.

123. As quoted in Pankhurst, *Life of Emmeline Pankhurst,* 104.

124. *Manchester Guardian,* May 1, 1913.

125. Marie Brackenbury, Account of the Militant Suffragettes Campaign, January 1930, 57, Suffragette Fellowship Collection, Museum of London.

126. Pankhurst, *My Own Story,* 222.

127. Christabel Pankhurst to Evelyn Sharp, March [1912?], Nevinson Papers, Bodleian Library.

128. Cheryl Jorgensen-Earp, *Speeches and Trials of the Militant Suffragettes* (London: Fairleigh Dickinson University Press, 1999), 152.

129. *Suffrage Speeches from the Dock,* WSPU pamphlet (London: Woman's Press, 1912), 3–4.

130. *Suffrage Speeches from the Dock,* 70.

131. Rosen estimates property damage at over one hundred thousand pounds in 1912 and 1913. *Rise Up Women,* 189–202.

132. Herbert Samuel to Reginald McKenna, March 3, 1913, Home Office report, Public Records Office, London.

133. R. Barrett, assistant editor of the *Suffragette,* to H. D. Harben, March 15, 1913, Additional Manuscripts Collection purchased from Dr. Andrew Rosen, British Library.

134. "The *Suffragette* to Be Suppressed," *Manchester Guardian,* May 1, 1913.

135. Forty thousand copies of a shortened version of the paper went out. Report of Proceedings, Rex vs. Sidney Granville Drew, May 5, 1913, Public Records Office.

136. Copy of *Suffragette* sent to Reginald McKenna, home secretary, May 2, 1913, Public Records Office. Brackets indicate words made difficult to read in original copy.

137. Samuel to McKenna, March 3, 1913.

138. The *Manchester Guardian* reported the government's "official policy" in "The *Suffragette* to be Suppressed."

139. Pankhurst, *Suffragette Movement,* 460.

140. A. E. Metcalfe, *Woman's Effort* (Oxford: Blackwell, 1917), 269.

141. *Newspaper World,* May 6, 1913.

142. "What We Think of the Raid on the WSPU," *Votes for Women,* May 1, 1913, 459.

143. "What We Think of the Raid on the WSPU," 459.

144. Ian Fletcher, "'A Star Changer of the Twentieth Century': Suffragettes, Liberals, and the 1908 'Rush the Commons' Case," *Journal of British Studies* 35 (October 1996), 528.

145. Damage costs from suffragette violence doubled after the raid in May 1913 from the previous month's figures. Rosen, *Rise Up Women,* 197.

146. Emmeline Pankhurst to readers of *Suffragette,* circular letter, March 27, 1914, Suffragette Fellowship Collection, Museum of London.

147. Eighth Annual Report, 1914, WSPU Papers.

148. Swanick, *I Have Been Young,* 221fn.

149. Fletcher, "'Prosecutions,'" 251.

150. The *Suffragette,* after ceasing publication for nine months, appeared again on April 16, 1915, as a prowar paper. On October 15 it changed its name to *Britannia.* Pankhurst, *Suffragette Movement,* 594.

151. Gullace, *"Blood of Our Sons,"* 118–19.

Chapter 5. Strategies of Dissent

1. A notable exception is Nicolleta Gullace's *"Blood of Our Sons,"* which reveals a more activist brand of prosuffrage agitation during World War I based on women's service to the nation. Sandra Holton, however, credits pragmatic negotiations of constitutionalists with the government with the granting of the franchise to women rather than their war work. Holton, *Feminism and Democracy.* Cheryl Law similarly has argued that suffrage continued to unify women's organizations after the war. *Suffrage and Power: The Women's Movement, 1918–1928* (London: 1997), 13–41.

2. Kent, *Making Peace,* claims that factionalism was the cause of interwar feminism's retreat. See also Smith, *British Feminism in the Twentieth Century,* and Pugh, *Women and the Women's Movement in Britain.*

3. Pugh, *Women and the Women's Movement in Britain,* 52.

4. Christabel Pankhurst ran as a "Women's Party" candidate after the war. Her unsuccessful election bid on a "patriotic platform" led to the party's disbanding in 1919.

5. Gullace, *"Blood of Our Sons,"* 9–10.

6. "The Paper," *Common Cause,* August 14, 1914, 386.

7. Seventh Annual Report, Common Cause Publishing Company, LSWS Papers. Other wartime reports indicate that although the paper did experience hardships during the war, such as paper shortages and loss of subscribers, it continued to pay contributors and maintain its sixteen-page format.

8. *Church Militant,* February 1919, 1.

9. Gullace, *"Blood of Our Sons,"* 140–41.

10. Holton, *Feminism and Democracy,* 1–8.

11. Gullace, *"Blood of Our Sons,"* 118.

12. Jenny Gould, "Women's Military Services in First World War Britain," in Higonnet, Jenson, Michel, and Weitz, *Behind the Lines,* 115–16.

13. *Common Cause,* August 14, 1914, 384.

14. Kent, *Making Peace,* chaps. 1 and 2.

15. See Holton, *Feminism and Democracy,* 146–48, for a detailed account of the campaign's revival.

16. Pankhurst, *Suffragette Movement,* 606.

17. Koss, *Rise and Fall of the Political Press in Britain,* 2:240–45, and Edward Cook, *The Press in War-Time* (London: Macmillan, 1920).

18. Koss, *Rise and Fall of the Political Press,* 243–45.

19. Official wartime press controls were loosened at the end of 1915, after which time legal responsibility for published statements was shifted to the newspapers themselves. As a result, according to Koss, "A high proportion of censorship operated on a voluntary basis in order to save time, money, and face for all concerned." *Rise and Fall of the Political Press,* 245.

20. Koss, *Rise and Fall of the Political Press,* 262.

21. Koss, *Fleet Street Radical,* 153.

22. Quinn, Superintendent, to Criminal Investigation Department, New Scotland Yard, March 8, 1916, Public Records Office.

23. "Confidential Notices to the Press," September 1915, Press Bureau, Public Records Office.

24. Deian Hopkin, "Domestic Censorship in the First World War," *Journal of Contemporary History* 5, 4 (1970), 156.

25. Over two thousand women attended the Kingsway Hall meeting, including Charlotte Despard, Mrs. Pethick-Lawrence, Olive Schreiner, and Mary MacArthur. Lord Robert Cecil to Fawcett, August 5, 1914, quoted in Oldfield, *Spinsters of This Parish,* 179.

26. "The Paper," 386.

27. "The Common Cause," *Common Cause,* August 14, 1914, 390.

28. "To Our Readers," *Vote,* August 14, 1914, 278.

29. "The Paper," 386.

30. "Organization," *Common Cause,* August 14, 1914, 385.

31. Ellen Garrett to NUWSS Society secretaries, October 15, 1915, LSWS Papers.

32. Holton, *Feminism and Democracy,* 130.

33. "Our Common Cause," *Common Cause,* August 14, 1914, 385.

34. Gould, "Women's Military Services in First World War Britain," 114–25.

35. "A Stream of Callers: The Votes Is Sold Out," *Vote,* August 28, 1914, 298

36. "The Prime Minister and the Vote," *Vote,* October 30, 1914, 301.

37. *Vote,* September 25, 1914.

38. "Maternity," *Vote,* September 25, 1914, 328.

39. According to Harrison, interwar feminists used "prudent" tactics to become the "quiet voices" of a movement no longer bound together by suffrage. *Prudent Revolutionaries,* 2.

40. Jean Chalaby, "Northcliffe: Proprietor as Journalist," in Catterall, Seymour-Ure, and Smith, *Northcliffe's Legacy,* 37.

41. See Holton, *Feminism and Democracy,* regarding pacifism and the NUWSS, 135–37. Swanick describes her role in the UDC in *I Have Been Young,* 417–65.

42. Leila Rupp, *Worlds of Women* (Princeton: Princeton University Press, 1997), 34.

43. Emmeline Pethick-Lawrence, *My Part in a Changing World,* 312–13.

44. Sheepshanks to Bertrand Russell, September 1914, as quoted in Sybil Oldfield, *Spinsters of this Parish,* 184.

45. Oldfield, "Mary Sheepshanks Edits an Internationalist Suffrage Monthly," 126.

46. Oldfield, *Spinsters of This Parish,* 176–80.

47. Oldfield, *Spinsters of This Parish,* 188–89.

48. *Jus Suffragii,* January 1915.

49. *Jus Suffragii,* [?], 1919, 197.

50. Sheepshanks, *Jus Suffragii,* October 1, 1914, as quoted in Oldfield, *Spinsters of This Parish,* 185.

51. Mary Sheepshanks to Alice Park, May 10, 1915, October 16, 1916, July 12, 1917, Sheepshanks Papers, Women's Library. Park, who resided in Palo Alto, California, described U.S. women's role in the League during this time. See also Carrie Chapman Catt to the International Woman Suffrage Alliance, circular letter, May 11, 1916, Autograph Letter Collection, Women's Library.

52. *Irish Citizen,* as quoted in Oldfield, *Spinsters of This Parish,* 188.

53. *Women's Dreadnought,* March 8, 1914, as reprinted in *Suffrage and the Pankhursts,* edited by Jane Marcus (London: Routledge, 1987), 241.

54. "Suffragette Sisters to Split," *Daily Sketch,* February 7, 1914, reprinted in Mackenzie, *Shoulder to Shoulder,* 270.

55. Sylvia originally wanted to call the paper *Worker's Mate,* but her supporters convinced her that *Women's Dreadnought* would best represent their cause to the public. Pankhurst, *Suffragette Movement,* 525.

56. Pankhurst, *Suffragette Movement,* 525.

57. Pankhurst, *Suffragette Movement,* 525.

58. Pankhurst, *Suffragette Movement,* 526.

59. Pankhurst, *Suffragette Movement,* 525.

60. Sylvia claimed a circulation of ten thousand. Winslow, *Sylvia Pankhurst,* 69.

61. Winslow, *Sylvia Pankhurst,* 68.

62. Sylvia took the *Dreadnought* to an East End printer, although Francis did publish later editions. Pankhurst, *Suffragette Movement,* 527.

63. Pankhurst, *Suffragette Movement,* 529. The police refused to allow the Federation to march in Trafalgar Square. A loosely organized men's group associated with them had engaged the Square for the group to march and distribute the *Dreadnought.*

64. Pankhurst, *Suffragette Movement,* 526–27; Margot Aswuith, ed., *Myself When Young* (London: Muller, 1938), 309.

65. Winslow, *Sylvia Pankhurst,* 80.

66. Winslow, *Sylvia Pankhurst,* 103.

67. Pankhurst, *Suffragette,* 595.

68. Speech Delivered by Christabel Pankhurst at Queen's Hall, November 7, 1917; see also "The Women's Party Victory, National Security, and Progress," *Britannia,* November 2, 1917; both reprinted in Mackenzie, *Shoulder to Shoulder,* 316–17.

69. "A Minimum Wage for Women," *Women's Dreadnought,* September 12, 1914, reprinted in Marcus, *Suffrage and the Pankhursts,* 266.

70. "The Sweating Scandal," *Women's Dreadnought,* October 4, 1914.

71. Culleton, *Working-Class Culture, Women, and Britain,* 102–8.

72. Winslow, *Sylvia Pankhurst,* 90.

73. Winslow, *Sylvia Pankhurst,* 72–73.

74. "Our Letter to Asquith," *Women's Dreadnought,* November 27, 1915.

75. Winslow, *Sylvia Pankhurst,* 103–4, 173.

Chapter 6. The New Feminist Reader and the Remaking of Women's Political Culture after World War I

1. See Pugh, *Women and the Women's Movement in Britain;* Kent, *Making Peace,* 140–43, 132–34; Harold Smith, "British Feminism in the 1920s," in Smith, *British Feminism in the Twentieth Century,* 47–65.

2. Kent, *Making Peace,* 117.

3. Smith, "British Feminism in the 1920s," 47–49.

4. See Gottlieb, *Feminine Fascism,* and Douglas, *Feminist Freikorp.*

5. Law, *Suffrage and Power,* 177.

6. Law, *Suffrage and Power,* 229.

7. John Eldrige, Jenny Kitzinger, and Kevin Williams, *The Mass Media and Power in Modern Britain* (Oxford: Oxford University Press, 1997), 28.

8. James Curran and Jean Seaton, *Power without Responsibility: The History of the Press and Broadcasting* (London: Routledge, 1991), 61.

9. Eldrige, Kitzinger, and Williams, *Mass Media and Power in Modern Britain,* 21–22.

10. Colin Seymour-Ure, "Northcliffe's Legacy," in Catterall, Seymour-Ure, and Smith, *Northcliffe's Legacy,* 10–11.

11. Dilwyn Porter offers the example of the *Mirror* headline "Stock Exchange Buoyant" being printed alongside "Jealous Woman's Gift: Sends her Rival Two Vipers in a Jewel Case." "Where There's a Tip There's a Tap," in Catterall, Seymour-Ure, and Smith, *Northcliffe's Legacy,* 72.

12. Advertising columns, *Westminster Gazette* and *Times,* c. 1919–25. Adrian Bingham has credited this move in the mainstream press with bringing the new woman voter into the public sphere in a limited though nevertheless significant way; *Gender, Modernity, and the Popular Press in Inter-War Britain* (Oxford: Oxford University Press, 2004), 143.

13. Williams, *Get Me a Murder a Day,* 102.

14. Pugh, *Women and the Women's Movement,* 209–10.

15. Janice Winship, "Women's Magazines," in *Nationalising Femininity: Culture, Sexuality, and British Cinema in the Second World War,* edited by Christine Gledhill and Gillian Swanson (Manchester, England: Manchester University Press, 1996), 128–29.

16. White, *Women's Magazines,* 93–99.

17. Oldfield, *Spinsters of This Parish,* 197.

18. Koss, *Rise and Fall of the Political Press in Britain,* 2:498.

19. Koss, *Rise and Fall of the Political Press in Britain,* 2:497.

20. Smith, *New Statesman,* 68.

21. Annual Report, 1918, Papers of the National Union of Societies for Equal Citizenship, Women's Library (hereafter cited as NUSEC Papers).

22. "'The Woman's Leader' and 'The Common Cause,'" *Common Cause,* January 30, 1920.

23. Annual Report, 1920, and Annual Report, 1918, NUSEC Papers.

24. According to the inaugural issue of the *Englishwoman,* "the *Englishwoman* is intended to reach the cultured public, and bring before it, in a convincing and moderate form, the case for the Enfranchisement of Women. . . . The *Englishwoman* is not addressed only to those who are already fully convinced of the justice of the Women's Movement and who have done their share in furthering the interests of women by their example and their work. It is intended for the general public."

25. Annual Report, 1927–28, NUSEC Papers.

26. Annual Report, 1920, NUSEC Papers. Although the paper was ostensibly independent from NUSEC, close financial ties continued between the two institutions.

27. "Recorded Comments of Reviews from the Press," 1925–26, NUSEC Papers.

28. "The Woman's Leader," *Common Cause,* January 30, 1920, 547.

29. Both articles appeared in the *Vote,* June 3, 1927.

30. Annual Report, April 24, 1926, 34, WFL Papers.

31. Annual Report, April 25, 1925, 20, WFL Papers.

32. According to WFL reports, slight increases in overall circulation that averaged around two thousand copies per week were achieved by means of street selling by members. The 1925 annual report, for example, estimated that sales for the year had increased by 4,735 copies.

33. *Vote,* April 6, 1928.

34. *Vote,* April 6, 1928.

35. Kent, *Making Peace,* 114–39.

36. Annual Report, 1928, and Annual Report, 1929, NUSEC Papers.

37. Annual Conference Report, April 25, 1925, 17, WFL Papers.

38. Linklater, *Unhusbanded Life,* 251.

39. Annual Report, 1930, NUSEC Papers.

40. Maggie Morgan, "The Women's Institute Movement," in *This Working-Day World: Women's Lives and Culture(s) in Britain, 1914–1945,* edited by Sybil Oldfield (London: Taylor and Francis, 1994), 37–38.

41. For more on the Townswomen's Guilds and Women's Institutes see Peter Gordon and David Doughan, eds., *Dictionary of British Women's Organisations, 1825–1960* (London: Woburn Press, 2001), 103–4, 141–42.

42. Spender, *Time and Tide Wait for No Man.*

43. Garner, *Dora Marsden,* 60–71. Marsden was from a lower-middle class background and attended Manchester Victoria University in 1900 with Christabel Pankhurst, Mary Gawthorpe, Theresa Billington-Greig, Rona Robinson, and Emily Wilding Davison. She abandoned her training as a teacher to become a salaried organizer for the WSPU in 1908. In 1911, Marsden moved to London, where she became involved with modernist literary culture. See Clarke, *Dora Marsden and Early Modernism,* 1–3.

44. Garner, *Dora Marsden,* 60–62. Lucy Delap understands the radicalism of the *Freewoman,* in part, as related to its attempts to redefine feminist politics, not only in its treatment of sexuality; "'Philosophical Vacuity and Political Ineptitude': The *Freewoman*'s Critique of the Suffrage Movement," *Women's History Review* 11, 4 (2002), 625.

45. West as quoted in Clarke, *Dora Marsden and Early Modernism,* 67.

46. *Freewoman,* November 23, 1911, as quoted in Garner, *Dora Marsden,* 62.

47. Clarke, *Dora Marsden and Early Modernism,* 91.

48. Clarke, *Dora Marsden and Early Modernism,* 129–31.

49. Lady Rhondda to Elizabeth Robins, August 8, 1920, Robins Papers, Fales Library.

50. They included Elizabeth Robins, Rebecca West, Cicely Hamilton, Maude Royden, Alexandra Chalmers-Watson, Helen Archdale, and Vera Laughton. Several writers also sat on the board of *Time and Tide,* a limited liability company—started with twenty thousand pounds in capital raised from the sale of one-pound shares—in which Rhondda held the controlling interest. Eoff, *Viscountess Rhondda,* 118–19.

51. Circular letter from *Time and Tide,* to papers including *London Times, Daily Dispatch, Daily Sketch, Evening Standard, Sunday Chronicle, Sunday Herald, Daily Telegraph,* January 6, 1920, Robins Papers.

52. Rhondda to Robins, December 1, 1919.

53. Circular letter from *Time and Tide* to press, March 16, 1920, Robins Papers.

54. In addition to sitting on the board of *Common Cause,* Rhondda wrote for a number of local and suffrage papers on the militant movement. "My Introduction to the Press," *Time and Tide,* October 31, 1924, 1051.

55. Rhondda served on the board from 1918 to 1920. Rhondda to Robins, December 6, 1919, December 8, 1919, July 14, 1919, Robins Papers.

56. "The Weekly Newspaper," *Time and Tide,* October 31, 1924.

57. "The Function of the Weekly Review," *Time and Tide,* December 9, 1927.

58. Eoff, *Viscountess Rhondda,* 121. The *New Statesman,* for example, sold ten thousand copies weekly during this period. Smith, *New Statesman,* 139.

59. "Review of *Time and Tide,*" *Yorkshire Post,* October 12, 1928.

60. "Lady Rhondda: Portraits Presented at Dinner," *Manchester Guardian,* February 24, 1933.

61. "Competition for Readers," *Time and Tide,* January 27, 1928, 85.

62. "Readers' Responses," *Time and Tide,* January 23, 1925.

63. "Why Your Friends Should Read *Time and Tide,*" *Time and Tide,* March 19, 1926, 289.

64. Vera Brittain to Winifred Holtby, August 20, 1926, in *Selected Letters of Winifred Holtby and Vera Brittain, 1920–1935* (London: Brown, 1960); Rhondda to Robins, February 9, 1920, Robins Papers.

65. "Extracts from Mr. St. John Ervine's Speech Proposing the Health of *Time and Tide,*" *Time and Tide,* July 10, 1925, 669.

66. Robins to Rhondda, February 16, 1920, Robins Papers.

67. Rhondda to Robins, August, 20, 1920, Robins Papers.

68. Rhondda to Robins, October 17, 1922, Robins Papers.

69. "Women and Public Affairs," *Time and Tide,* October 14, 1921, 978.

70. "The Sex Disqualification (Removal) Act," *Time and Tide,* August 3, 1923, 776.

71. Cicely Hamilton, "The Backwash of Feminism," *Time and Tide,* September 8, 1922, 853.

72. Rebecca West, "On a Form of Nagging," *Time and Tide,* October 31, 1924, reprinted in Spender, *Time and Tide Wait for No Man,* 58.

73. "*Time and Tide,*" *Time and Tide,* May 14, 1920.

74. *Time and Tide,* June 25, 1920, 144–45.

75. *Time and Tide,* May 20, 1927, 470.

76. "Our Men's Page," *Time and Tide,* January 4, 1924, 17.

77. Letter to editor of the Men's Page, "Sir Duffer D'Amboring," "Men's Page," *Time and Tide,* January 11, 1924.

78. "Men's Page," January 11, 1924.

79. "Advertisement," *Time and Tide,* December 5, 1924, 1207. *Time and Tide* board members observed in 1919 that Northcliffe's failure to draw in women readers resulted from his lack of attention to issues such as women's employment and education. Lady Rhondda to Members of the Board, March 16, 1920, Robins Papers.

80. Fredrick Pethick-Lawrence to Elizabeth Robins, October 16, 1926, Robins Papers.

81. Eoff, *Viscountess Rhondda,* 118.

82. Lady Rhondda, introduction to *Time and Tide Anthology,* edited by Anthony Lejeune (London: Deutsch, 1956), 11.

83. Rhondda to Virginia Woolf, quoted in Eoff, *Viscountess Rhondda,* 133.

84. Graham Murdock and Peter Golding, "The Structure, Ownership, and Control of the Press, 1914–76," in Boyce, Curran, and Wingate, *Newspaper History,* 130–37, 146–48.

85. "Lady Rhondda: Champion of Her Sex," *London Times,* July 21, 1958; "Viscountess Rhondda: Suffragette and Business Woman," *Daily Telegraph,* July 21, 1958; "Viscountess Rhondda," *Manchester Guardian,* July 21, 1958; Eoff, *Viscountess Rhondda,* 128.

86. "Lady Rhondda: Portraits Presented at Dinner," *Manchester Guardian,* February 24, 1923.

87. "Lady Rhondda: Champion of Her Sex," *London Times,* July 21, 1958.

88. "Viscountess Rhondda," *Manchester Guardian,* July 21, 1958.

89. *Daily Telegraph,* May 19, 1941.

90. Birkenhead, "Letters to the Editor," *Time and Tide,* July 26, 1958.

91. "Viscountess Rhondda: Suffragette and Business Woman," *Daily Telegraph,* July 21, 1958, and Doughan and Sanchez, *Feminist Periodicals,* 45.

Conclusion

1. Michelene Wandor, *Once a Feminist* (London: Virago, 1990), 6. A very similar experience inspired the founding of *Ms.* magazine in the United States in 1972; Mary Thom, *Inside Ms.* (New York: Holt, 1997), 1–19.

2. Marsha Rowe, *Spare Rib Reader* (London: Penguin, 1982), 13, 14.

3. Doughan and Sanchez, *Feminist Periodicals,* 67–261.

4. Doughan and Sanchez, *Feminist Periodicals,* 52.

5. Rowe, *Spare Rib Reader,* 16; Doughan and Sanchez, *Feminist Periodicals,* 86. Circulation figures are from 1983.

6. Quoted in Pamela Freeman, "Spare Rib," in *Consumer Magazines of the British Isles,* edited by Sam Riley (Westport, Conn.: Greenwood, 1993), 194.

7. Paul Anderson, "Second Time Lucky?" *New Statesman,* May 20, 1990, 12–13.

8. Loretta Loach, "Eve's Revenge," *New Statesman,* June 26, 1987, 38–39.

9. Margaret Cousins and James Cousins, *We Two Together* (Madras, India: Ganesh, 1950), 129–30.

10. George Boyce, "The Fourth Estate," in Boyce, Curran, and Wingate, *Newspaper History,* 20–21.

11. Jean Chalaby, *The Invention of Journalism* (London: Macmillan, 1998), 77–78.

12. Anderson, "Second Time Lucky," 13.

Bibliography

Manuscript Sources

Beinecke Library, Yale University
  Rebecca West Collection
Bodleian Library, University of Oxford
  Correspondence and Papers of Evelyn Sharp Nevinson, 1888– 1955; John Johnson
    Collection/Women's Suffrage
British Library, London
  Letters and Papers of Mrs. Elizabeth Wolstenholme Elmy (1881–1914); Additional
    Manuscripts Collection purchased from Dr. Andrew Rosen; Papers and Cor-
    respondence of Charles Wentworth Dilke; Maud Arncliffe-Sennett Collection
    (suffrage ephemera and pamphlets)
William Andrews Clark Memorial Library, University of California, Los Angeles
  Oscar Wilde and His Literary Collection of Papers, 1819–1995
Devon Record Office, Exeter, England
  Miss M. P. Willcocks Correspondence
Fales Library and Special Collections, New York University
  Elizabeth Robins Papers
Girton College Archive, University of Cambridge
  Helen Blackburn Collection; Papers of Barbara Leigh Smith Bodichon; Davies
    Papers; Papers of Bessie Rayner Parkes; Papers of the Society for Promoting
    the Training of Women
Hull Public Library, Hull, England
  Winifred Holtby Collection
Huntington Library, San Marino, California
  Anthony Family Papers; Papers of Richard Carlile, 1819–1900; Francis Power Cobbe
    Correspondence, 1855–1904; Woman's Press pamphlets

University of Liverpool, Liverpool, England
 Josephine Butler Collection; Papers of Eleanor Rathbone
Manchester Central Reference Library, Manchester, England
 Lydia Becker Newspaper Cutting Collection; Papers of Millicent Garrett Fawcett;
  Papers of the Manchester Society for Women's Suffrage
Museum of London, London
 Suffragette Fellowship Collection
Public Records Office, London
 Home Office Papers; Papers of the Treasury Solicitor, War Office, Cabinet Office
John Rylands Research Institute, Manchester, England
 Uncatalogued suffrage documents and correspondence
Wellcome Institute Library, London
 Florence Fenwick Miller Collection, 1854–1935
Women's Library, London
 Personal Papers of Dame Margery Corbett Ashby; Autograph Letter Collection;
  Personal Papers of Lydia Ernestine Becker; Personal Papers of Fiona Billington-
  Greig; Papers of the Central Committee of the National Society for Women's
  Suffrage; Papers of the Consultive Committee of Constitutional Women's Suf-
  frage Societies, 1916–19; Personal Papers of Charlotte Despard; Personal Papers
  of Emily Faithfull; Personal Papers of Dame Millicent Fawcett; Personal Papers
  of Winifred Holtby; Personal Papers of Edith How-Martyn; Papers of the London Society for Women's Suffrage/Service, 1907–26; Personal Papers of Harriet
  McIlquham; Papers of the National Union of Societies for Equal Citizenship,
  1919–46; Papers of the National Union of Women's Suffrage Societies, 1896–19;
  Papers of the Open Door Council, 1926–65; Personal Papers of Eleanor Rathbone; Personal Papers of Maude A. Royden; Personal Papers of Mary Sheepshanks; Papers of the Six Point Group, 1919–81; Papers of the Townswomen's
  Guild; Personal Papers of Rebecca West; Papers of the Women's Freedom League,
  1907–61; Universal Decimal Classification (UDC) Pamphlets

Selected Books and Articles

Adburgham, Alison. *Women in Print: Writing Women and Women's Magazines from the Restoration to the Accession of Victoria.* London: Allen and Unwin, 1972.
A. J. R. *The Suffrage Annual and Women's Who's Who.* London: Stanley Paul, 1913.
Aldred, Guy. *Richard Carlile: Agitator.* London: Pioneer Press, 1923.
Anderson, Benedict. *Imagined Communities.* London: Verso, 1992.
Atkinson, Diane. *Suffragettes in Purple, White, and Green, 1906–1914.* London: Museum of London, 1992.
———. *Votes for Women.* Cambridge: Cambridge University Press, 1988.
Barrows, Susanna, and Robin Room, eds. *Drinking Behavior and Belief in Modern History.* Berkeley: University of California Press, 1991.

Beadnell, Henry. *A Guide to Typography, in Two Parts, Literary and Practical; or The Reader's Handbook and the Compositor's Vade-mecum.* London: F. Bowering, 1859.

Becker, Lydia. *The Rights and Duties of Women in Local Government: A Paper by Miss Becker.* Manchester: A. Ireland, 1879.

Beetham, Margaret. *A Magazine of Her Own? Domesticity and Desire in the Woman's Magazine, 1800–1914.* London: Routledge, 1996.

Bell, E. Moberly. *Josephine Butler: Flame of Fire.* London: Constable, 1962.

Belloc, Hillare. *Lambkin's Remains.* Oxford: J. Vincent, 1900.

Benjamin, Ionie. *The Black Press in Britain.* Stoke-on-Trent: Trentham Books, 1995.

Besant, Annie. *Annie Besant: An Autobiography.* London: T. Fisher Unwin, 1893.

Bettany, F. G. *Stewart Headlam: A Biography.* London: John Murray, 1926.

Black, Clementina. *Married Women's Work: Being the Report of an Enquiry Undertaken by the Women's Industrial Council.* London: G. Bell, 1915.

Blackburn, Helen, ed. *A Handbook for Women Engaged in Social and Political Work.* London: Edward Stanford, 1895.

———. *A Handy Book of Reference for Irishwomen.* London: Irish Exhibition, 1888.

———. *Preface to Women under the Factory Act.* London: Williams and Norgate, 1903.

———. *Women's Suffrage: A Record of the Women's Suffrage Movement in the British Isles with Biographical Sketches of Miss Becker.* London: Williams and Norgate, 1902.

———. *Words of a Leader: Being Extracts from the Writings of the late Miss Lydia Becker.* Bristol: J. W. Arrowsmith, 1897.

Blair, W. T. *Female Suffrage: An Article Reprinted from the "Victoria Magazine" of 1874 with Some Remarks on the Late Debate in the House of Commons.* London: Victoria Press, 1876.

Bland, Lucy. *Banishing the Beast.* New York: New Press, 1995.

Bodichon, Barbara [Leigh Smith]. *Reasons for and against the Enfranchisement of Women.* London: M'Corquodale, 1872.

———. *Women and Work, Improvement of Women.* London: Bosworth and Harrison, 1857.

Bonner, Hypatia Bradlaugh. *Charles Bradlaugh: A Record of His Life and Work by His Daughter.* Vol. 1. London: T. Fisher Unwin, 1894.

Boucherett, Jessie. *Hints on Self-Help; A Book for Young Women.* London: S. W. Partridge, 1863.

Boyce, George, James Curran, and Pauline Wingate, eds. *Newspaper History from the Seventeenth Century to the Present Day.* London: Constable, 1978.

Bremner, Christina. *Divorce and Morality.* London: Frank Palmer, 1912.

———. *Education of Girls and Women.* London: Swan Sonnenschein, 1897.

———. *A Month in a Dandi: A Woman's Wanderings in Northern India.* London: Simpkin, Marshall, Hamilton, Kent, 1891.

Brewer, John. *Party Ideology and Popular Politics at the Accession of George III.* Cambridge: Cambridge University Press, 1976.

Brittain, Vera. *Selected Letters of Winifred Holtby and Vera Brittain, 1920–1935.* London: A. Brown, 1960.

Brown, Lucy. *Victorian News and Newspapers.* Oxford: Clarendon Press, 1985.

Burrett, Edward. *Full Point: A Typographer Remembers.* Esher: Penmiel Press, 1976.

Burton, Antoinette. *Burdens of History: British Feminists, Indian Women, and Imperial Culture, 1865–1915.* Chapel Hill: University of North Carolina Press, 1994.

Butler, A. S. G. *Portrait of Josephine Butler.* London: Faber and Faber, 1954.

Butler, Josephine, ed. *Woman's Work and Culture: A Series of Essays.* London: Macmillan, 1869.

Calhoun, Craig, ed. *Habermas and the Public Sphere.* Cambridge, Mass.: MIT Press, 1992.

Carlile Campbell, Theophila. *The Battle of the Press: As Told through the Life of Richard Carlile.* London: Bonner, 1899.

Catterall, Peter, Colin Seymour-Ure, and Adrian Smith, eds. *Northcliffe's Legacy: Aspects of the British Popular Press, 1896–1996.* New York: St. Martin's Press, 2000.

Chalaby, Jean. *The Invention of Journalism.* London: Macmillan, 1998.

Chappell, Jennie. *Noble Work by Noble Women.* London: S. W. Partridge, 1900.

Clarke, Bruce. *Dora Marsden and Early Modernism.* Ann Arbor: University of Michigan Press, 1996.

Clear, Gwen. *The Story of W. H. Smith and Son.* London: Printed for private circulation, 1949.

Clough, Blanche Athena. *A Memoir of Anne Jemima Clough.* London: Edward Arnold, 1897.

Coates, Chris. "The Things That They Have Wrought." *Spare Rib,* December 1986, 36–38.

Cole, G. D. H. *Richard Carlile.* Biographical Series Issued by the Fabian Society. Vol. 13. London: Victor Gollancz, 1942.

Colley, Linda. *Britons, Forging the Nation, 1707–1837.* New Haven: Yale University Press, 1992.

Cooke, C. A. *Corporation, Trust, and Company.* Manchester: Manchester University Press, 1950.

Cott, Nancy. *The Bonds of Womanhood: "Woman's Sphere" in New England, 1780–1835.* New Haven: Yale University Press, 1977.

Cranfield, G. A. *The Press and Society.* London: Longman, 1978.

Cudlipp, Hugh. *Publish and Be Damned! The Astonishing Story of the Daily Mirror.* London: Andrew Dakers, 1953.

Culleton, Claire A. *Working-Class Culture, Women, and Britain, 1914–1921.* New York: St. Martin's Press, 1999.

Cunningham, Gail. *The New Woman and the Victorian Novel.* London: Macmillan Press, 1978.

DeVinne, Theodore. *Printing in the Nineteenth Century.* New York: Lead Mould Electrotype Foundry, 1924.

DiCenzo, Maria. "Gutter Politics: Women Newsies and the Suffrage Press." *Women's History Review* 12, 1 (2003), 14–34.

Dijkstra, Bram. *Idols of Perversity: Fantasies of Feminine Evil in Fin-de-Siècle Culture.* Oxford: Oxford University Press, 1986.

Dooley, Allan C. *Author and Printer in Victorian England.* Charlottesville: University of Virginia Press, 1992.

Doughan, David, and Denise Sanchez. *Feminist Periodicals, 1855–1984.* New York: New York University Press, 1987.

Douglas, R. M. *Feminist Freikorps.* London: Praeger, 1999.

Dubois, Ellen. "Considering the State of U.S. Women's History," *Journal of Women's History* 15, 1 (Spring 2003), 151–52.

Duckworth, Eleanor. *Poems and Sketches.* Edinburgh: William Winter, 1856.

Eisenstein, Zillah. *The Radical Future of Liberal Feminism.* New York: Longman, 1981.

Eldridge, John, Jenny Kitzinger, and Kevin Williams *The Mass Media and Power in Modern Britain.* Oxford: Oxford University Press, 1997.

Ellsworth, Edward. *Liberators of the Female Mind: The Shirreff Sisters, Educational Reform, and the Women's Movement.* Westport, Conn.: Greenwood Press, 1979.

Elshtain, Jean Bethke. *Public Man, Private Woman: Women in Social and Political Thought.* Princeton: Princeton University Press, 1981.

Eoff, Shirley. *Viscountess Rhondda, Equalitarian Feminist.* Columbus: Ohio State University Press, 1991.

Epstein, James. *Radical Expression: Political Language, Ritual, and Symbol in England, 1790–1850.* Oxford: Oxford University Press, 1994.

Ethington, Philip. "Hypothesis from Habermas: Notes on Reconstructing American Political and Social History, 1890–1920." *Intellectual History Newsletter* 14 (1992), 21–39.

Faithfull, Emily. *Three Visits to America.* Edinburgh: David Douglas, 1884.

Finnegan, Margaret. *Selling Suffrage: Consumer Culture and Votes for Women.* Columbia: Columbia University Press, 1999.

Fitzpatrick, Kathleen. *Lady Henry Somerset.* London: Jonathan Cape, 1923.

Fletcher, Ian Christopher. "'Prosecutions . . . Are Always Risky Business': Labor, Liberals and the 1912 'Don't Shoot' Prosecutions." *Albion* 28, 2 (1996): 251–78.

———. "'A Star Chamber for the Twentieth Century': Suffragettes, Liberals and the 1908 'Rush the Commons' Case.'" *Journal of British Studies* 35, 4 (1996), 504–30.

Flint, Kate. *The Woman Reader, 1837–1914.* Oxford: Clarendon Press, 1993.

Fredeman, William. "Emily Faithfull and the Victoria Press." *Library* 29 (June 1973), 139–64.

Freedman, Estelle. "Separatism as Strategy: Female Institution Building and American Feminism." *Feminist Studies* 5, 3 (1979), 512–29.

Gallagher, Catherine. *The Industrial Reformation of English Fiction.* Chicago: University of Chicago Press, 1980.

———. *Nobody's Story.* Berkeley: University of California Press, 1994.

Garner, Les. *Dora Marsden: A Brave and Beautiful Spirit.* Aldershot, England: Avebury, 1990.

Gillespie, Sarah. *A Hundred Years of Progress: The Record of the Scottish Typographical Association, 1853–1952.* Glasgow: Robert Maclehose, 1953.

Girton College. *Girton College Register, 1869–1946.* Cambridge: Privately printed for Girton College, 1948.

Gleadle, Kathryn. *The Early Feminists: Radical Unitarians and the Emergence of the Women's Rights Movement, 1831–51.* London: St. Martin's Press, 1995.

Glendinning, Victoria. *Rebecca West: A Life.* London: Weidenfeld and Nicolson, 1987.

Goldman, Harold. *Emma Paterson.* London: Lawrence and Wishart, 1974.

Goldman, Lawrence. *Science Reform and Politics in Victorian Britain: The Social Science Association, 1857–1886.* Cambridge: Cambridge University Press, 2002.

———. "The Social Science Association, 1857–1886." *English Historical Review* 101 (January 1986), 95–134.

Gottlieb, Julie. *Feminine Fascism.* London: I. B. Tauris, 2000.

Gould, Joseph. *The Compositor's Guide and Pocket Book.* London: Farrington, 1878.

Green, Barbara. *Spectacular Confessions: Autobiography, Performative Activism, and the Sites of Suffrage, 1905–1938.* New York: St. Martin's Press, 1997.

Gullace, Nicoletta F. *"The Blood of Our Sons": Men, Women, and the Renegotiation of British Citizenship during the Great War.* London: Palgrave, 2002.

Gurney, Peter. *Co-operative Culture and the Politics of Consumption in England, 1870–1830.* Manchester: Manchester University Press, 1996.

Grogan, Mercy. *How Women May Earn a Living.* London: Cassell, Petter, and Galpin, 1880.

Habermas, Jürgen. *The Structural Transformation of the Public Sphere.* Cambridge, Mass.: MIT Press, 1993.

Hall, Catherine, Keith McClelland, and Jane Rendall, eds. *Defining the Victorian Nation: Class, Race, Gender and the Reform Act of 1867.* Cambridge: Cambridge University Press, 2000.

Hall, S. C. *The Worn Thimble: A Story of Woman's Duty and Woman's Influence.* London: William Tweedie, 1853.

Hampton, Mark. *Visions of the Press in Britain, 1850–1950.* Illinois: University of Illinois Press, 2004.

Handover, Phyllis. *Printing in London: From 1476 to Modern Times.* London: Allen and Unwin, 1960.

Harris, Michael, and Alan Lee, eds. *The Press in English Society from the Seventeenth to Nineteenth Centuries.* Rutherford, N.J.: Fairleigh Dickinson University Press, 1986.

Harrison, Brian. *Drink and the Victorians: The Temperance Question in England.* London: Faber and Faber, 1971.

―――. *Prudent Revolutionaries: Portraits of British Feminists between the Wars.* Oxford: Clarendon Press, 1987.

―――. *Separate Spheres: The Opposition to Women's Suffrage in Britain.* London: Croom Helm, 1978.

Hays, Frances. *Women of the Day: A Biographical Dictionary of Notable Contemporaries.* London: Chatto and Windus, 1885.

Higonnet, Margaret Randolph, Jane Jenson, Sonya Michel, and Margaret Collins Weitz, eds. *Behind the Lines: Gender and the Two World Wars.* New Haven: Yale University Press, 1987.

Holcombe, Lee. *Victorian Ladies at Work.* Hamden, Conn.: Archon Books, 1973.

Hollis, Patricia. *The Pauper Press.* Oxford: Oxford University Press, 1970.

Holmes, Marion. *Lydia Becker: A Cameo Life Sketch.* London: Women's Freedom League, [19??].

―――. *Josephine Butler: A Cameo Life Sketch.* London: Women's Freedom League, [19??].

Holton, Sandra. *Feminism and Democracy: Women's Suffrage and Reform Politics in Britain, 1900–1918.* Cambridge: Cambridge University Press, 1986.

―――. *Suffrage Days: Stories from the Suffrage Movement.* London: Routledge, 1997.

Holyoake, George Jacob. *The Principles of Secularism.* London: Austin, 1871.

Hubbard, Louisa. *The Year Book of Women's Work.* Vol. 1. London: "Labour News" Publishing Office, 1875.

Huss, Richard. *The Development of Printers' Mechanical Typesetting Methods, 1822–1925.* Charlottesville: University of Virginia Press, 1973.

Jameson, Anna. *Sisters of Charity and The Communion of Labour: Two Lectures on the Social Employments of Women.* London: Longman, 1859.

Janes, Emily. *The Year Book of Women's Work: 1899, 1904, 1901.* London: Adam and Charles Black.

Joannou, Maroula, and June Purvis, eds. *The Women's Suffrage Movement: New Feminist Perspectives.* Manchester: Manchester University Press, 1998.

John, Angela. *Elizabeth Robins: Staging a Life.* London: Routledge, 1995.

―――, ed. *Unequal Opportunities: Women's Employment in England 1800–1918.* Oxford: Blackwell, 1986.

Jones, Aled. *Powers of the Press: Newspapers, Power, and the Public in Nineteenth-Century England.* Aldershot, England: Scolar, 1996.

Johnson, George W., and Lucy A. Johnson, eds. *Josephine E. Butler: An Autobiographical Memoir.* Bristol: J. W. Arrowsmith, 1909.

Jordan, Ellen. "The Christening of the New Woman." *Victorian Newsletter* 63 (Spring 1983), 19–21.

———. *The Women's Movement and Women's Employment in Nineteenth-Century Britain.* London: Routledge, 1999.

Kelly, Audrey. *Lydia Becker and the Cause.* Lancaster, England: University of Lancaster, 1992.

Kent, Susan. *Making Peace: The Reconstruction of War in Interwar Britain.* Princeton: Princeton University Press, 1993.

———. *Sex and Suffrage in Britain, 1860–1914.* Princeton: Princeton University Press, 1987.

Koss, Stephen. *Fleet Street Radical: A. G. Gardiner and the Daily News.* London: Allen Lane, 1973.

———. *The Rise and Fall of the Political Press in Britain.* Vols. 1 and 2. London: Hamish Hamilton, 1981.

Laqueur, Tom. *Making Sex: Body and Gender from the Greeks to Freud.* Cambridge, Mass.: Harvard University Press, 1990.

Law, Cheryl. *Suffrage and Power: The Women's Movement, 1918–1928.* London: Tauris, 2000.

Lawrence, Arthur. *Journalism as a Profession.* London: Hodder and Stoughton, 1903.

Lee, Alan. *The Origins of the Popular Press in England, 1855–1914.* London: Croom Helm, 1976.

Legg, Marie-Louise. *Newspapers and Nationalism: The Irish Provincial Press, 1850–1992.* Portland, Ore.: Four Courts Press, 1999.

LeMahieu, D. L. *A Culture for Democracy: Mass Communication and the Cultivated Mind in Britain between the Wars.* Oxford: Clarendon Press, 1988.

Leonard, Tom. *News for All.* Oxford: Oxford University Press, 1995.

Levine, Philippa. *Feminist Lives in Victorian England.* Oxford: Blackwell, 1990.

———. "'The Humanising Influences of Five O'Clock Tea': Victorian Feminist Periodicals." *Victorian Studies* 33 (Winter 1990), 293–306.

Lidderdale, Jane, and Mary Nicholson. *Dear Mrs. Weaver: Harriet Shaw Weaver, 1876–1961.* New York: Viking Press, 1970.

Linklater, Andro. *An Unhusbanded Life: Charlotte Despard.* London: Huchinson, 1980.

Lloyd, M. A. *Susanna Meredith: A Record of Vigorous Life.* London: Hodder and Stoughton, 1903.

London Feminist History Group, eds. *The Sexual Dynamics of History.* London: Pluto Press, 1983.

Lowndes, M. Belloc. *I, Too, Have Lived in Arcadia.* London: Pan Books, 1941.

MacDonald, J. Ramsey. *Women in the Printing Trades: A Sociological Study.* London: P. S. King, 1904.

MacKenzie, Midge. *Shoulder to Shoulder: A Documentary.* New York: Knopf, 1975.

MacQuoid, Katherine. *Women Novelists of Queen Victoria's Reign.* London: Hurst and Blackett, 1897.

Mayhall, Laura E. Nym. *The Militant Suffrage Movement: Citizenship and Resistance in Britain, 1860–1930.* Oxford: Oxford University Press, 2003.

McCalman, Iain. *Radical Underworld: Prophets, Revolutionaries and Pornographers in London, 1795–1840.* Oxford: Clarendon Press, 1993.

McCrone, Kathleen. "The National Association for the Promotion of Social Science and the Advancement of Women." *Atlantis* 8, 1 (Fall 1982), 44–66.

McPhee, Carol, and Ann FitzGerald, eds. *The Non-Violent Militant: Selected Writings of Teresa Billington-Greig.* London: Routledge, 1987.

Merriman, Dorothy. *Godiva's Ride: Women of Letters in England, 1830–1880.* Bloomington: Indiana University Press, 1993.

Midgley, Clare, ed. *Gender and Imperialism.* Manchester: Manchester University Press, 1998.

Miller, Florence Fenwick. *Harriet Martineau.* London: W. H. Allen, 1884.

———. *In Ladies' Company: Six Interesting Women.* London: Ward and Downey, 1892.

———. *Readings in Social Economy: For Schools and Beginners.* London: Longmans, Green, 1884.

Mitton, G. E. *The Year Book of Women's Work.* London: Adam and Charles Black, 1910.

Montefiore, Dora. *From a Victorian to a Modern.* London: E. Archer, 1927.

Mulvihill, Margaret. *Charlotte Despard: A Biography.* London: Pandora, 1989.

Murphy, Cliona. *The Women's Suffrage Movement and Irish Society in the Early Twentieth Century.* Philadelphia: Temple University Press, 1989.

Neale, R. S. *Class in English History, 1680–1850.* Oxford: Blackwell, 1981.

Nestor, Pauline. "A New Departure in Women's Publishing: The *English Woman's Journal* and the *Victoria Magazine.*" *Victorian Periodicals Review* 15 (Fall 1982), 93–106.

Oldfield, Sybil. "Mary Sheepshanks Edits an Internationalist Suffrage Monthly in Wartime: *Jus Suffragii* 1914–1919." *Women's History Review* 12, 1 (2003), 119–30.

———. *Spinsters of This Parish: The Life and Times of F. M. Mayor and Mary Sheepshanks.* London: Virago, 1984.

Orel, Harold. *The Literary Achievement of Rebecca West.* London: Macmillan, 1986.

Owens, Rosemary. *Smashing Times: A History of the Irish Women's Suffrage Movement, 1889–1922.* Dublin: Attic Press, 1984.

Palmegiano, E. M. *Women and British Periodicals, 1832–1867: A Bibliography.* New York: Garland, 1976.

Pankhurst, Dame Christabel. *Unshackled: The Story of How We Won the Vote.* London: Hutchinson of London, 1959.

Pankhurst, Emmeline. *My Own Story.* Westport, Conn.: Greenwood Press, 1985.

Pankhurst, E. Sylvia. *The Life of Emmeline Pankhurst.* London: T. Werner Laurie, 1935.

————. *The Suffragette: The History of the Women's Militant Suffrage Movement: 1905–1910.* New York: Sturgis and Walton, 1911.

————. *The Suffragette Movement.* London: Longmans, 1931.

Parkes, Bessie Rayner. *Essays on Women's Work.* London: Alexander Strahan, 1865.

————. *Vignettes: Twelve Biographical Sketches.* London: Alexander Strahan, 1866.

Pedersen, Susan, and Peter Mandler, eds. *After the Victorians.* London: Routledge, 1994.

Pethick-Lawrence, Emmeline. *My Part in a Changing World.* London: Victor Gollancz, 1938.

Pethick-Lawrence, F. W. *Fate Has Been Kind.* London: Hutchinson, 1943.

Philipps, Mrs. *A Dictionary of Employments Open to Women.* London: Women's Institute, 1898.

Pincus, Steve. "Coffee Politicians Does Create: Coffeehouses and Restoration Political Culture." *Journal of Modern History* 67 (December 1995), 807–34.

Poovey, Mary. *Uneven Developments: The Ideological Work of Gender in Mid-Victorian England.* Chicago: University of Chicago Press, 1988.

Pratt, Edwin A. *A Woman's Work for Women, Being the Aims, Efforts and Aspirations of "L.M.H." (Miss Louisa M. Hubbard).* London: George Newnes, 1898.

Priestley, Mary, ed. *The Female Spectator: Being Selections from Mrs. Eliza Haywood's Periodical (1744–1746).* London: John Lane, 1929.

Prochaska, F. K. *Royal Bounty: The Making of the Welfare Monarchy.* New Haven: Yale University Press, 1995.

————. *Women and Philanthropy in Nineteenth-Century England.* Oxford: Clarendon, 1980.

Procter, Adelaide, ed. *The Victoria Regia: A Volume of Original Contributions in Poetry and Prose.* London: Victoria Press, 1861.

Pugh, Martin. *The March of Women: A Revisionist Analysis of the Campaign for Women's Suffrage, 1866–1914.* Oxford: Oxford University Press, 2000.

————. *Women and the Women's Movement in Britain, 1914–1959.* New York: Paragon, 1992.

Rae, Lettice Milne. *Ladies in Debate: Being a History of the Ladies' Edinburgh Debating Society: 1865–1935.* Edinburgh: Oliver and Boyd, 1936.

Raeburn, Antonia. *The Suffragette View.* New York: St. Martin's Press, 1976.

Rakow, Lana F., ed. *Women Making Meaning: New Feminism Directions in Communication.* New York: Routledge, 1992.

Rappaport, Erika Diane. *Shopping for Pleasure: Women in the Making of London's West End.* Princeton: Princeton University Press, 2000.

Reckitt, Maurice, ed. *For Christ and the People: Studies of Four Socialist Priests and Profits of the Church of England between 1870 and 1930.* London: SPCK, 1968.

Rendall, Jane, ed. *Equal or Different: Women's Politics 1800–1914.* Oxford: Blackwell, 1987.

Reynolds, Sian. *Britannica's Typesetters: Women Compositors in Edinburgh.* Edinburgh: Edinburgh University Press, 1989.

Robins, Elizabeth. *Both Sides of the Curtain: Memoirs of Elizabeth Robins.* London: Heinemann, 1940.

Rosen, Andrew. *Rise Up Women! The Militant Campaign of the WSPU, 1903–1914.* London: Routledge and Kegan Paul, 1974.

Rubinstein, David. *Before the Suffragettes: Women's Emancipation in the 1890s.* Brighton, England: Harvester Press, 1986.

Ryan, Mary. *Women in Public: Between Ballots and Banners.* Baltimore: Johns Hopkins University Press, 1990.

Sapiro, Virginia. *A Vindication of Political Virtue: The Political Theory of Mary Wollstonecraft.* Chicago: University of Chicago Press, 1992.

Schudson, Michael. *The Power of News.* Cambridge, Mass.: Harvard University Press, 1995.

Shanley, Mary Lyndon. *Feminism, Marriage, and the Law in Victorian England, 1850–1895.* Princeton: Princeton University Press, 1989.

Sharp, Evelyn. *Unfinished Adventure: Selected Reminiscences from an Englishwoman's Life.* London: John Lane, 1933.

Shattock, Joanne, and Michael Wolff, eds. *The Victorian Periodical Press: Samplings and Soundings.* Toronto: University of Toronto Press, 1982.

Shevelow, Kathryn. *Women and Print Culture: The Construction of Femininity in the Early Periodical.* London: Routledge, 1989.

Shirreff, Emily. *Intellectual Education and Its Influence on the Character and Happiness of Women.* London: Smith and Elder, 1862.

Showalter, Elaine. *Sexual Anarchy: Gender and Culture in the Fin de Siècle.* New York: Penguin, 1990.

Six Point Group. *Dorothy Evans and the Six Point Group.* London: Claire Madden, 1946.

Smith, Adrian. *The New Statesman: Portrait of a Political Weekly.* London: Frank Cass, 1996.

Smith, Harold L., ed. *British Feminism in the Twentieth Century.* Aldershot, England: Edward Elgar, 1990.

Solomon, Martha, ed. *A Voice of Their Own: The Women Suffrage Press, 1840–1910.* Tuscaloosa: University of Alabama Press, 1991.

Somerset, Lady Henry. *Beauty for Ashes.* London: L. Upcott Gill, 1913.

Spender, Dale. *Time and Tide Wait for No Man.* London: Pandora Press, 1984.

Stanley, Liz. *The Life and Death of Emily Wilding Davison.* London: Women's Press, 1988.

Stanton, Theodore, ed. *The Woman Question in Europe: A Series of Original Essays.* London: Sampson Low, Marston, Searle, and Rivington, 1884.

Staves, Susan. "Chattel Property Rules and the Construction of Englishness, 1660–1800." *Law and History Review* 12 (Spring 1994), 123–53.

Swanwick, H. M. *I Have Been Young.* London: Victor Gollancz, 1935.

Taylor, Barbara. *Eve and the New Jerusalem: Socialism and Feminism in the Nineteenth Century.* London: Virago, 1983.

Taylor, Mary. *The First Duty of Women: A Series of Articles Reprinted from the "Victoria Magazine," 1865–1870.* London: Emily Faithfull, 1870.

Thomas, Clara. *Love and Work Enough: The Life of Anna Jameson.* Toronto: University of Toronto Press, 1967.

Tickner, Lisa. *The Spectacle of Women: Imagery of the Suffrage Campaign, 1907–14.* Chicago: University of Chicago Press, 1988.

Tidcombe, Marianne. *Women Bookbinders, 1880–1920.* London: British Library, 1996.

Tulloch, Gail. *Mill and Sexual Equality.* Boulder, Colo.: Lynne Rienner, 1989.

Tunstall, Jeremy. *The Media in Britain.* New York: Columbia University Press, 1983.

Turner, Cheryl. *Living by the Pen: Women Writers in the Eighteenth Century.* London: Routledge, 1992.

Vann, J. Don, and Rosemary Van Arsdel. *Victorian Periodicals and Victorian Society.* Toronto: University of Toronto Press, 1994.

Van Arsdel, Rosemary. *Florence Fenwick Miller: Victorian Feminist, Journalist, and Educator.* Aldershot, England: Ashgate, 2001.

———. "Mrs. Florence Fenwick-Miller and the *Woman's Signal,* 1895–1899." *Victorian Periodicals Review* 15 (Fall 1982), 107–18.

Vicinus, Martha. *Independent Women: Work and Community for Single Women, 1850–1920.* Chicago: University of Chicago, 1985.

Vickery, Amanda, ed. *Women, Privilege and Power: British Politics, 1750 to the Present.* Stanford: Stanford University Press, 2001.

Walkowitz, Judith. *City of Dreadful Delight: Narratives of Sexual Danger in Late Victorian London.* Chicago: University of Chicago Press, 1992.

———. "Going Public: Shopping, Street Harassment, and Streetwalking in Late-Victorian London," *Representations* 62 (Spring 1998), 1–30.

———. *Prostitution and Victorian Society: Women, Class, and the State.* Cambridge: Cambridge University Press, 1980.

Waters, Chris. *British Socialists and the Politics of Popular Culture, 1884–1990.* Stanford: Stanford University Press, 1990.

Watts, Ruth. *Gender, Power, and the Unitarians in England, 1760–1860.* London: Longman, 1998.

Whicher, George Frisbie. *The Life and Romances of Mrs. Eliza Haywood.* New York: Columbia University Press, 1915.

White, Cynthia. *Women's Magazines, 1693–1968.* London: Michael Joseph, 1970.

Williams, Kevin. *Get Me a Murder a Day! A History of Mass Communication in Britain.* London: Arnold Press, 1998.

Williams, Raymond. *Communications.* 3rd ed. Middlesex, England: Penguin Press, 1982.

Wilson, Charles. *First with the News: The History of W. H. Smith.* Garden City, N.Y.: Doubleday, 1986.

Winslow, Barbara. *Sylvia Pankhurst: Sexual Politics and Political Activism.* New York: St. Martin's Press, 1996.

Yeo, Eileen. *The Contest for Social Science.* London: Rivers Oram, 1996.

Theses and Dissertations

Brady, Norman. "*Shafts* and the Quest for a New Morality." M.A. thesis, University of Warwick, 1978.

Dingsdale, Ann. "Generous and Lofty Sympathies: The Kensington Society, the 1866 Women's Suffrage Petition and the Development of Mid-Victorian Feminism." Ph.D. diss., University of Greenwich, 1995.

Harrington, Elizabeth. "Towards a Sane Feminism: The Early Works of Rebecca West." Graduate student thesis paper, Yale University, 1971.

Hume, Leslie. "The National Union of Women's Suffrage Societies, 1897–1914." Ph.D. diss., Stanford University, 1979.

Parker, Joan Elizabeth. "Lydia Becker: Her Work for Women." Ph.D. diss., Manchester University, 1990.

Walker, Linda. "The Employment Question and the Woman's Movement in Late Victorian and Edwardian Society with Particular Reference to the *English Woman's Review.*" M.A. thesis, University of Manchester, 1974.

Worzala, Diane. "The Langham Place Circle: The Beginnings of the Organized Women's Movement in England, 1854–1870." Ph.D. diss., University of Wisconsin, 1982.

Index

THE HISTORY OF COMMUNICATION

MICHELLE ELIZABETH TUSAN is an assistant professor of history at the University of Nevada, Las Vegas. She is the author of articles on women's political newspapers and journalists, including "Reforming Work: Gender, Class and the Printing Trade in Victorian Britain," *Journal of Women's History;* "Writing *Stri Dharma:* International Feminism, Nationalist Politics, and Women's Press Advocacy in Colonial India," *Women's History Review;* "Not the Ordinary Victorian Charity," *History Workshop Journal;* and "Inventing the New Woman," *Victorian Periodicals Review.*

The University of Illinois Press
is a founding member of the
Association of American University Presses.

———————————————————————

Composed in 10.5/13 Adobe Minion
with Meta display
at the University of Illinois Press
Manufactured by Thomson-Shore, Inc.

University of Illinois Press
1325 South Oak Street
Champaign, IL 61820-6903
www.press.uillinois.edu